Skip·Beat!

Shojo Beat

Skip·Beat!

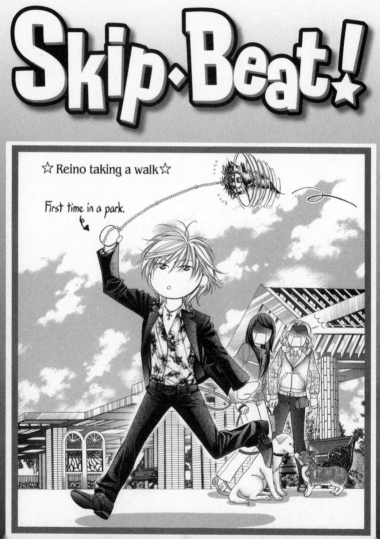

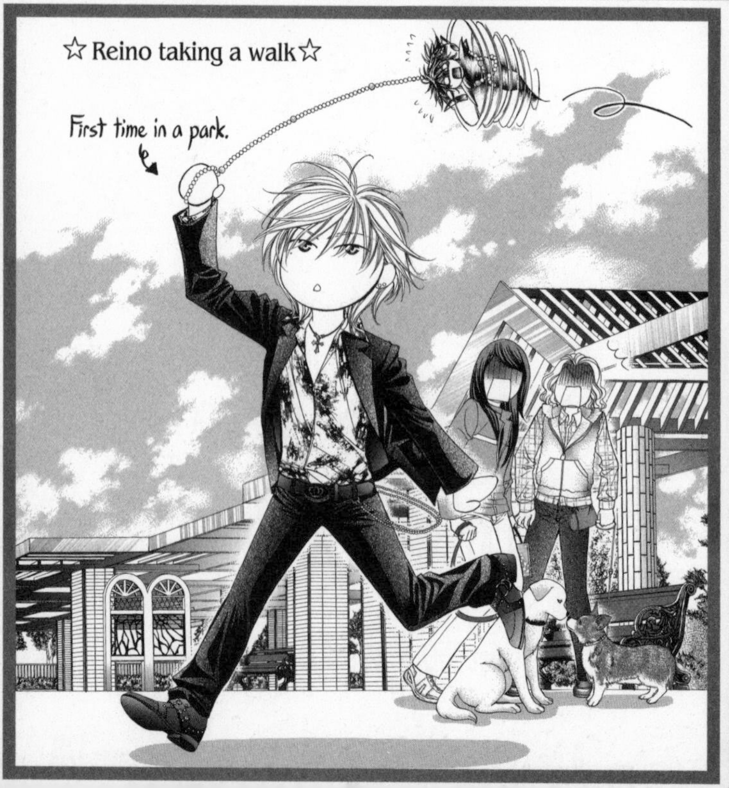
☆Reino taking a walk☆
First time in a park.

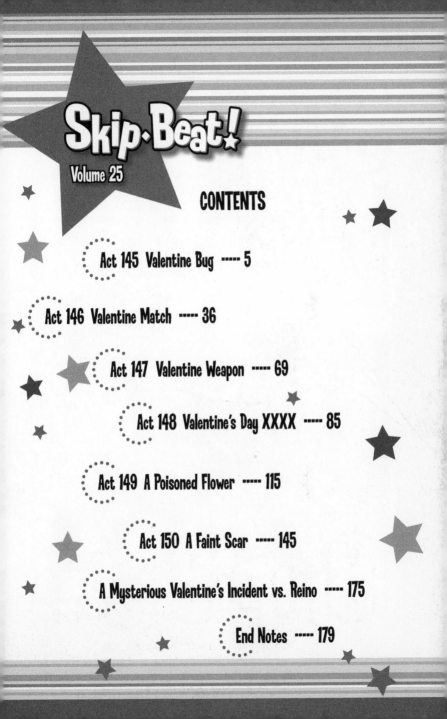

Skip·Beat!
Volume 25

CONTENTS

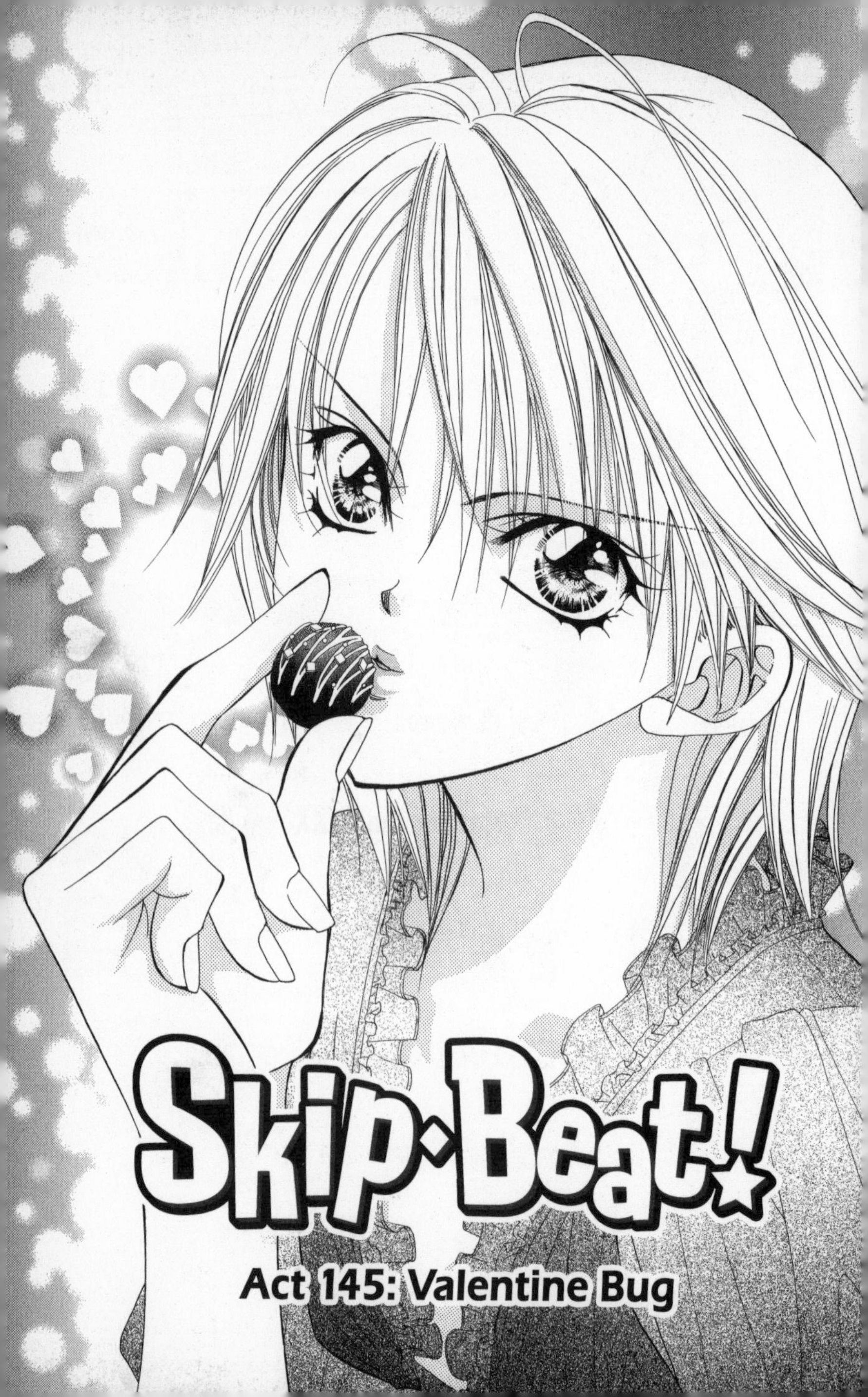
Skip·Beat!
Act 145: Valentine Bug

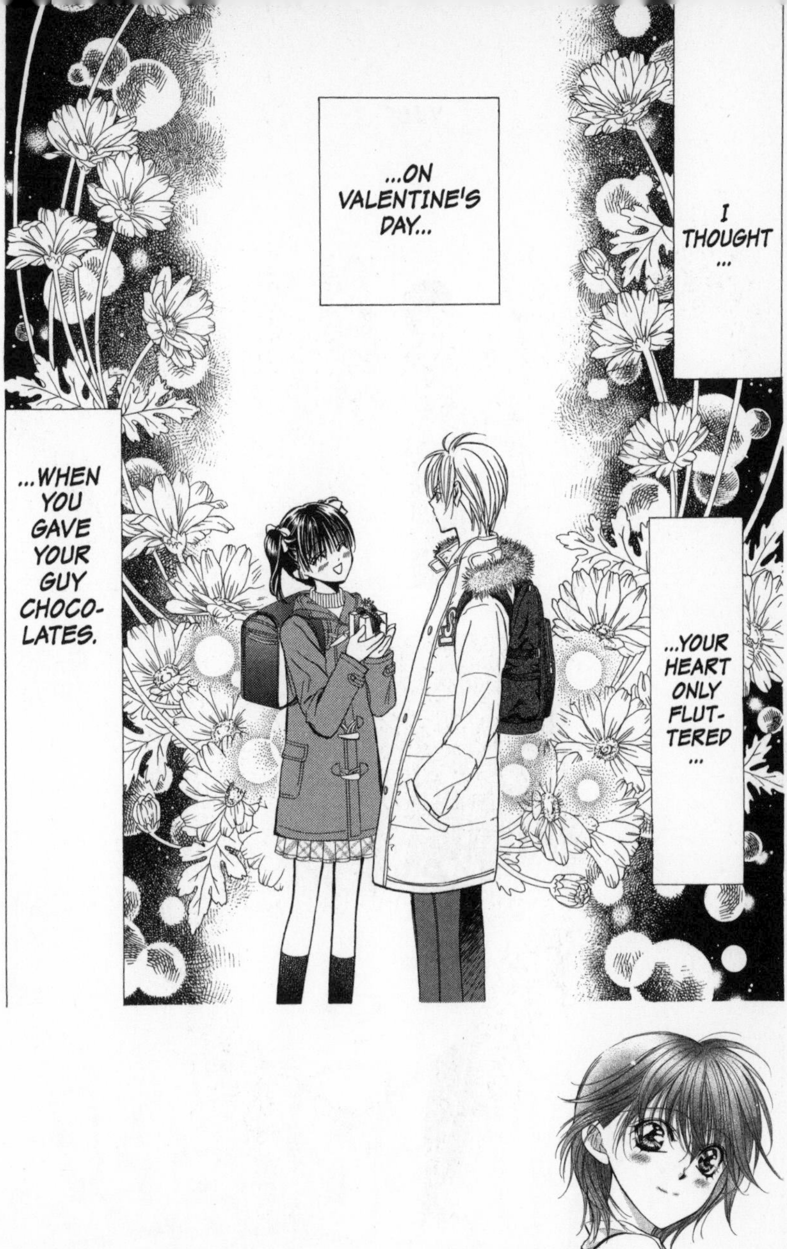
I THOUGHT ...
...ON VALENTINE'S DAY...
...YOUR HEART ONLY FLUT-TERED ...
...WHEN YOU GAVE YOUR GUY CHOCO-LATES.

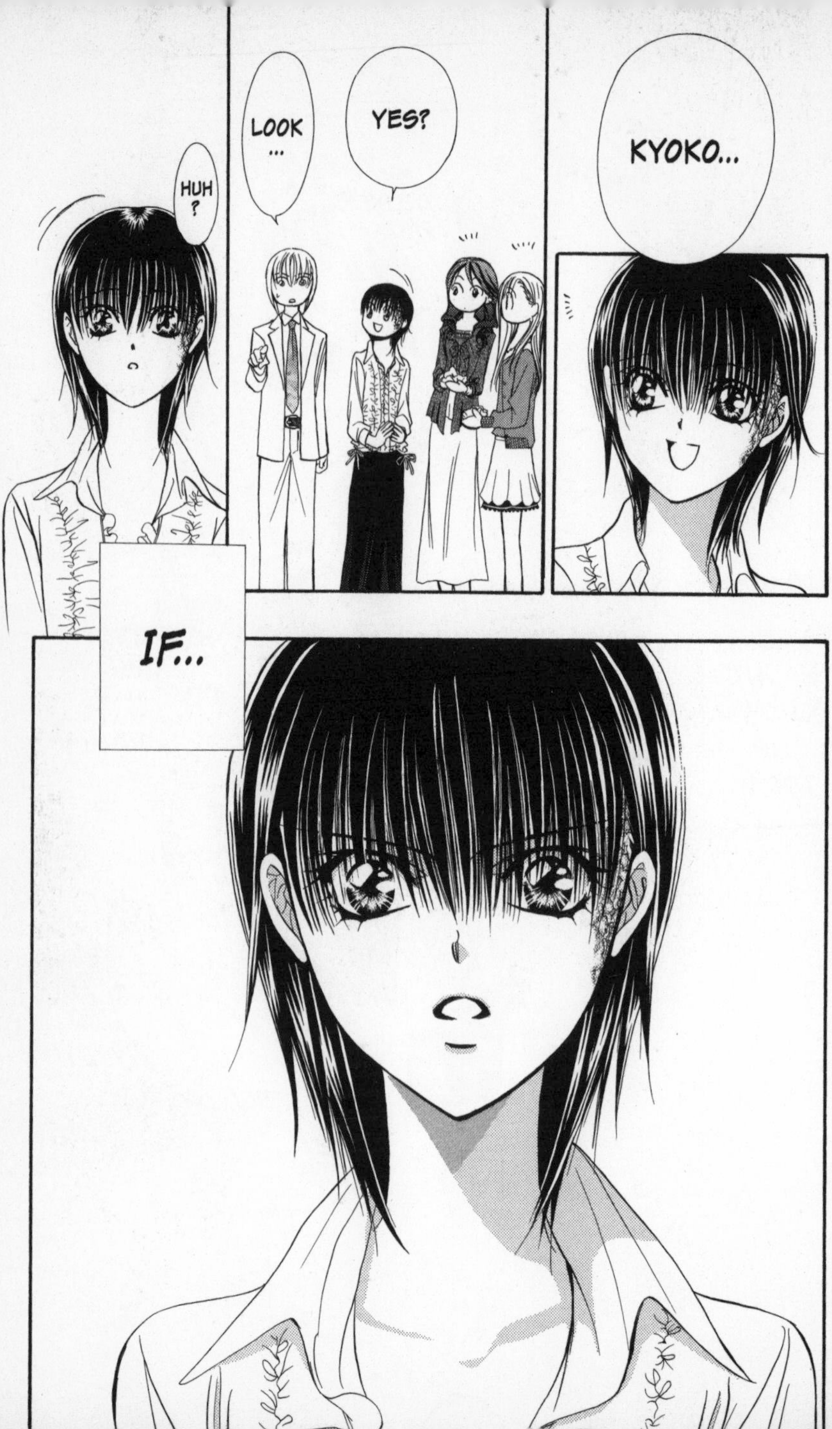
KYOKO...
YES?
LOOK ...
HUH ?
IF...

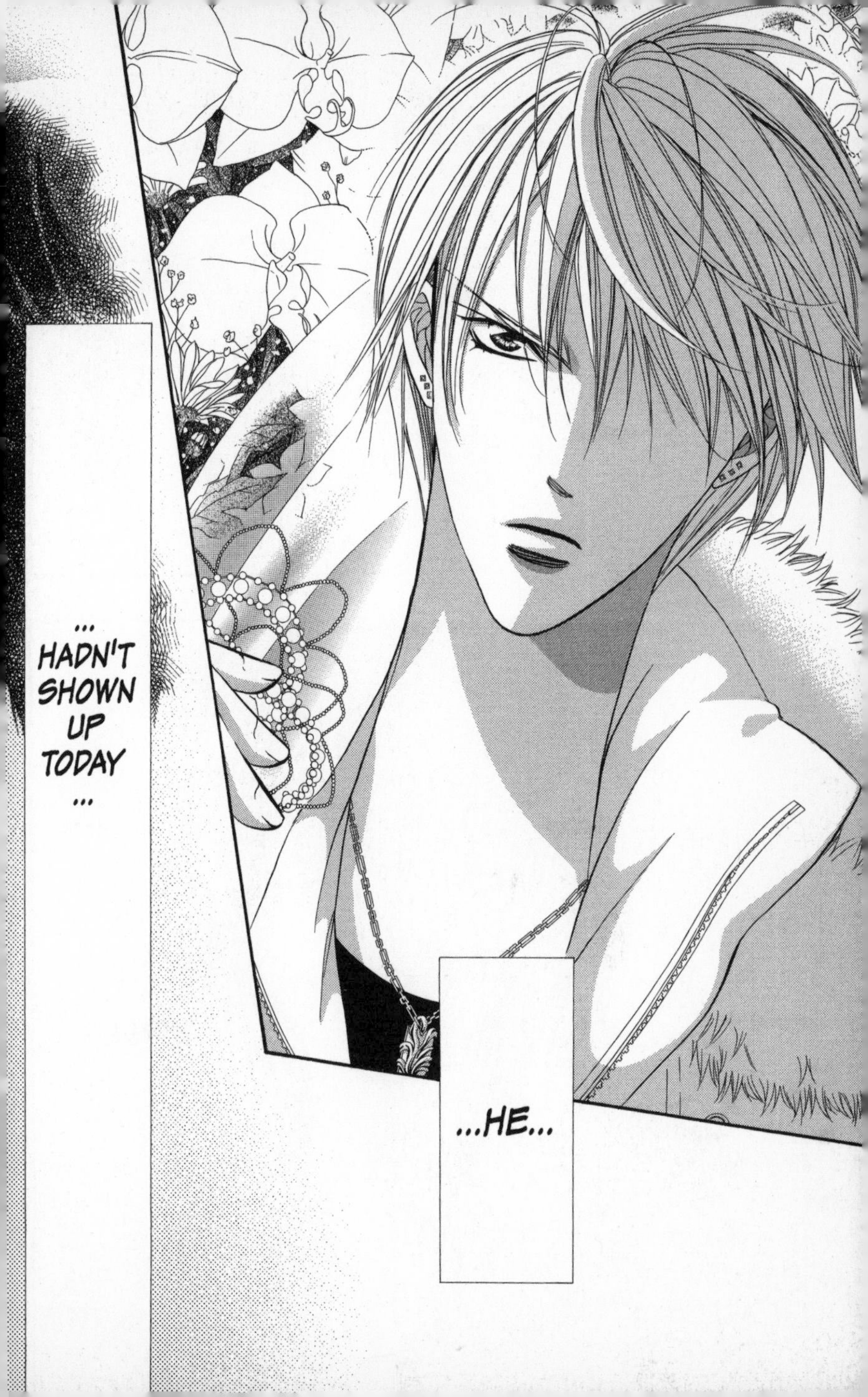
...HE...
... HADN'T SHOWN UP TODAY ...

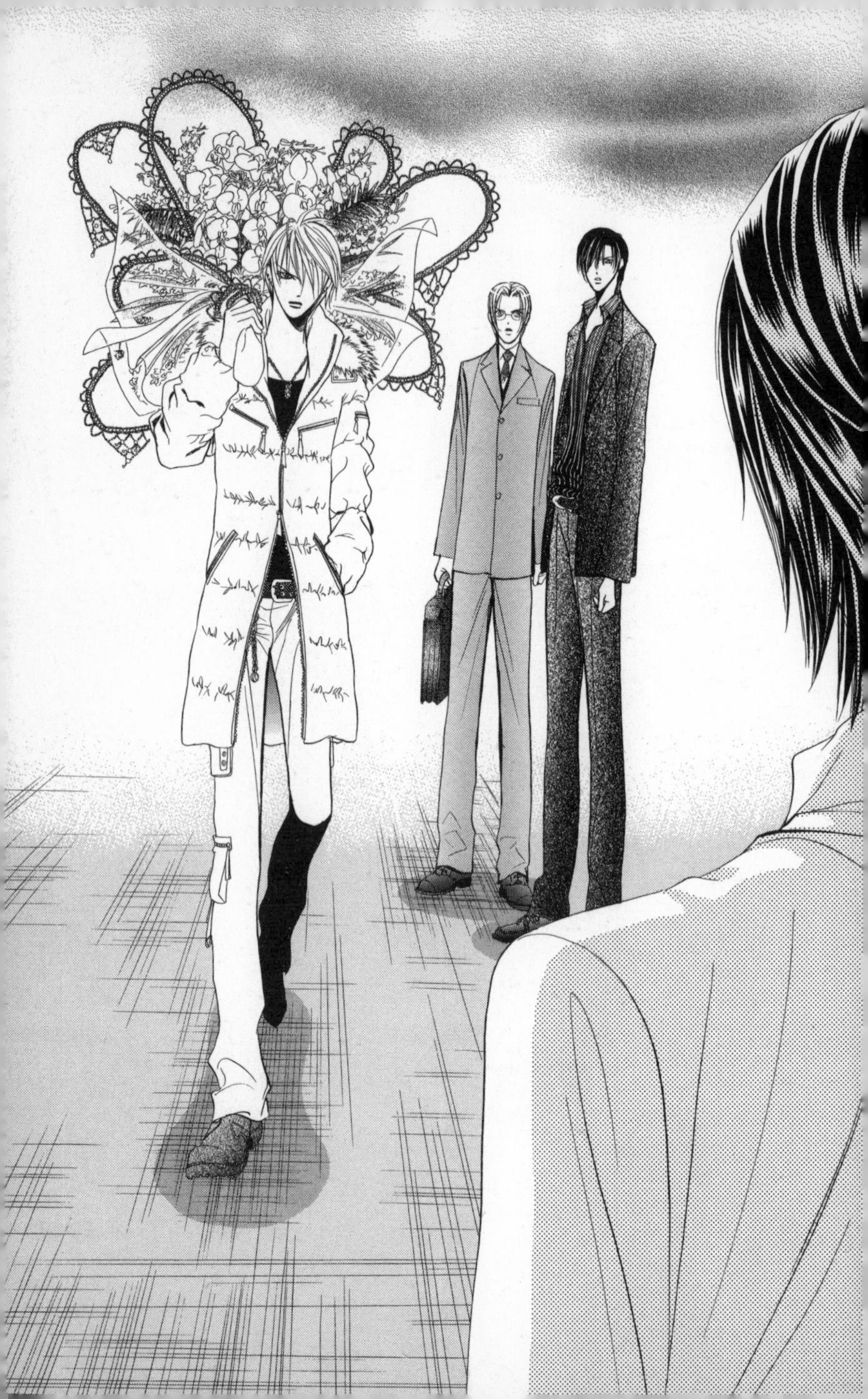

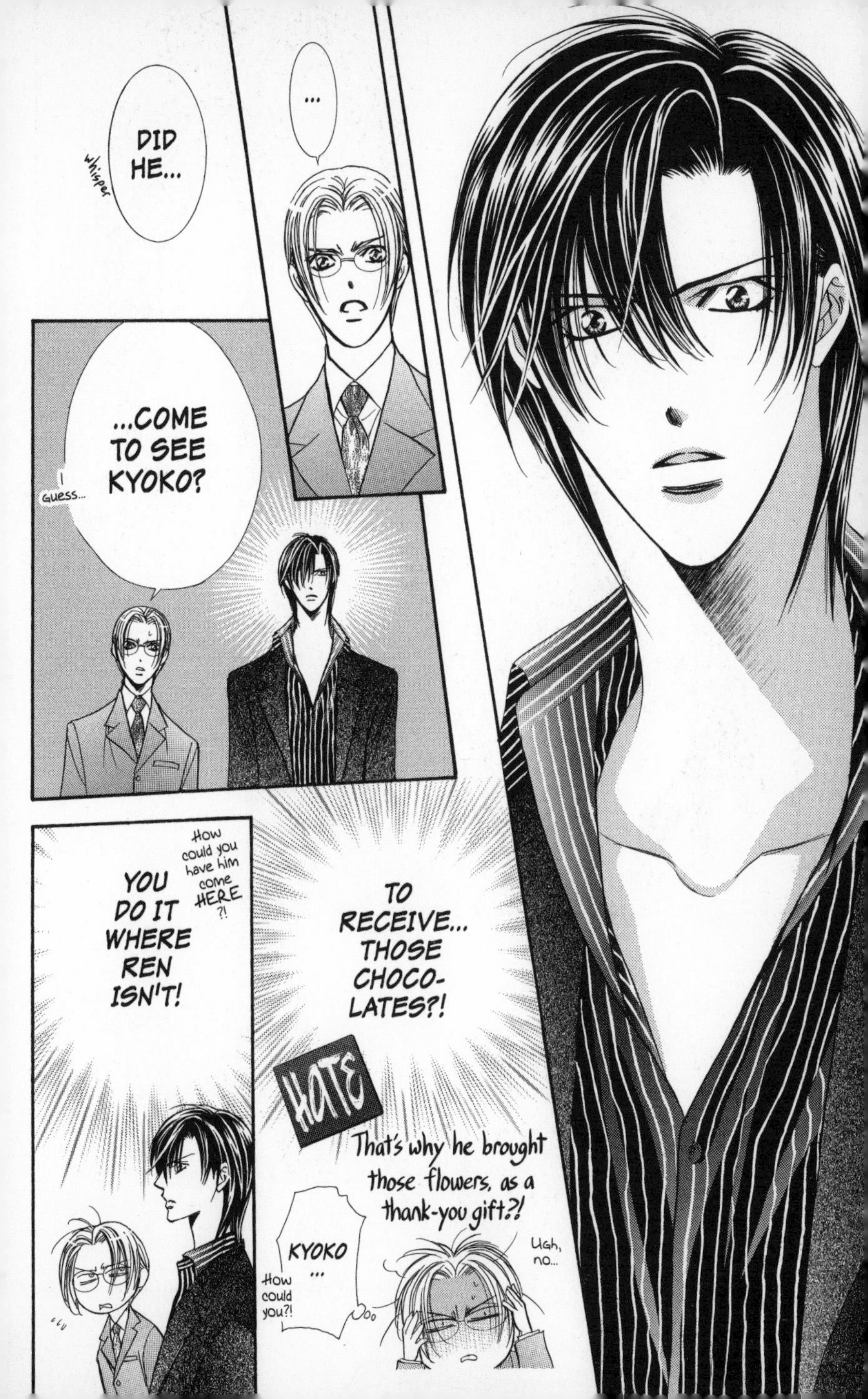
...
whisper
DID HE...
...COME TO SEE KYOKO?
I guess...
TO RECEIVE... THOSE CHOCO-LATES?!
HATE
That's why he brought those flowers, as a thank-you gift?!
Ugh, no...
KYOKO...
How could you?!
How could you have him come HERE?!
YOU DO IT WHERE REN ISN'T!

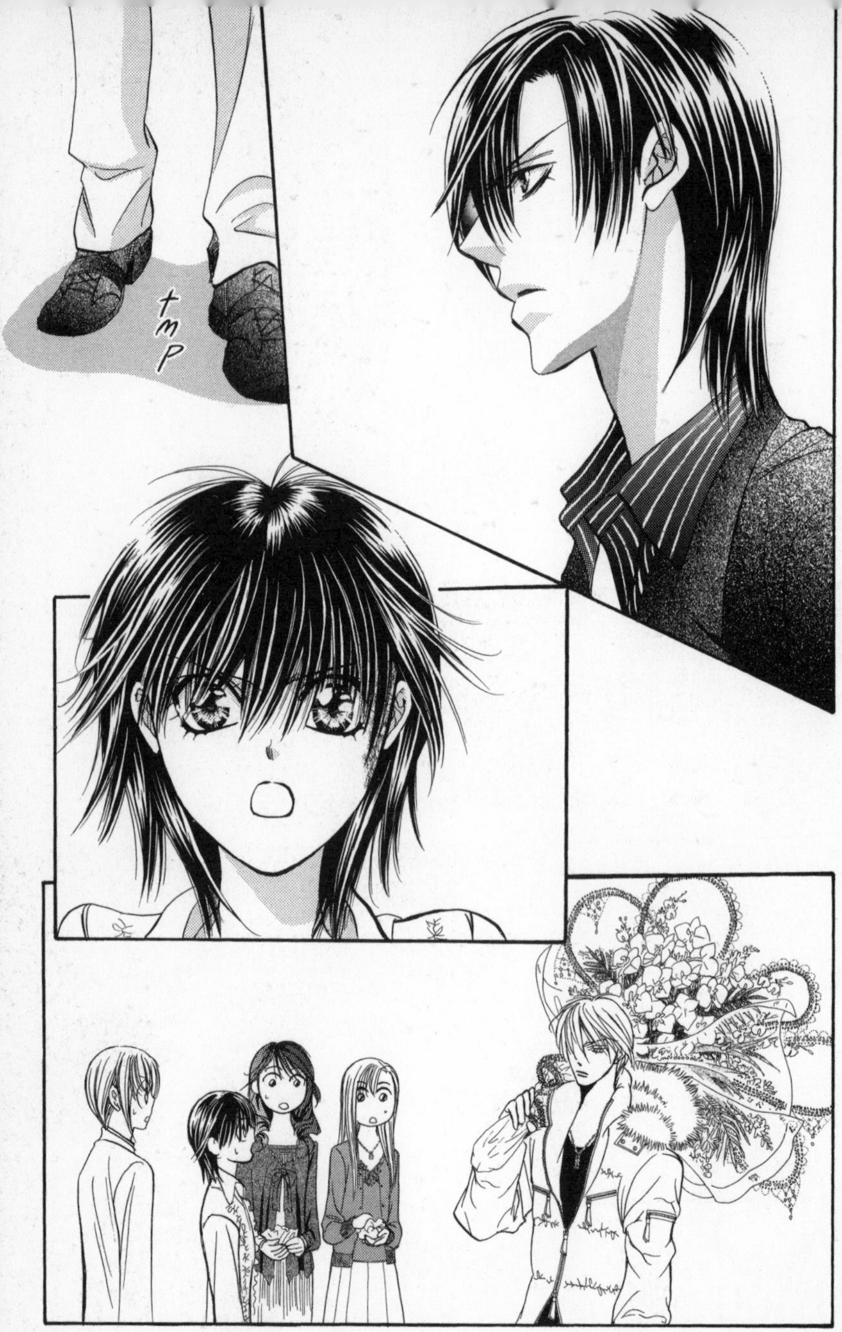
tmp

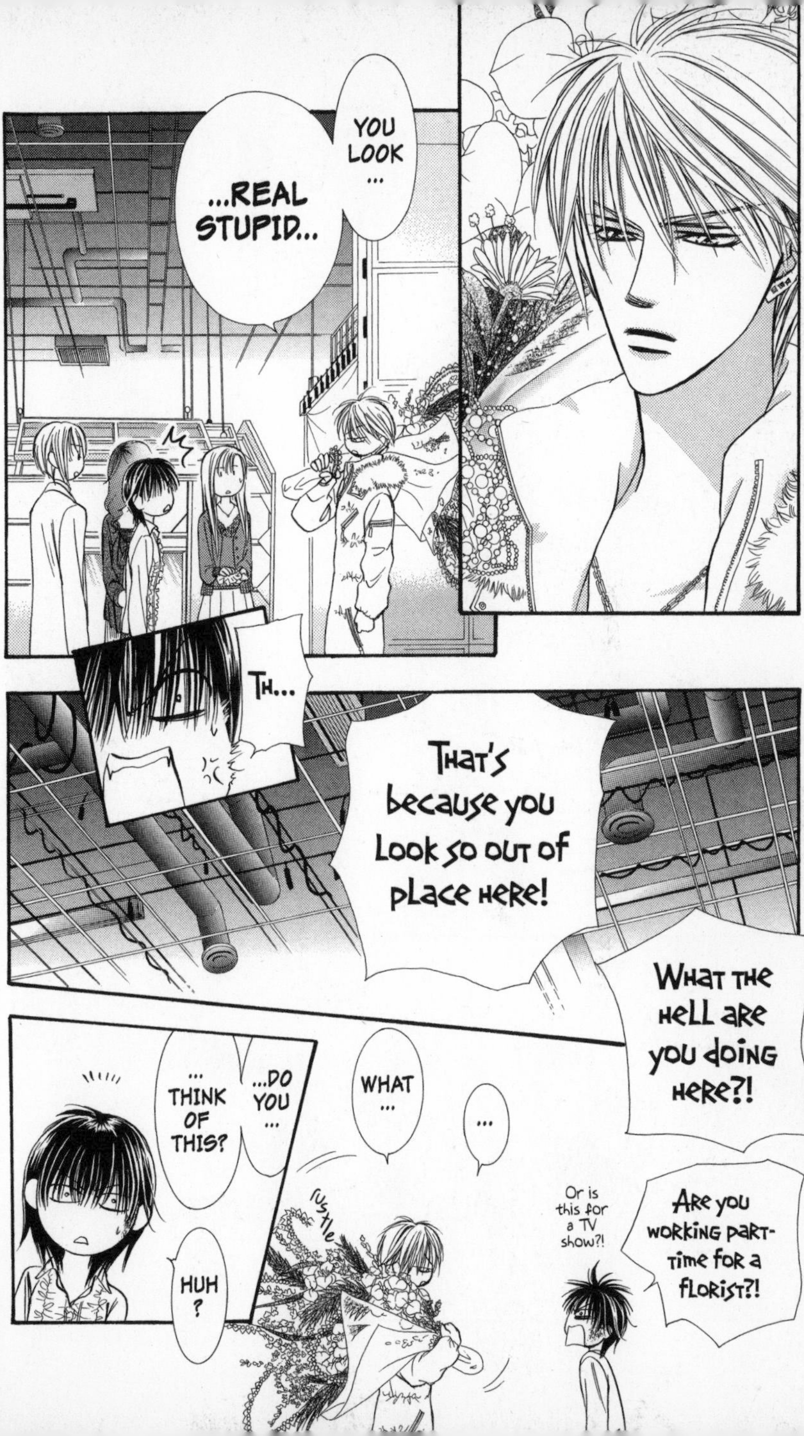
YOU LOOK ...
...REAL STUPID...
TH...
That's because you look so out of place here!
What the hell are you doing here?!
Are you working part-time for a florist?!
Or is this for a TV show?!
...
WHAT ...
rustle
...DO YOU ...
... THINK OF THIS?
HUH ?

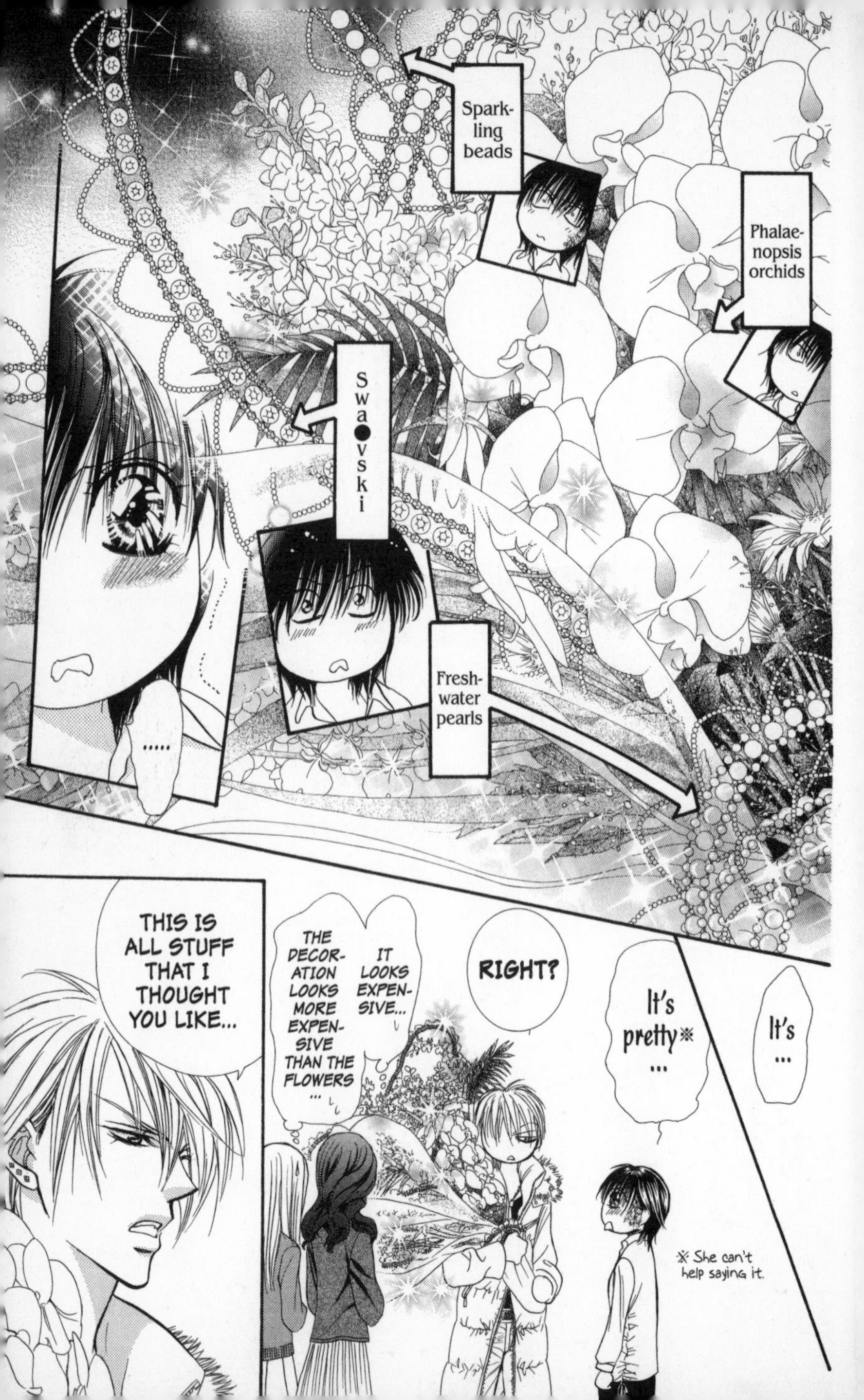
Sparkling beads
Phalaenopsis orchids
Swa●vski
Freshwater pearls
.....
It's ...
※ She can't help saying it.
It's pretty※ ...
RIGHT?
IT LOOKS EXPENSIVE...
THE DECORATION LOOKS MORE EXPENSIVE THAN THE FLOWERS ...
THIS IS ALL STUFF THAT I THOUGHT YOU LIKE...

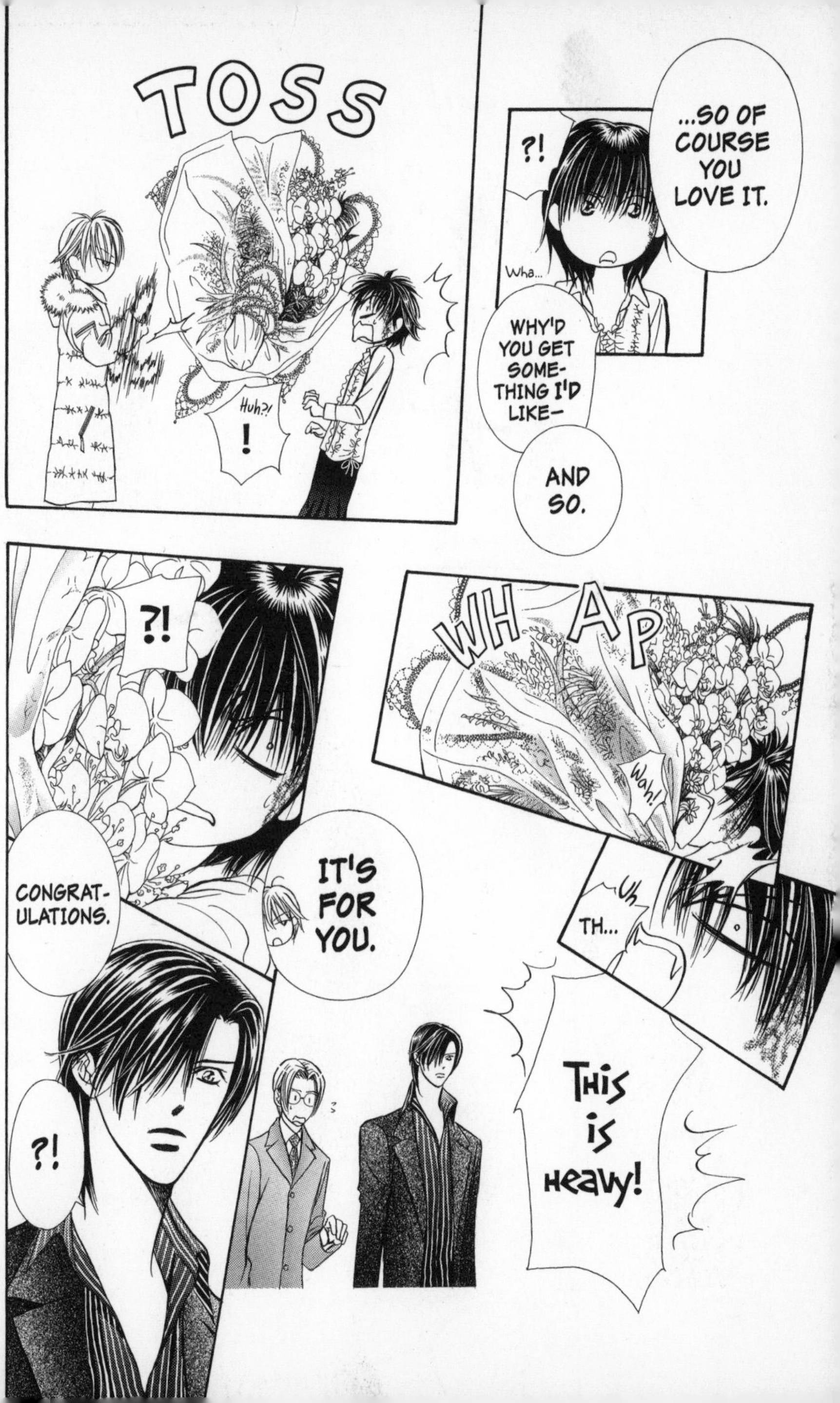
...SO OF COURSE YOU LOVE IT.
?!
Wha...
WHY'D YOU GET SOMETHING I'D LIKE–
AND SO.
TOSS
Huh?!
!
WHAP
Wah!
?!
Uh
TH...
THIS IS HEAVY!
IT'S FOR YOU.
CONGRATULATIONS.
?!

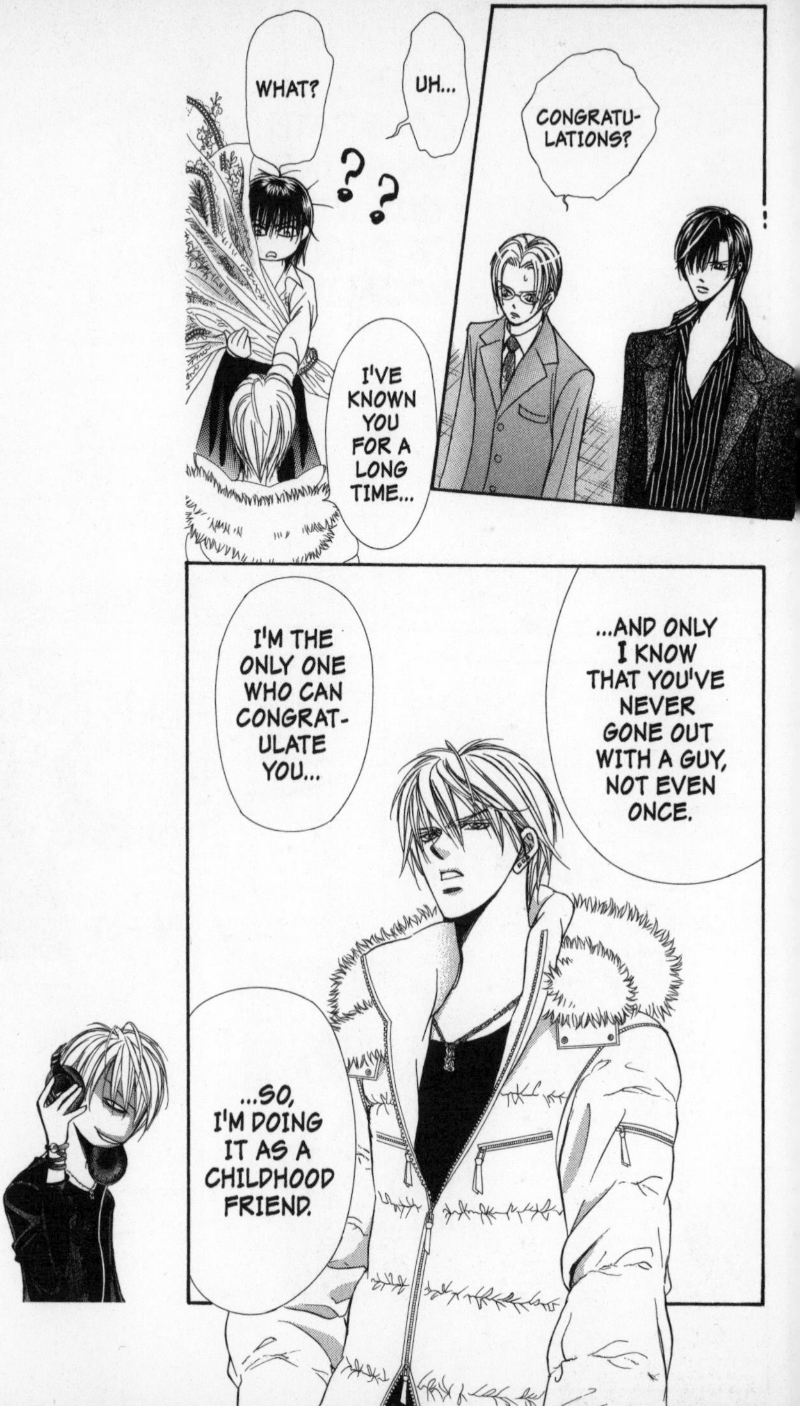
CONGRATU-LATIONS?
UH...
WHAT?
??
I'VE KNOWN YOU FOR A LONG TIME...
...AND ONLY I KNOW THAT YOU'VE NEVER GONE OUT WITH A GUY, NOT EVEN ONCE.
I'M THE ONLY ONE WHO CAN CONGRAT-ULATE YOU...
...SO, I'M DOING IT AS A CHILDHOOD FRIEND.

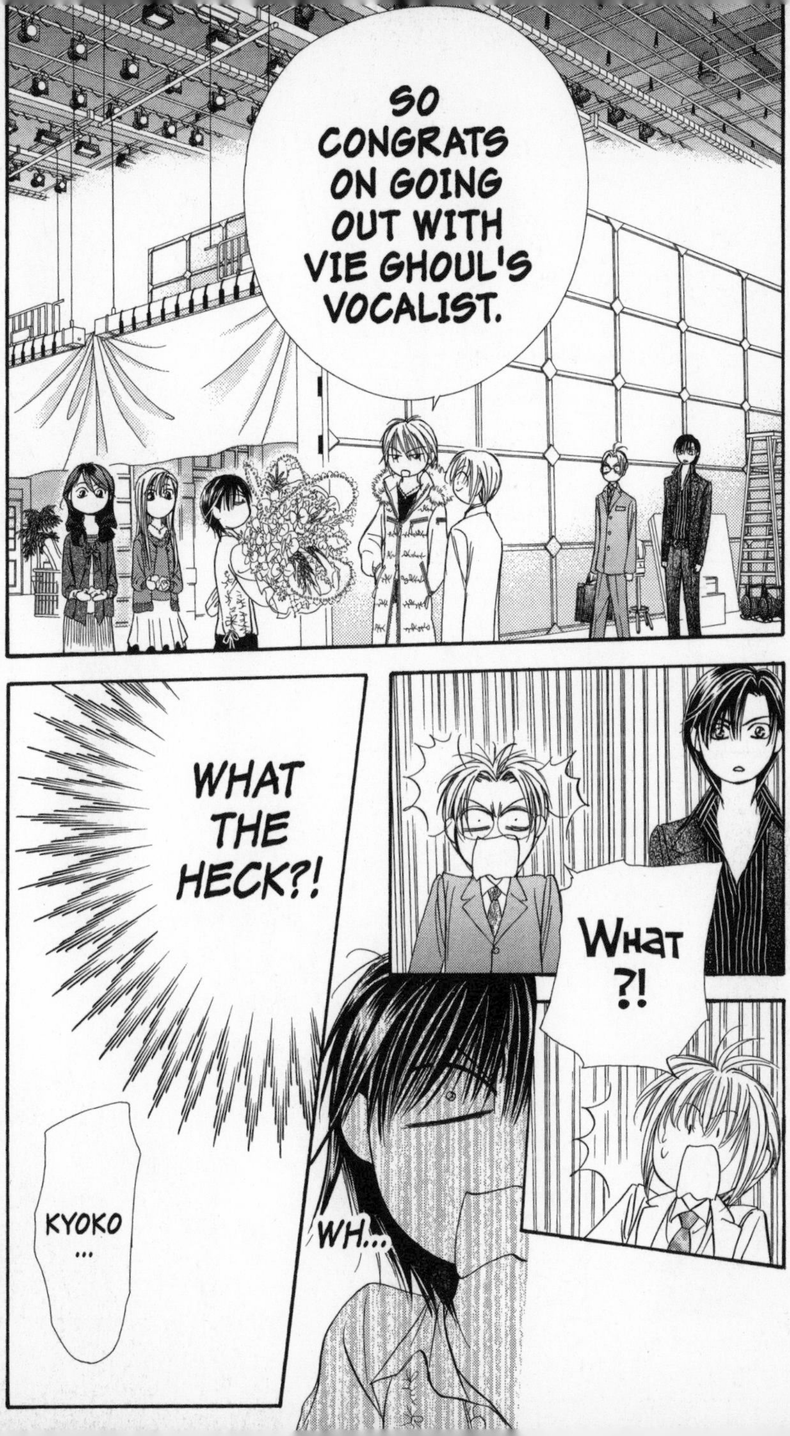
SO CONGRATS ON GOING OUT WITH VIE GHOUL'S VOCALIST.
WHAT ?!
WHAT THE HECK?!
WH...
KYOKO ...

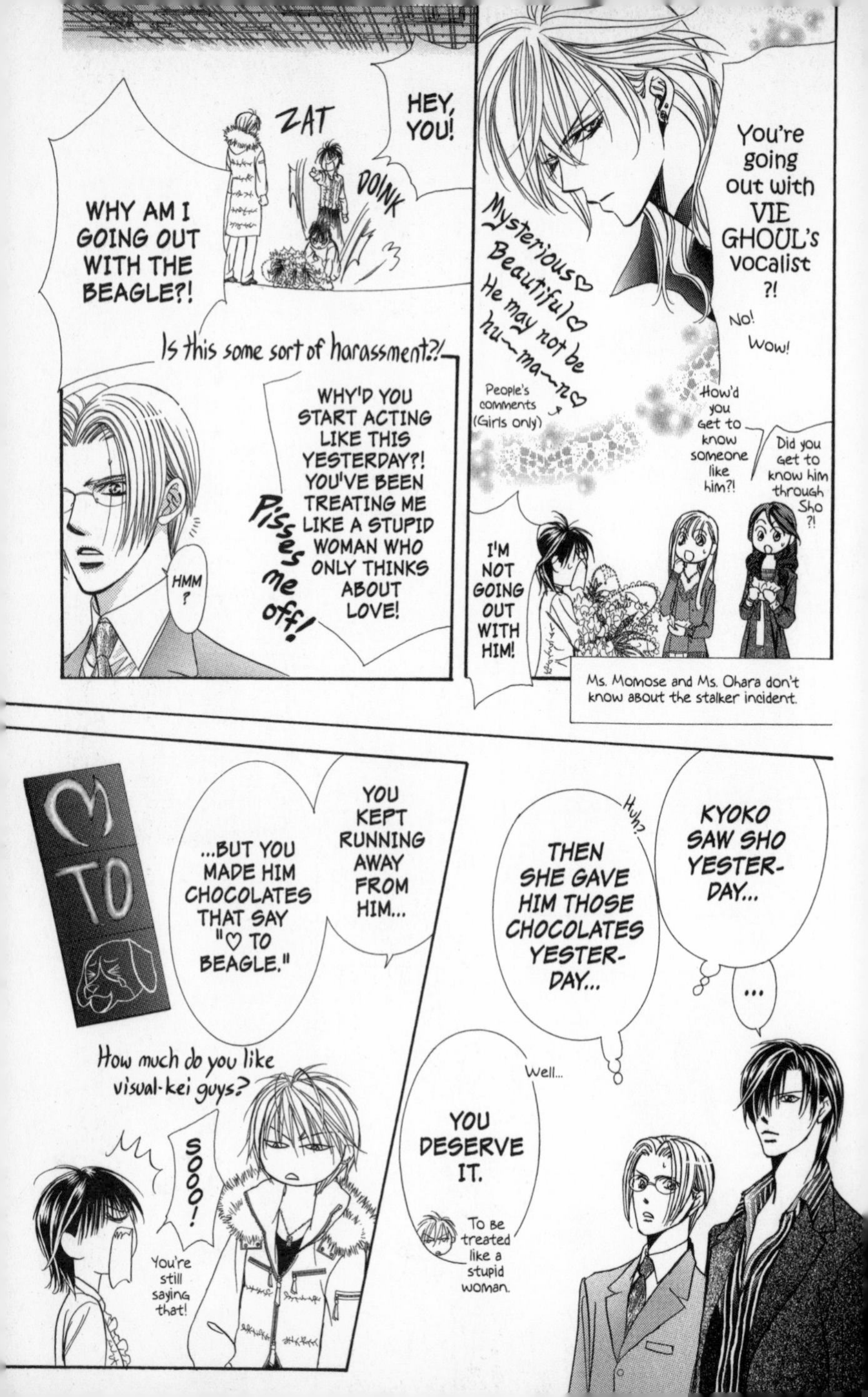
You're going out with VIE GHOUL's vocalist?!
No!
Wow!
Mysterious♡ Beautiful♡ He may not be hu~ma~n♡
People's comments (Girls only)
How'd you get to know someone like him?!
Did you get to know him through Sho?!
I'M NOT GOING OUT WITH HIM!
Ms. Momose and Ms. Ohara don't know about the stalker incident.
HEY, YOU!
ZAT
DOINK
WHY AM I GOING OUT WITH THE BEAGLE?!
Is this some sort of harassment?!
WHY'D YOU START ACTING LIKE THIS YESTERDAY?! YOU'VE BEEN TREATING ME LIKE A STUPID WOMAN WHO ONLY THINKS ABOUT LOVE!
Pisses me off!
HMM?
KYOKO SAW SHO YESTER-DAY...
...
Huh?
THEN SHE GAVE HIM THOSE CHOCOLATES YESTER-DAY...
Well...
YOU DESERVE IT.
To be treated like a stupid woman.
YOU KEPT RUNNING AWAY FROM HIM...
...BUT YOU MADE HIM CHOCOLATES THAT SAY "♡ TO BEAGLE."
♡ TO
How much do you like visual-kei guys?
SOOO!
You're still saying that!

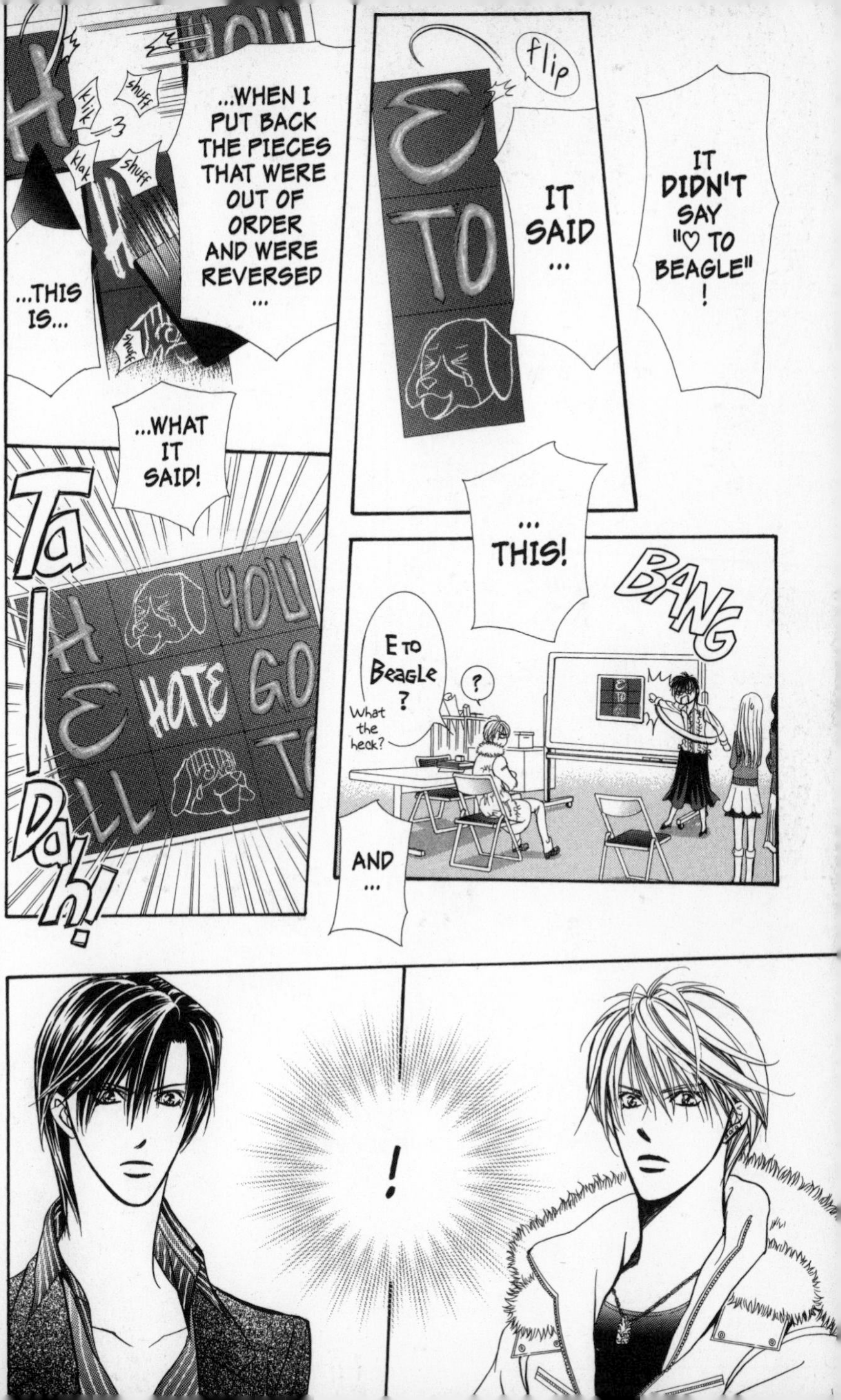
IT DIDN'T SAY "♡ TO BEAGLE"!
flip
IT SAID ...
shuff
klik
klak
shuff
...WHEN I PUT BACK THE PIECES THAT WERE OUT OF ORDER AND WERE REVERSED ...
...THIS IS...
shuff
...WHAT IT SAID!
Ta-Dah!
... THIS!
BANG
?
E TO Beagle?
What the heck?
AND ...
!

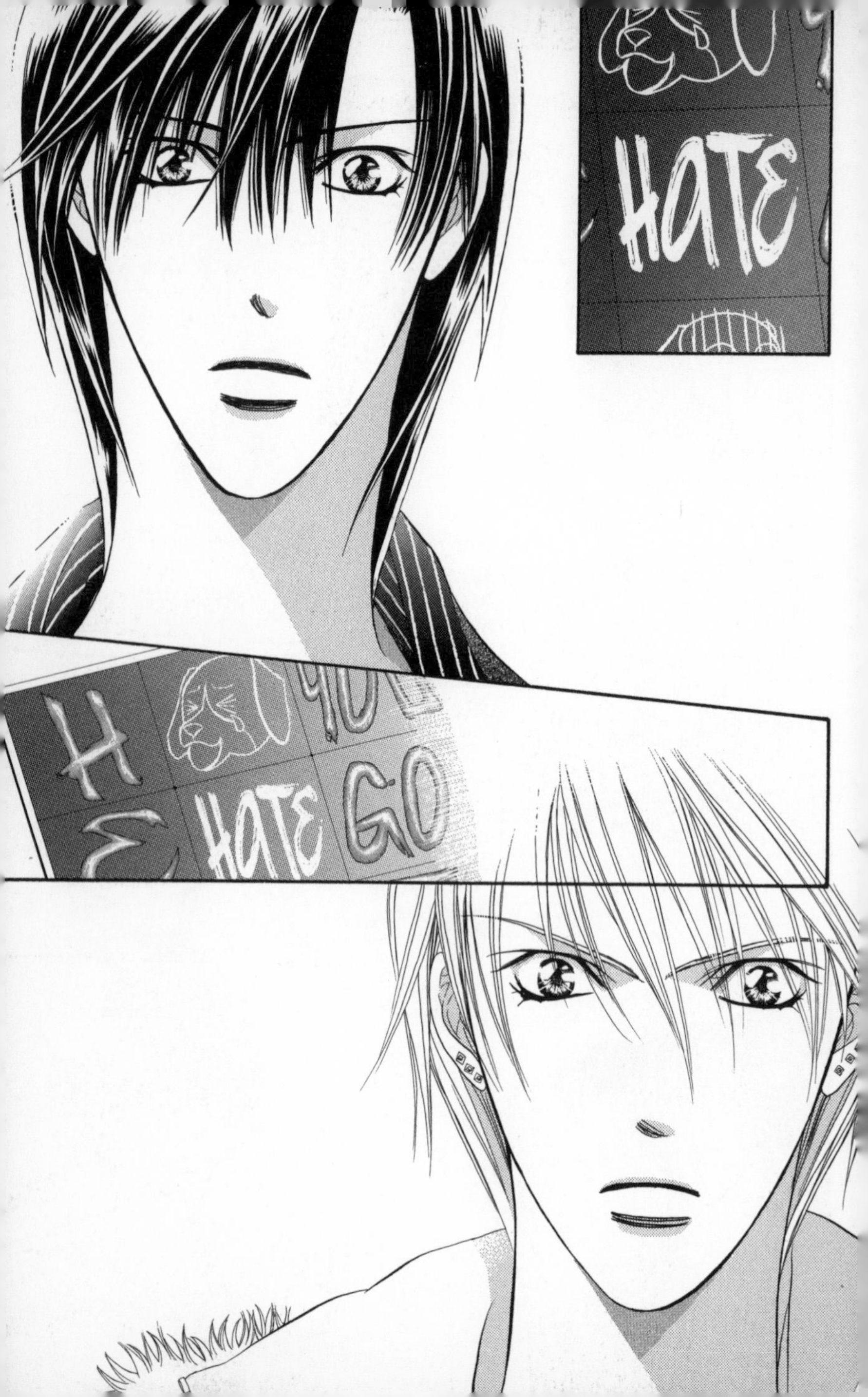
HATE
H
GO
HATE

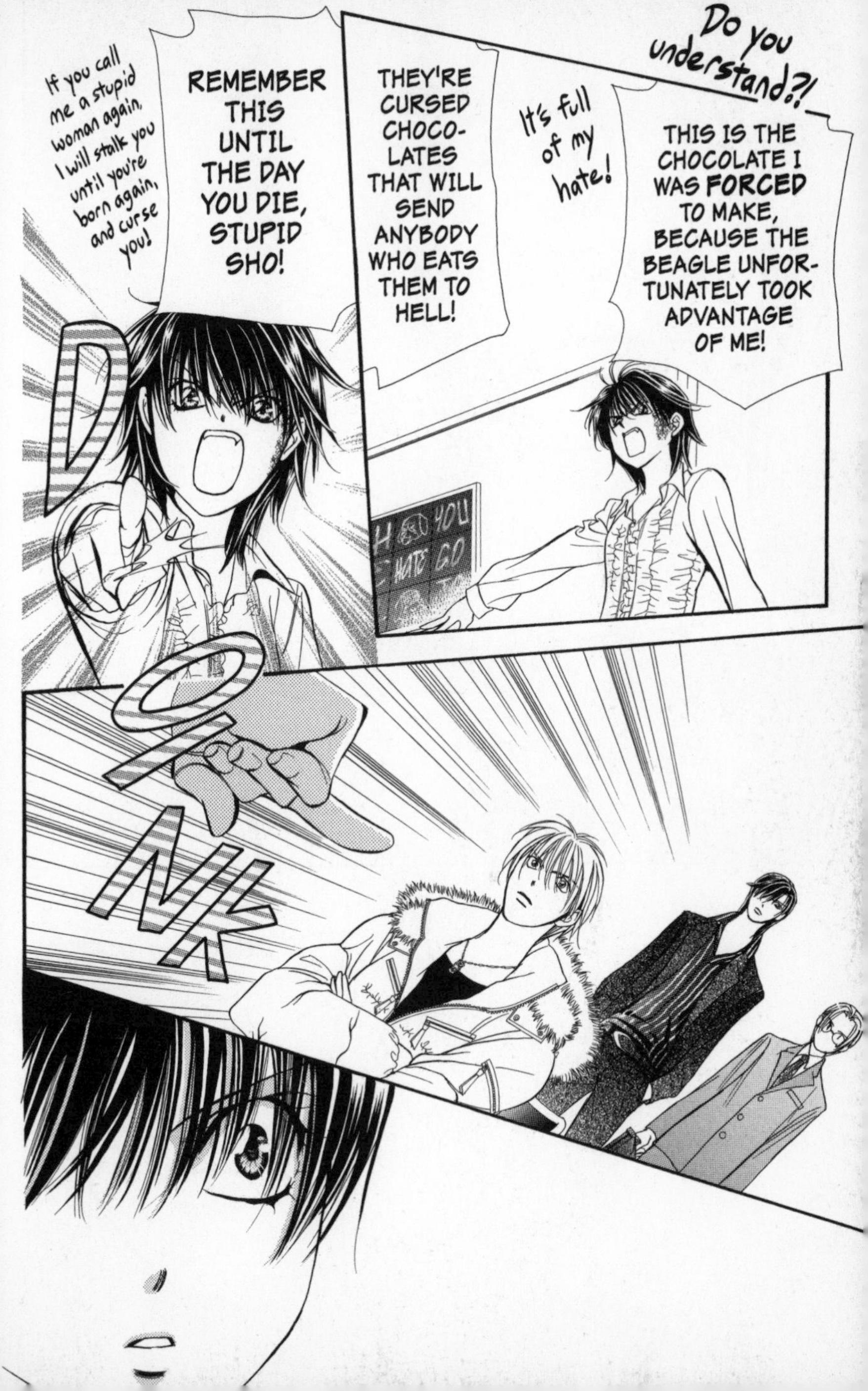
Do you understand?!
THIS IS THE CHOCOLATE I WAS **FORCED** TO MAKE, BECAUSE THE BEAGLE UNFORTUNATELY TOOK ADVANTAGE OF ME!
It's full of my hate!
THEY'RE CURSED CHOCOLATES THAT WILL SEND ANYBODY WHO EATS THEM TO HELL!
REMEMBER THIS UNTIL THE DAY YOU DIE, STUPID SHO!
If you call me a stupid woman again, I will stalk you until you're born again, and curse you!
DOINK

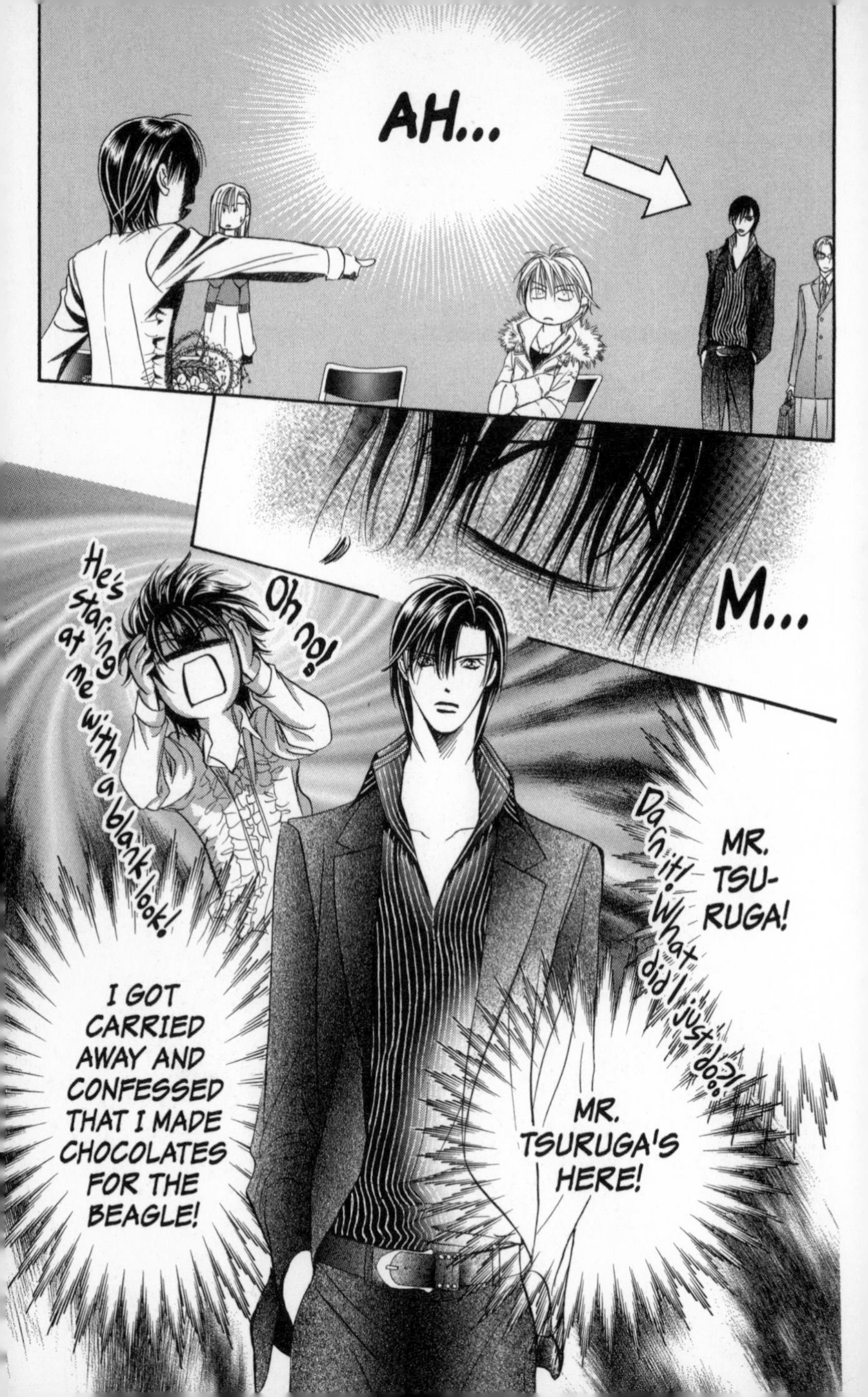
AH...
M...
MR. TSURUGA!
Darn it! What did I just do?!
MR. TSURUGA'S HERE!
Oh no!
He's staring at me with a blank look!
I GOT CARRIED AWAY AND CONFESSED THAT I MADE CHOCOLATES FOR THE BEAGLE!

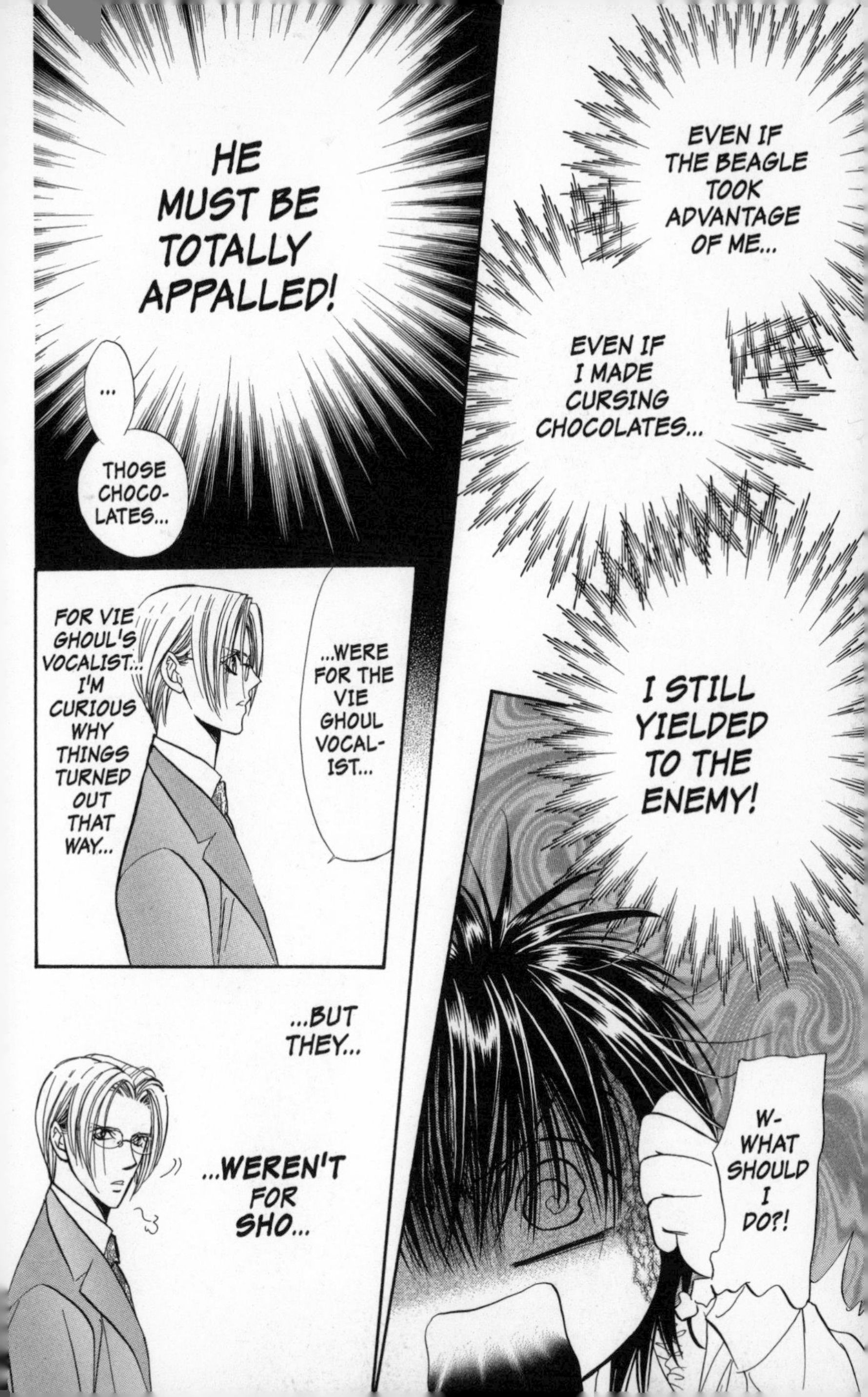
EVEN IF THE BEAGLE TOOK ADVANTAGE OF ME...
EVEN IF I MADE CURSING CHOCOLATES...
I STILL YIELDED TO THE ENEMY!
W-WHAT SHOULD I DO?!
HE MUST BE TOTALLY APPALLED!
...
THOSE CHOCOLATES...
...WERE FOR THE VIE GHOUL VOCALIST...
FOR VIE GHOUL'S VOCALIST... I'M CURIOUS WHY THINGS TURNED OUT THAT WAY...
...BUT THEY...
...WEREN'T FOR SHO...

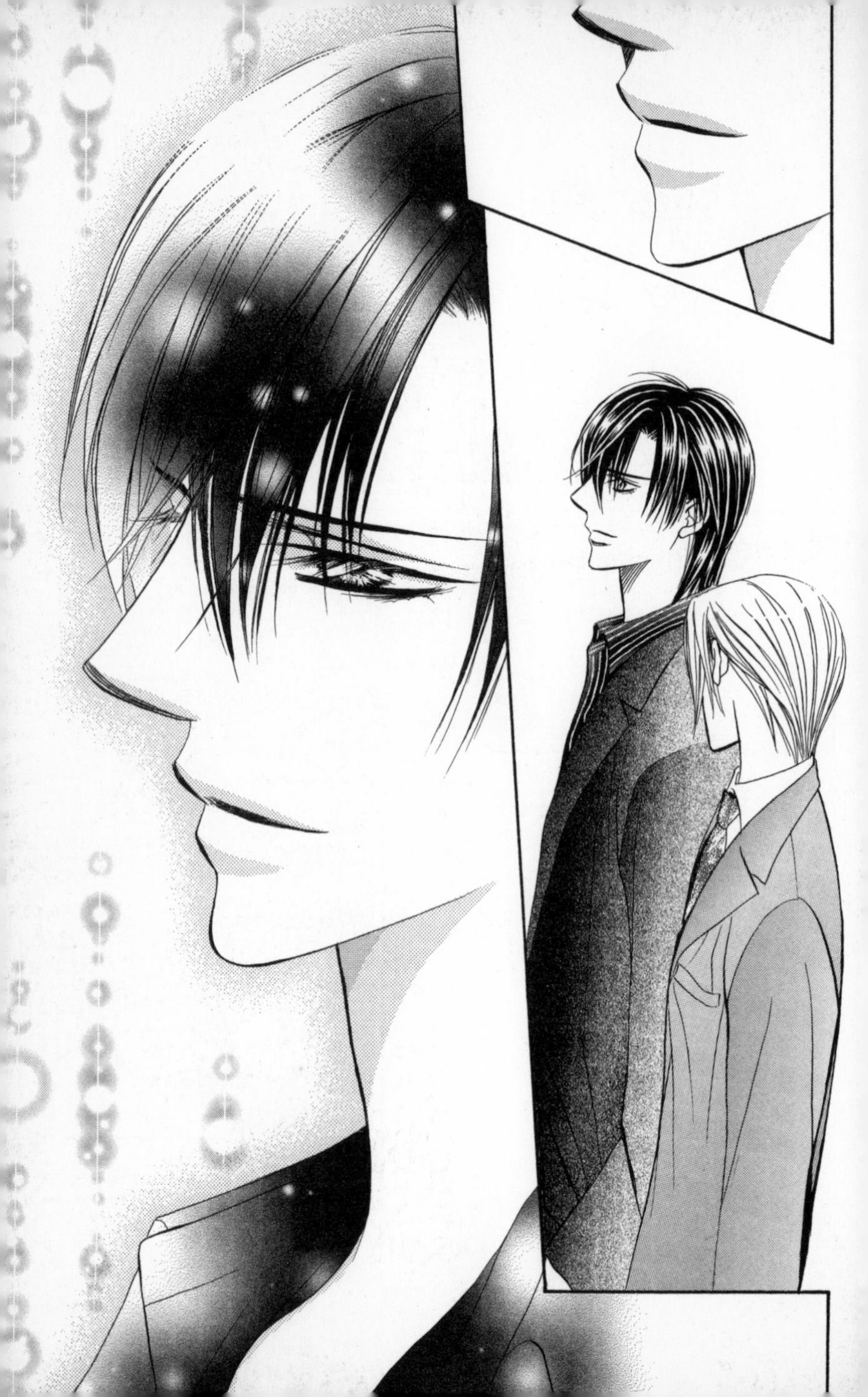

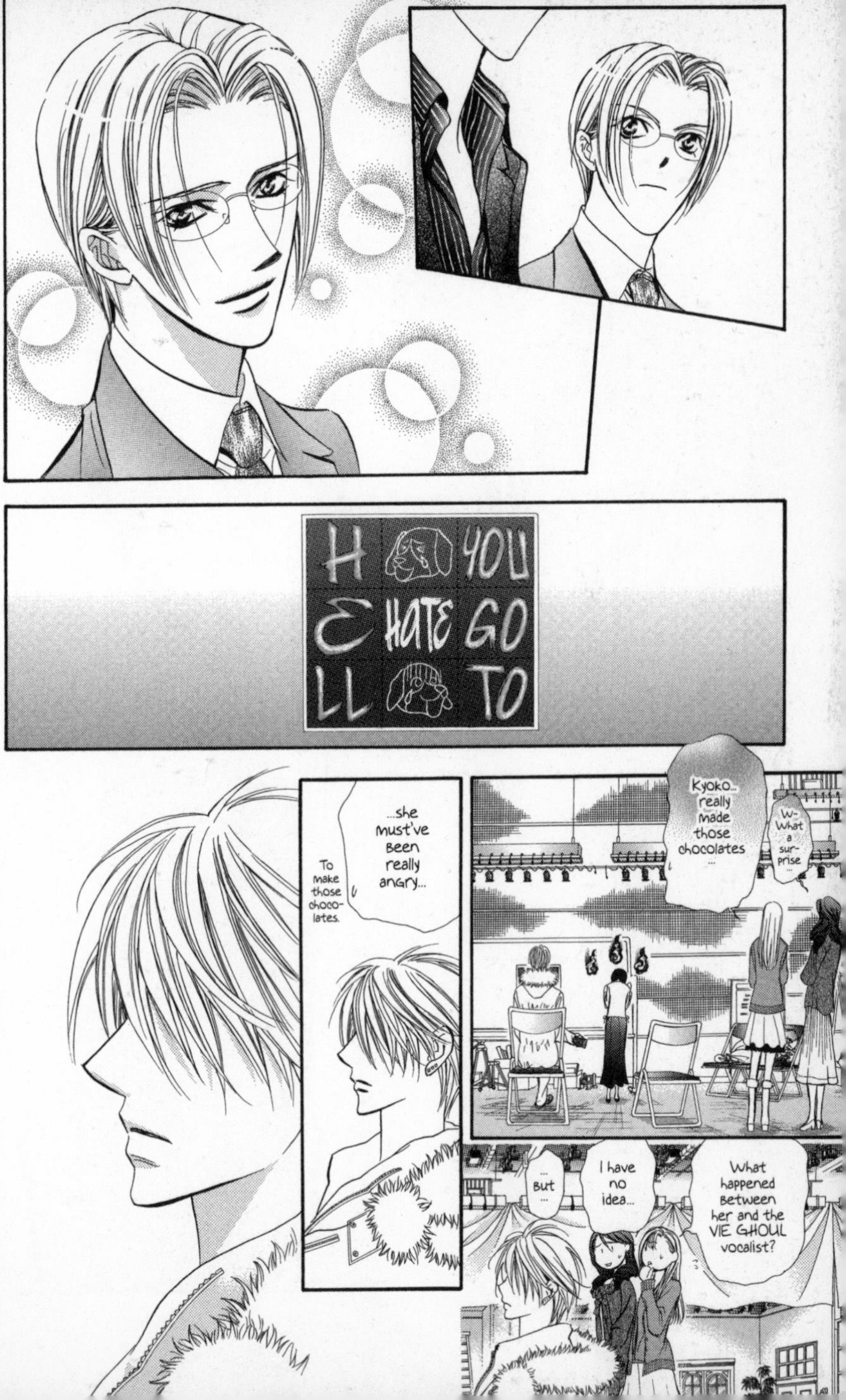
H YOU
E HATE GO
LL TO
Kyoko... really made those chocolates ...
W-What a sur-prise ...
What happened between her and the VIE GHOUL vocalist?
I have no idea...
... But ...
...she must've been really angry...
To make those choco-lates.

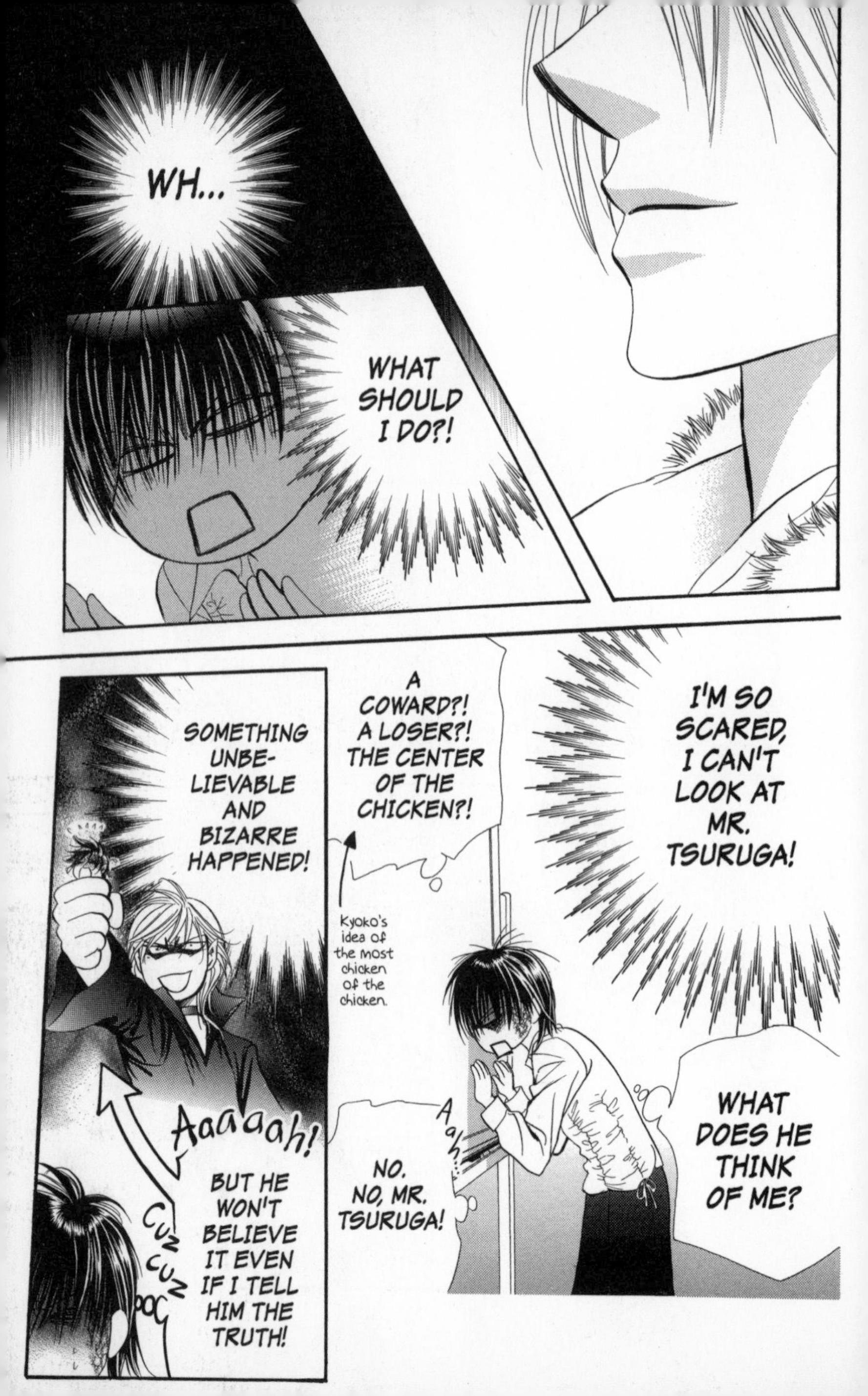
WH...
WHAT SHOULD I DO?!
I'M SO SCARED, I CAN'T LOOK AT MR. TSURUGA!
A COWARD?! A LOSER?! THE CENTER OF THE CHICKEN?!
Kyoko's idea of the most chicken of the chicken.
WHAT DOES HE THINK OF ME?
Aah...
NO. NO, MR. TSURUGA!
SOMETHING UNBE-LIEVABLE AND BIZARRE HAPPENED!
Aaaaah!
BUT HE WON'T BELIEVE IT EVEN IF I TELL HIM THE TRUTH!
CUZ CUZ DOC

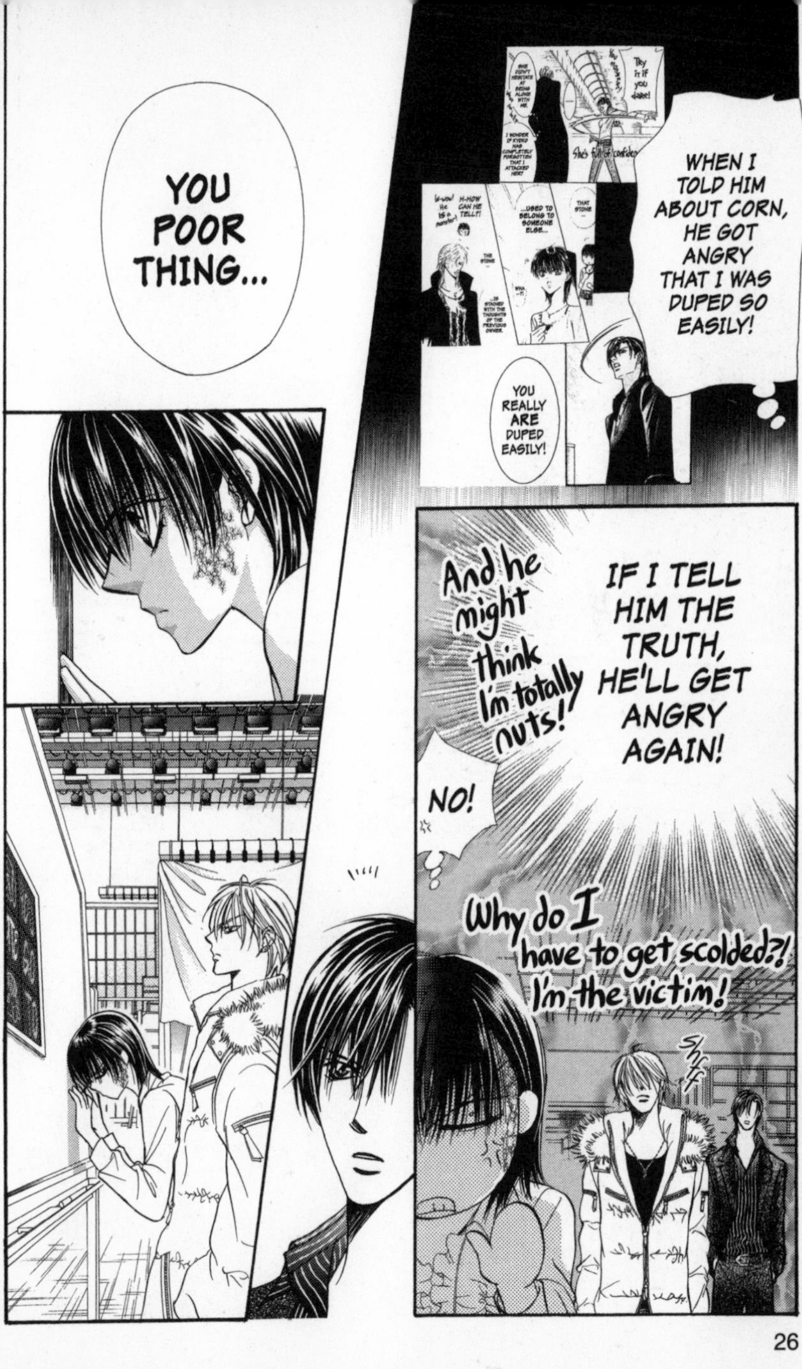
WHEN I TOLD HIM ABOUT CORN, HE GOT ANGRY THAT I WAS DUPED SO EASILY!
Try it if you dare!
She's full of confide
SHE DIDN'T HESITATE AT BEING ALONE WITH ME.
I WONDER IF KYOKO HAS COMPLETELY FORGOTTEN THAT I ATTACKED HER!
THAT STONE...
...USED TO BELONG TO SOMEONE ELSE...
WHA-?!
THE STONE...
...IS STAINED WITH THE THOUGHTS OF THE PREVIOUS OWNER.
H-HOW CAN HE TELL?!
W-wow! He is a monster!
YOU REALLY ARE DUPED EASILY!
IF I TELL HIM THE TRUTH, HE'LL GET ANGRY AGAIN!
And he might think I'm totally nuts!
NO!
Why do I have to get scolded?! I'm the victim!
Shff
YOU POOR THING...

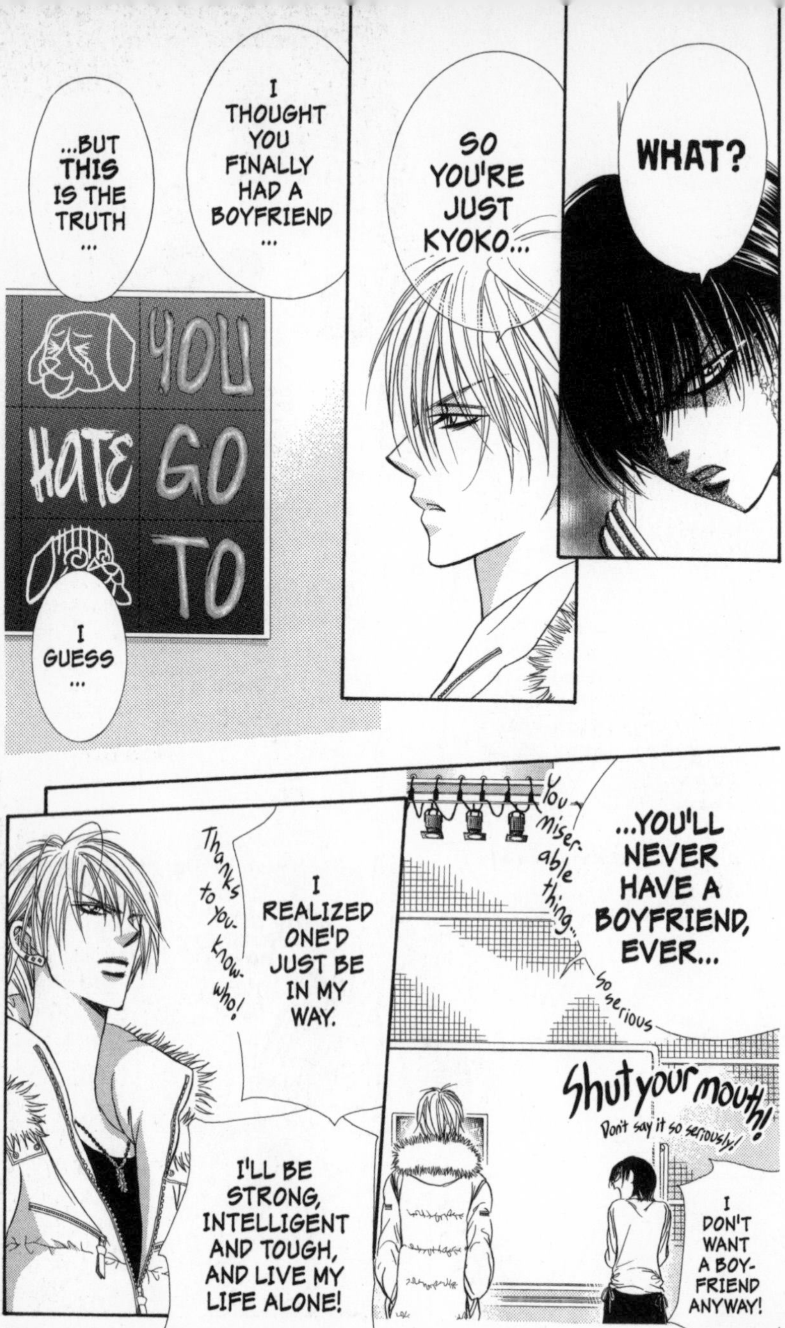
WHAT?
SO YOU'RE JUST KYOKO...
I THOUGHT YOU FINALLY HAD A BOYFRIEND...
...BUT THIS IS THE TRUTH...
YOU
HATE GO
TO
I GUESS...
You miserable thing...
...YOU'LL NEVER HAVE A BOYFRIEND, EVER...
So serious
Shut your mouth!
Don't say it so seriously!
I DON'T WANT A BOY-FRIEND ANYWAY!
Thanks to you-know-who!
I REALIZED ONE'D JUST BE IN MY WAY.
I'LL BE STRONG, INTELLIGENT AND TOUGH, AND LIVE MY LIFE ALONE!

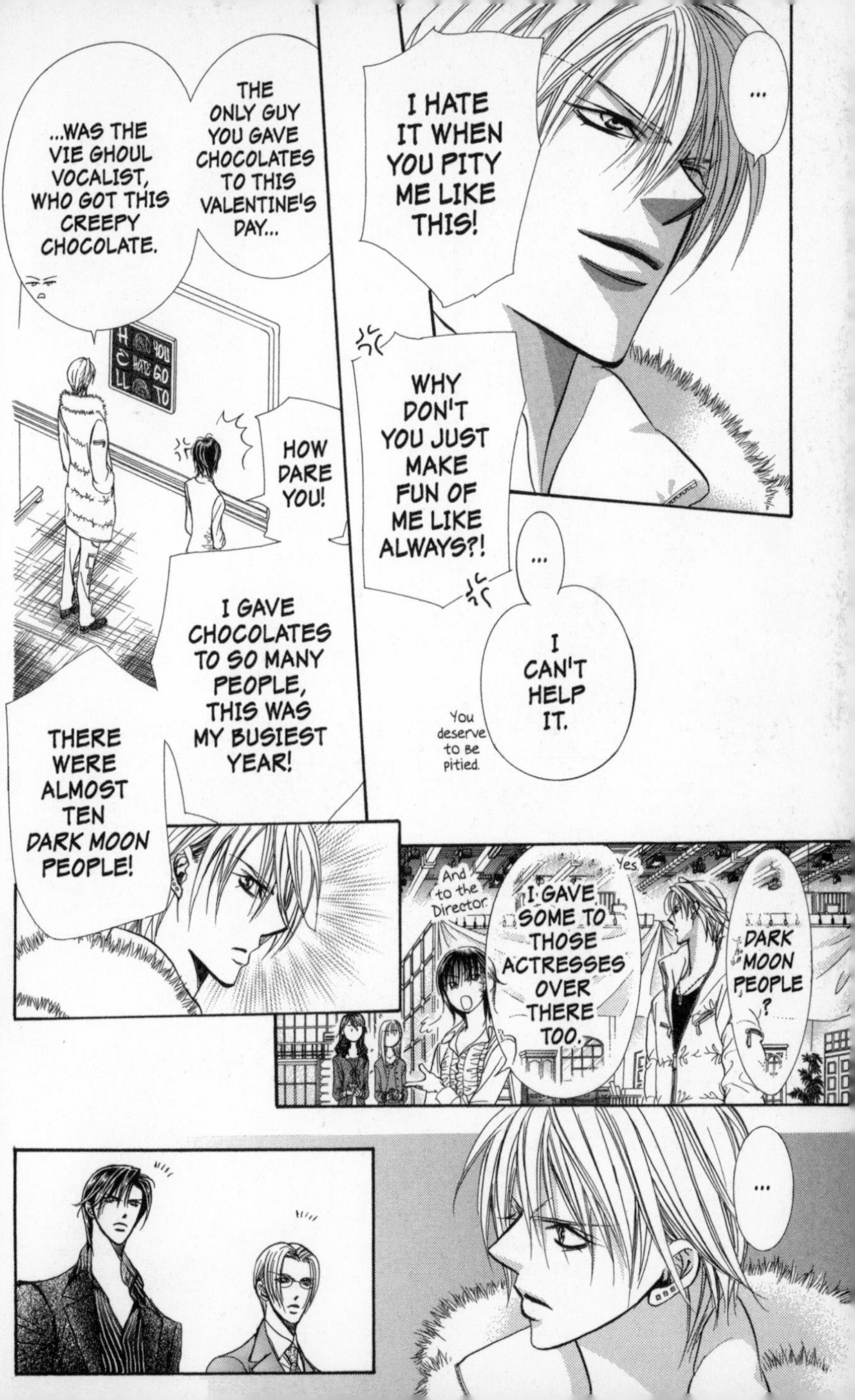
...
I HATE IT WHEN YOU PITY ME LIKE THIS!
WHY DON'T YOU JUST MAKE FUN OF ME LIKE ALWAYS?!
...
I CAN'T HELP IT.
You deserve to be pitied.
THE ONLY GUY YOU GAVE CHOCOLATES TO THIS VALENTINE'S DAY...
...WAS THE VIE GHOUL VOCALIST, WHO GOT THIS CREEPY CHOCOLATE.
HOW DARE YOU!
I GAVE CHOCOLATES TO SO MANY PEOPLE, THIS WAS MY BUSIEST YEAR!
THERE WERE ALMOST TEN DARK MOON PEOPLE!
DARK MOON PEOPLE?
Yes.
I GAVE SOME TO THOSE ACTRESSES OVER THERE TOO.
And to the Director.
...

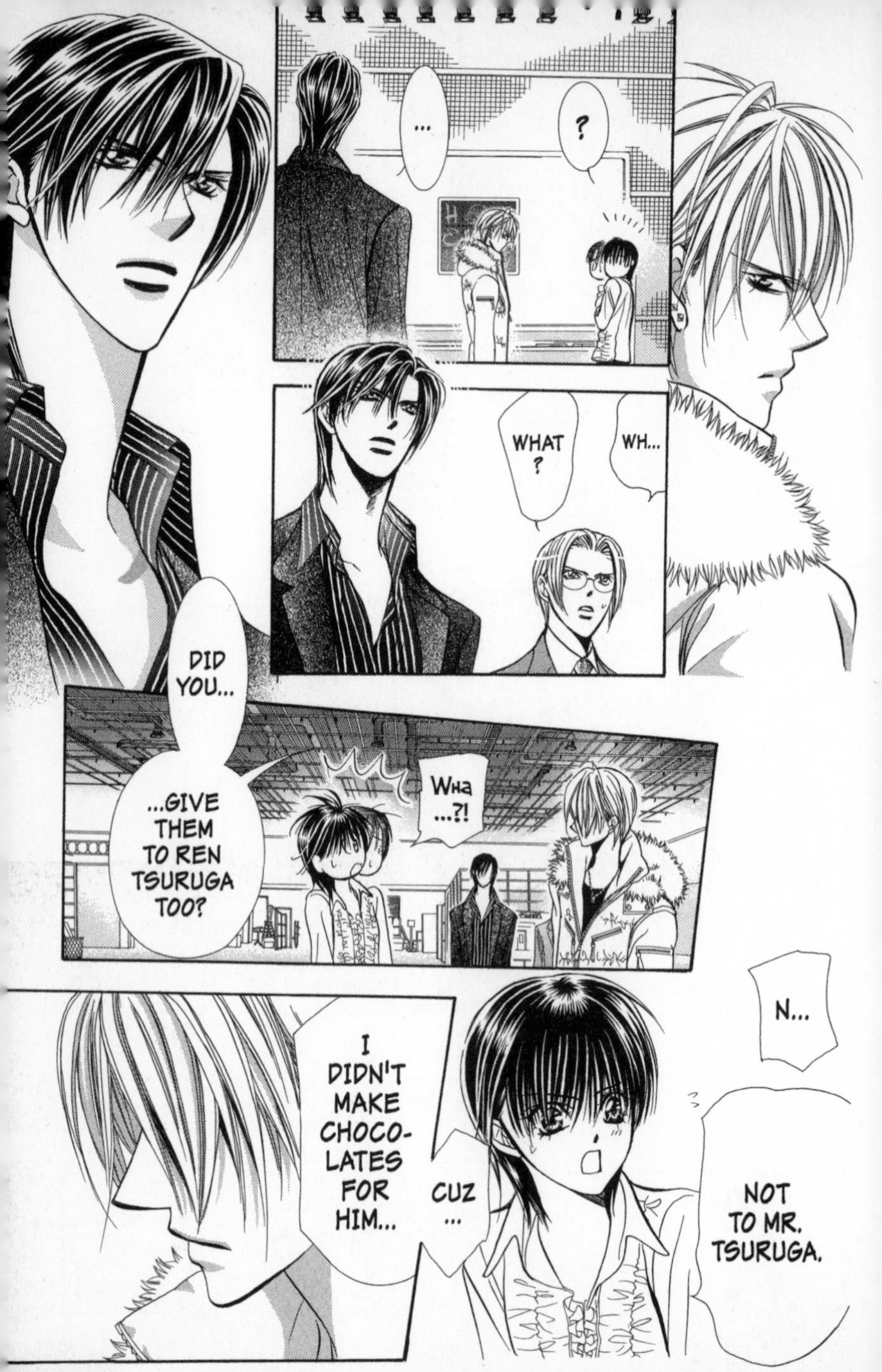
?
...
WH...
WHAT ?
DID YOU...
...GIVE THEM TO REN TSURUGA TOO?
Wha ...?!
N...
NOT TO MR. TSURUGA.
CUZ ...
I DIDN'T MAKE CHOCO-LATES FOR HIM...

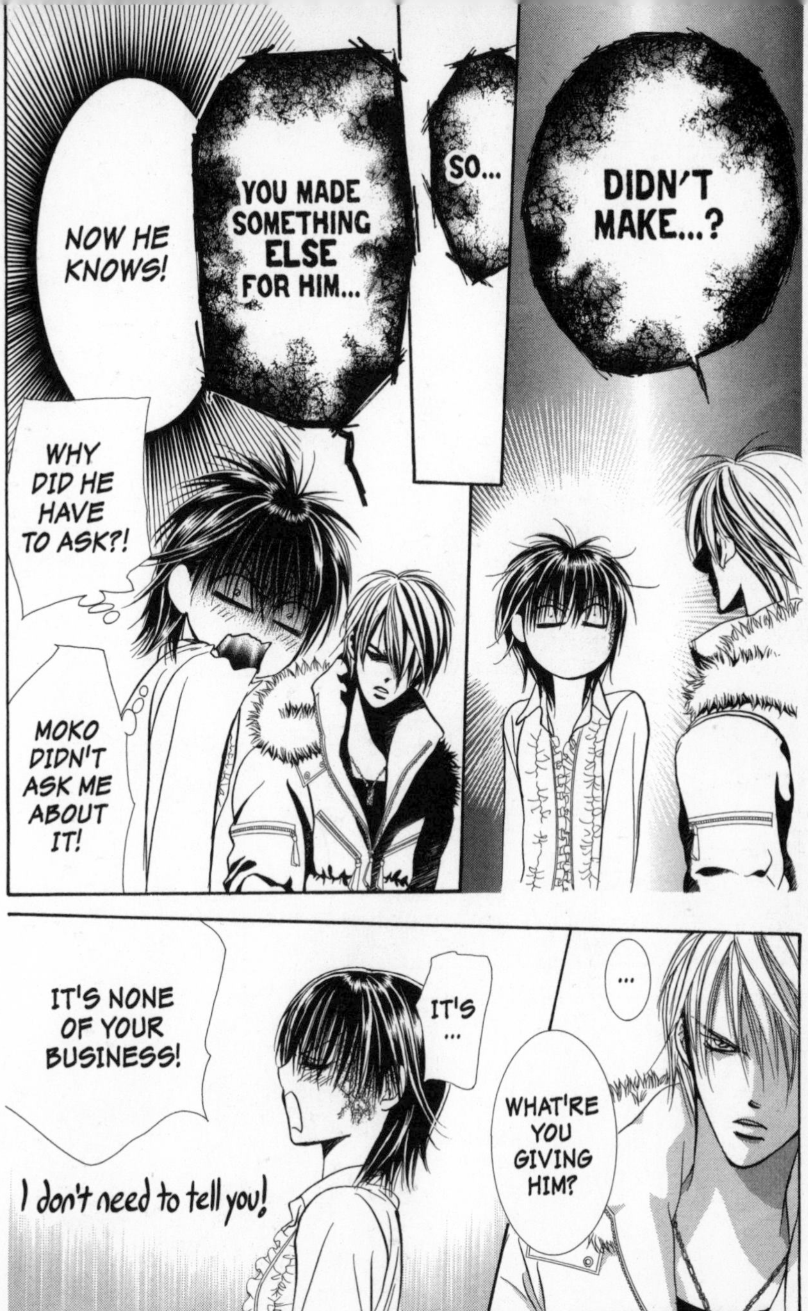
DIDN'T MAKE...?
SO...
YOU MADE SOMETHING ELSE FOR HIM...
NOW HE KNOWS!
WHY DID HE HAVE TO ASK?!
MOKO DIDN'T ASK ME ABOUT IT!
...
WHAT'RE YOU GIVING HIM?
IT'S ...
IT'S NONE OF YOUR BUSINESS!
I don't need to tell you!

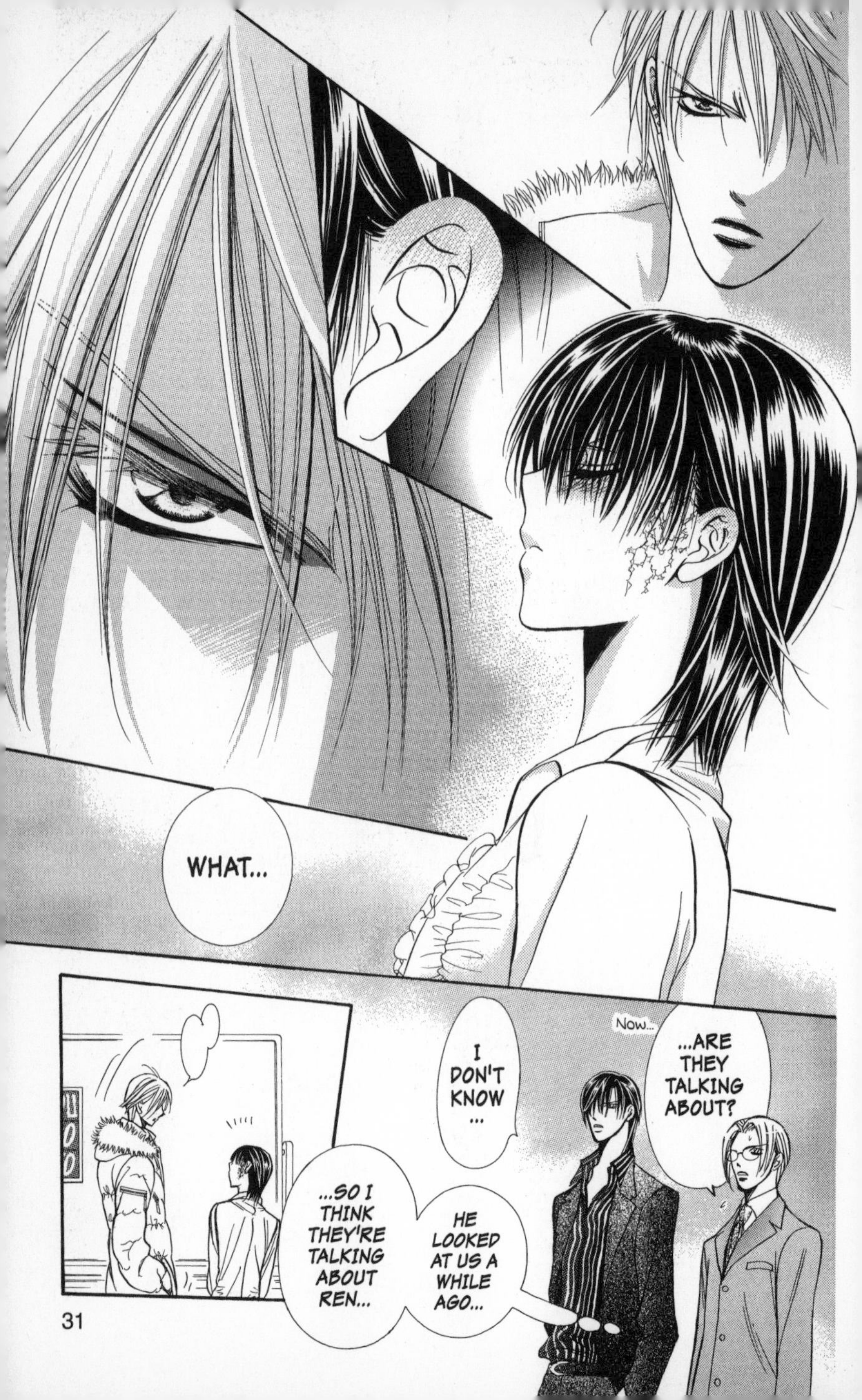
WHAT...
Now...
...ARE THEY TALKING ABOUT?
I DON'T KNOW ...
HE LOOKED AT US A WHILE AGO...
...SO I THINK THEY'RE TALKING ABOUT REN...

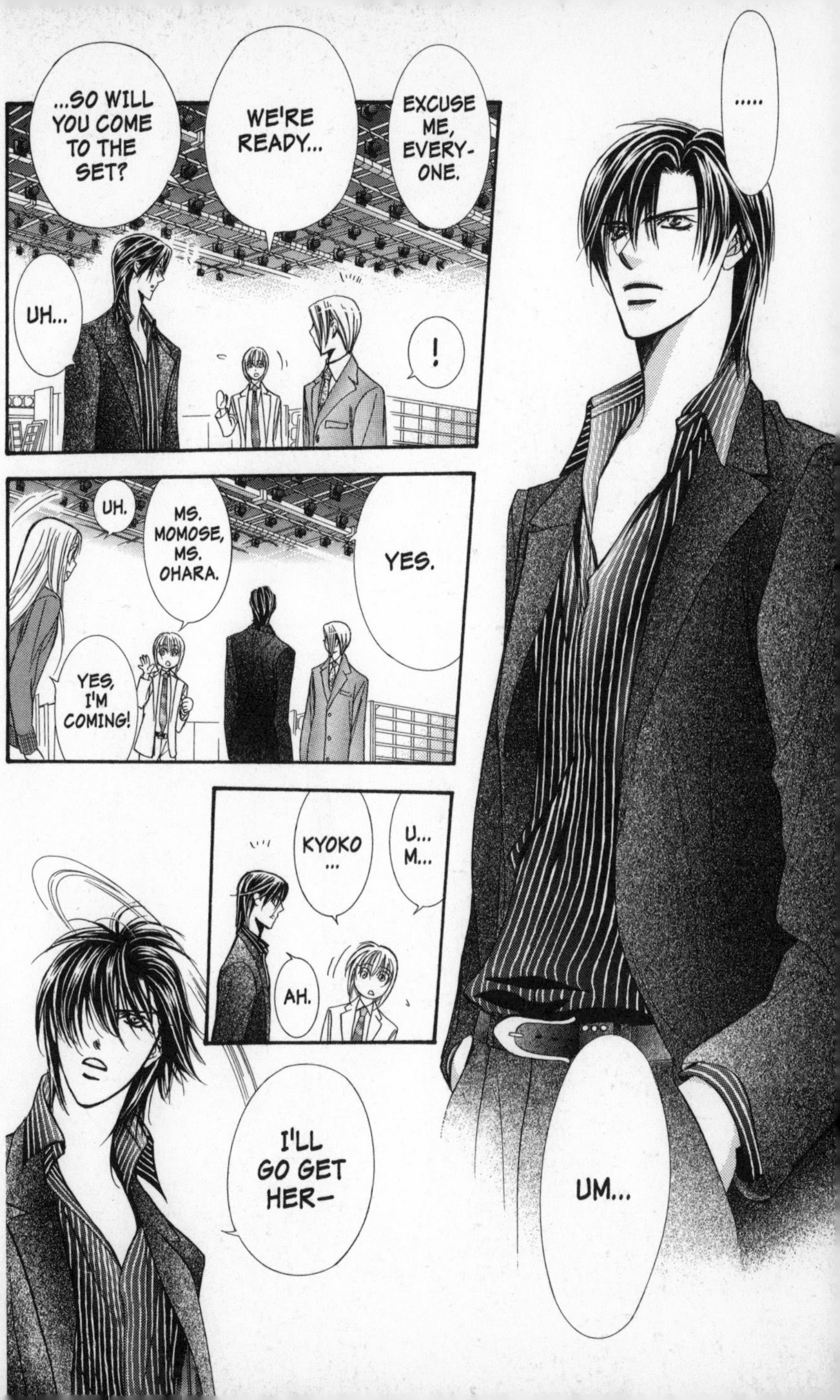
.....
UM...
EXCUSE ME, EVERYONE.
WE'RE READY...
...SO WILL YOU COME TO THE SET?
!
UH...
YES.
MS. MOMOSE, MS. OHARA.
UH.
YES, I'M COMING!
U... M...
KYOKO ...
AH.
I'LL GO GET HER-

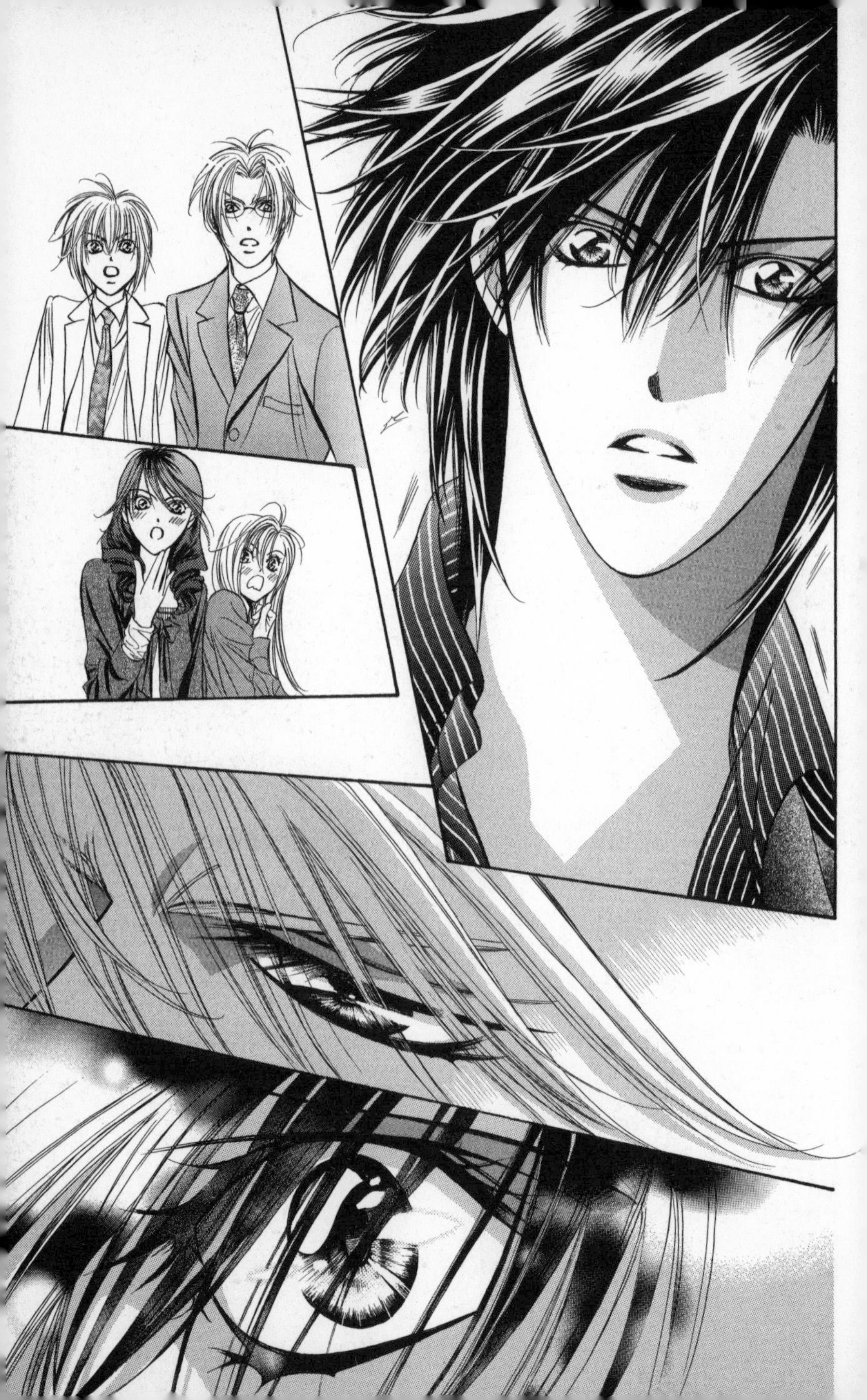

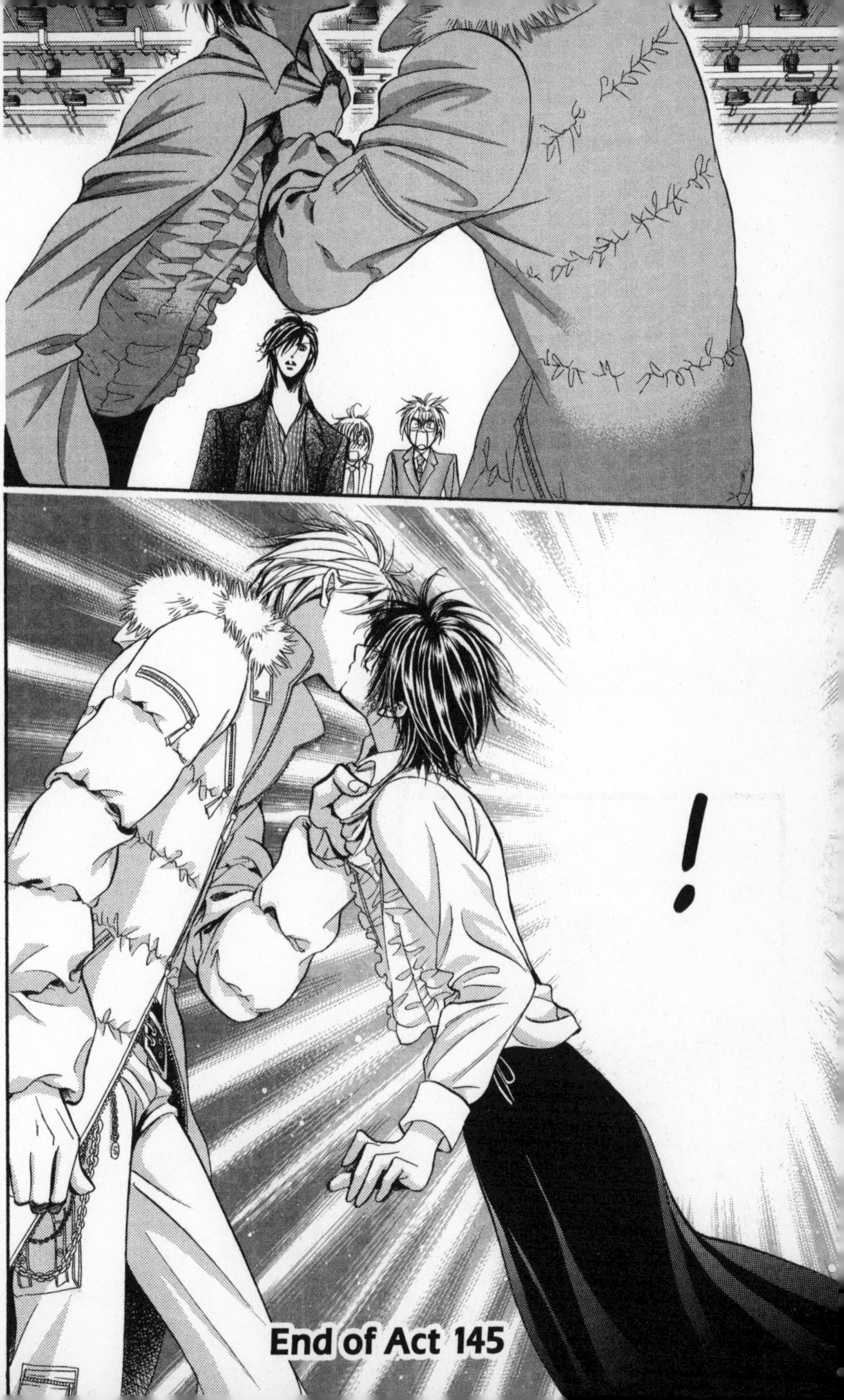
!

End of Act 145

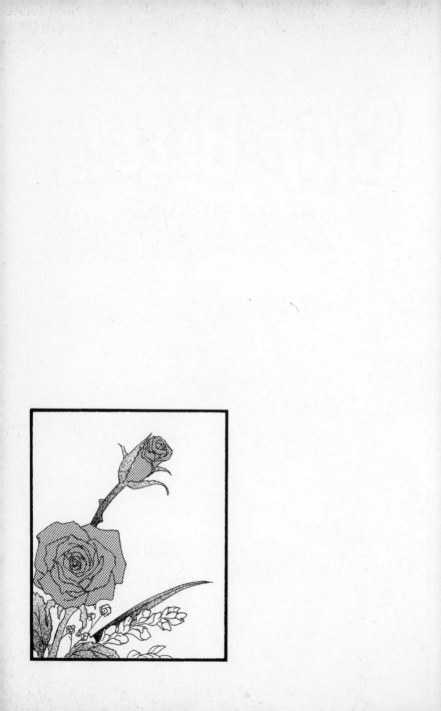

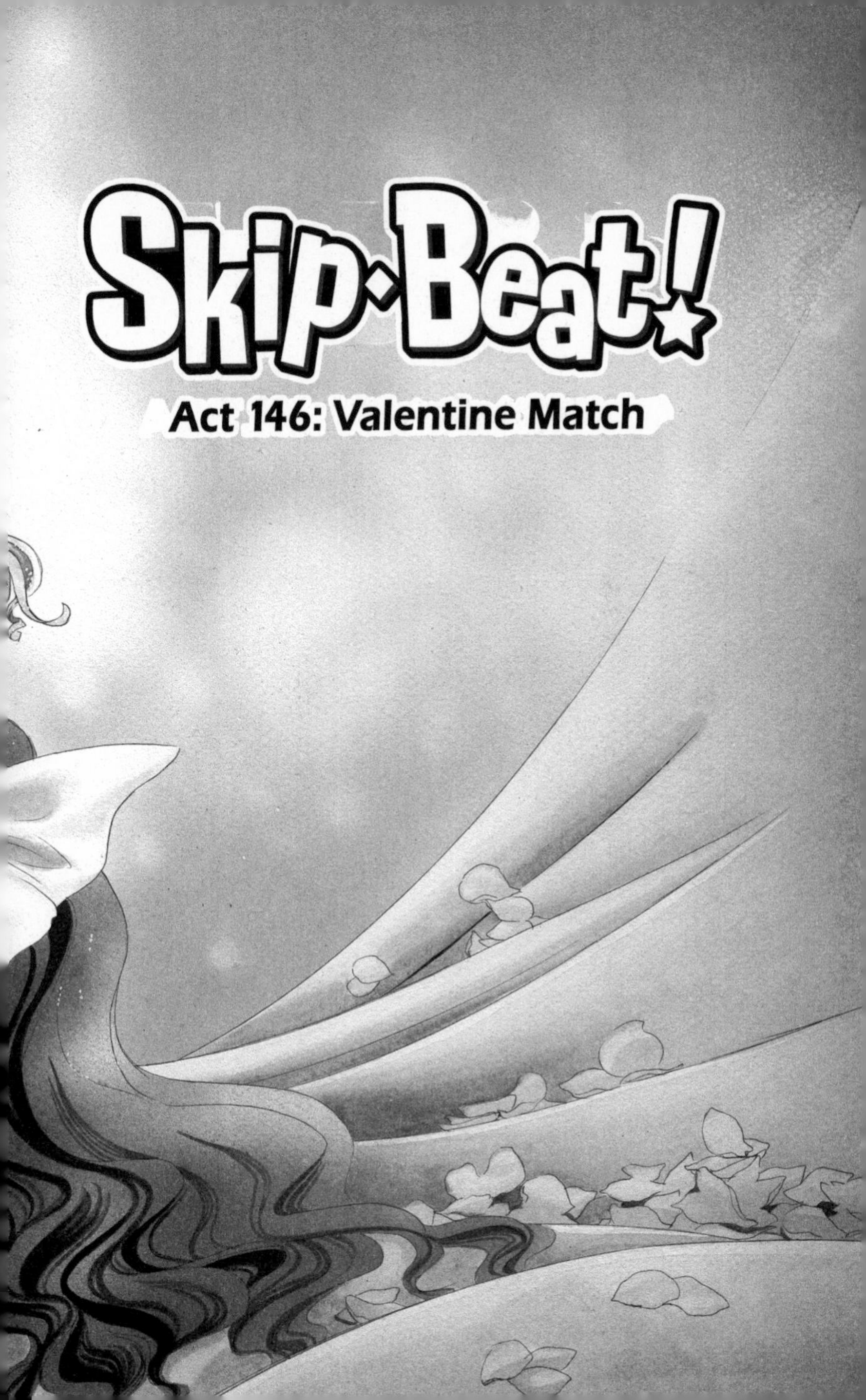
Skip·Beat!
Act 146: Valentine Match

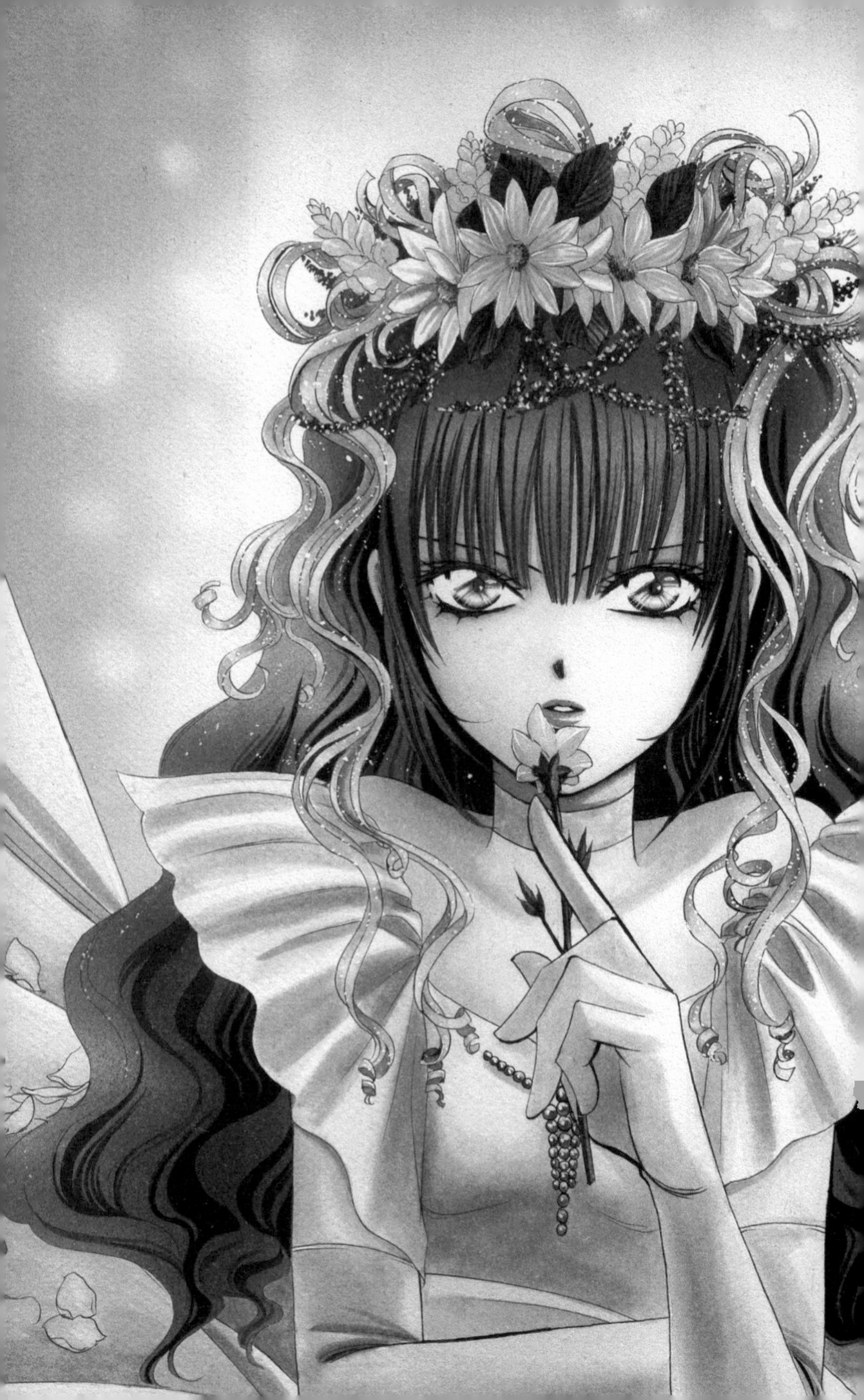

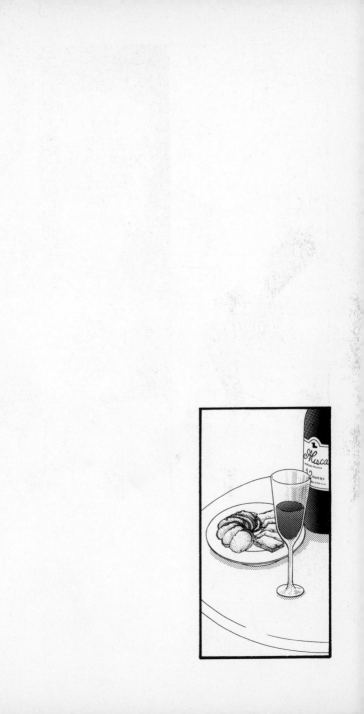

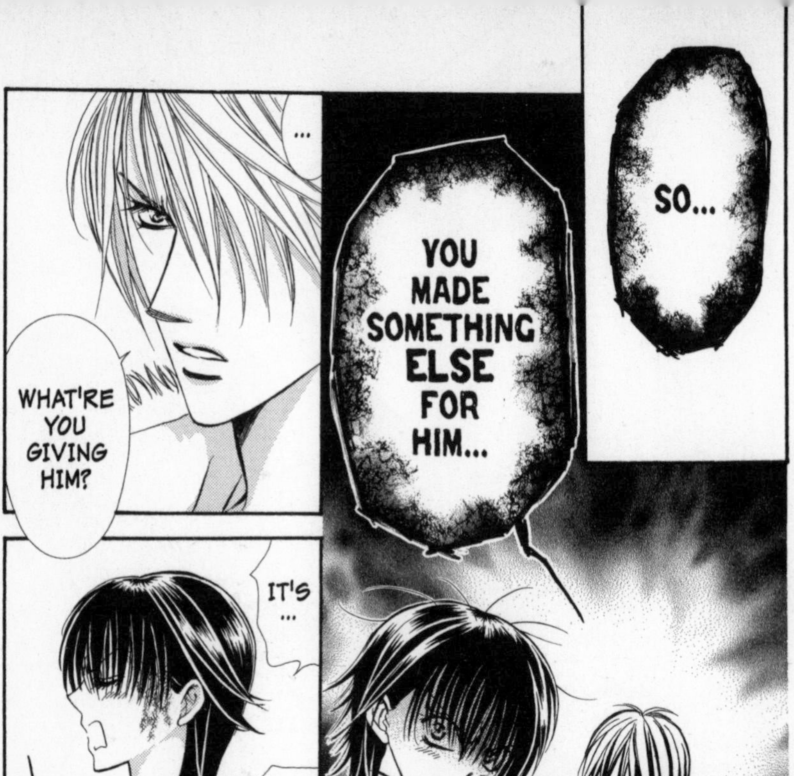
SO...
YOU MADE SOMETHING ELSE FOR HIM...
...
WHAT'RE YOU GIVING HIM?
IT'S ...
IT'S NONE OF YOUR BUSINESS!
I don't need to tell you!

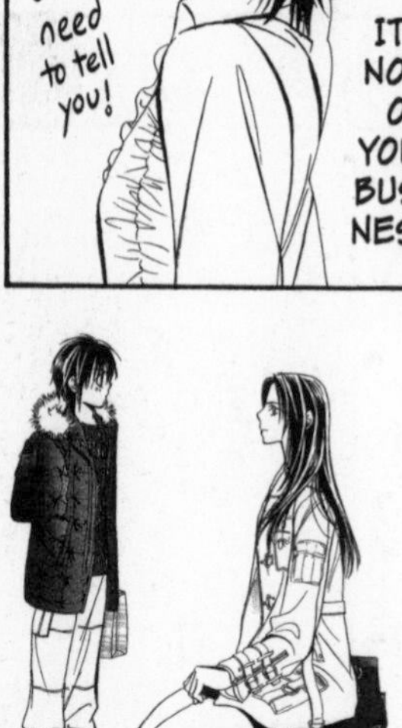

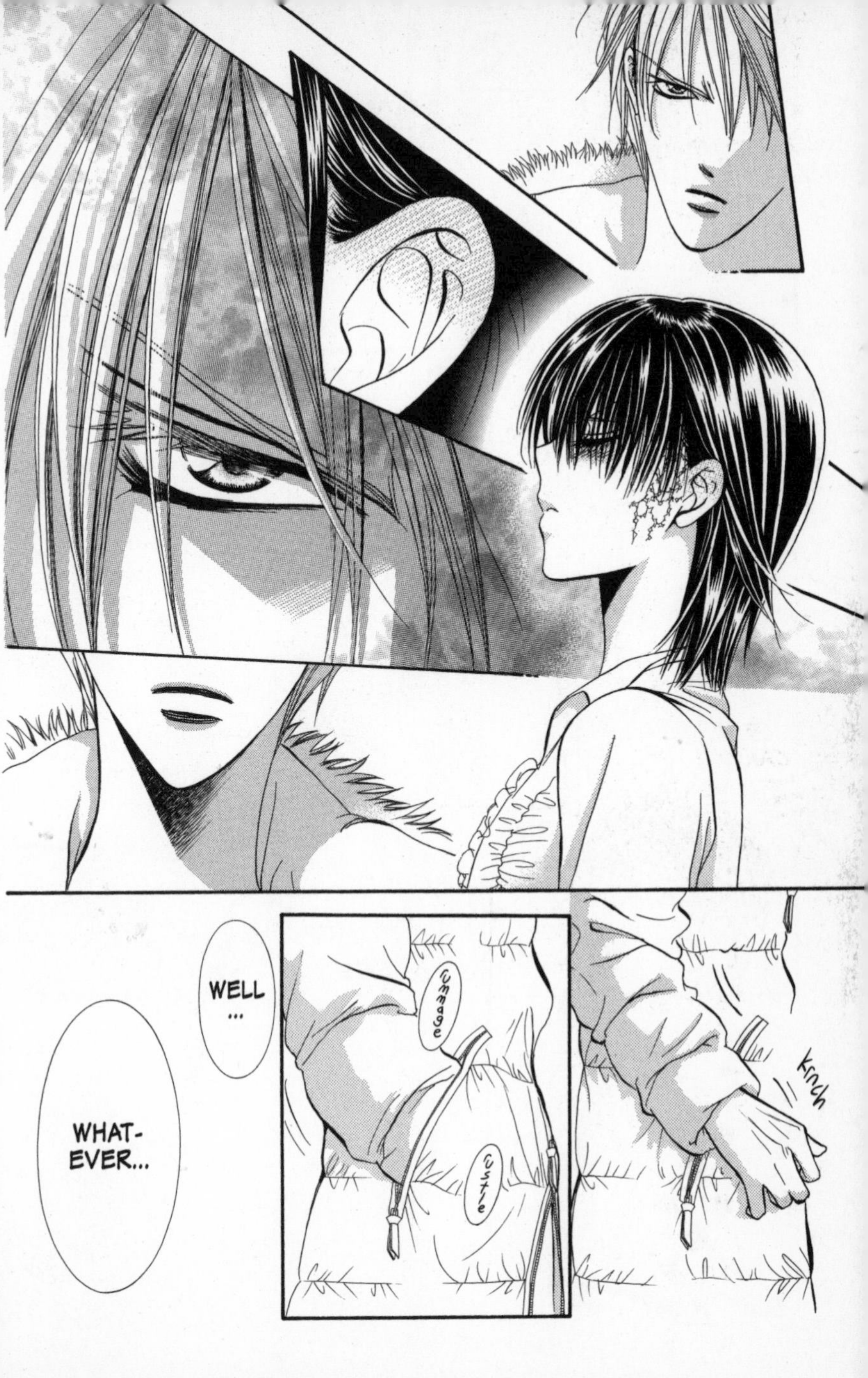
krnch
rummage
rustle
WELL...
WHAT-EVER...

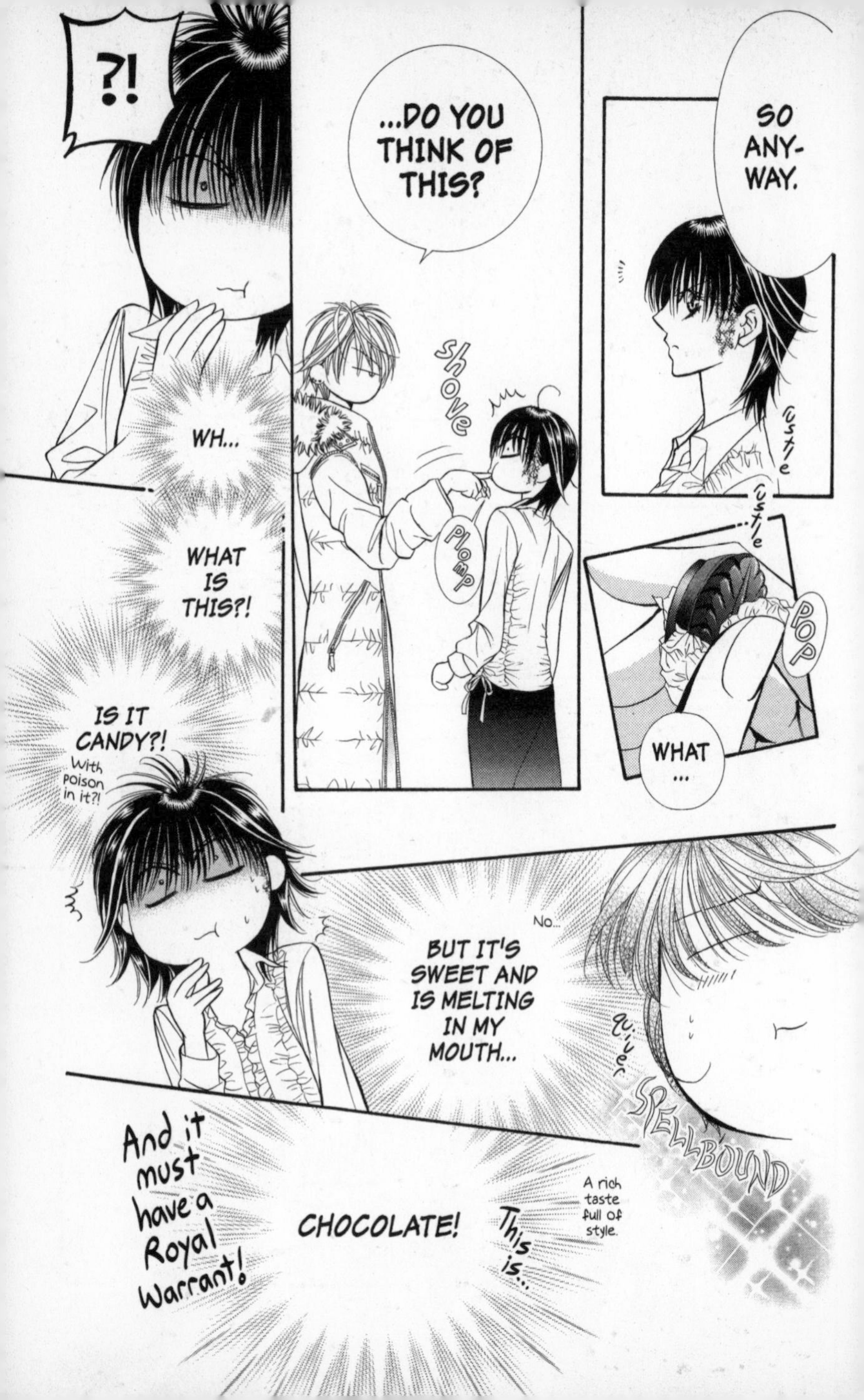
SO ANY-WAY.
rustle
rustle
POP
WHAT...
...DO YOU THINK OF THIS?
shove
Plomp
?!
WH...
WHAT IS THIS?!
IS IT CANDY?!
With poison in it?!
Quiver
SPELLBOUND
No...
BUT IT'S SWEET AND IS MELTING IN MY MOUTH...
A rich taste full of style.
This is...
CHOCOLATE!
And it must have a Royal Warrant!

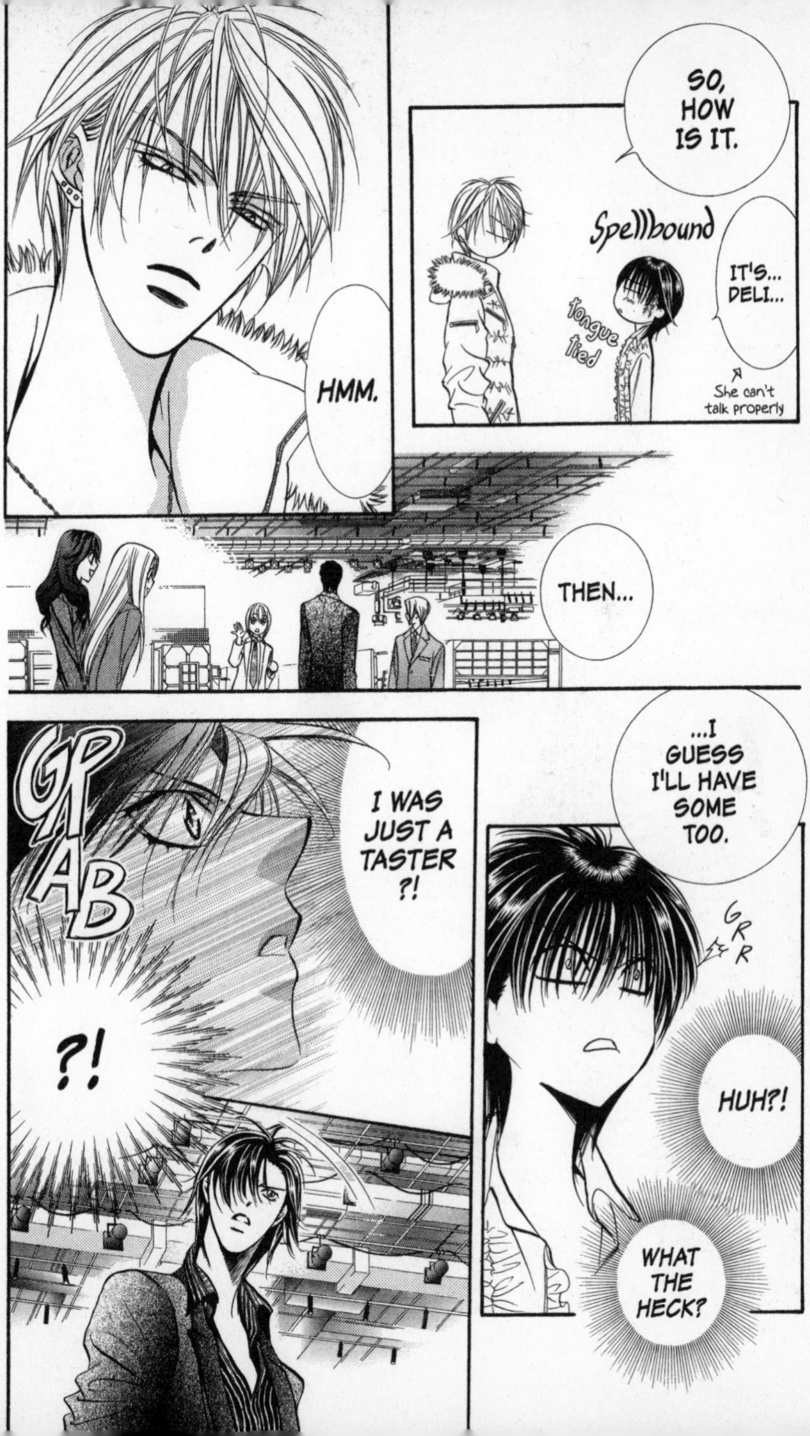

SO, HOW IS IT.
Spellbound
IT'S... DELI...
tongue tied
She can't talk properly
HMM.
THEN...
...I GUESS I'LL HAVE SOME TOO.
GRR
HUH?!
WHAT THE HECK?
GRAB
I WAS JUST A TASTER?!
?!

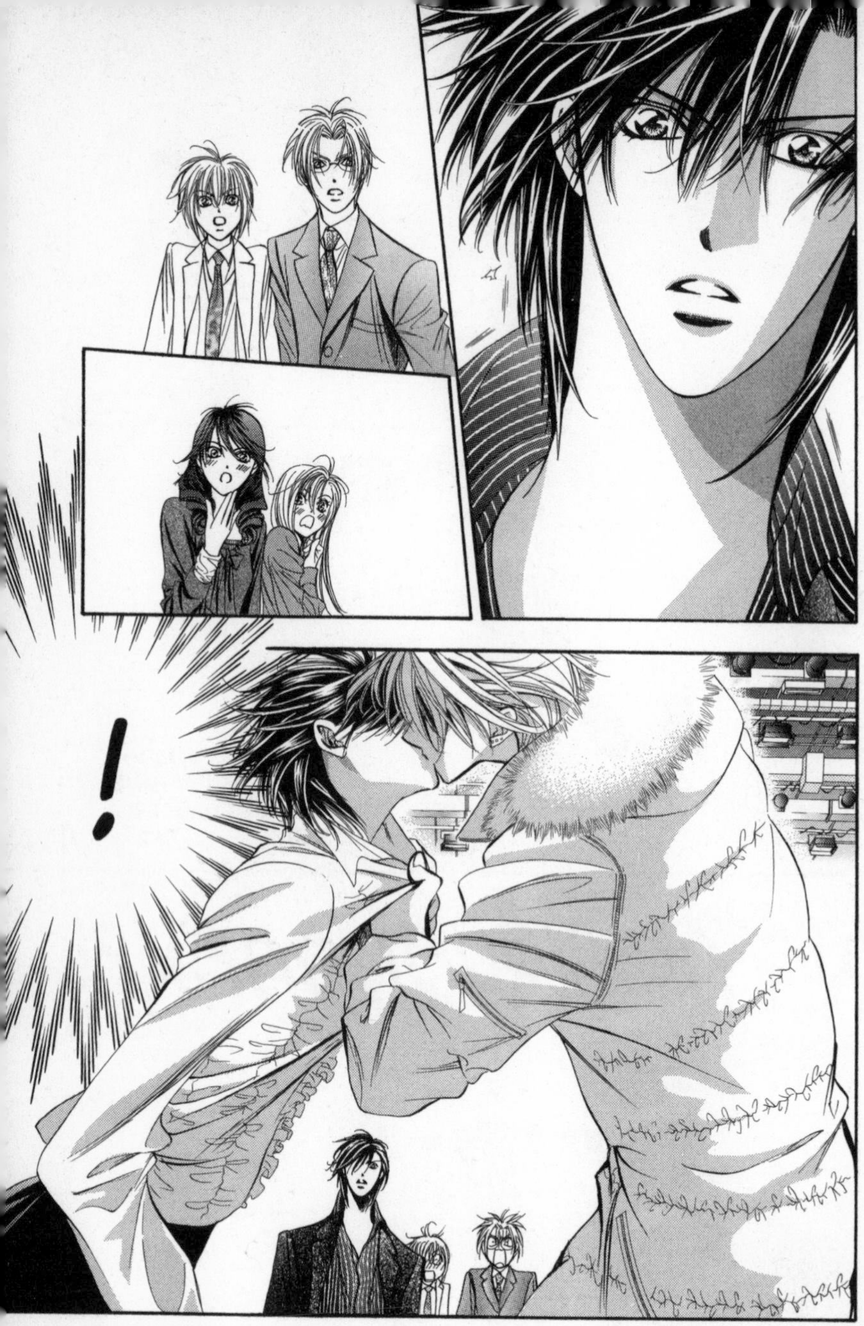
!

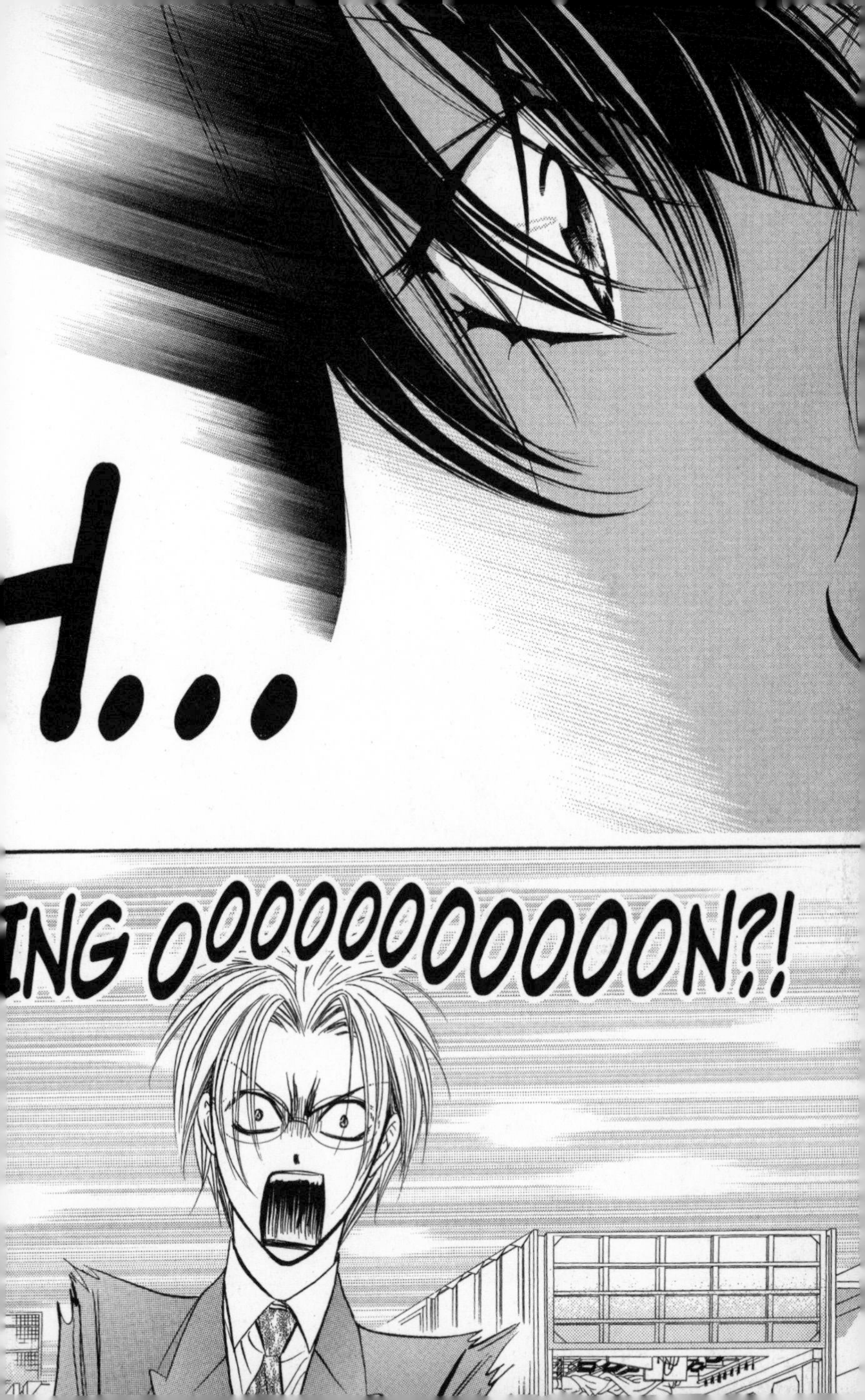
ING OOOOOOOOOOON?!

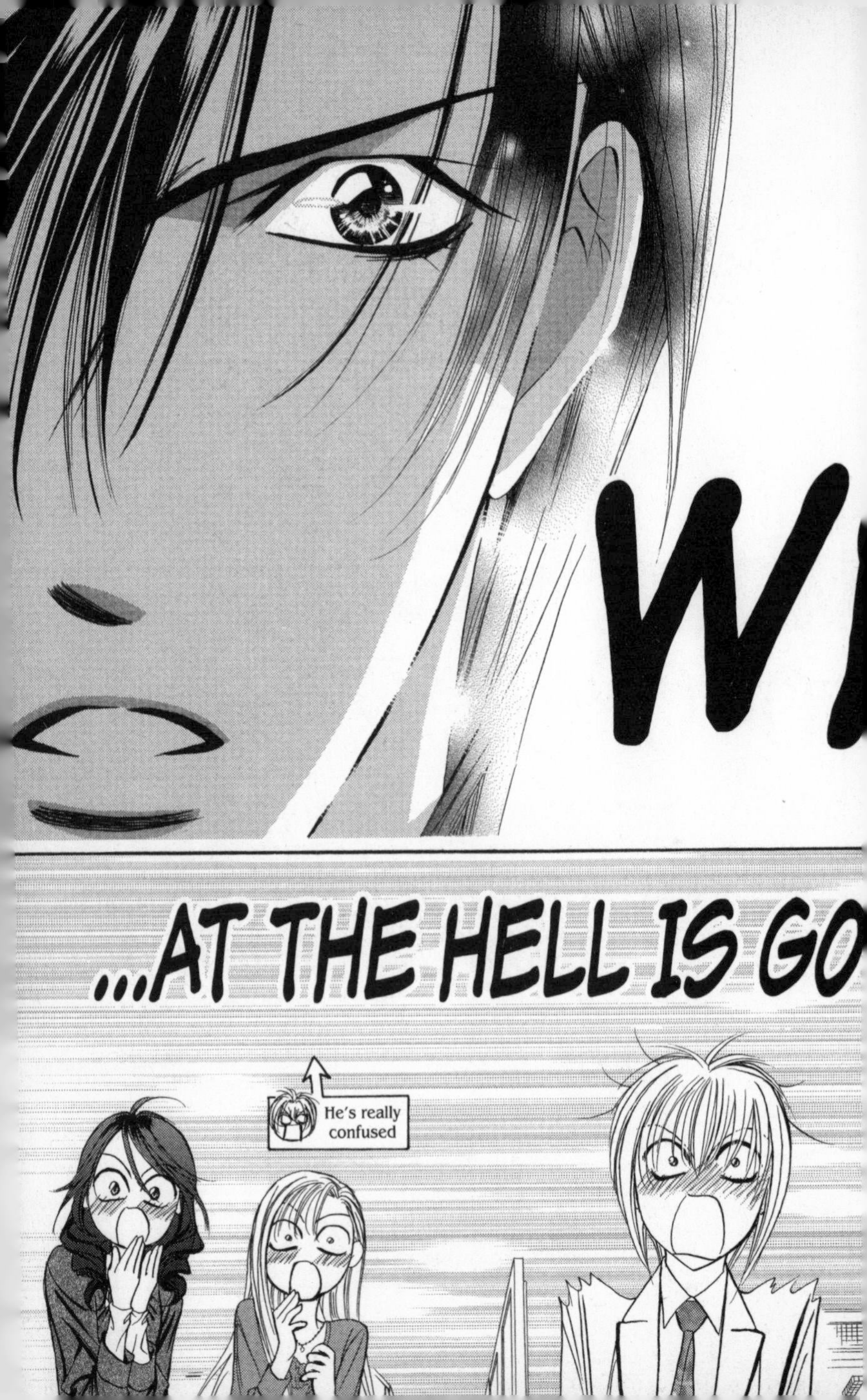
WH
...AT THE HELL IS GO
He's really confused

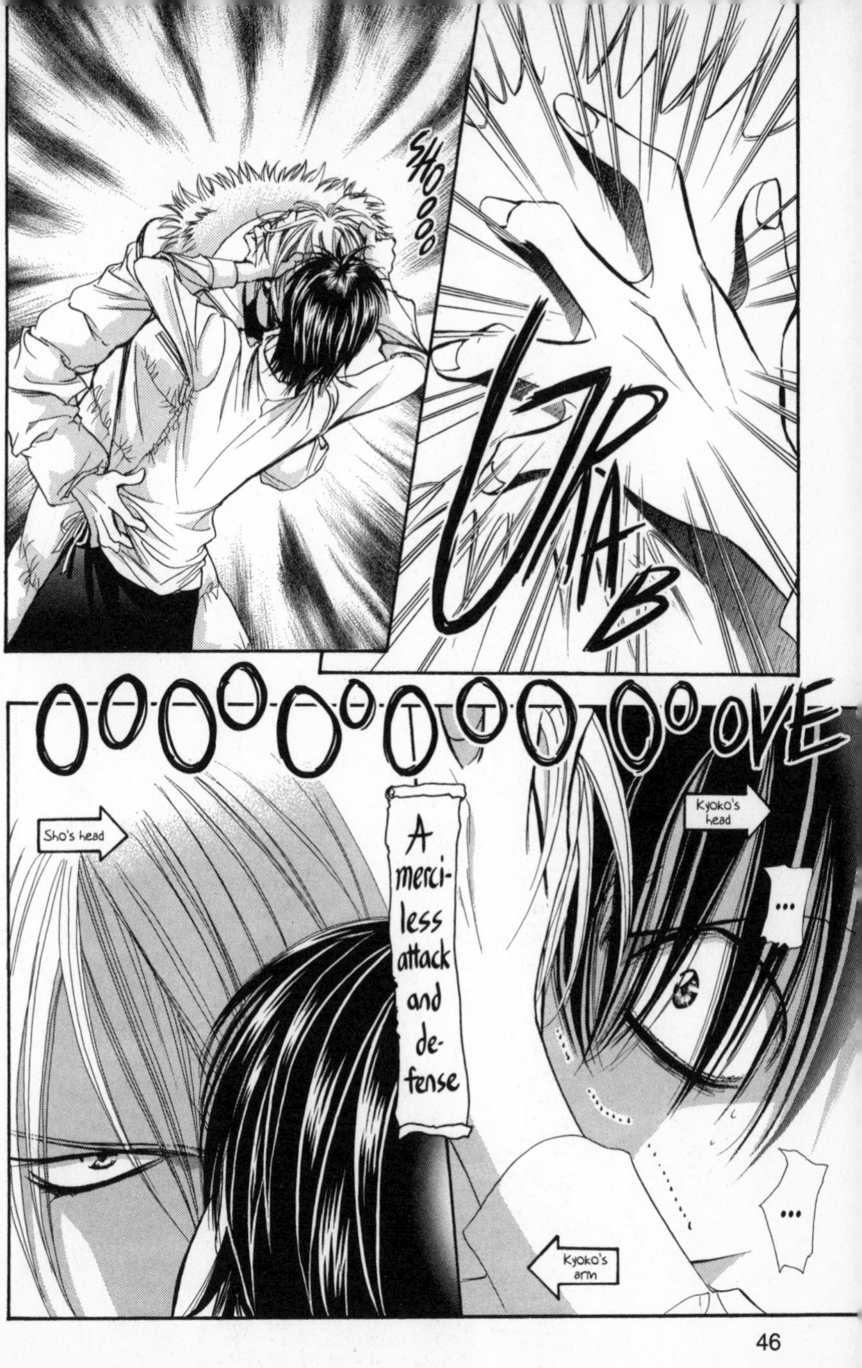
GRAB
SHOOOOO
OOOOOOOOOOOOOVE
A merciless attack and defense
Kyoko's head
...
...
Sho's head
Kyoko's arm

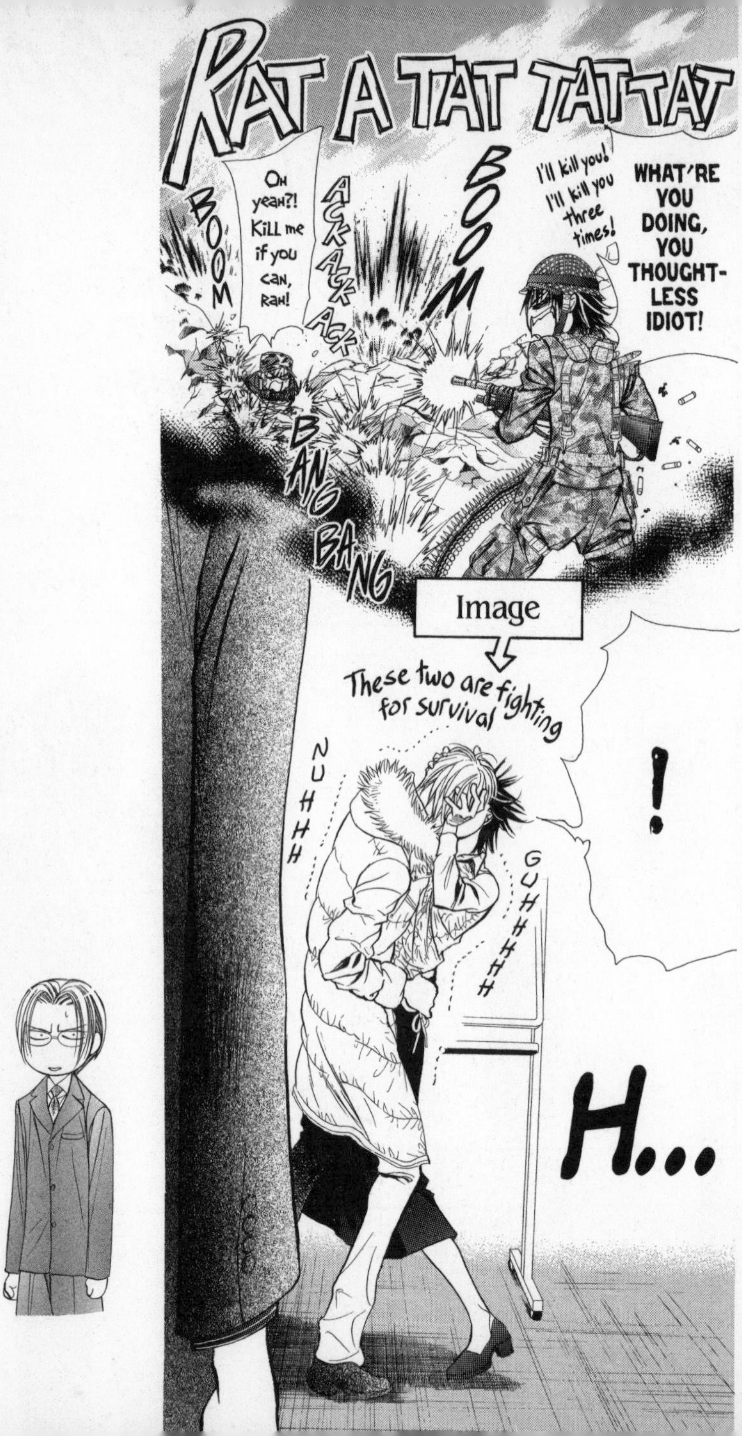
RAT A TAT TAT TAT
WHAT'RE YOU DOING, YOU THOUGHTLESS IDIOT!
I'll kill you! I'll kill you three times!
BOOM
ACK ACK ACK
Oh yeah?! Kill me if you can, Rah!
BOOM
BANG BANG
Image
These two are fighting for survival
!
NUHHHH
GUHHHHHH
H...

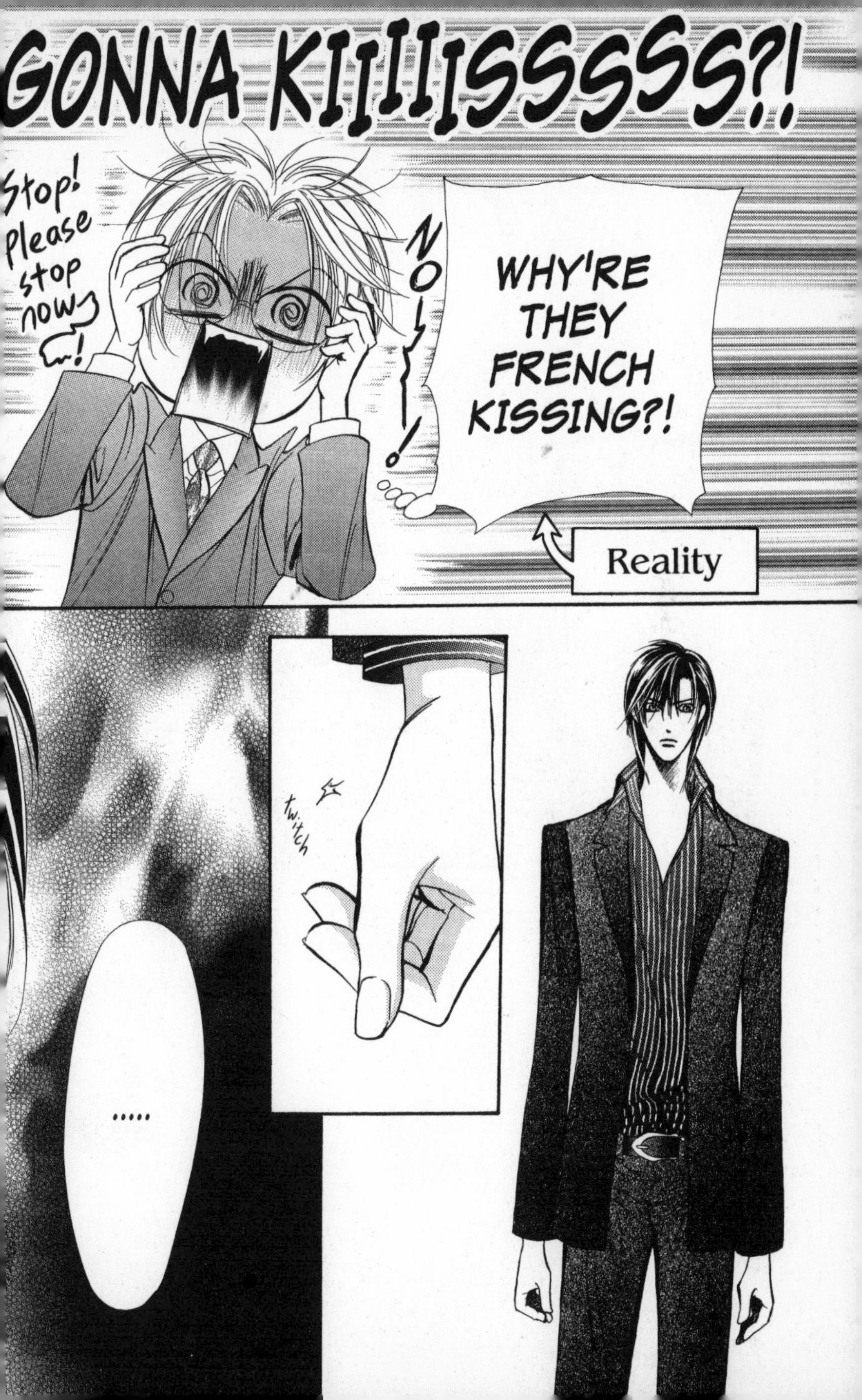
GONNA KIIIIISSSSSS?!
WHY'RE THEY FRENCH KISSING?!
NO~~~!
Reality
Stop! Please stop now~!
twitch
.....

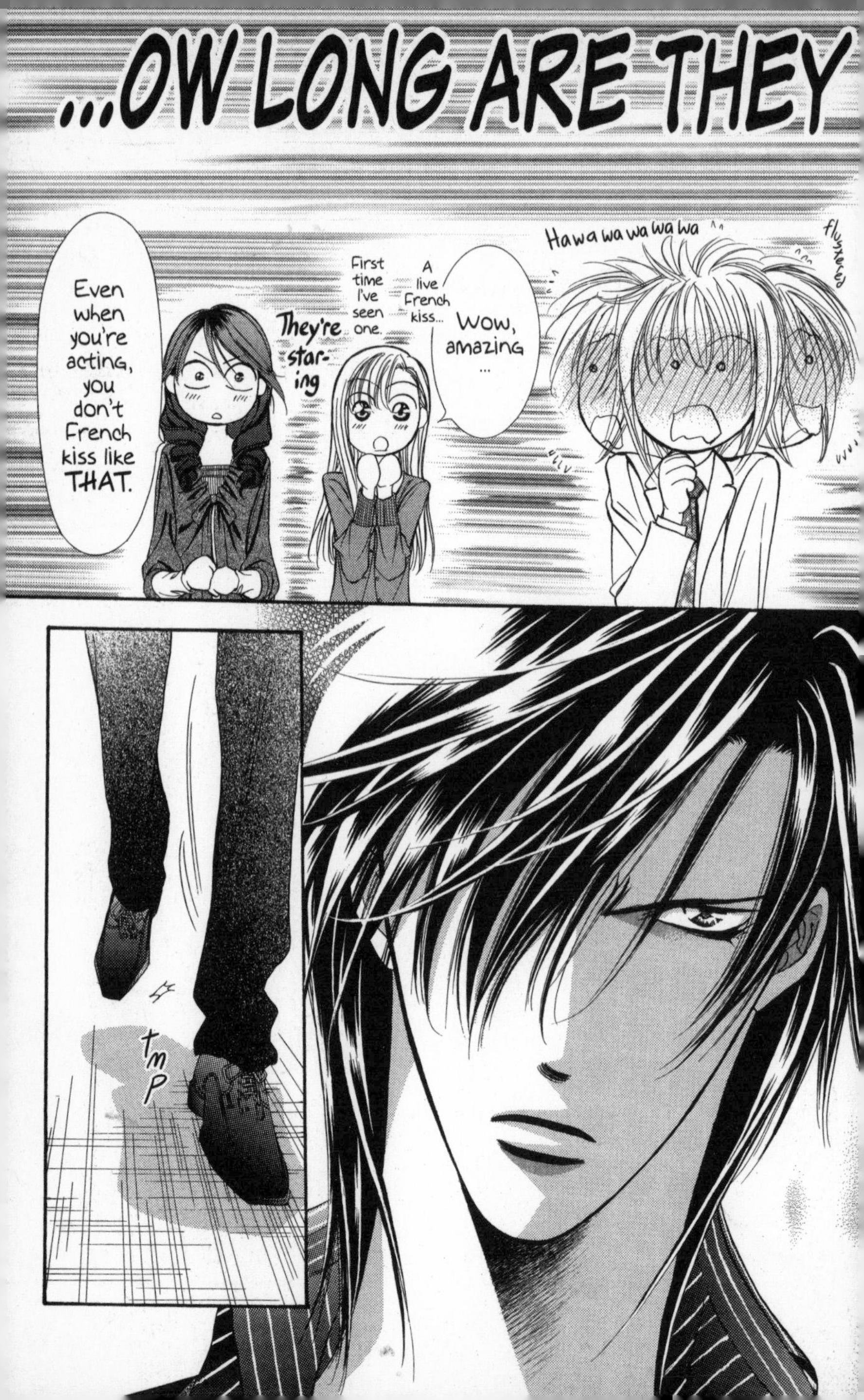
...OW LONG ARE THEY
Hawawawawawa
flustered
A live French kiss...
Wow, amazing...
First time I've seen one.
They're star- ing
Even when you're acting, you don't French kiss like THAT.
TMP

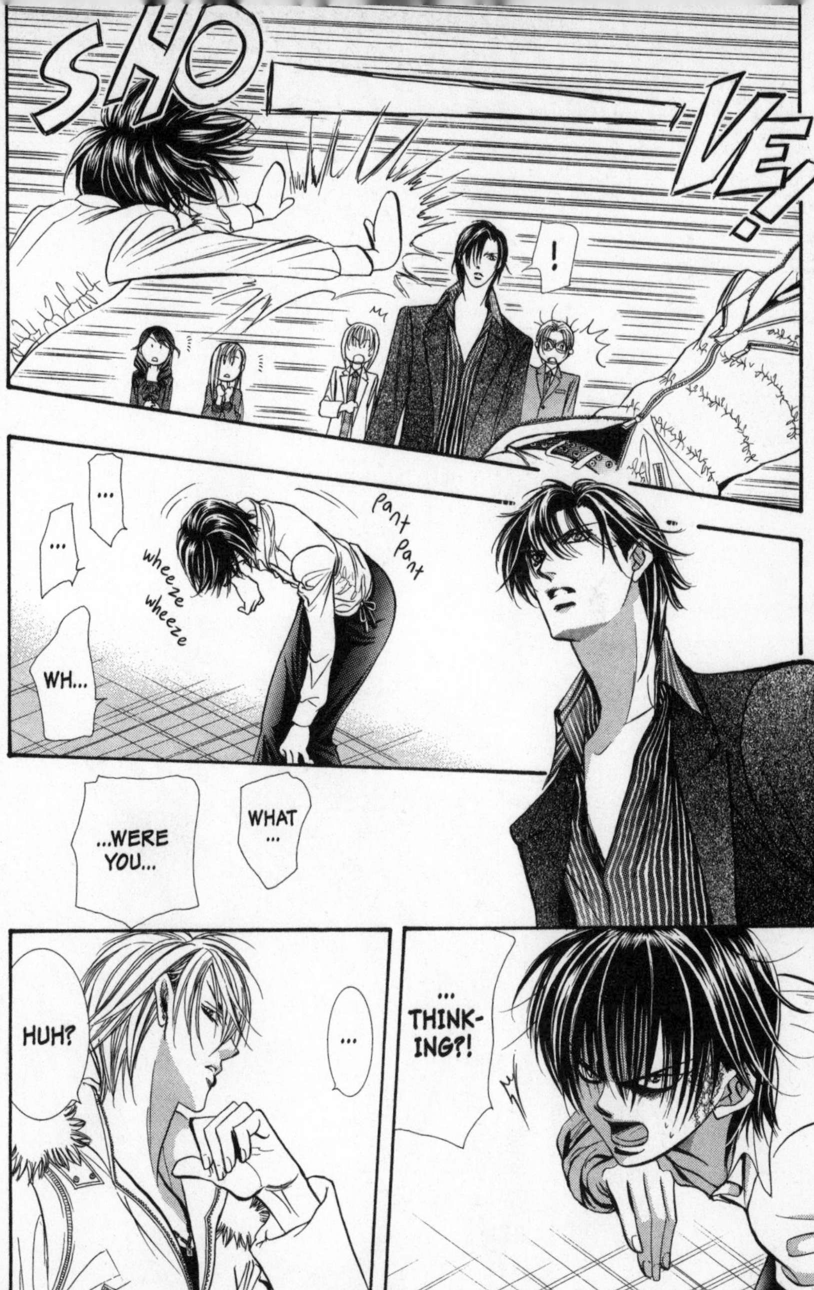
SHO
VE!
!
pant pant
wheeze wheeze
...
...
WH...
WHAT ...
...WERE YOU...
... THINKING?!
...
HUH?

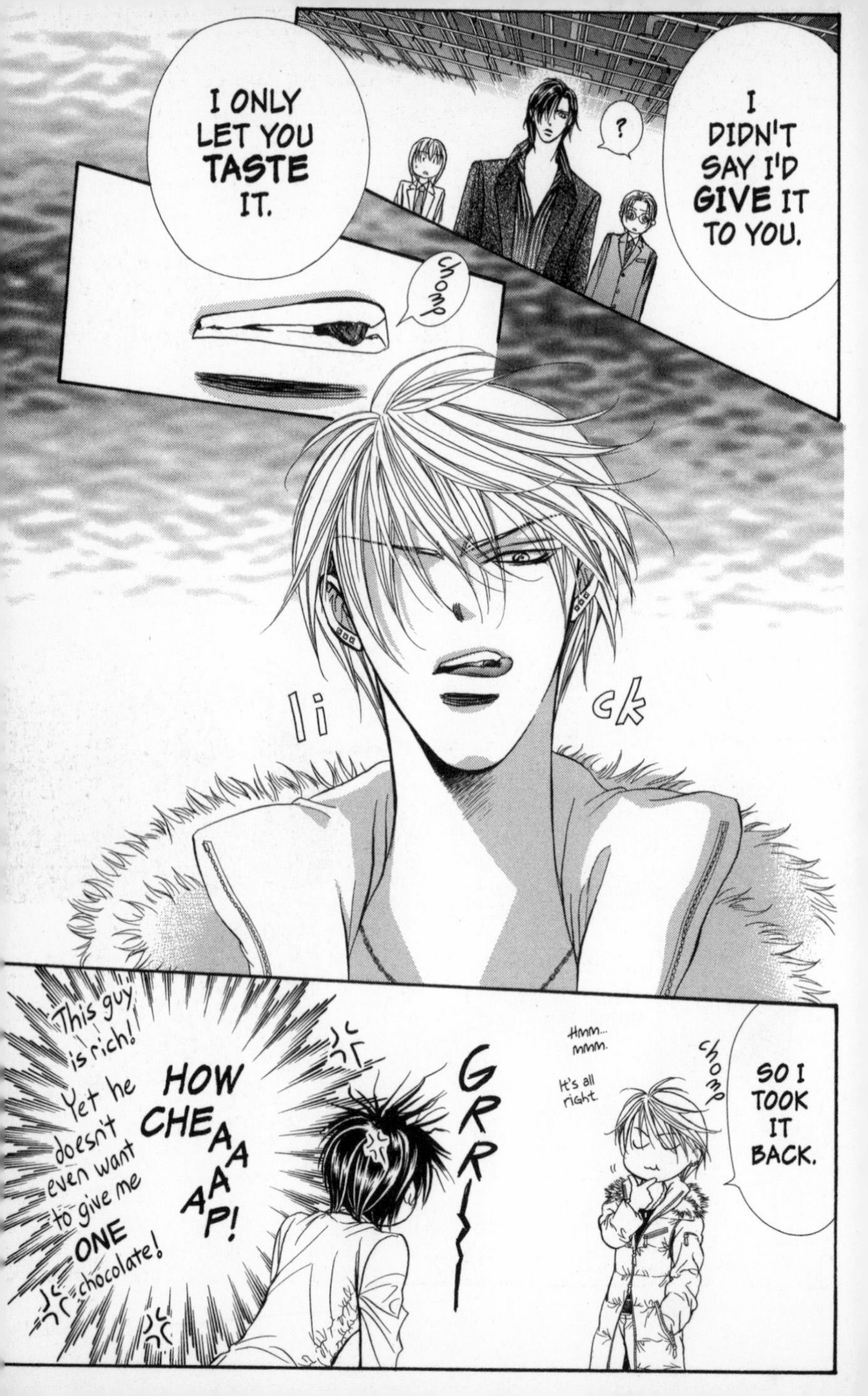
I DIDN'T SAY I'D GIVE IT TO YOU.
?
I ONLY LET YOU TASTE IT.
chomp
li ck
SO I TOOK IT BACK.
chomp
Hmm... mmm.
It's all right.
GRRR
HOW CHEAAAAP!
This guy is rich! Yet he doesn't even want to give me ONE chocolate!

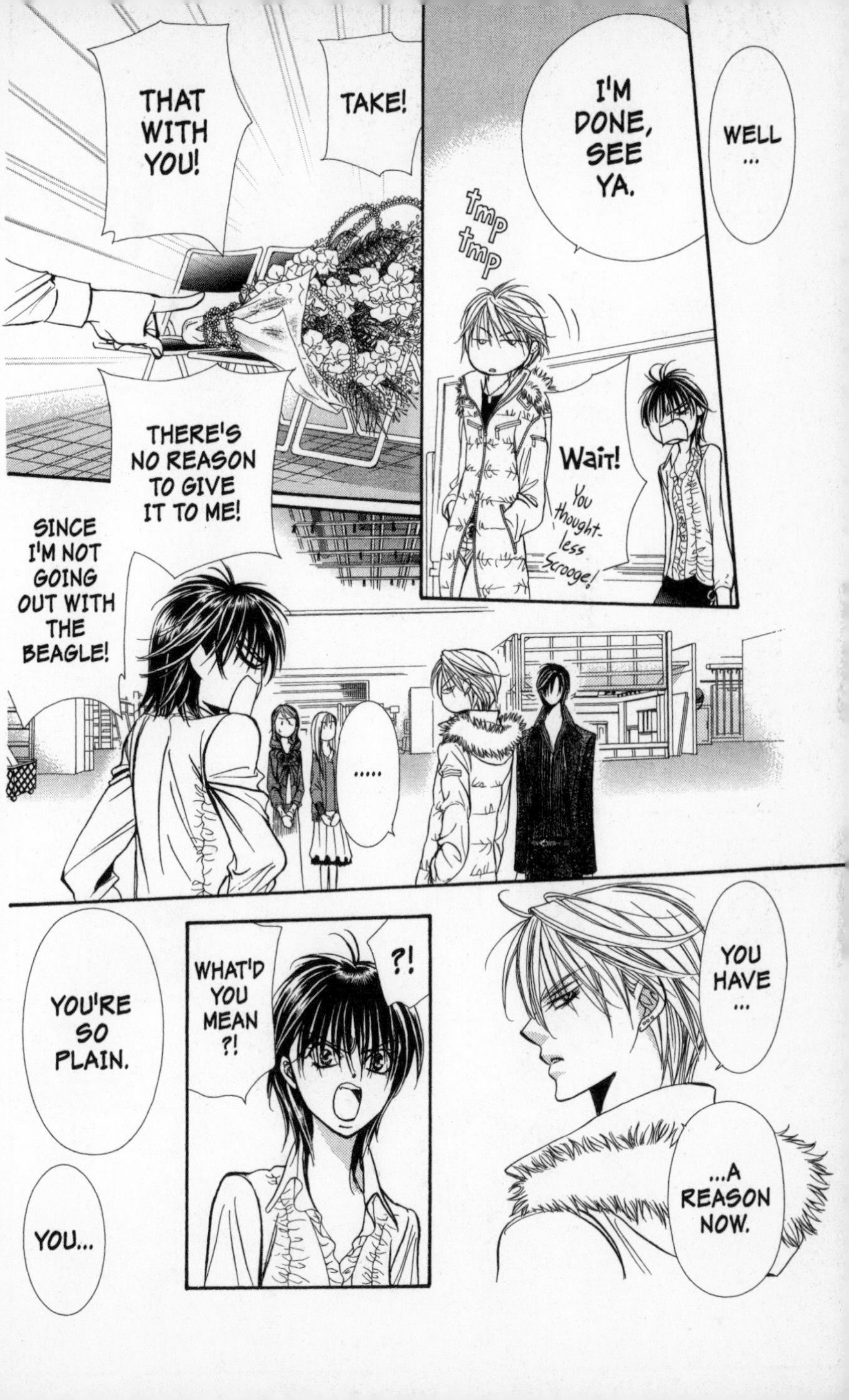
WELL ...
I'M DONE, SEE YA.
tmp tmp
Wait!
You thoughtless Scrooge!
TAKE!
THAT WITH YOU!
THERE'S NO REASON TO GIVE IT TO ME!
SINCE I'M NOT GOING OUT WITH THE BEAGLE!
.....
YOU HAVE ...
...A REASON NOW.
?!
WHAT'D YOU MEAN ?!
YOU'RE SO PLAIN.
YOU...

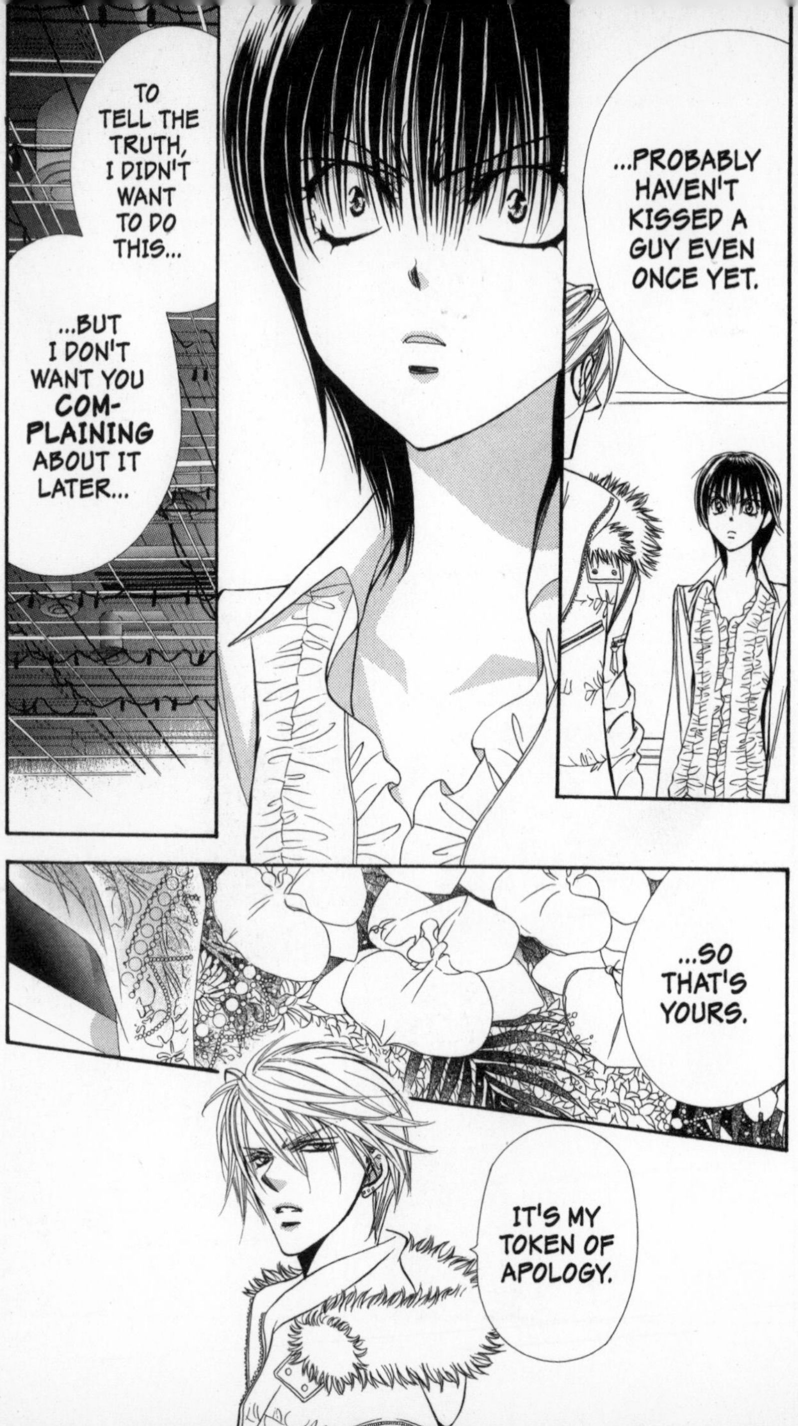
...PROBABLY HAVEN'T KISSED A GUY EVEN ONCE YET.
TO TELL THE TRUTH, I DIDN'T WANT TO DO THIS...
...BUT I DON'T WANT YOU **COM-PLAINING** ABOUT IT LATER...
...SO THAT'S YOURS.
IT'S MY TOKEN OF APOLOGY.

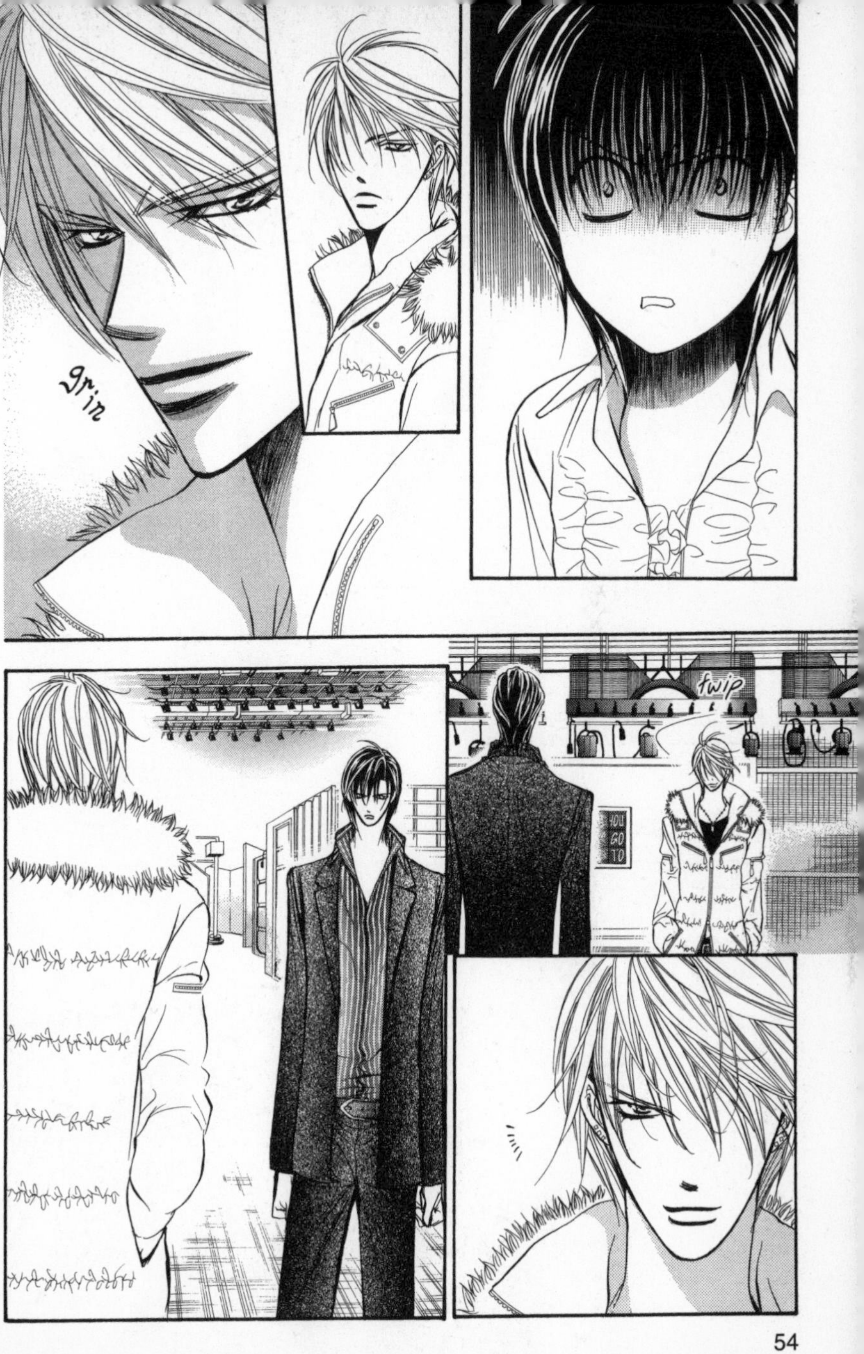
grin
fwip
YOU GO TO

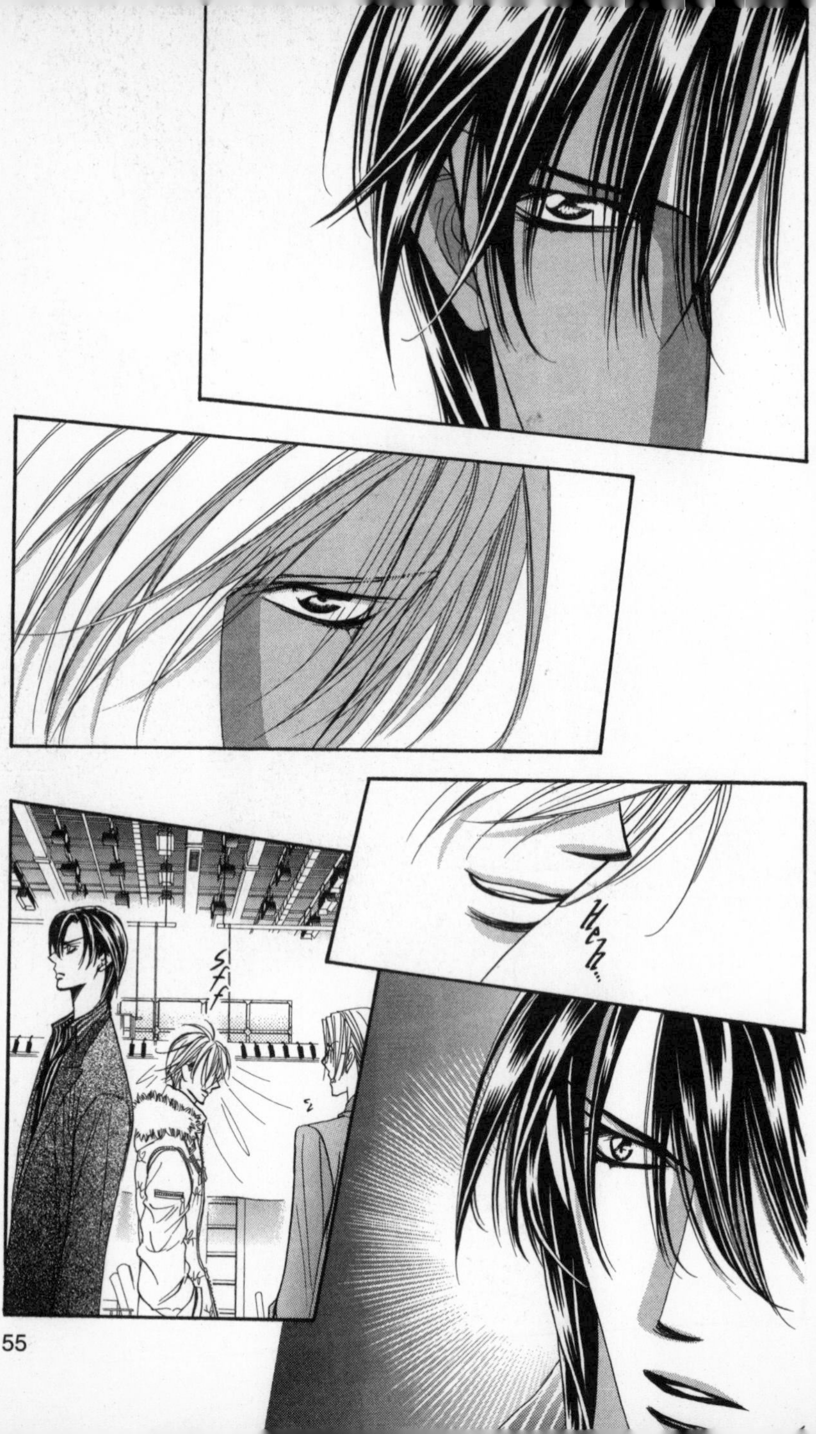
Heh...
Sff

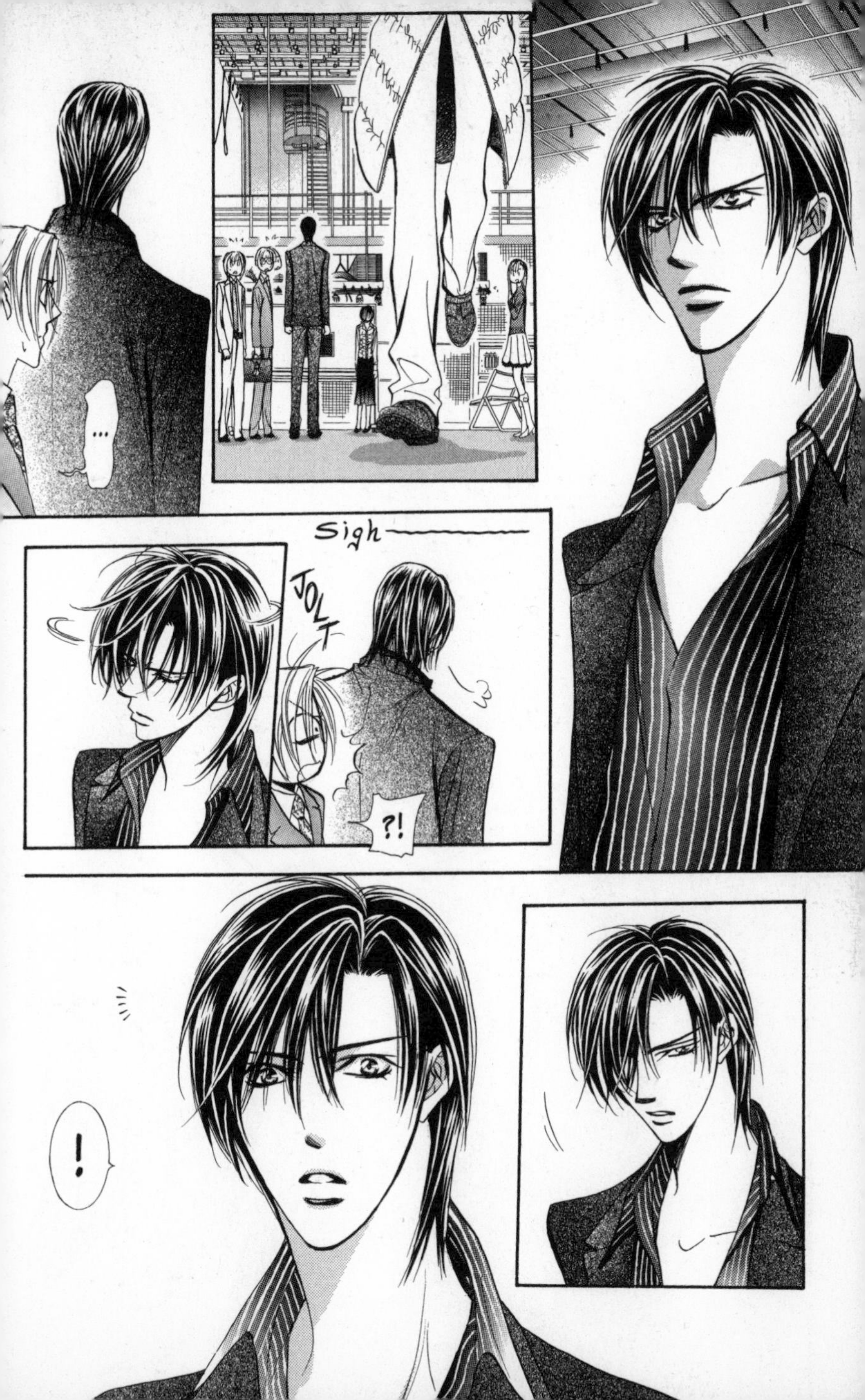
...
Sigh
JOLT
?!
!

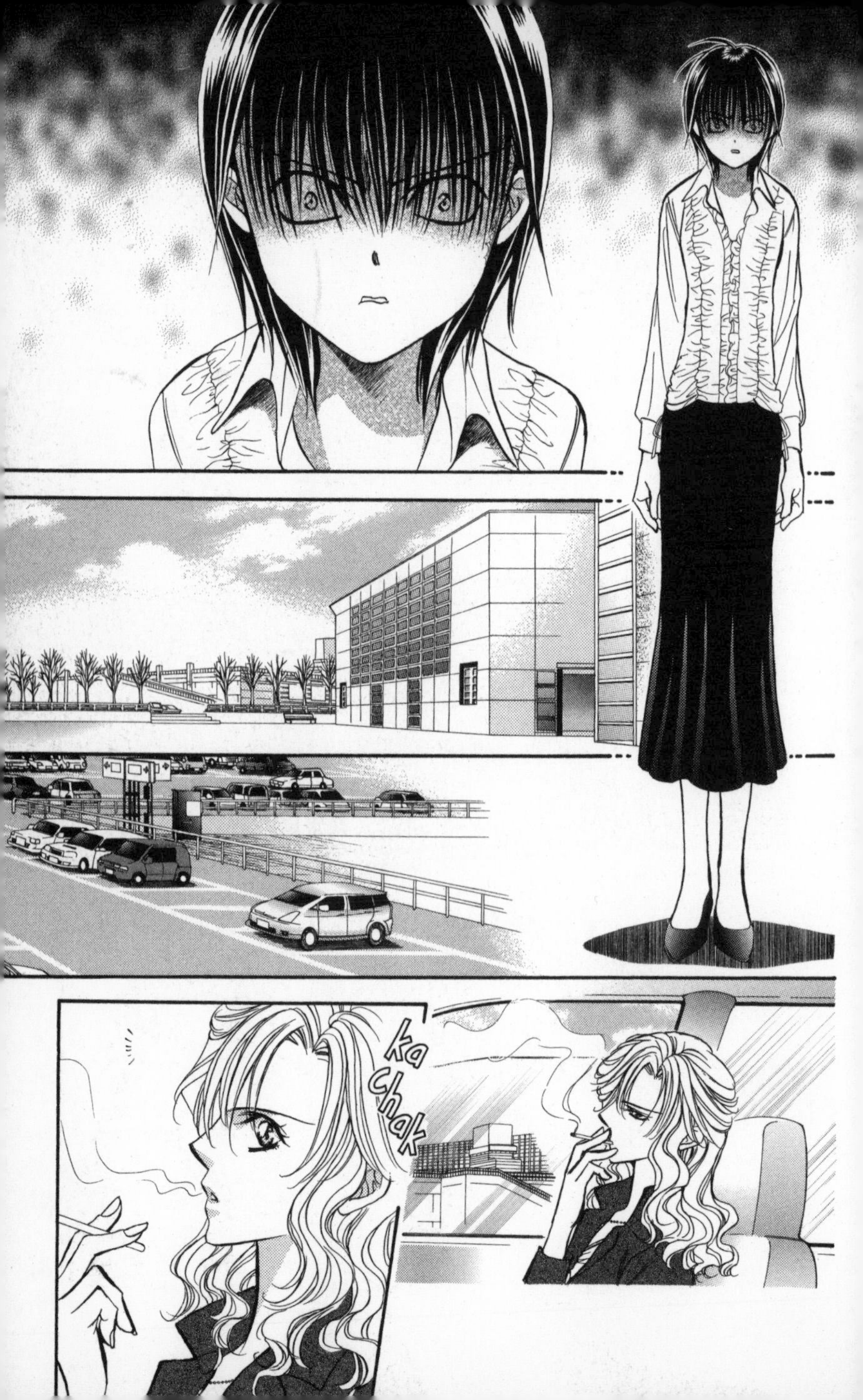
ka chak

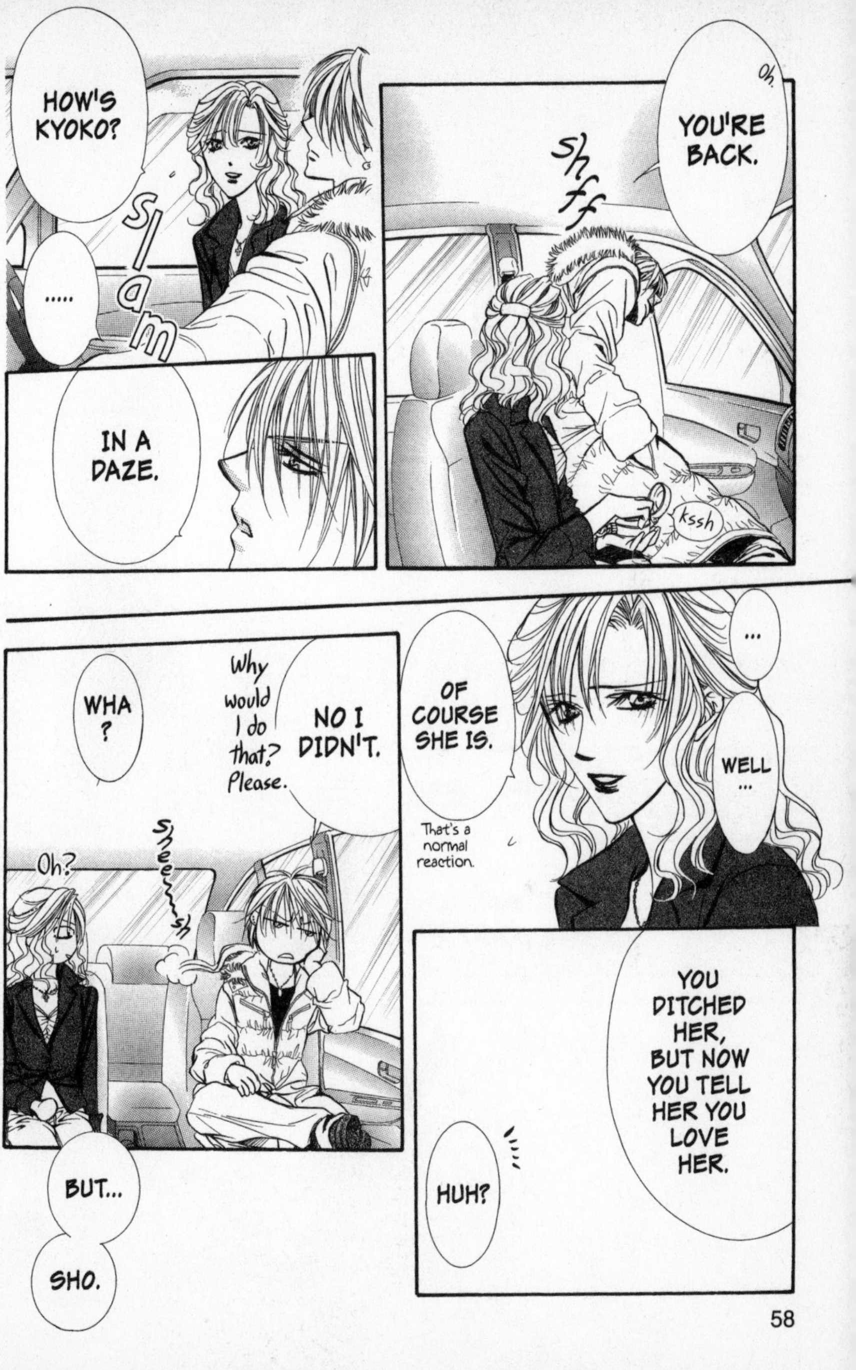

Oh.
YOU'RE BACK.
shff
kssh
HOW'S KYOKO?
.....
slam
IN A DAZE.
...
WELL...
OF COURSE SHE IS.
That's a normal reaction.
YOU DITCHED HER, BUT NOW YOU TELL HER YOU LOVE HER.
HUH?
NO I DIDN'T.
Why would I do that? Please.
WHA?
sheesh
Oh?
BUT...
SHO.

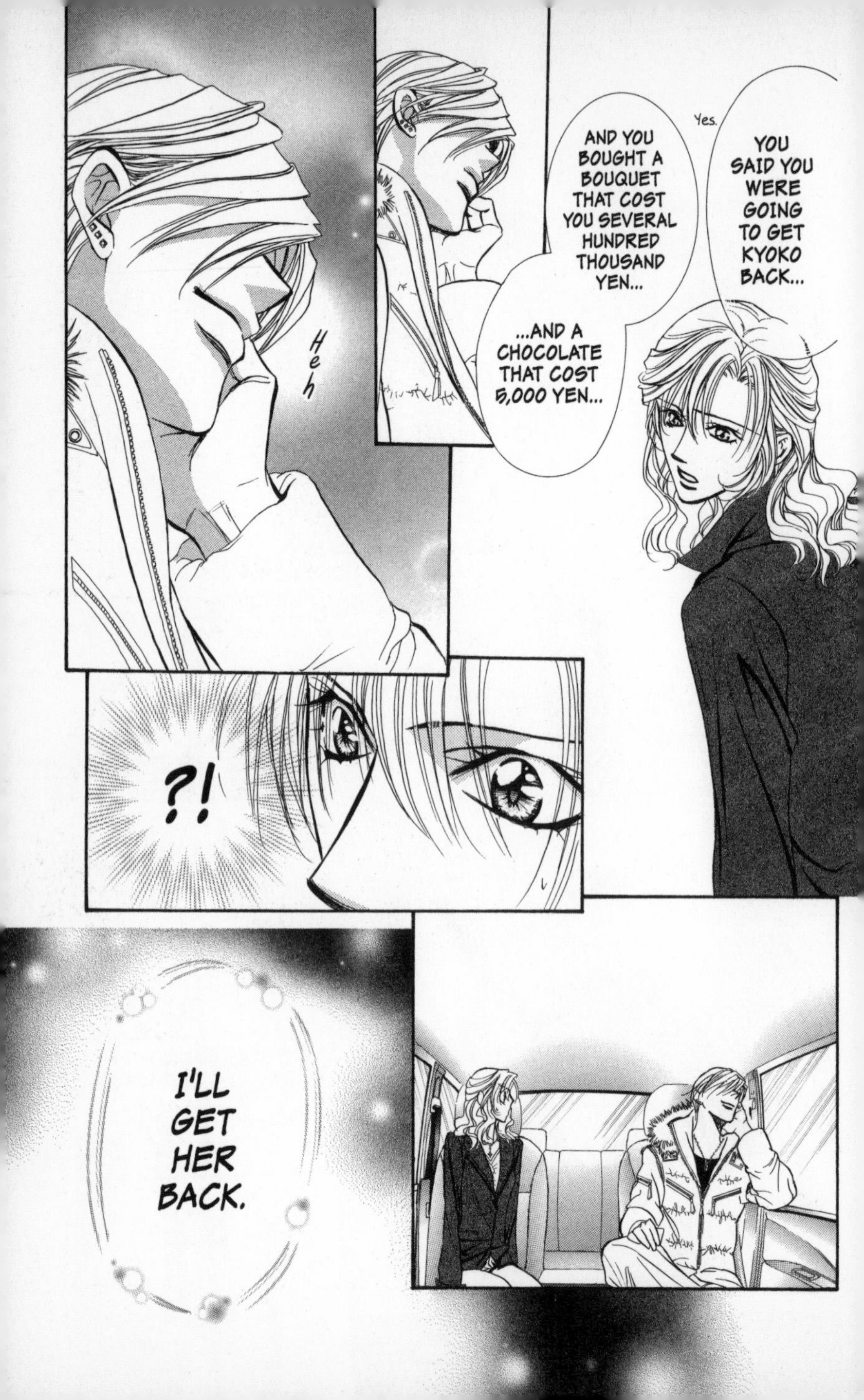
YOU SAID YOU WERE GOING TO GET KYOKO BACK...
Yes.
AND YOU BOUGHT A BOUQUET THAT COST YOU SEVERAL HUNDRED THOUSAND YEN...
...AND A CHOCOLATE THAT COST 5,000 YEN...
Heh
?!
I'LL GET HER BACK.

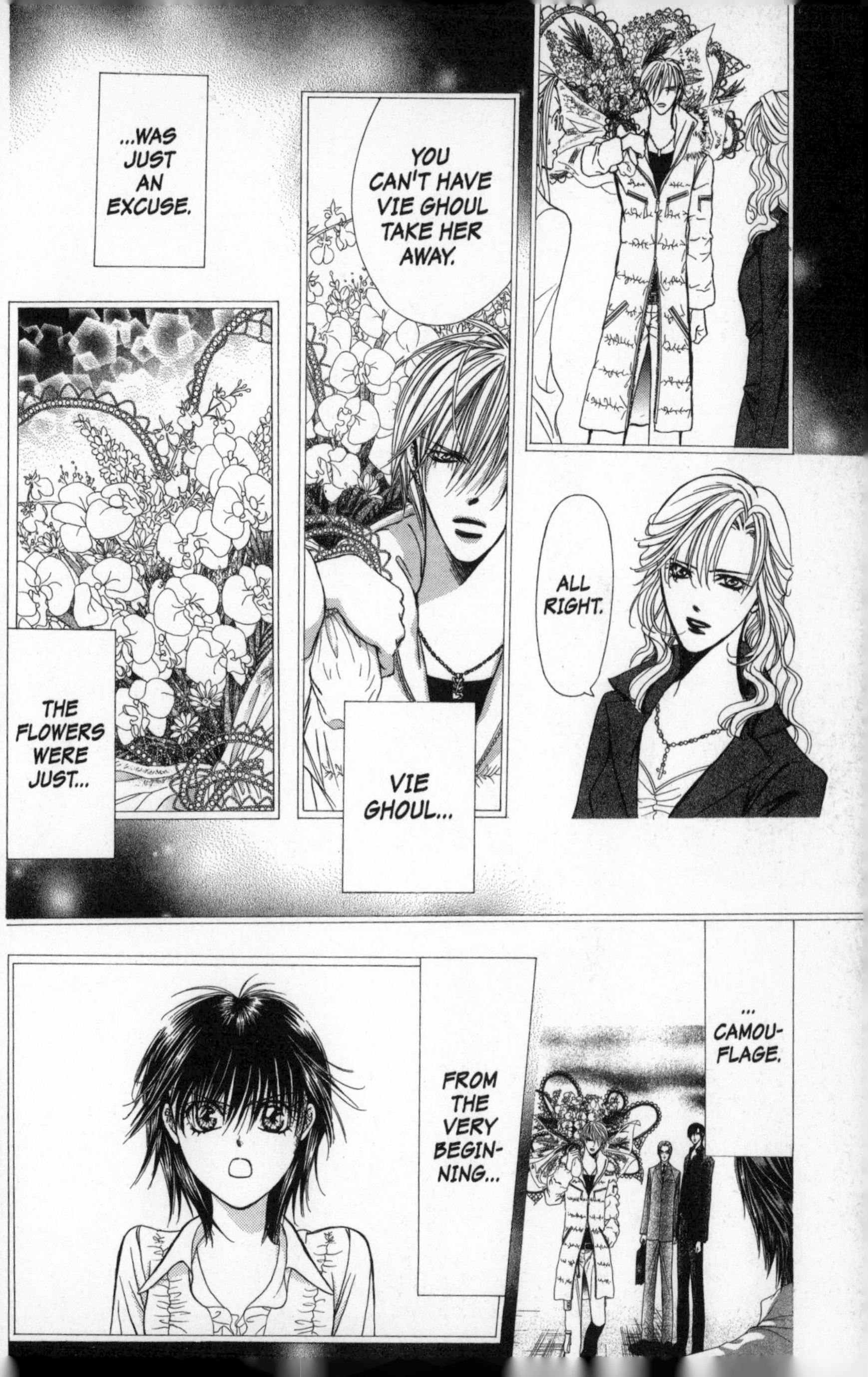
YOU CAN'T HAVE VIE GHOUL TAKE HER AWAY.
ALL RIGHT.
VIE GHOUL...
...WAS JUST AN EXCUSE.
THE FLOWERS WERE JUST...
...CAMOUFLAGE.
FROM THE VERY BEGINNING...

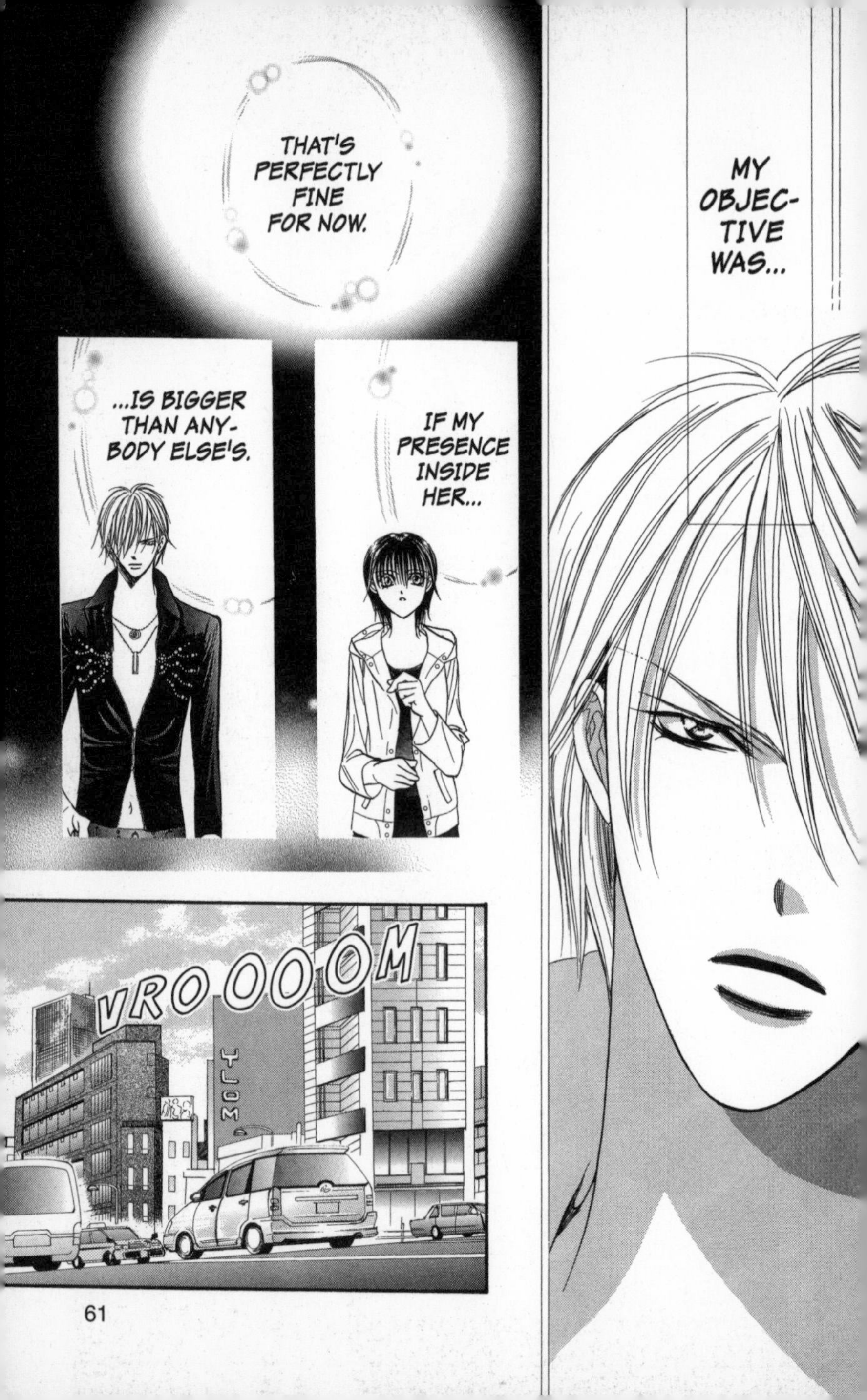
MY OBJEC-TIVE WAS...
THAT'S PERFECTLY FINE FOR NOW.
IF MY PRESENCE INSIDE HER...
...IS BIGGER THAN ANY-BODY ELSE'S.
VROOOOOM

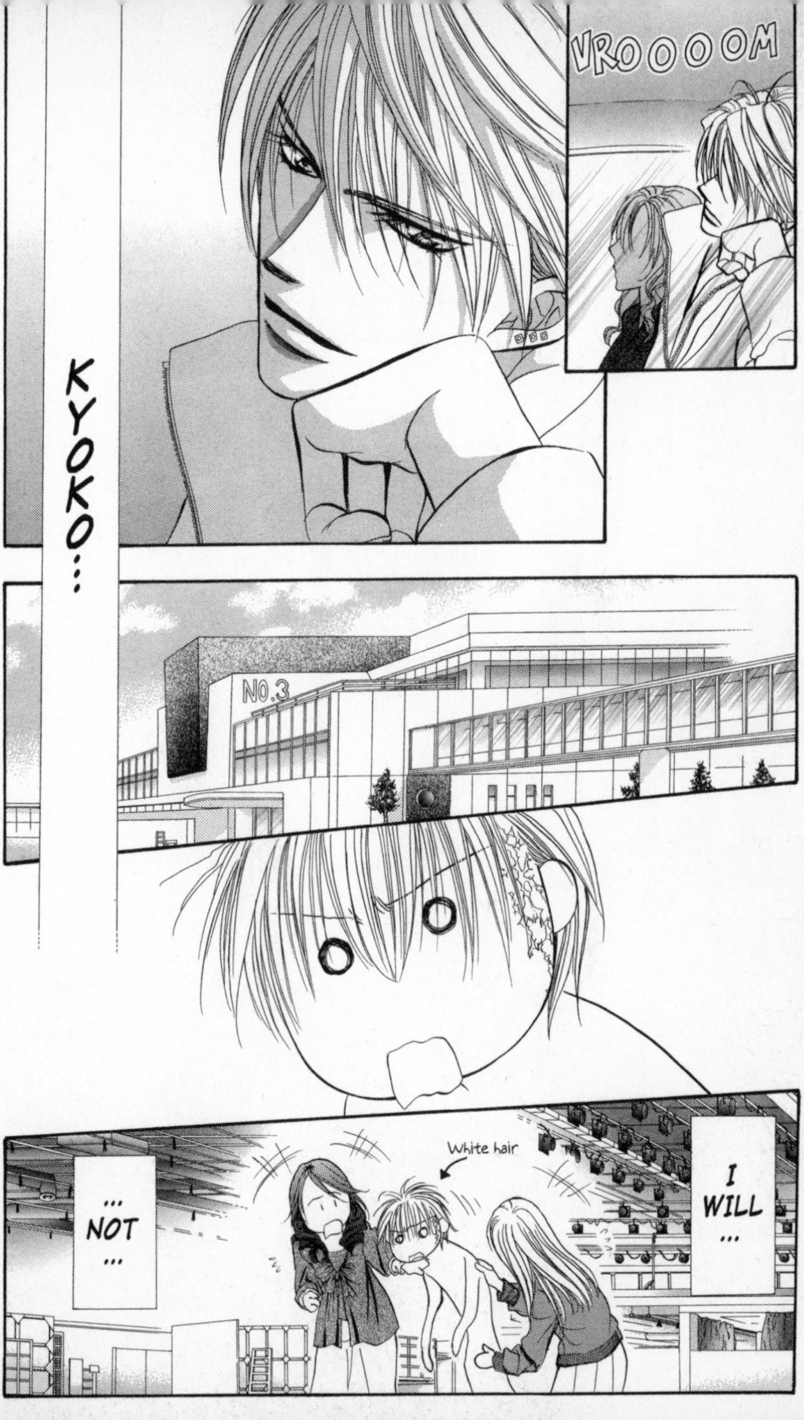
VROOOOM
KYOKO...
NO.3
I WILL ...
White hair
... NOT ...

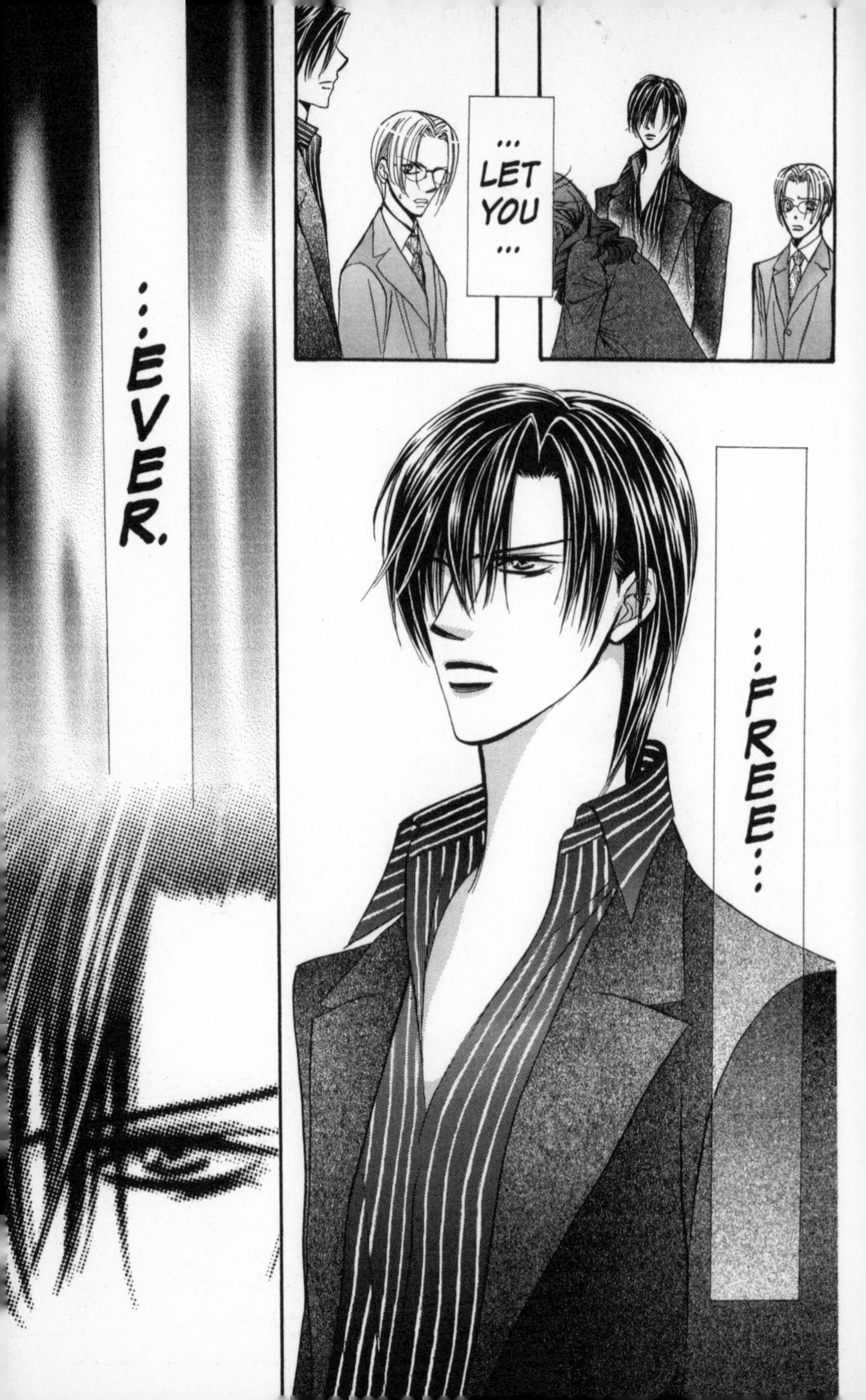
... LET YOU ...
...FREE...
...EVER.

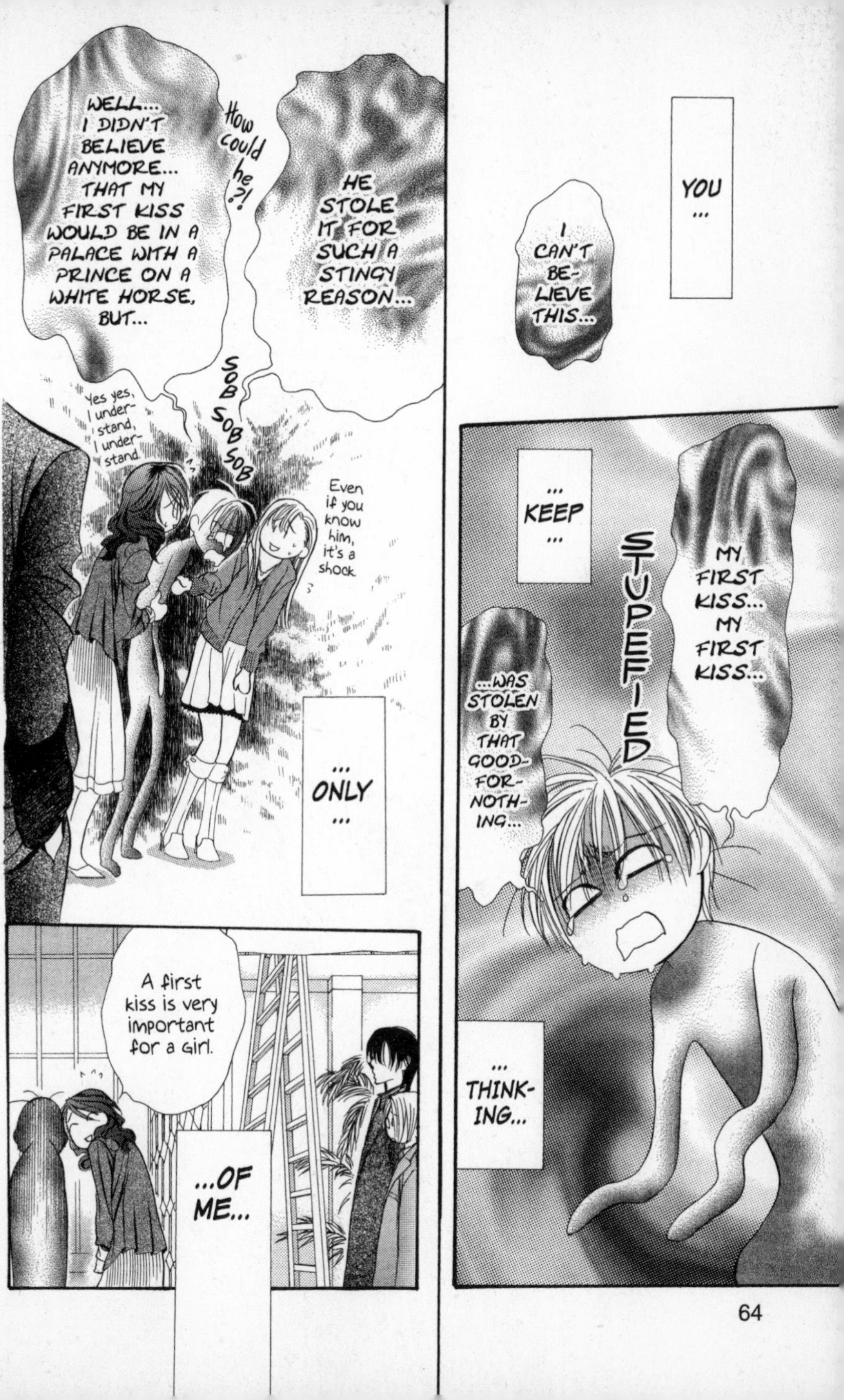
YOU...
I CAN'T BE-LIEVE THIS...
...KEEP...
MY FIRST KISS... MY FIRST KISS...
STUPEFIED
...WAS STOLEN BY THAT GOOD-FOR-NOTHING...
...THINKING...
HE STOLE IT FOR SUCH A STINGY REASON...
How could he?!
WELL... I DIDN'T BELIEVE ANYMORE... THAT MY FIRST KISS WOULD BE IN A PALACE WITH A PRINCE ON A WHITE HORSE, BUT...
SOB SOB SOB
Even if you know him, it's a shock.
Yes yes, I under-stand, I under-stand.
...ONLY...
A first kiss is very important for a girl.
...OF ME...

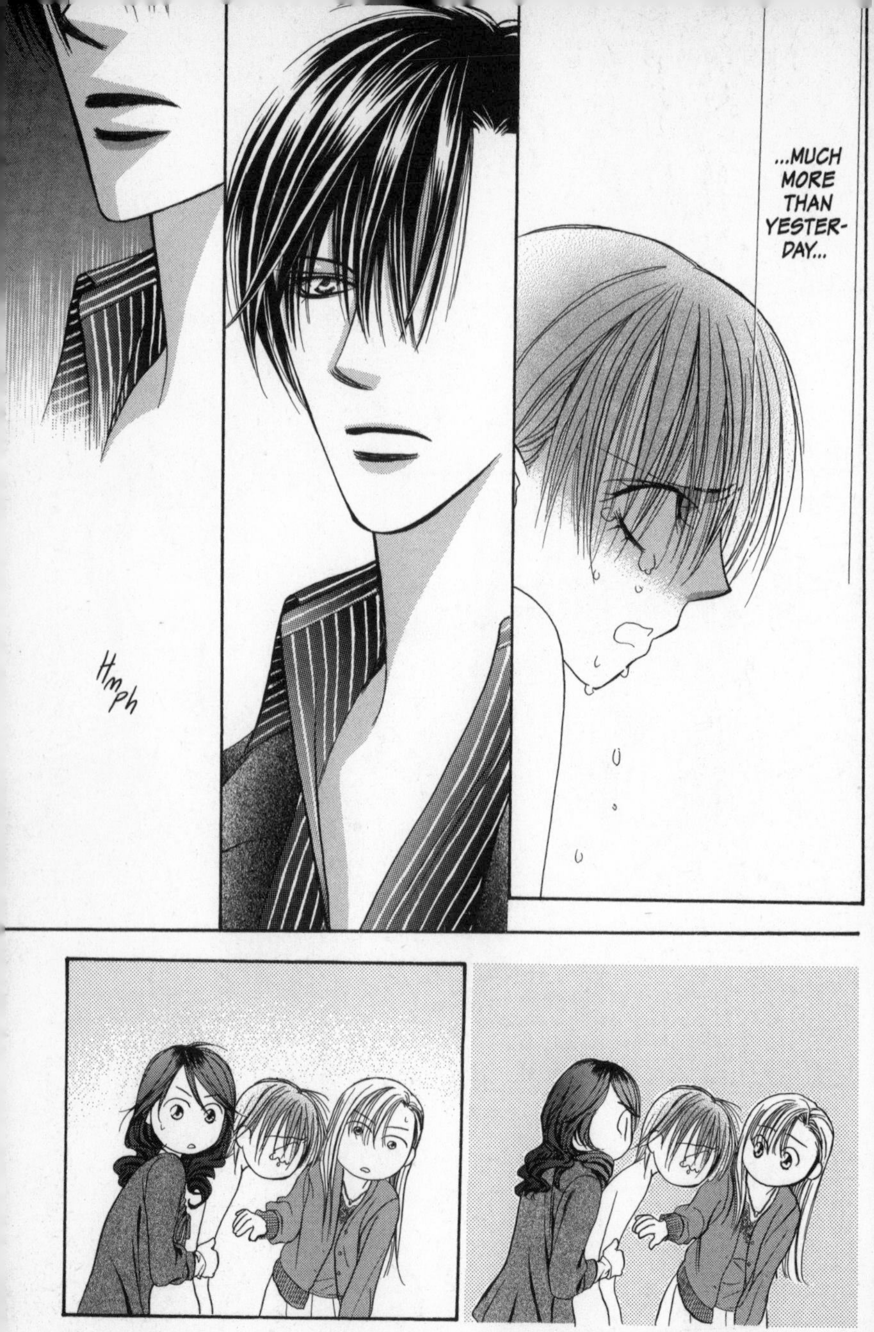
...MUCH MORE THAN YESTER-DAY...
Hmph

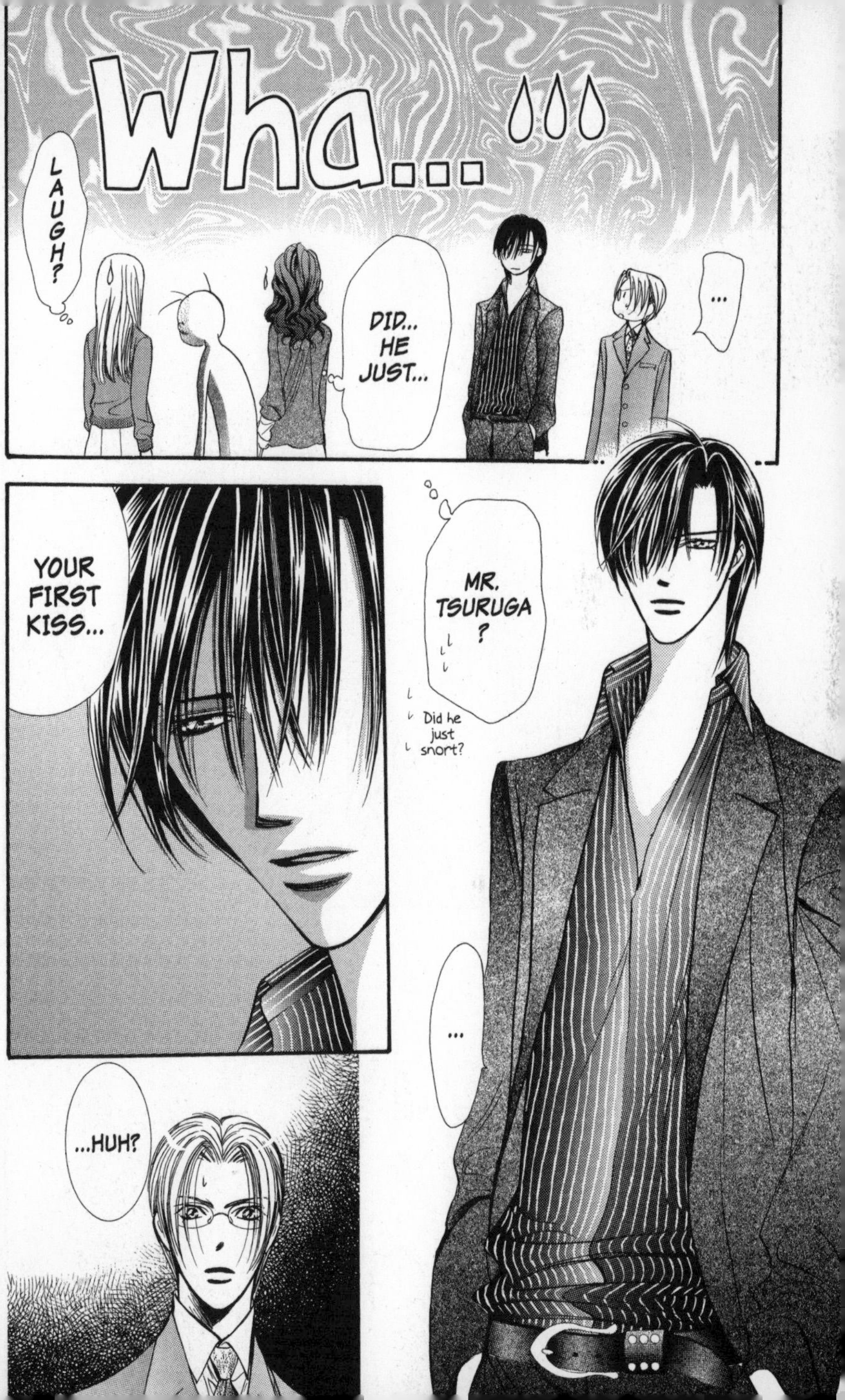
Wha...
...
DID... HE JUST...
LAUGH?
MR. TSURUGA?
Did he just snort?
...
YOUR FIRST KISS...
...HUH?

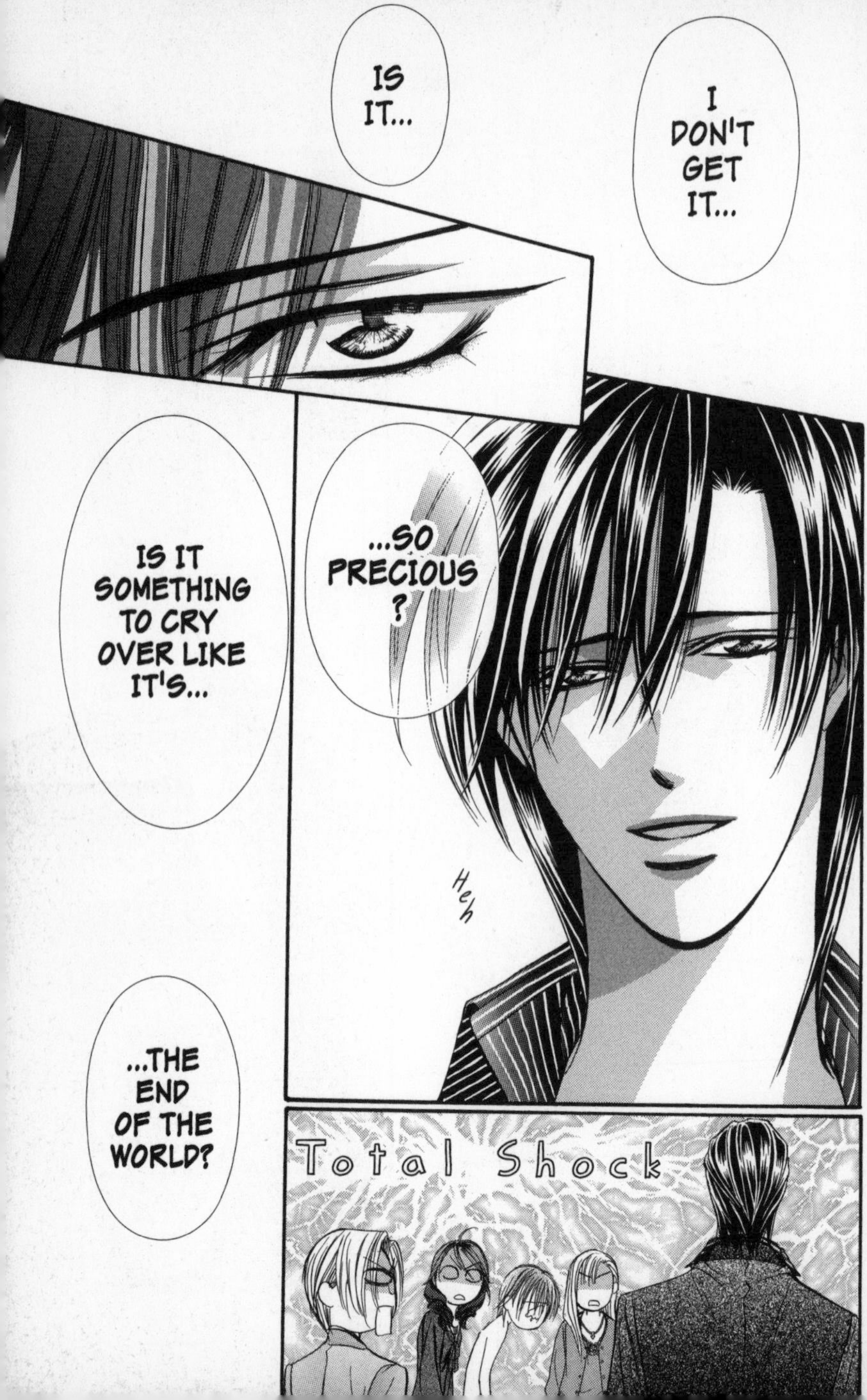
I DON'T GET IT...
IS IT...
IS IT SOMETHING TO CRY OVER LIKE IT'S...
...SO PRECIOUS?
Heh
...THE END OF THE WORLD?
Total Shock

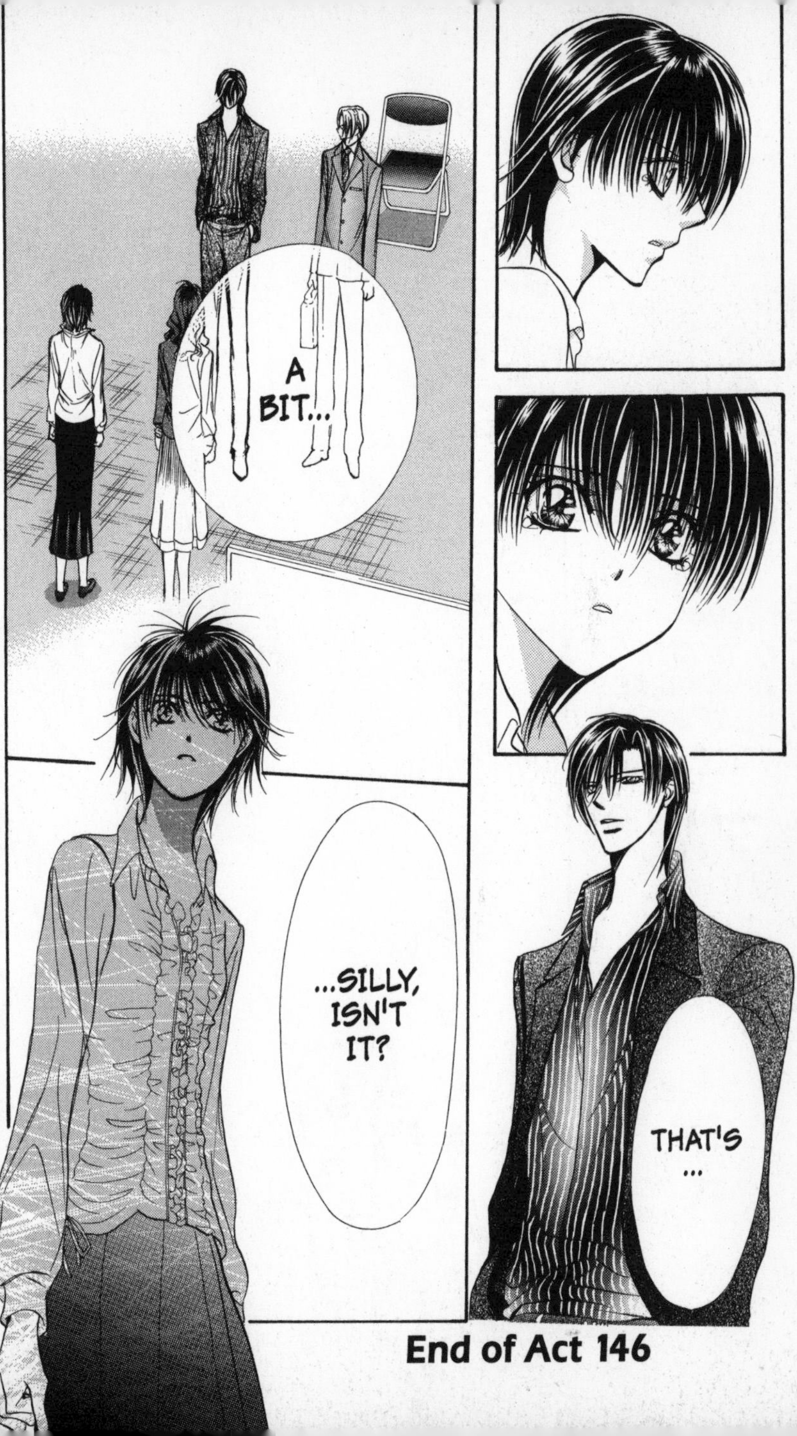
A BIT...
THAT'S ...
...SILLY, ISN'T IT?

End of Act 146

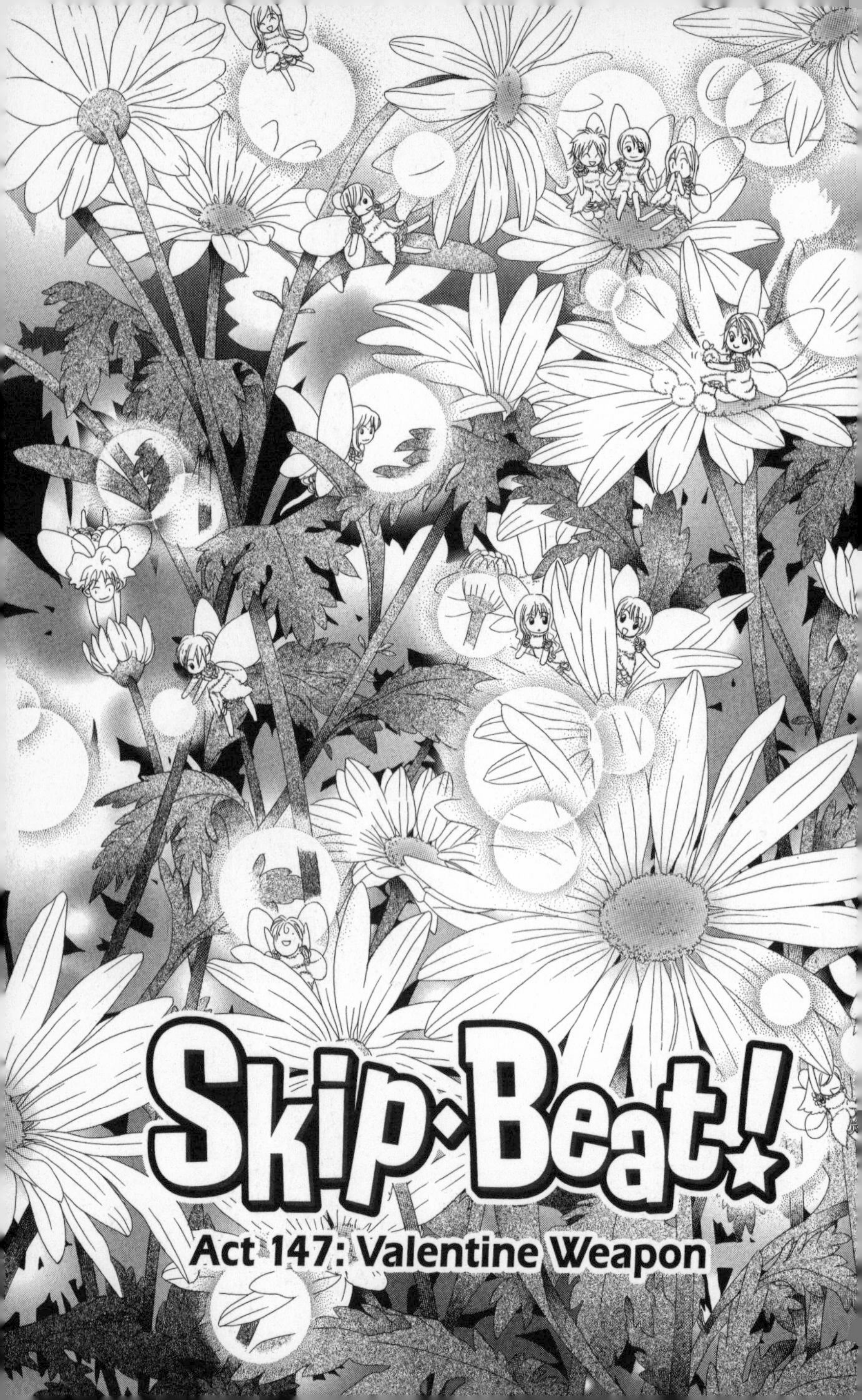
Skip·Beat!
Act 147: Valentine Weapon

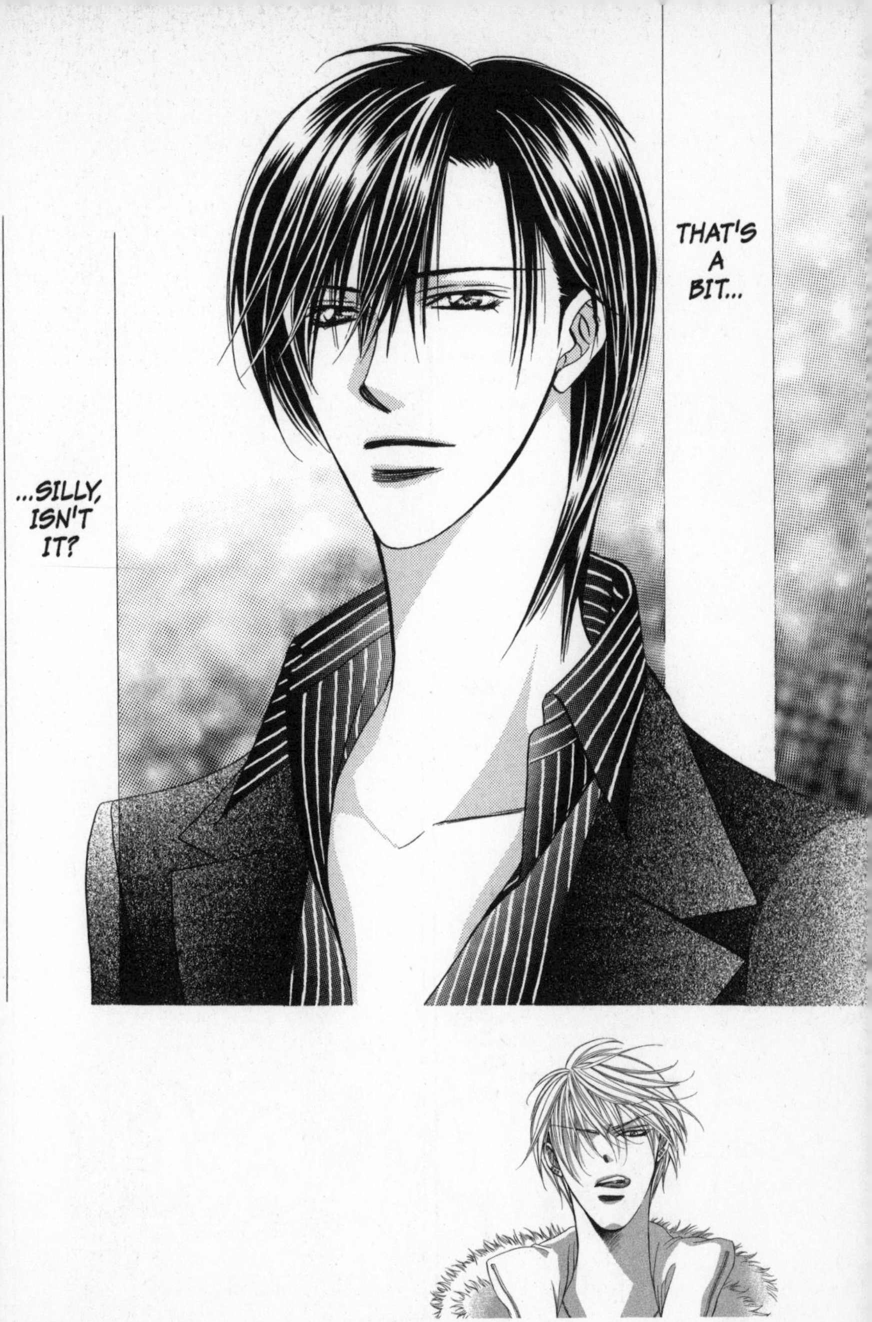
THAT'S A BIT...
...SILLY, ISN'T IT?

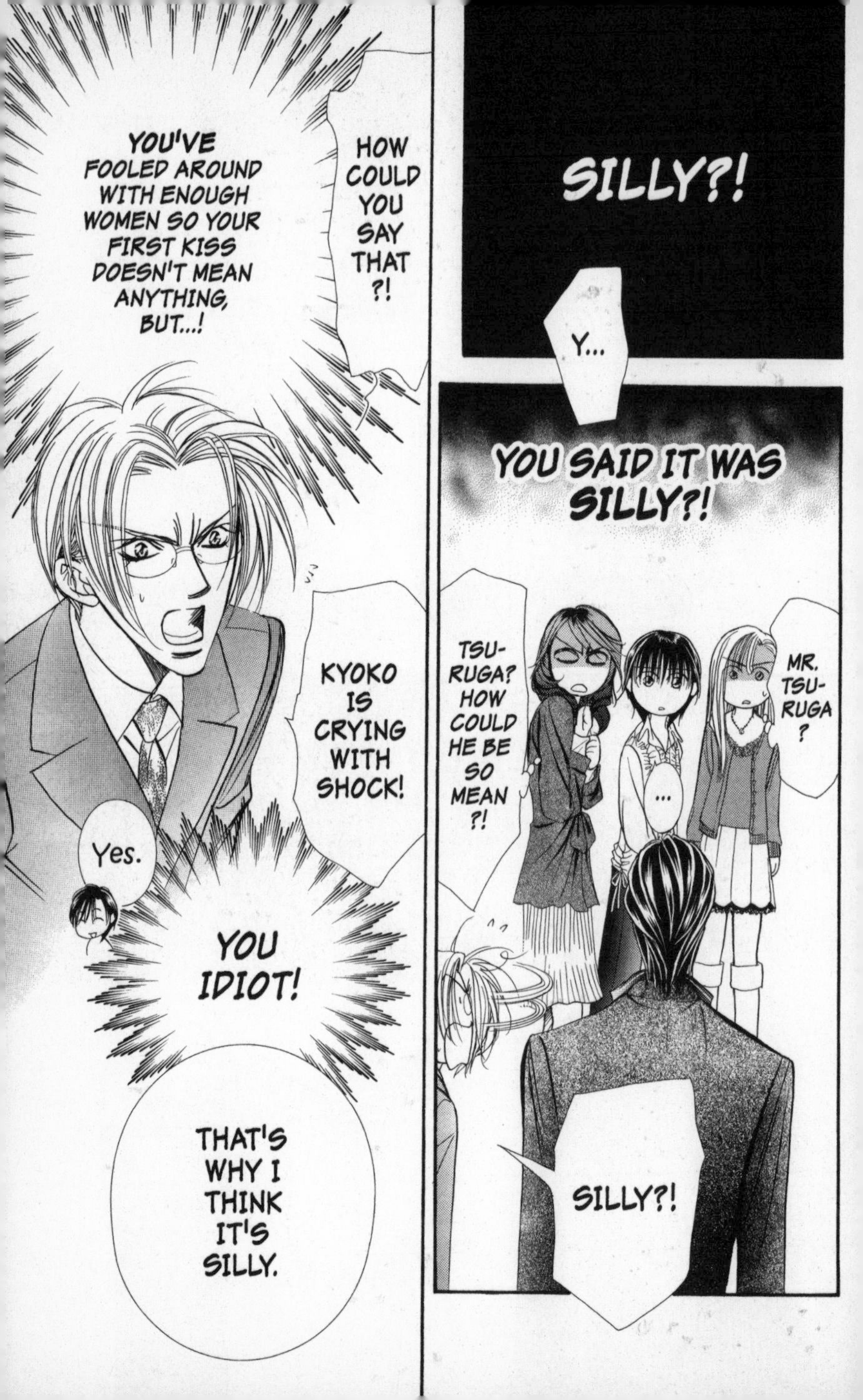
YOU'VE FOOLED AROUND WITH ENOUGH WOMEN SO YOUR FIRST KISS DOESN'T MEAN ANYTHING, BUT...!
HOW COULD YOU SAY THAT?!
KYOKO IS CRYING WITH SHOCK!
Yes.
YOU IDIOT!
THAT'S WHY I THINK IT'S SILLY.
SILLY?!
Y...
YOU SAID IT WAS SILLY?!
MR. TSU-RUGA?
...
TSU-RUGA? HOW COULD HE BE SO MEAN?!
SILLY?!

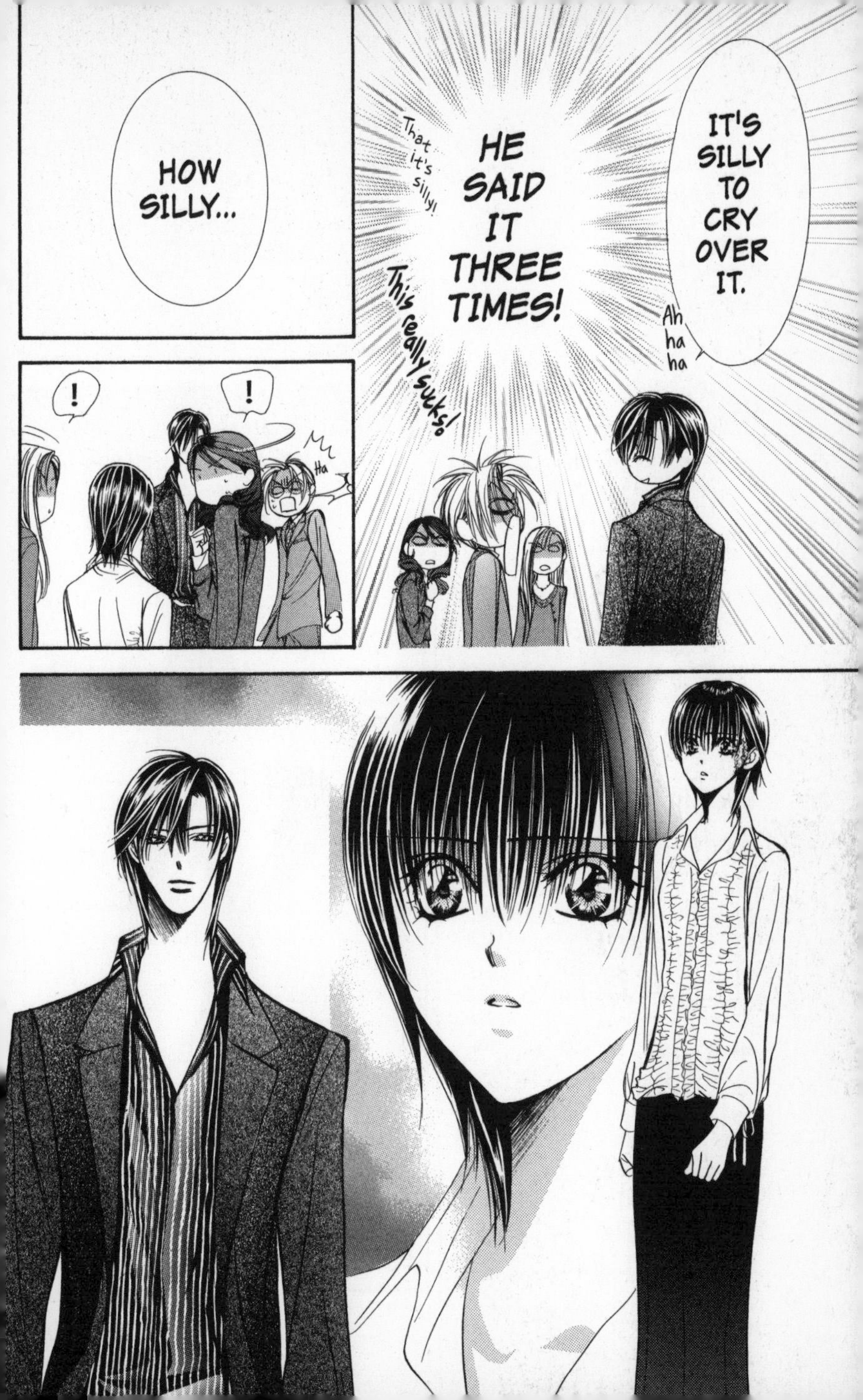
IT'S SILLY TO CRY OVER IT.
Ah ha ha
HE SAID IT THREE TIMES!
That it's silly!
This really sucks!
HOW SILLY...
!
!
Ha

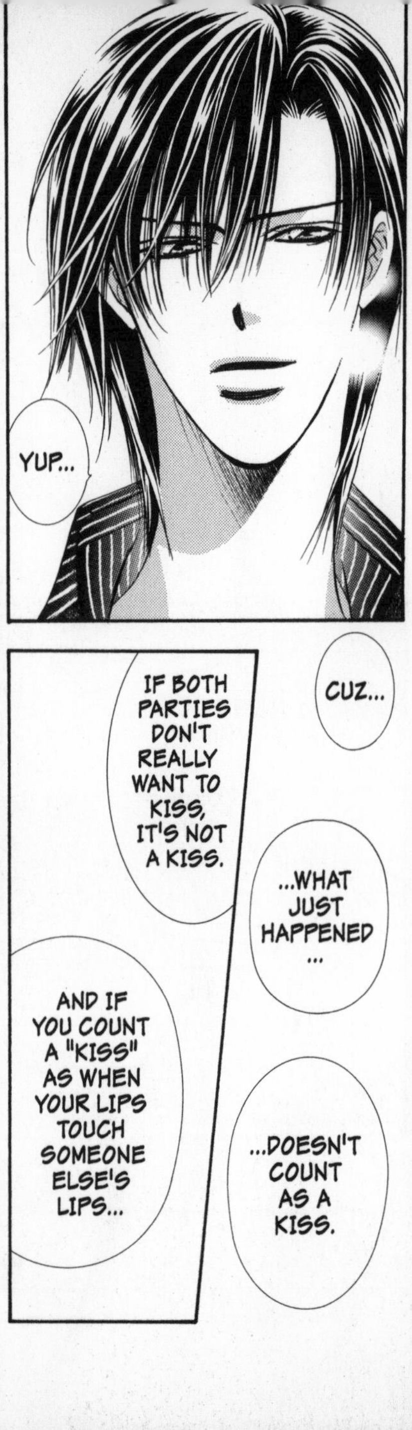
YUP...
CUZ...
IF BOTH PARTIES DON'T REALLY WANT TO KISS, IT'S NOT A KISS.
...WHAT JUST HAPPENED ...
AND IF YOU COUNT A "KISS" AS WHEN YOUR LIPS TOUCH SOMEONE ELSE'S LIPS...
...DOESN'T COUNT AS A KISS.

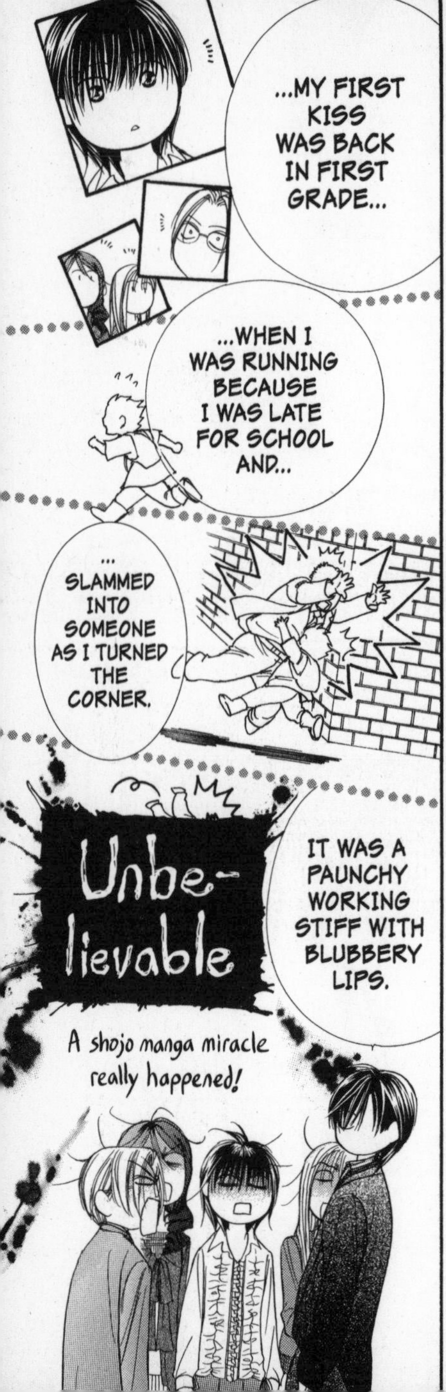
...MY FIRST KISS WAS BACK IN FIRST GRADE...
...WHEN I WAS RUNNING BECAUSE I WAS LATE FOR SCHOOL AND...
... SLAMMED INTO SOMEONE AS I TURNED THE CORNER.
IT WAS A PAUNCHY WORKING STIFF WITH BLUBBERY LIPS.
Unbe-lievable
A shojo manga miracle really happened!

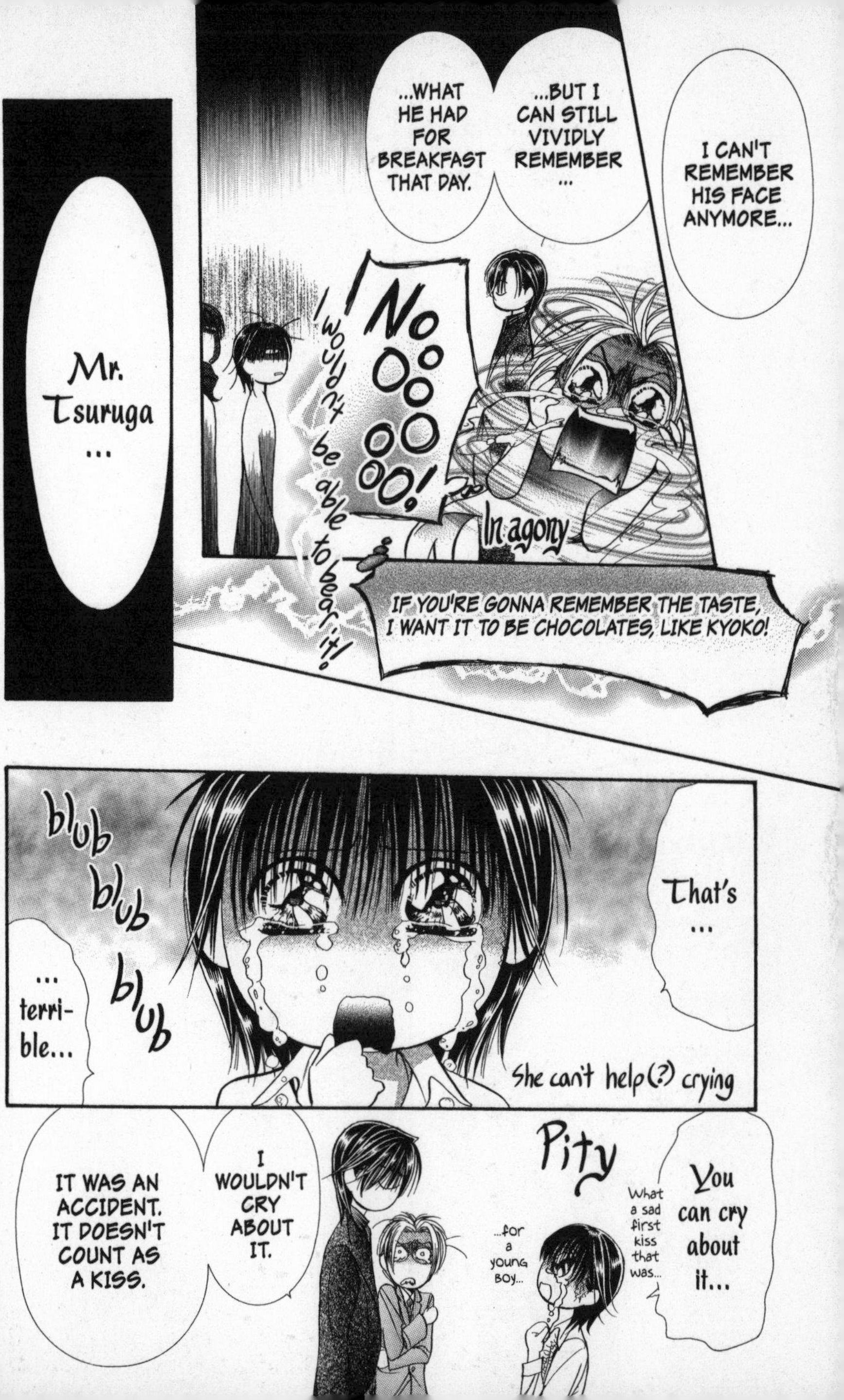
I CAN'T REMEMBER HIS FACE ANYMORE...
...BUT I CAN STILL VIVIDLY REMEMBER...
...WHAT HE HAD FOR BREAKFAST THAT DAY.
NoOOOOOOOO!
I wouldn't be able to bear it!
In agony
IF YOU'RE GONNA REMEMBER THE TASTE, I WANT IT TO BE CHOCOLATES, LIKE KYOKO!
Mr. Tsuruga...
That's...
She can't help(?) crying
blub blub blub
...terrible...
You can cry about it...
What a sad first kiss that was...
...for a young boy...
Pity
I WOULDN'T CRY ABOUT IT.
IT WAS AN ACCIDENT. IT DOESN'T COUNT AS A KISS.

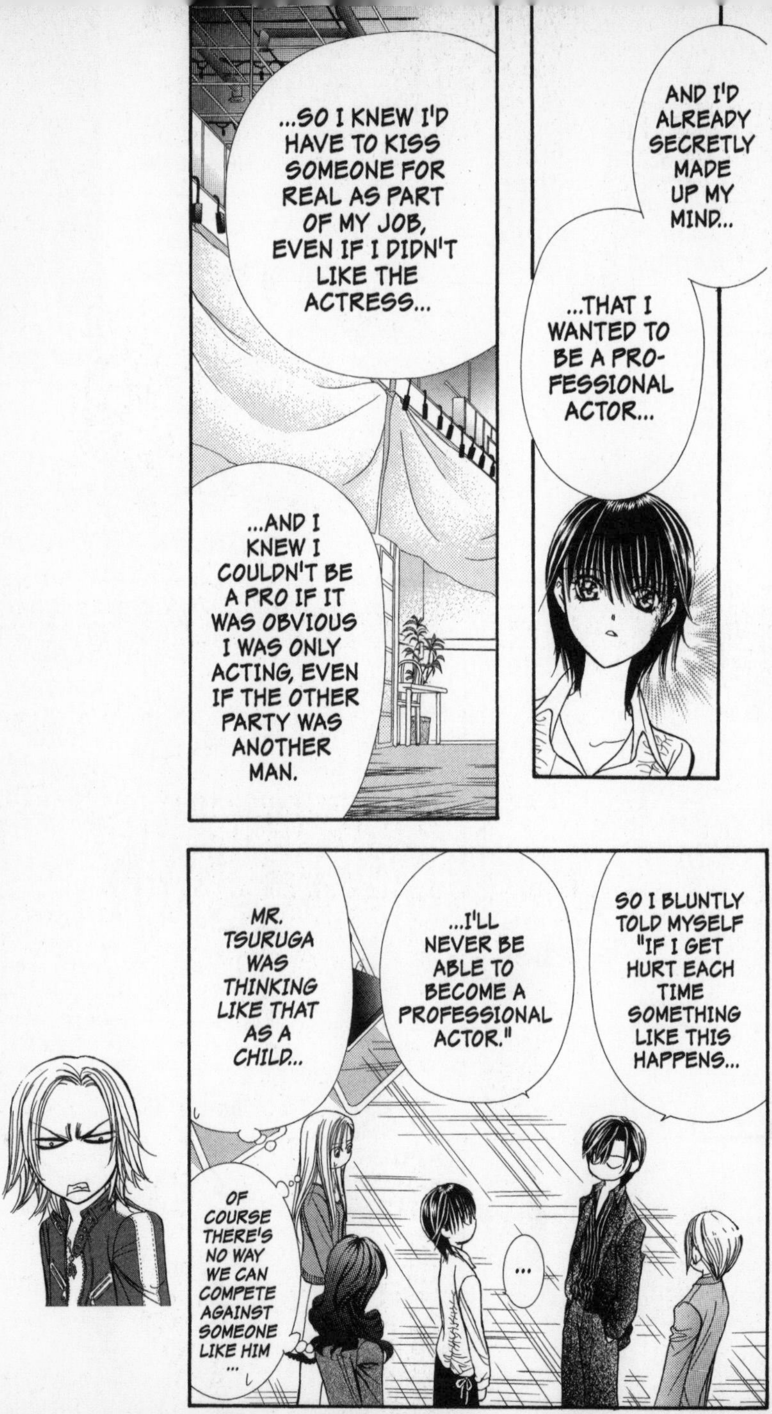
AND I'D ALREADY SECRETLY MADE UP MY MIND...
...THAT I WANTED TO BE A PRO-FESSIONAL ACTOR...
...SO I KNEW I'D HAVE TO KISS SOMEONE FOR REAL AS PART OF MY JOB, EVEN IF I DIDN'T LIKE THE ACTRESS...
...AND I KNEW I COULDN'T BE A PRO IF IT WAS OBVIOUS I WAS ONLY ACTING, EVEN IF THE OTHER PARTY WAS ANOTHER MAN.
SO I BLUNTLY TOLD MYSELF "IF I GET HURT EACH TIME SOMETHING LIKE THIS HAPPENS...
...I'LL NEVER BE ABLE TO BECOME A PROFESSIONAL ACTOR."
MR. TSURUGA WAS THINKING LIKE THAT AS A CHILD...
...
OF COURSE THERE'S NO WAY WE CAN COMPETE AGAINST SOMEONE LIKE HIM ...

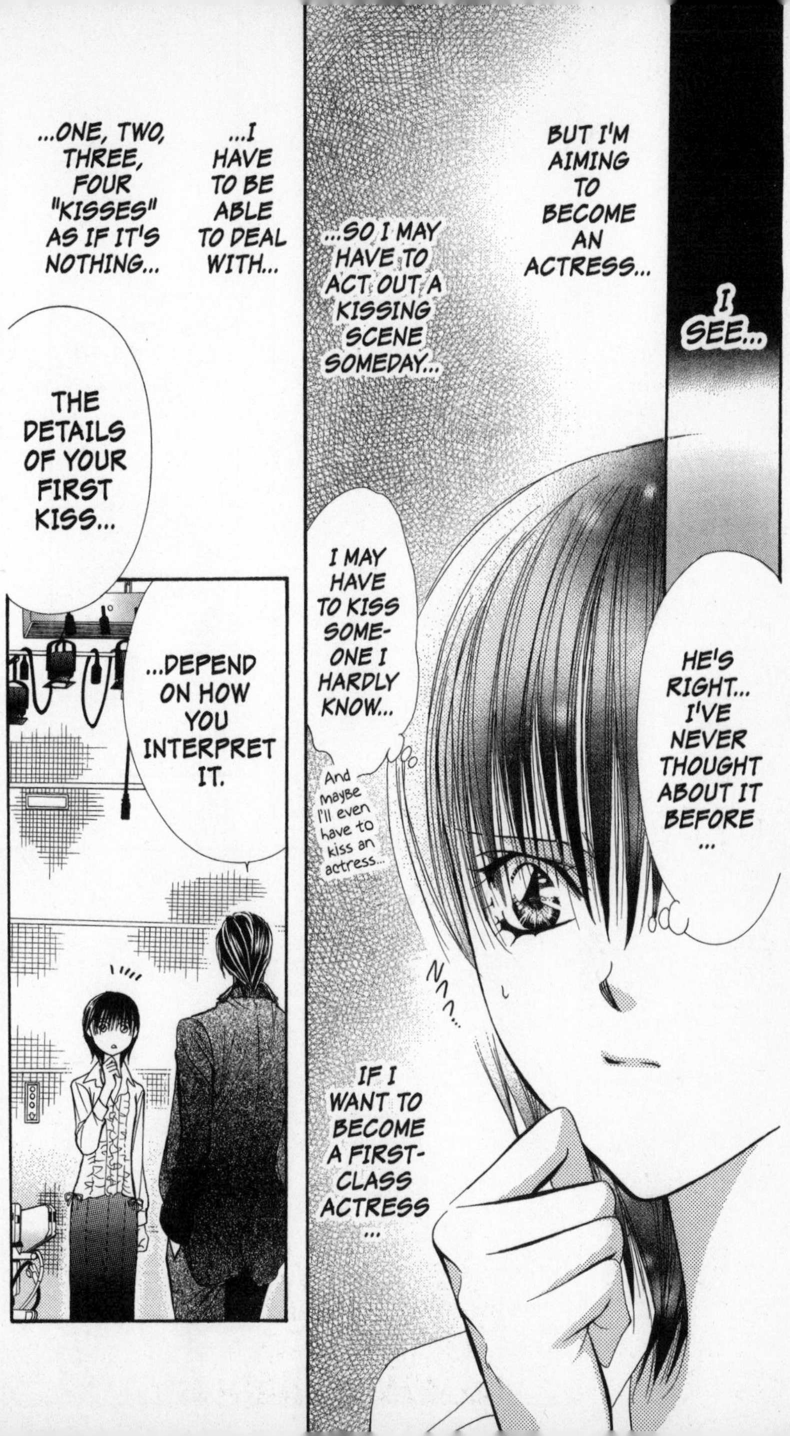
I SEE...
BUT I'M AIMING TO BECOME AN ACTRESS...
...SO I MAY HAVE TO ACT OUT A KISSING SCENE SOMEDAY...
HE'S RIGHT... I'VE NEVER THOUGHT ABOUT IT BEFORE ...
I MAY HAVE TO KISS SOME-ONE I HARDLY KNOW...
And maybe I'll even have to kiss an actress...
Nnn...
IF I WANT TO BECOME A FIRST-CLASS ACTRESS ...
...I HAVE TO BE ABLE TO DEAL WITH...
...ONE, TWO, THREE, FOUR "KISSES" AS IF IT'S NOTHING...
THE DETAILS OF YOUR FIRST KISS...
...DEPEND ON HOW YOU INTERPRET IT.

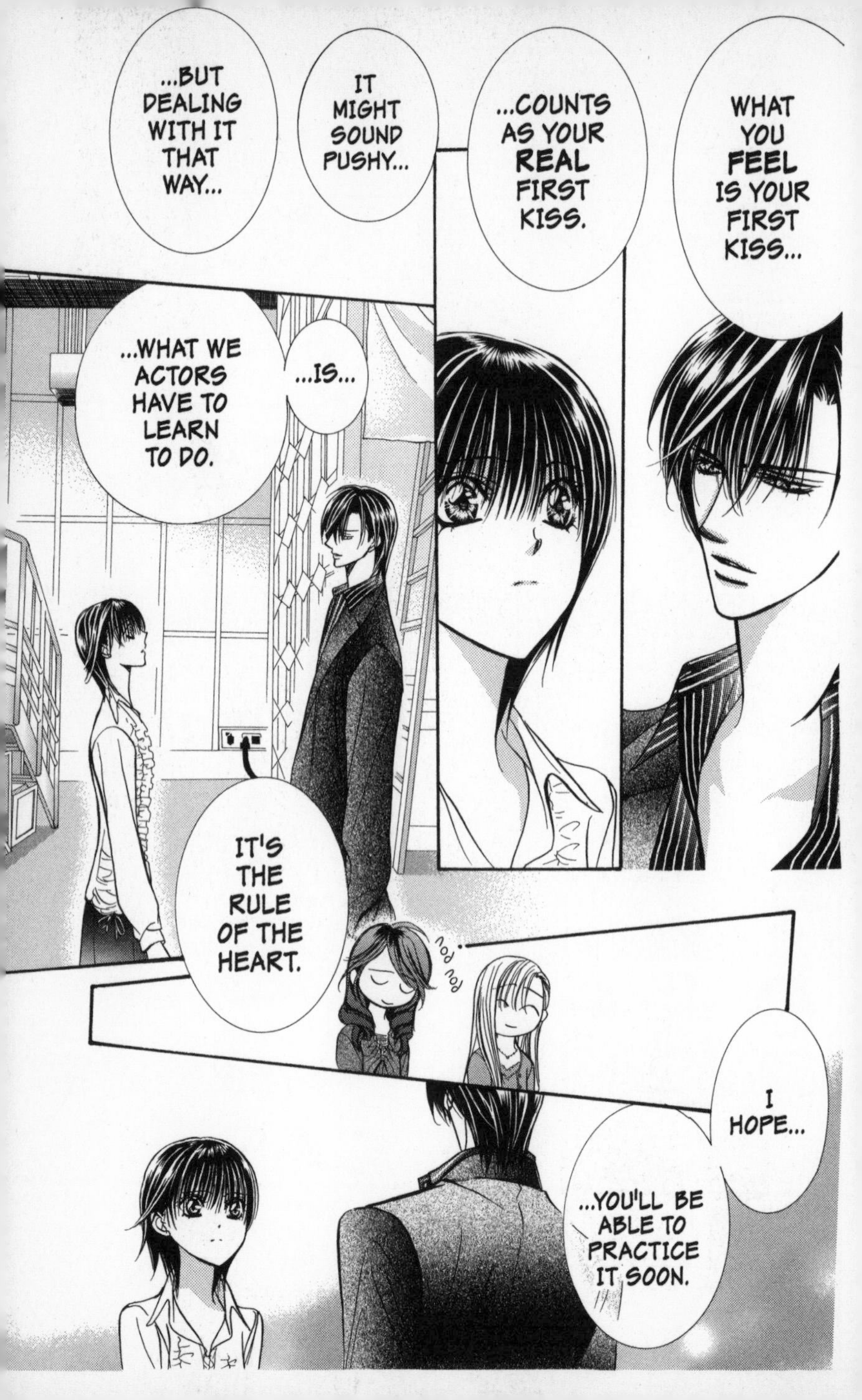
WHAT YOU FEEL IS YOUR FIRST KISS...
...COUNTS AS YOUR REAL FIRST KISS.
IT MIGHT SOUND PUSHY...
...BUT DEALING WITH IT THAT WAY...
...IS...
...WHAT WE ACTORS HAVE TO LEARN TO DO.
IT'S THE RULE OF THE HEART.
pou pou
I HOPE...
...YOU'LL BE ABLE TO PRACTICE IT SOON.

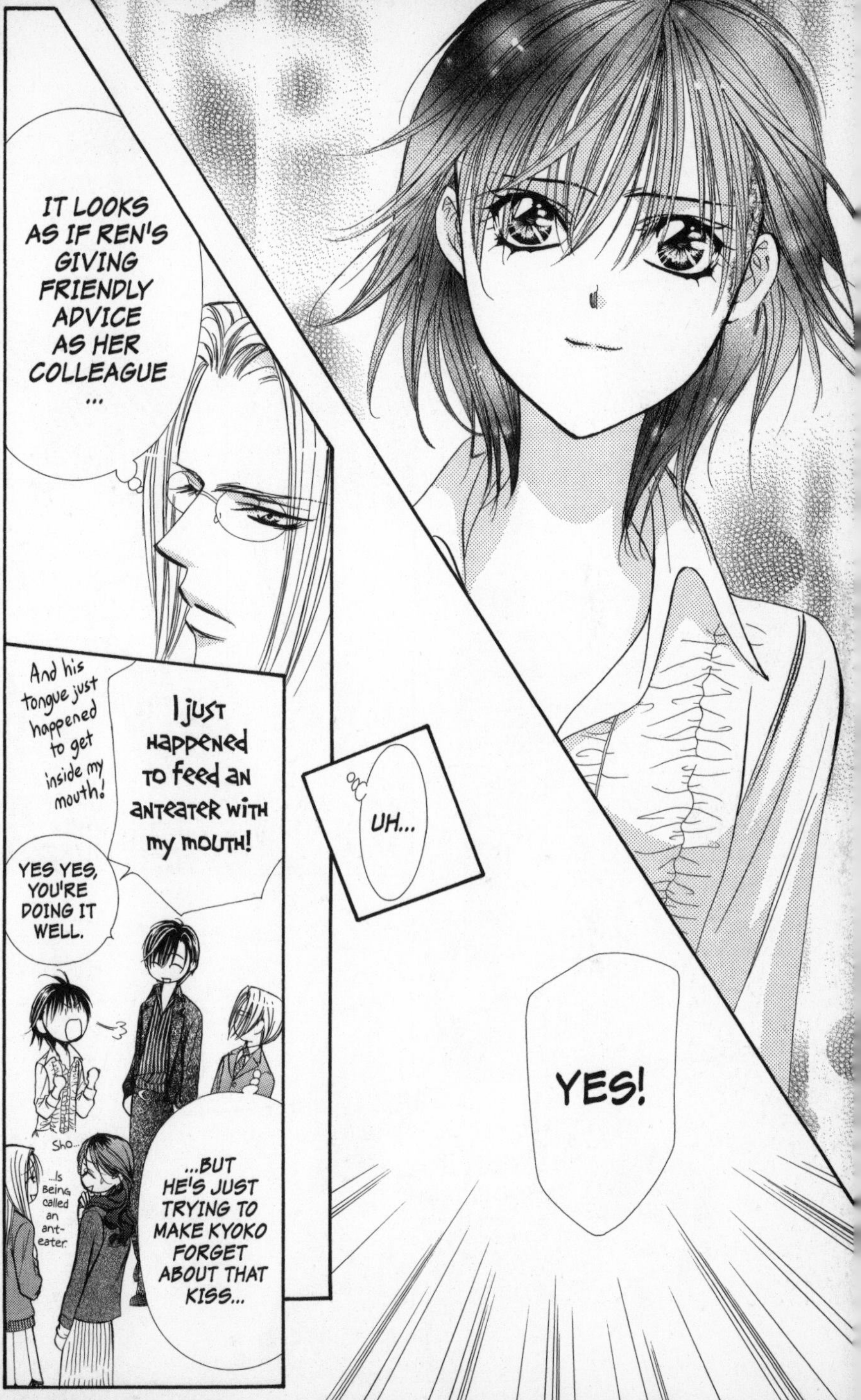
UH...
YES!
IT LOOKS AS IF REN'S GIVING FRIENDLY ADVICE AS HER COLLEAGUE ...
I just happened to feed an anteater with my mouth!
And his tongue just happened to get inside my mouth!
YES YES, YOU'RE DOING IT WELL.
...BUT HE'S JUST TRYING TO MAKE KYOKO FORGET ABOUT THAT KISS...
Sho...
...Is being called an ant-eater.

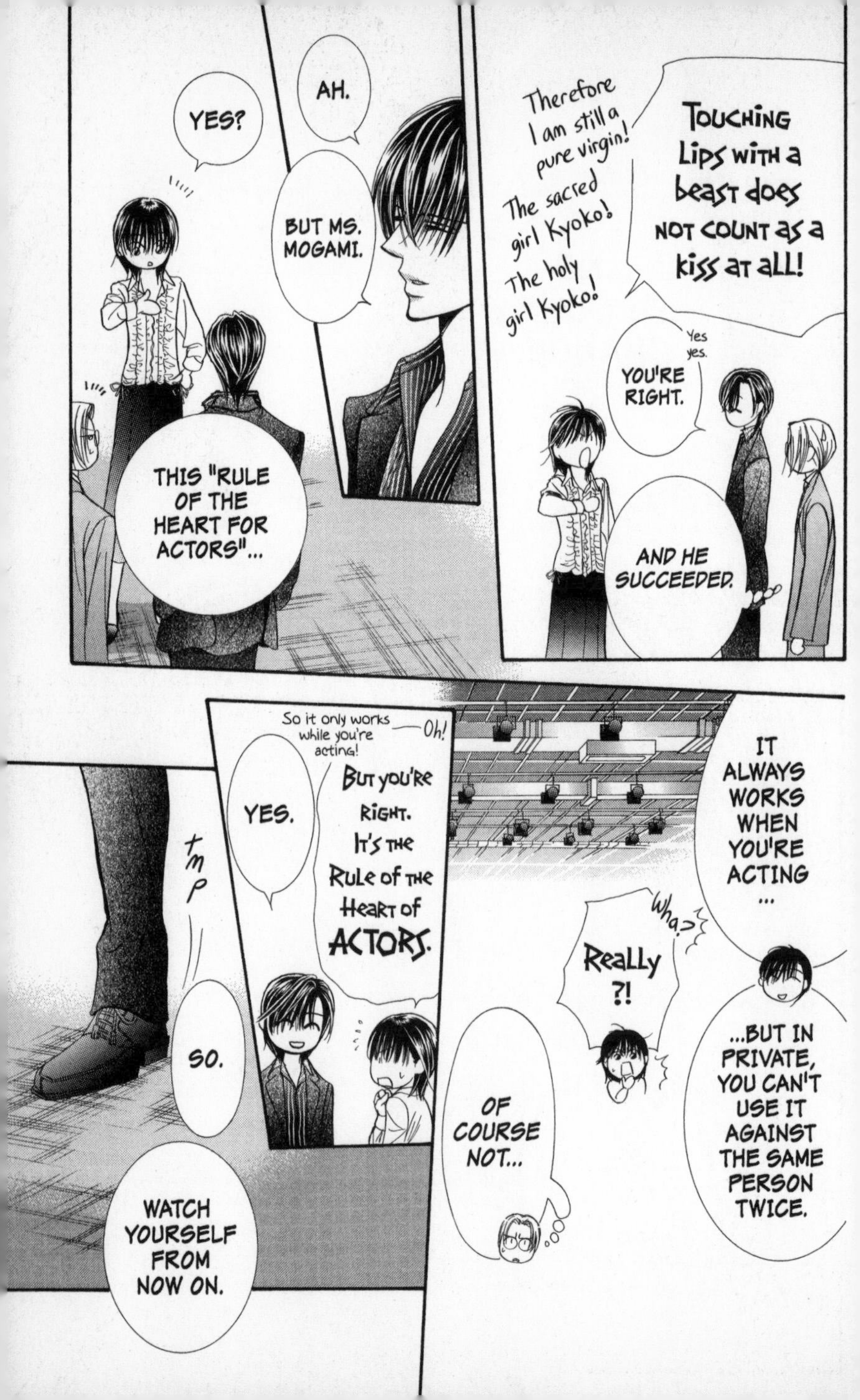
TOUCHING LIPS WITH A BEAST DOES NOT COUNT AS A KISS AT ALL!
Therefore I am still a pure virgin! The sacred girl Kyoko! The holy girl Kyoko!
YOU'RE RIGHT.
Yes yes.
AND HE SUCCEEDED.
AH.
BUT MS. MOGAMI.
YES?
THIS "RULE OF THE HEART FOR ACTORS"...
IT ALWAYS WORKS WHEN YOU'RE ACTING...
Wha?
Really?!
...BUT IN PRIVATE, YOU CAN'T USE IT AGAINST THE SAME PERSON TWICE.
OF COURSE NOT...
Oh!
So it only works while you're acting!
But you're right. It's the Rule of the Heart of ACTORS.
YES.
tmp
SO.
WATCH YOURSELF FROM NOW ON.

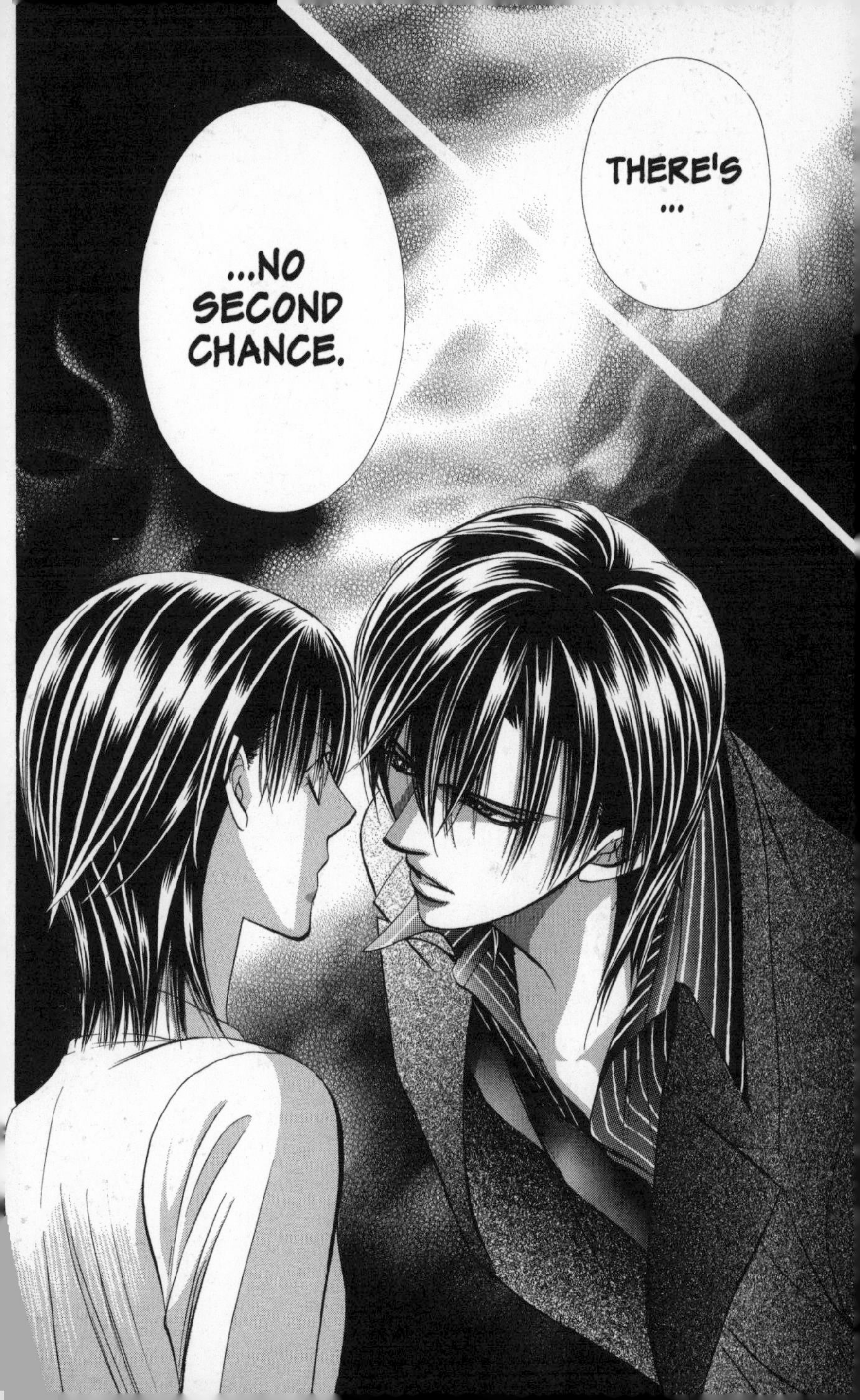
THERE'S ...
...NO SECOND CHANCE.

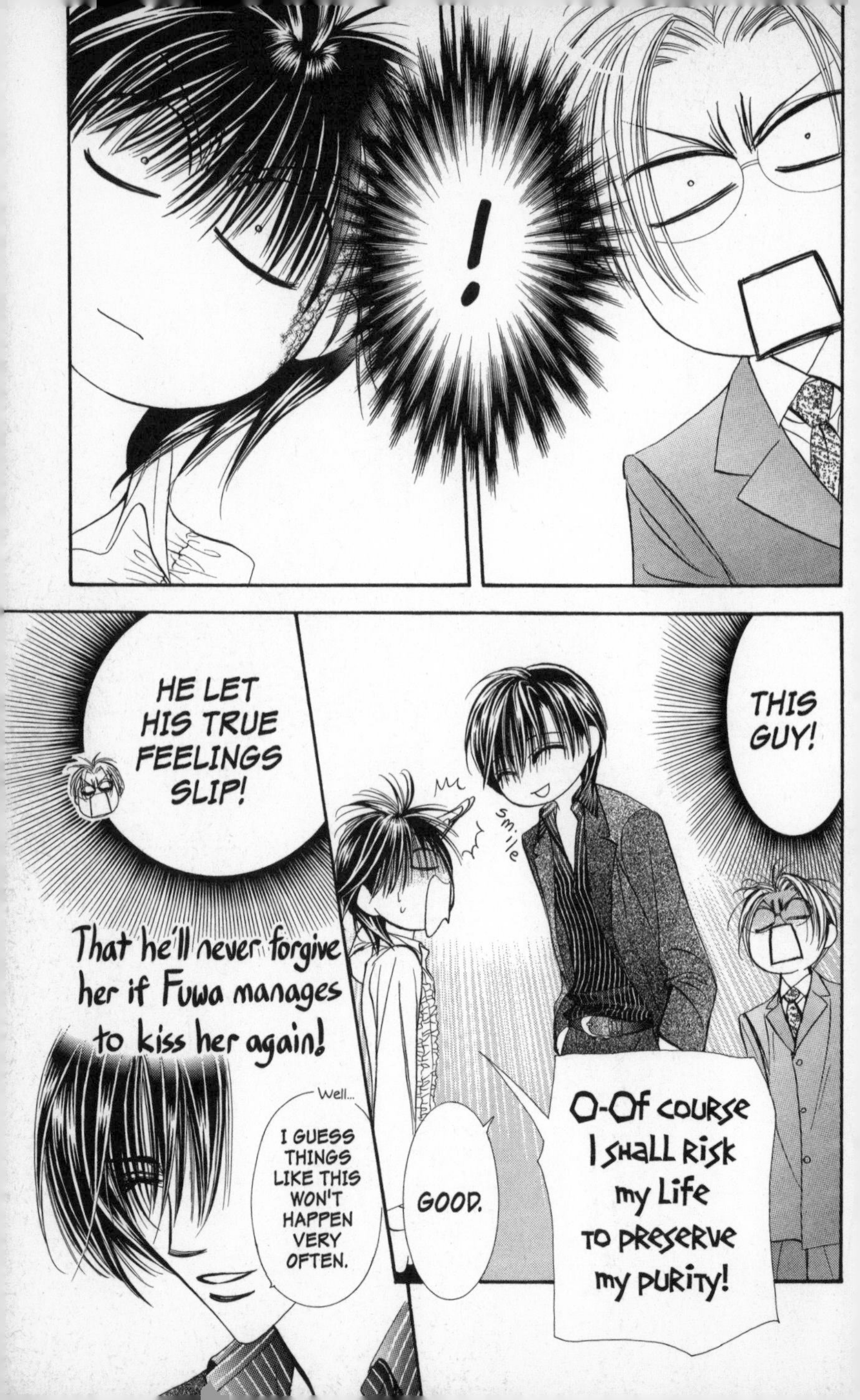
!
THIS GUY!
smile
O-Of course I shall risk my life to preserve my purity!
GOOD.
HE LET HIS TRUE FEELINGS SLIP!
That he'll never forgive her if Fuwa manages to kiss her again!
Well...
I GUESS THINGS LIKE THIS WON'T HAPPEN VERY OFTEN.

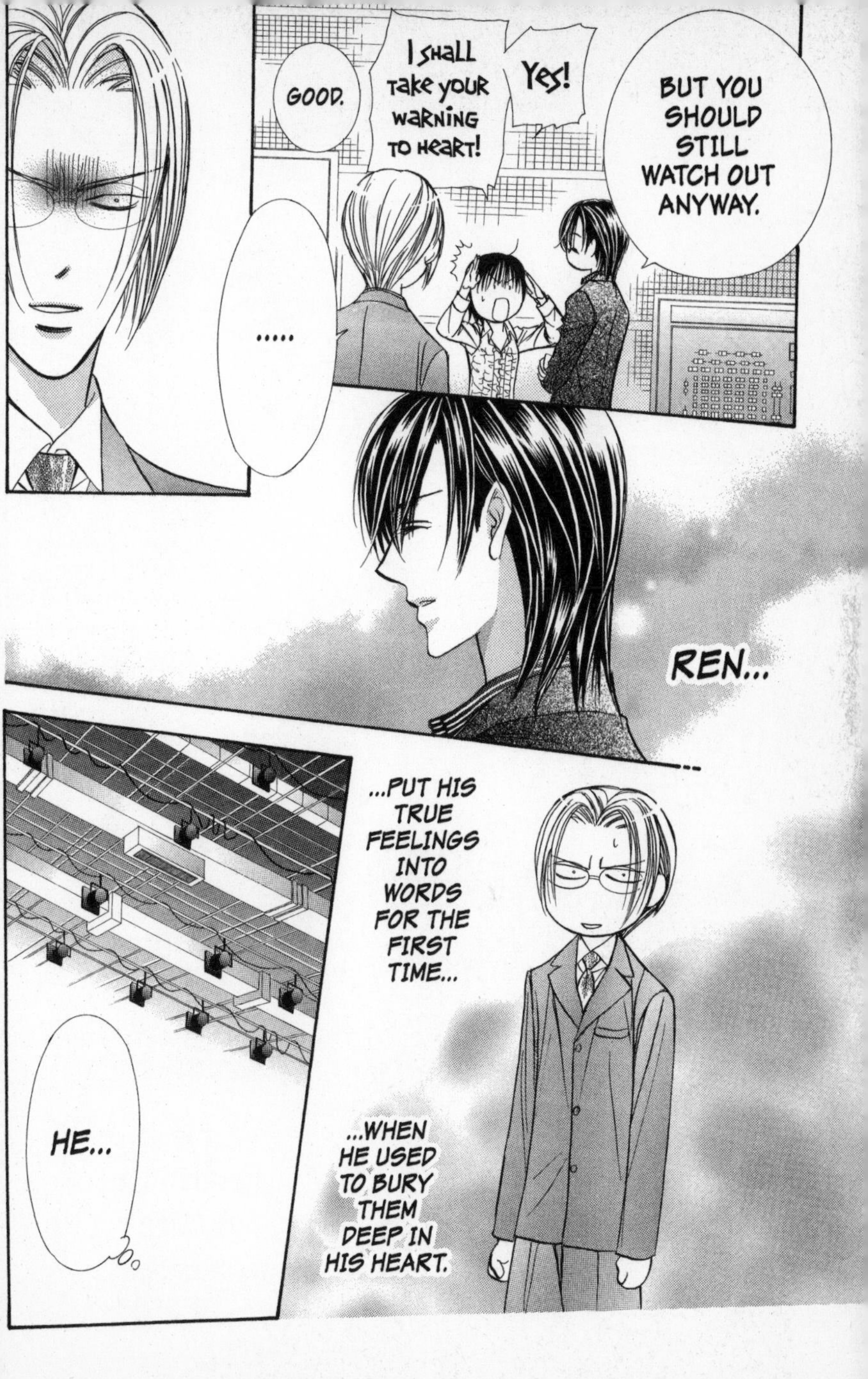
BUT YOU SHOULD STILL WATCH OUT ANYWAY.
Yes!
I shall take your warning to heart!
GOOD.
.....
REN...
...PUT HIS TRUE FEELINGS INTO WORDS FOR THE FIRST TIME...
...WHEN HE USED TO BURY THEM DEEP IN HIS HEART.
HE...

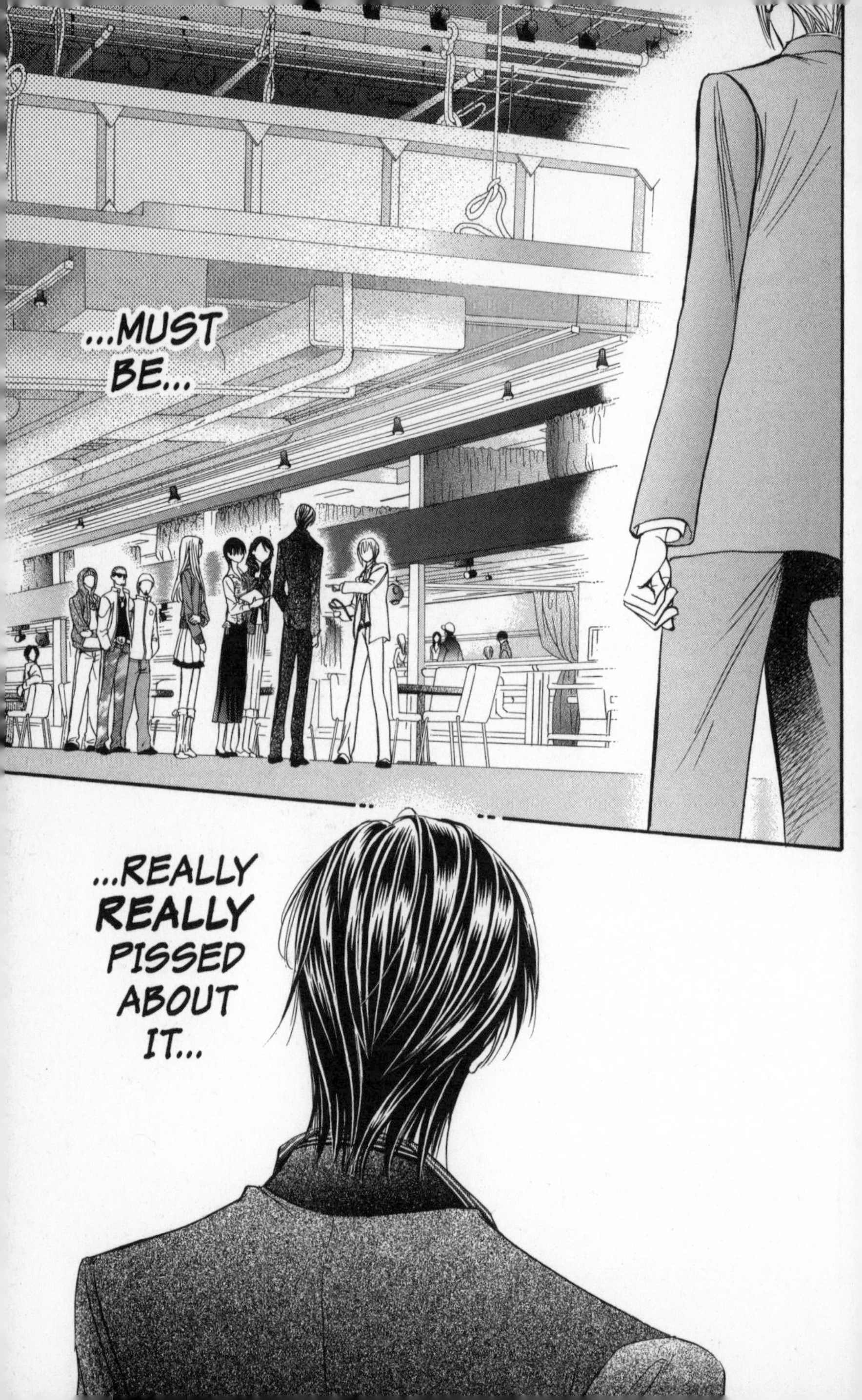
...MUST BE...
...REALLY REALLY PISSED ABOUT IT...

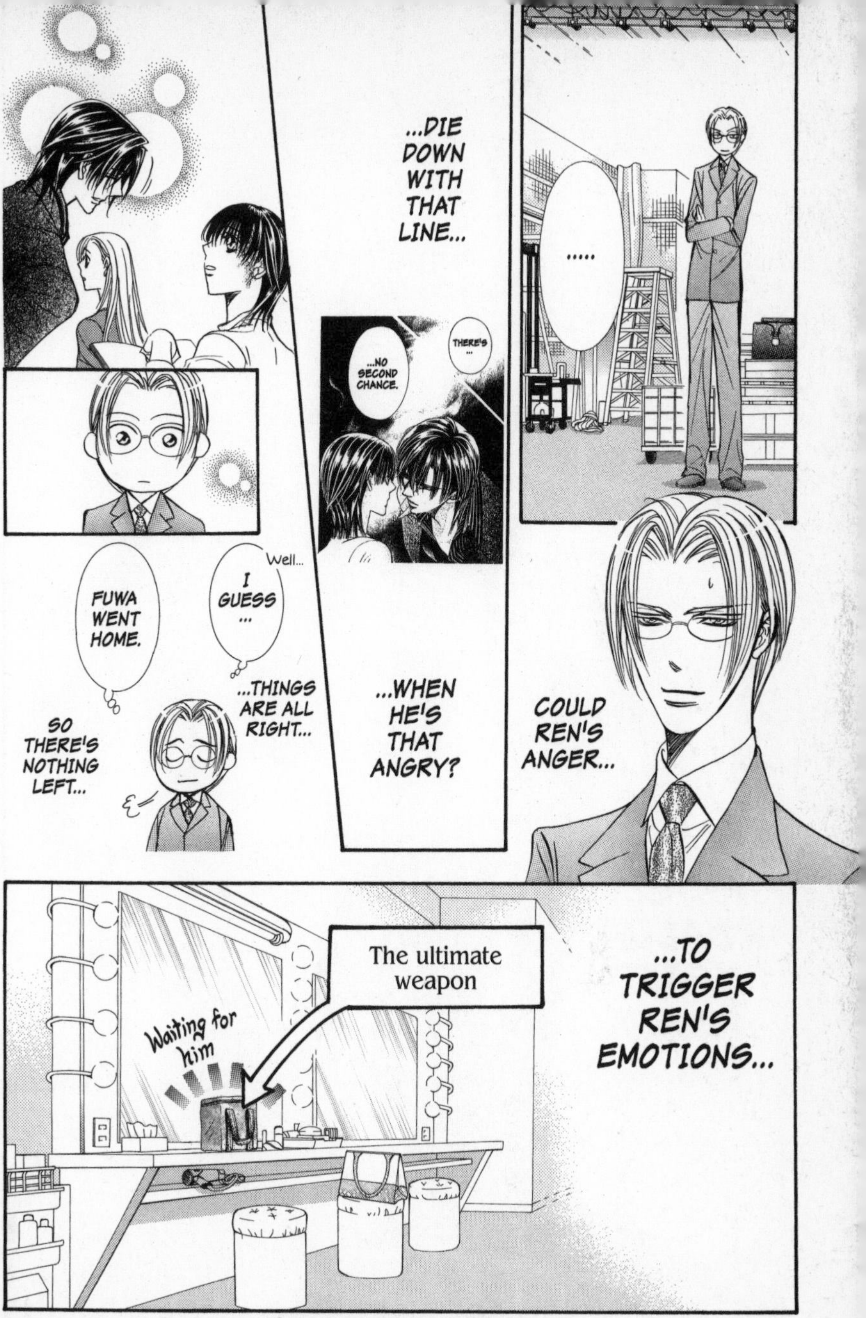
.....
COULD REN'S ANGER...
...DIE DOWN WITH THAT LINE...
THERE'S ...
...NO SECOND CHANCE.
...WHEN HE'S THAT ANGRY?
Well... I GUESS ...
...THINGS ARE ALL RIGHT...
FUWA WENT HOME.
SO THERE'S NOTHING LEFT...
...TO TRIGGER REN'S EMOTIONS...
The ultimate weapon
Waiting for him

End of Act 147

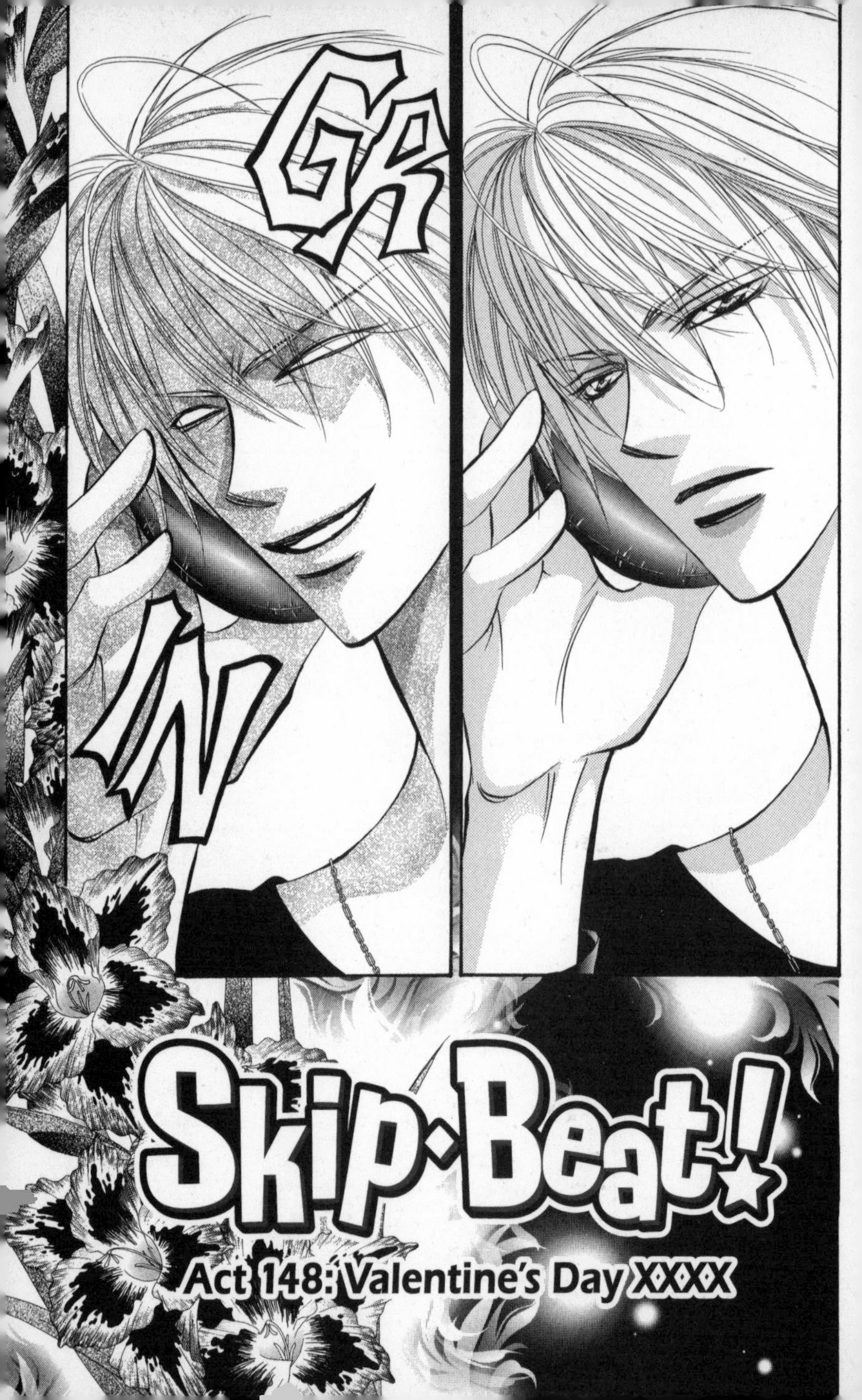
GRIN
Skip·Beat!
Act 148: Valentine's Day XXXX

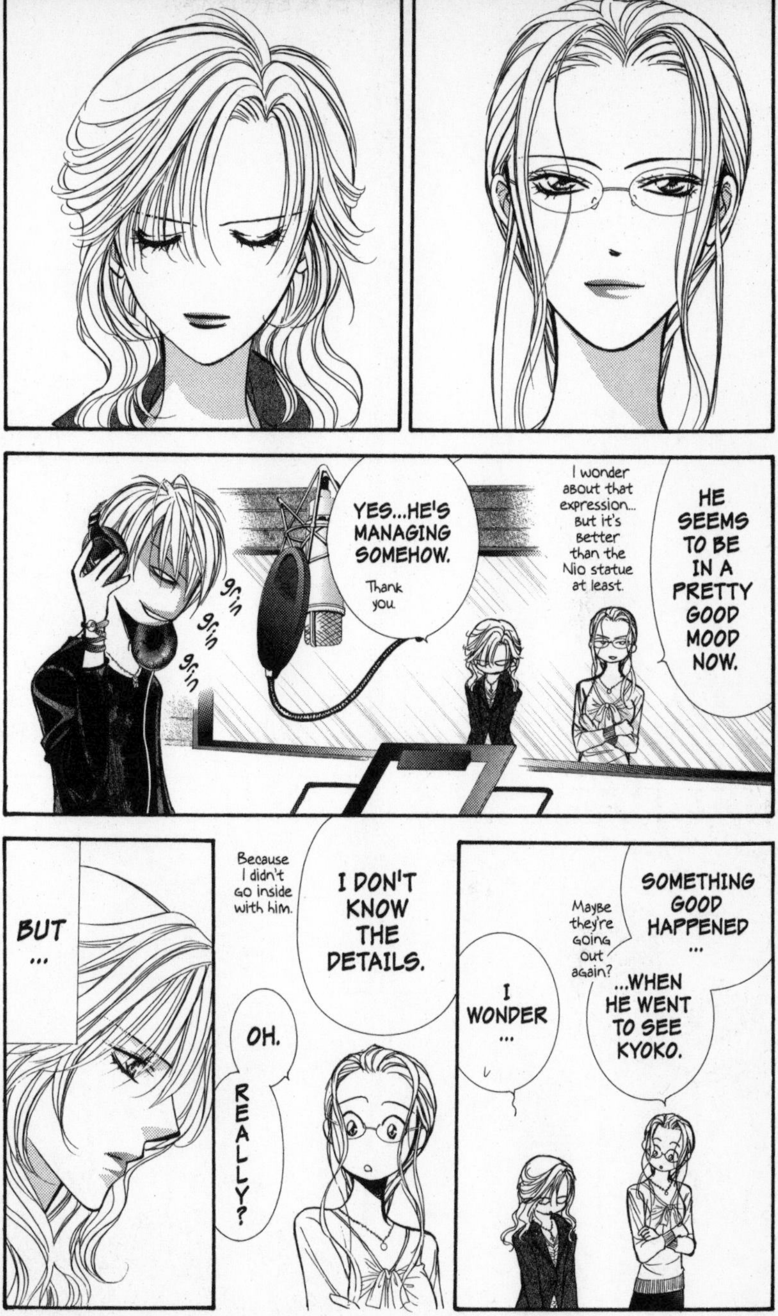
HE SEEMS TO BE IN A PRETTY GOOD MOOD NOW.
I wonder about that expression... But it's better than the Nio statue at least.
YES...HE'S MANAGING SOMEHOW.
Thank you.
grin grin grin
SOMETHING GOOD HAPPENED ...
...WHEN HE WENT TO SEE KYOKO.
Maybe they're going out again?
I WONDER ...
I DON'T KNOW THE DETAILS.
Because I didn't go inside with him.
OH.
REALLY?
BUT ...

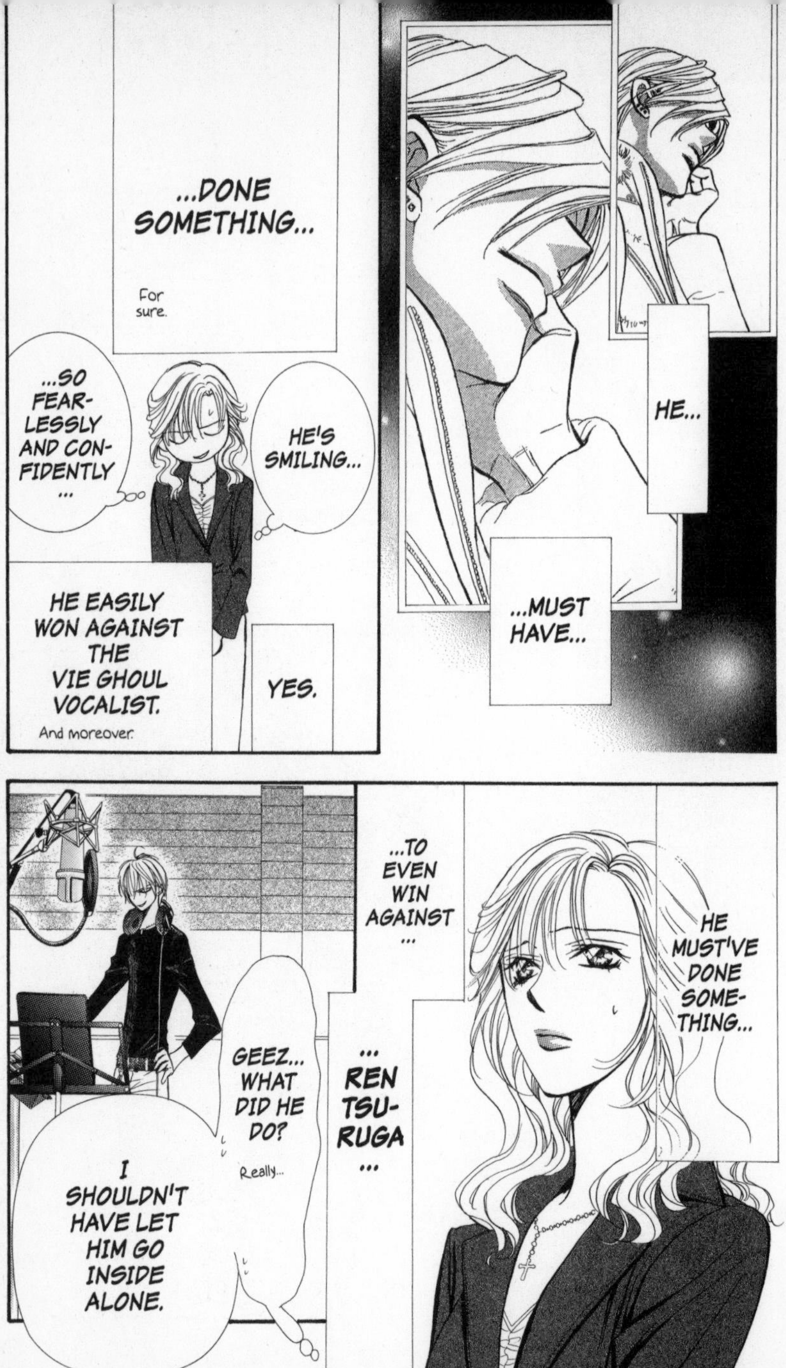
HE...
...MUST HAVE...
...DONE SOMETHING...
For sure.
HE'S SMILING...
...SO FEARLESSLY AND CONFIDENTLY...
YES.
HE EASILY WON AGAINST THE VIE GHOUL VOCALIST.
And moreover.
HE MUST'VE DONE SOMETHING...
...TO EVEN WIN AGAINST...
...REN TSURUGA...
GEEZ... WHAT DID HE DO?
Really...
I SHOULDN'T HAVE LET HIM GO INSIDE ALONE.

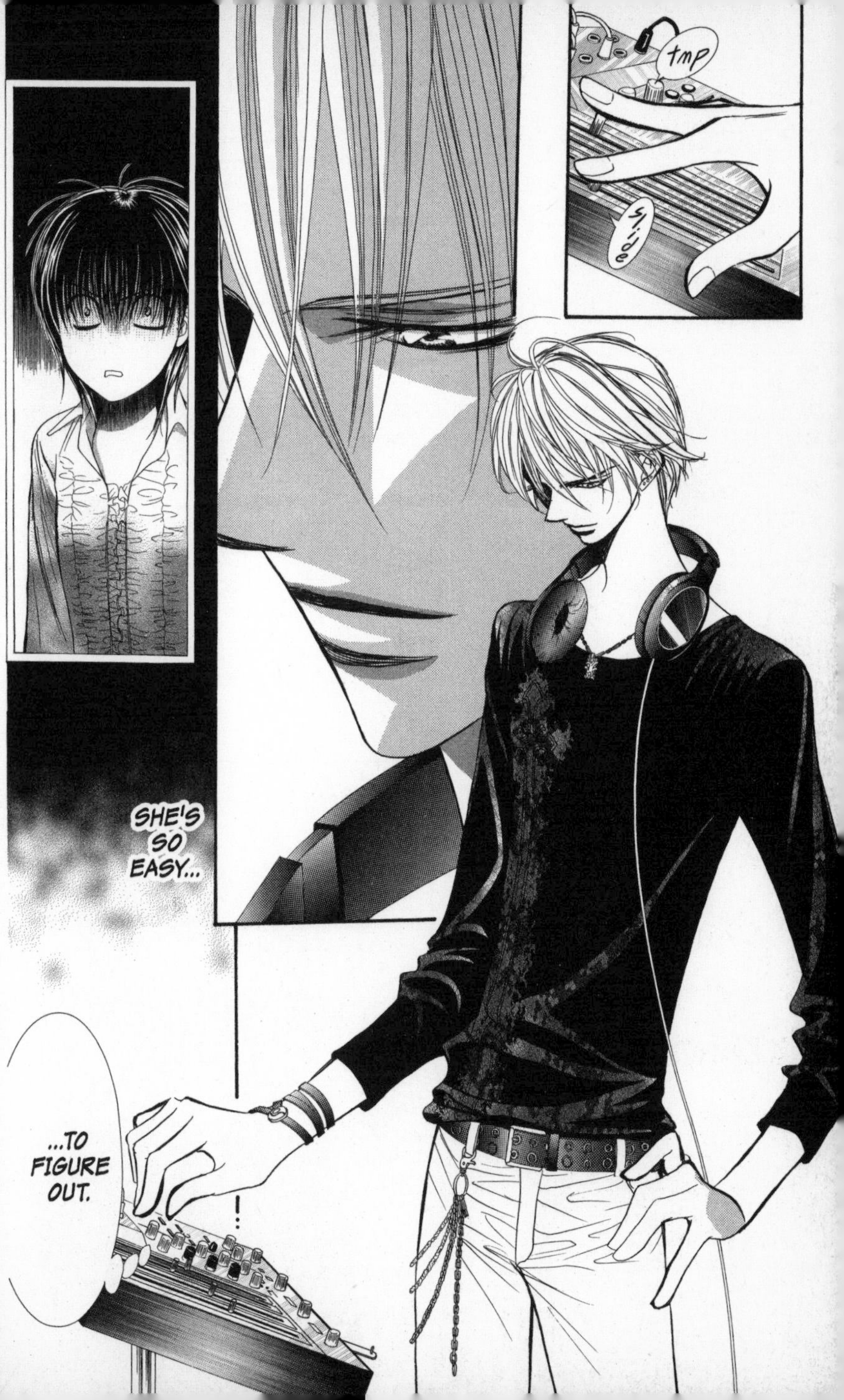
tmp
slide
SHE'S SO EASY...
...TO FIGURE OUT.

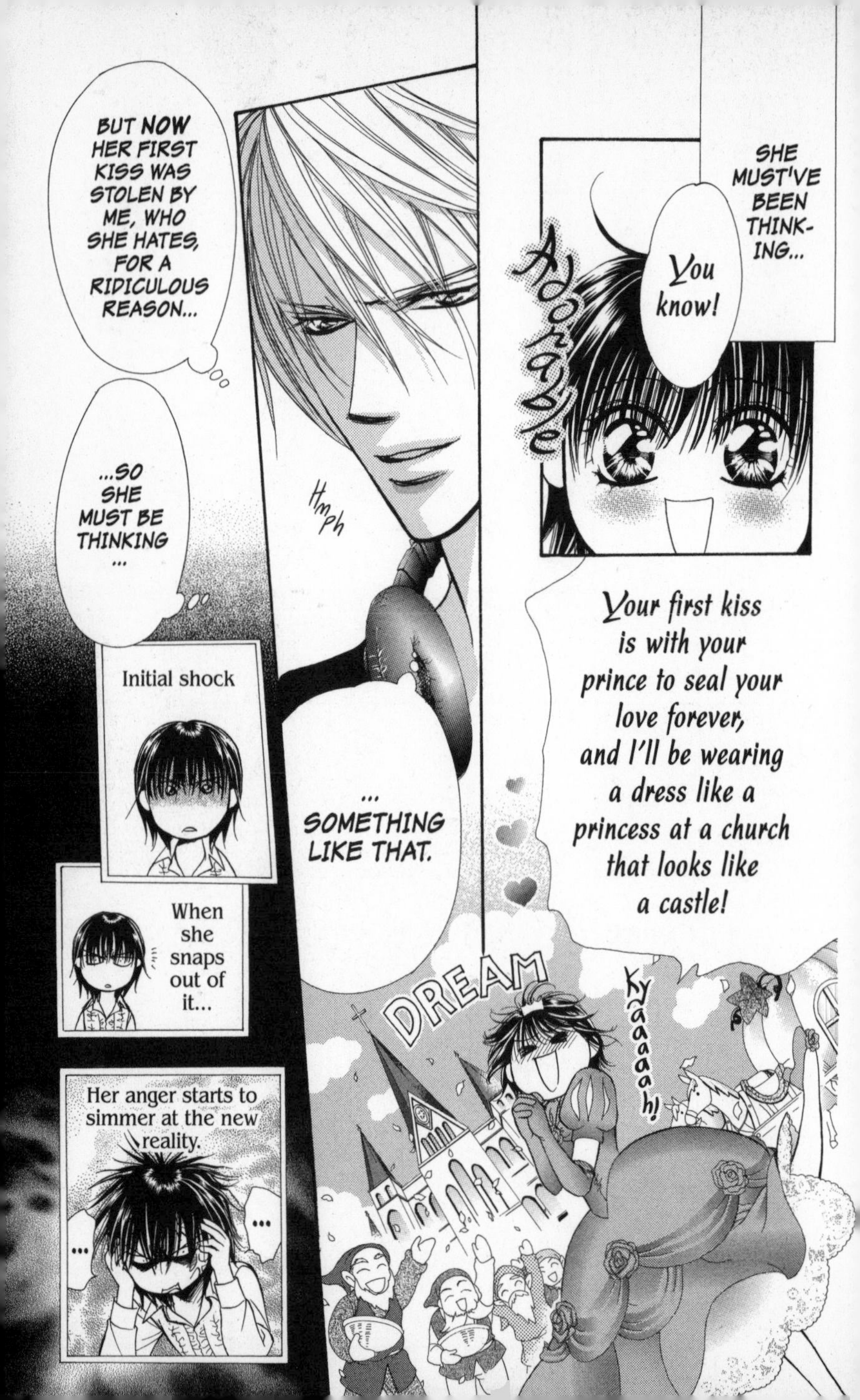

SHE MUST'VE BEEN THINKING...
You know!
Adorable
Your first kiss is with your prince to seal your love forever, and I'll be wearing a dress like a princess at a church that looks like a castle!
DREAM
Kyaaaaaah!
Hmph
... SOMETHING LIKE THAT.
BUT NOW HER FIRST KISS WAS STOLEN BY ME, WHO SHE HATES, FOR A RIDICULOUS REASON...
...SO SHE MUST BE THINKING ...
Initial shock
When she snaps out of it...
Her anger starts to simmer at the new reality.
...
...

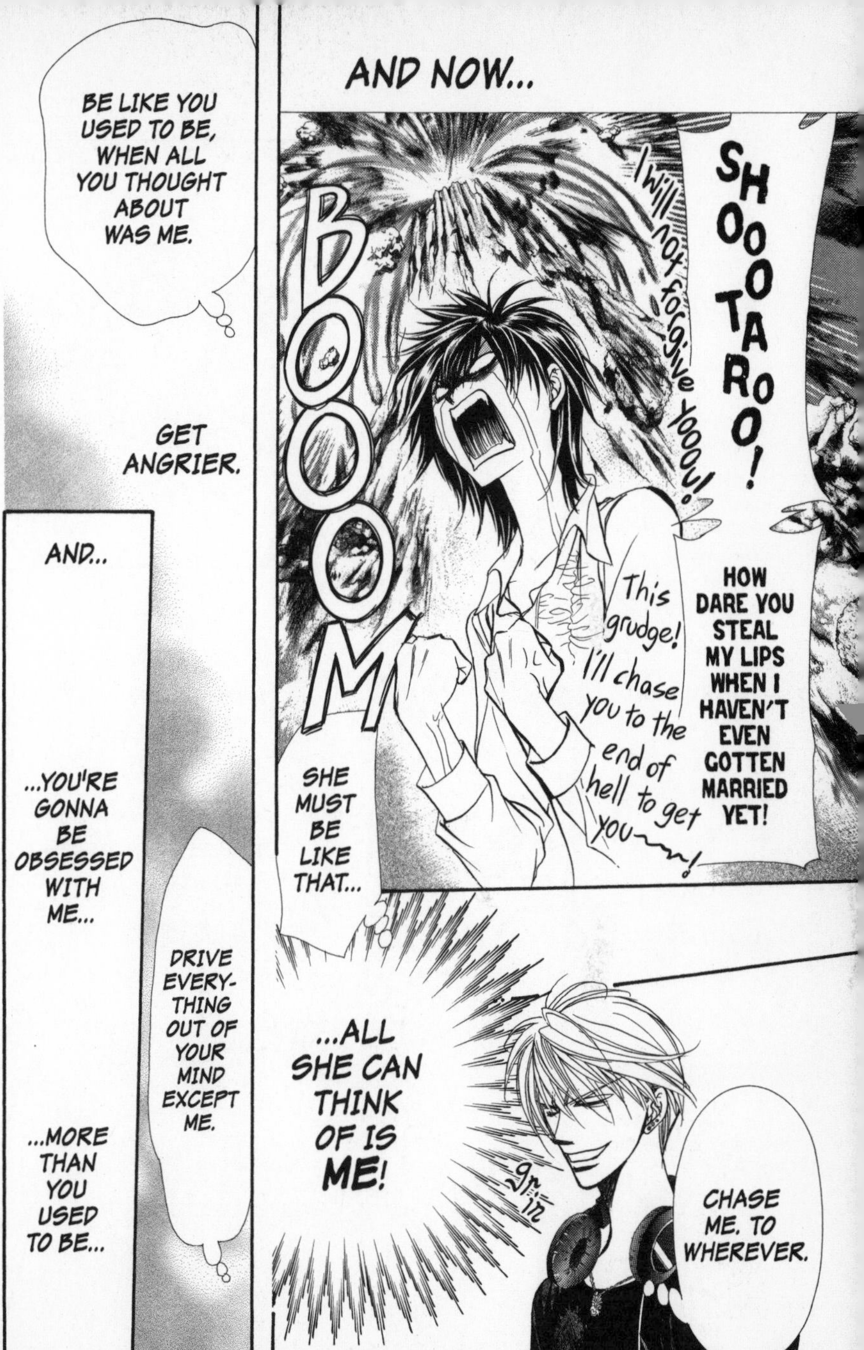
AND NOW...
SHOOOTAROO!
I will not forgive yoooou!
BOOOOM
HOW DARE YOU STEAL MY LIPS WHEN I HAVEN'T EVEN GOTTEN MARRIED YET!
This grudge! I'll chase you to the end of hell to get you~~!
SHE MUST BE LIKE THAT...
...ALL SHE CAN THINK OF IS ME!
grin
CHASE ME. TO WHEREVER.
BE LIKE YOU USED TO BE, WHEN ALL YOU THOUGHT ABOUT WAS ME.
GET ANGRIER.
AND...
...YOU'RE GONNA BE OBSESSED WITH ME...
DRIVE EVERY-THING OUT OF YOUR MIND EXCEPT ME.
...MORE THAN YOU USED TO BE...

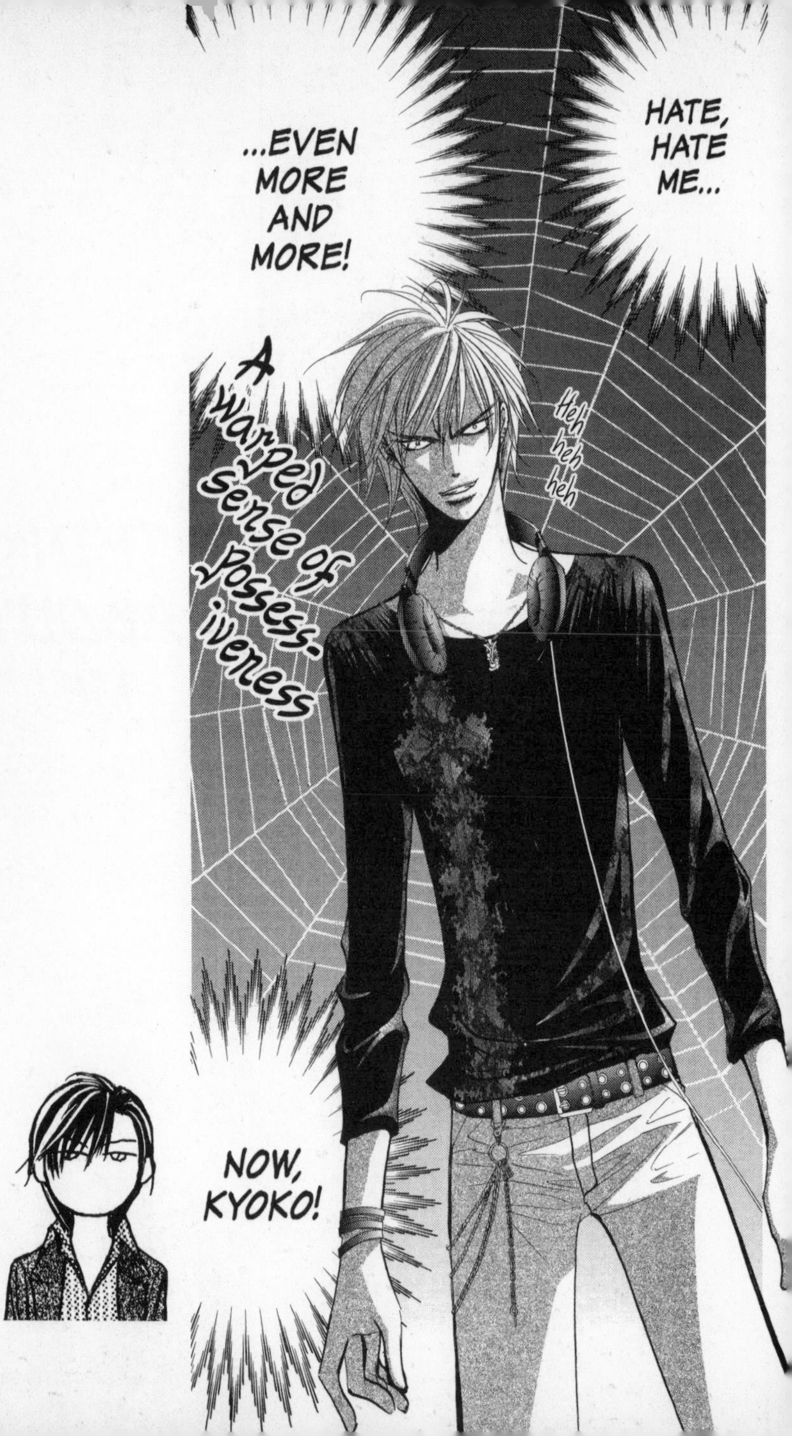
HATE, HATE ME...
...EVEN MORE AND MORE!
Heh heh heh
A warped sense of possess-iveness
NOW, KYOKO!

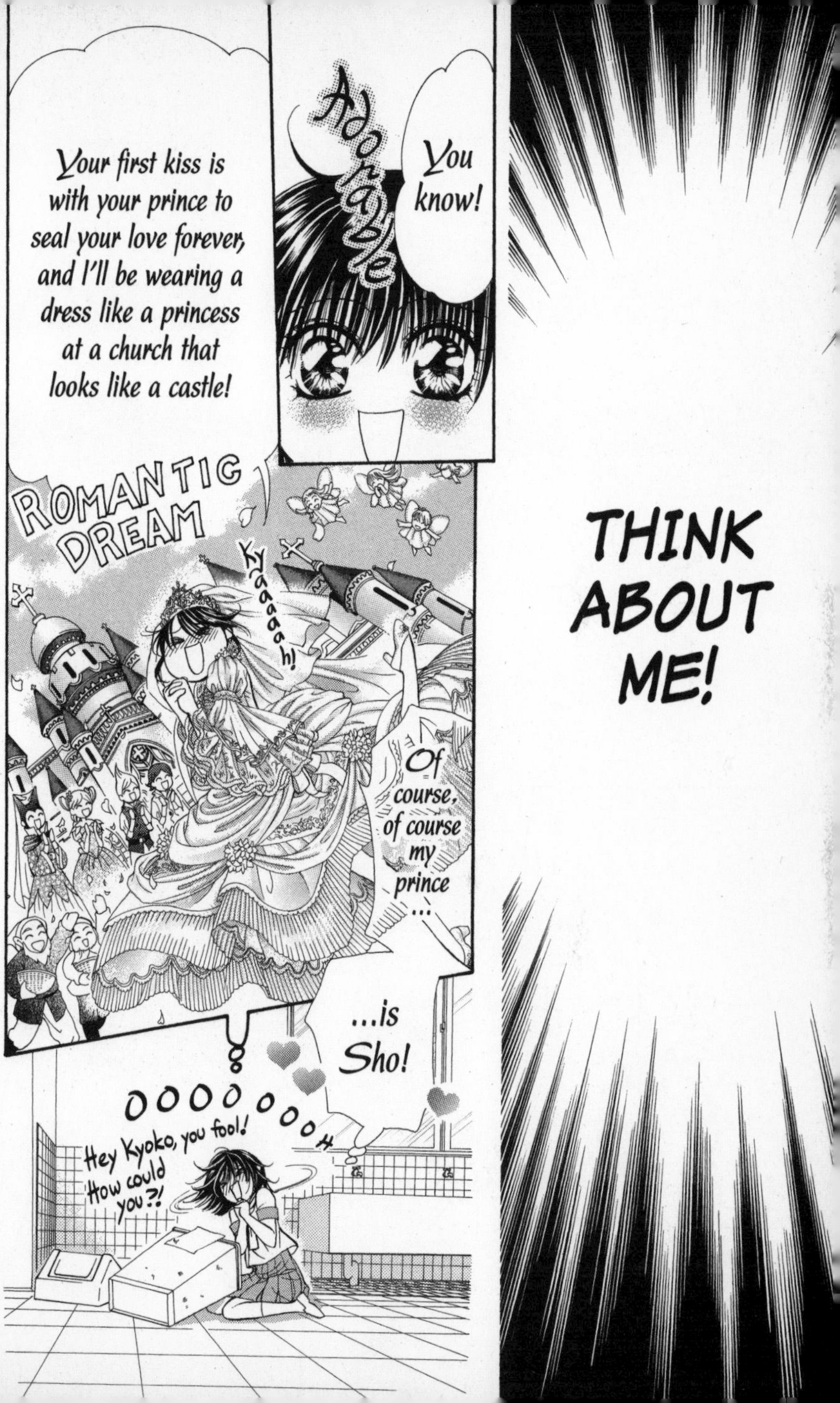
THINK ABOUT ME!
You know!
Adorable
Your first kiss is with your prince to seal your love forever, and I'll be wearing a dress like a princess at a church that looks like a castle!
ROMANTIC DREAM
Kyaaaaaah!
Of course, of course my prince...
...is Sho!
OOOOOOOOH
Hey Kyoko, you fool! How could you?!

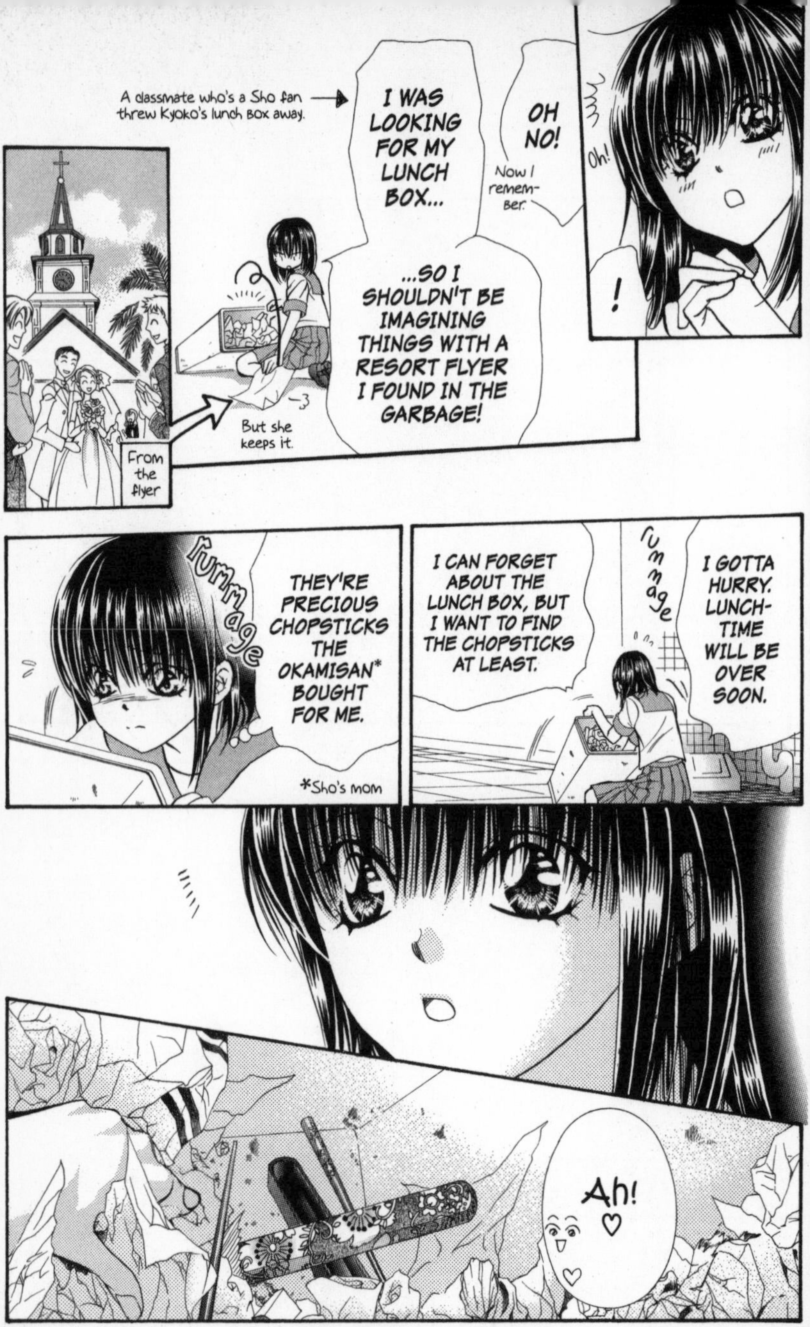
Oh!
!
OH NO!
Now I remember.
I WAS LOOKING FOR MY LUNCH BOX...
A classmate who's a Sho fan threw Kyoko's lunch box away.
...SO I SHOULDN'T BE IMAGINING THINGS WITH A RESORT FLYER I FOUND IN THE GARBAGE!
But she keeps it.
From the flyer
I GOTTA HURRY. LUNCHTIME WILL BE OVER SOON.
rummage
I CAN FORGET ABOUT THE LUNCH BOX, BUT I WANT TO FIND THE CHOPSTICKS AT LEAST.
THEY'RE PRECIOUS CHOPSTICKS THE OKAMISAN* BOUGHT FOR ME.
rummage
*Sho's mom
Ah!

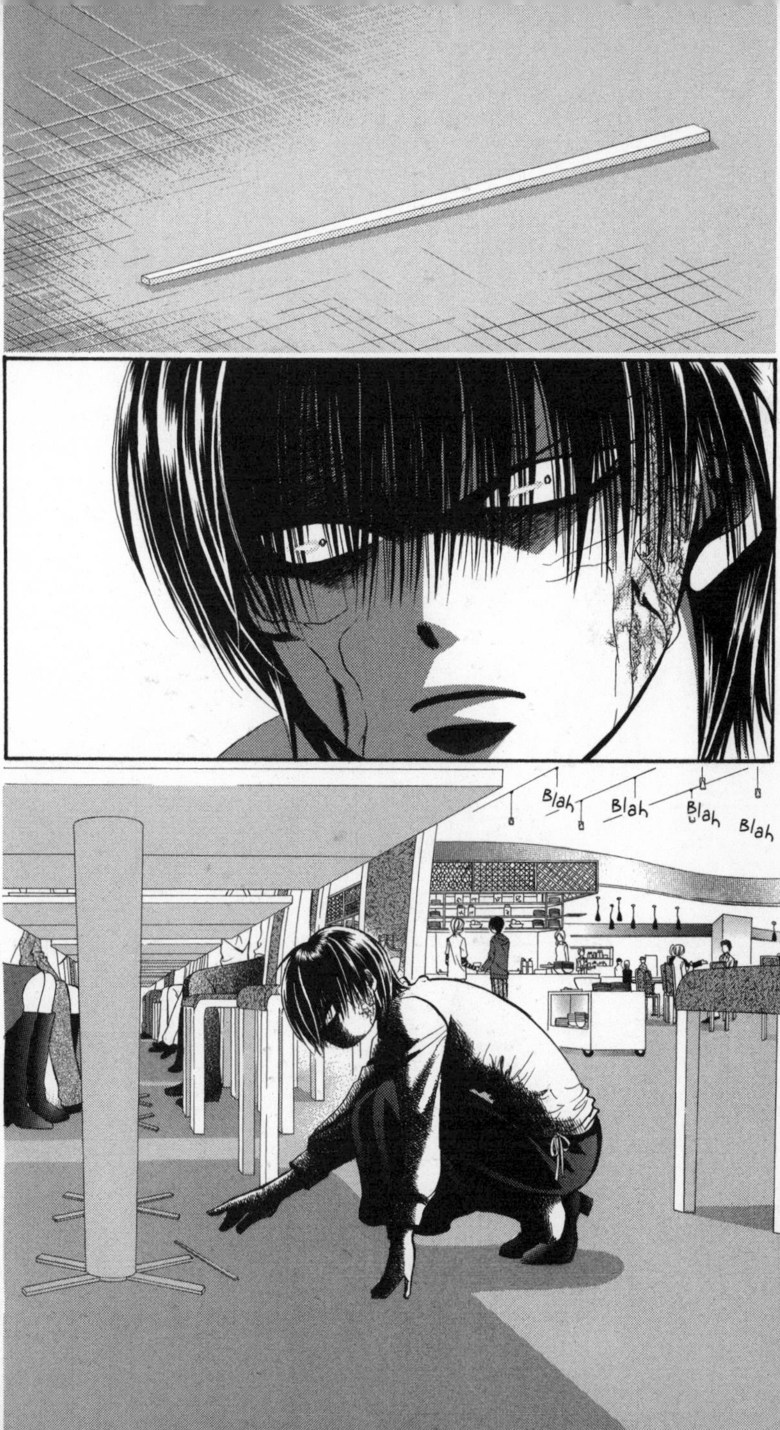
Blah
Blah
Blah
Blah

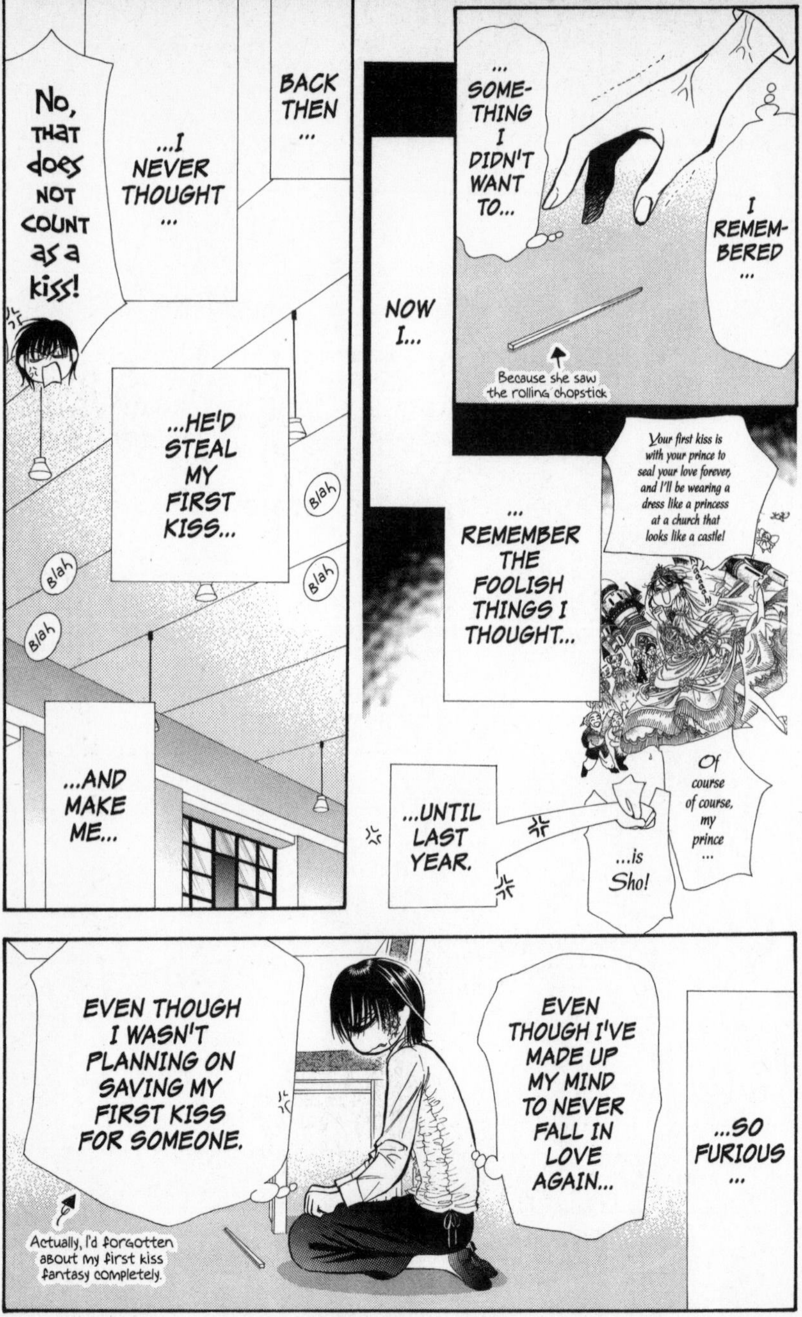
I REMEMBERED...
...SOMETHING I DIDN'T WANT TO...
Because she saw the rolling chopstick
NOW I...
Your first kiss is with your prince to seal your love forever, and I'll be wearing a dress like a princess at a church that looks like a castle!
...REMEMBER THE FOOLISH THINGS I THOUGHT...
Of course of course, my prince...
...is Sho!
...UNTIL LAST YEAR.
BACK THEN...
...I NEVER THOUGHT...
No, that does not count as a kiss!
...HE'D STEAL MY FIRST KISS...
Blah
Blah
Blah
Blah
...AND MAKE ME...
...SO FURIOUS...
EVEN THOUGH I'VE MADE UP MY MIND TO NEVER FALL IN LOVE AGAIN...
EVEN THOUGH I WASN'T PLANNING ON SAVING MY FIRST KISS FOR SOMEONE.
Actually, I'd forgotten about my first kiss fantasy completely.

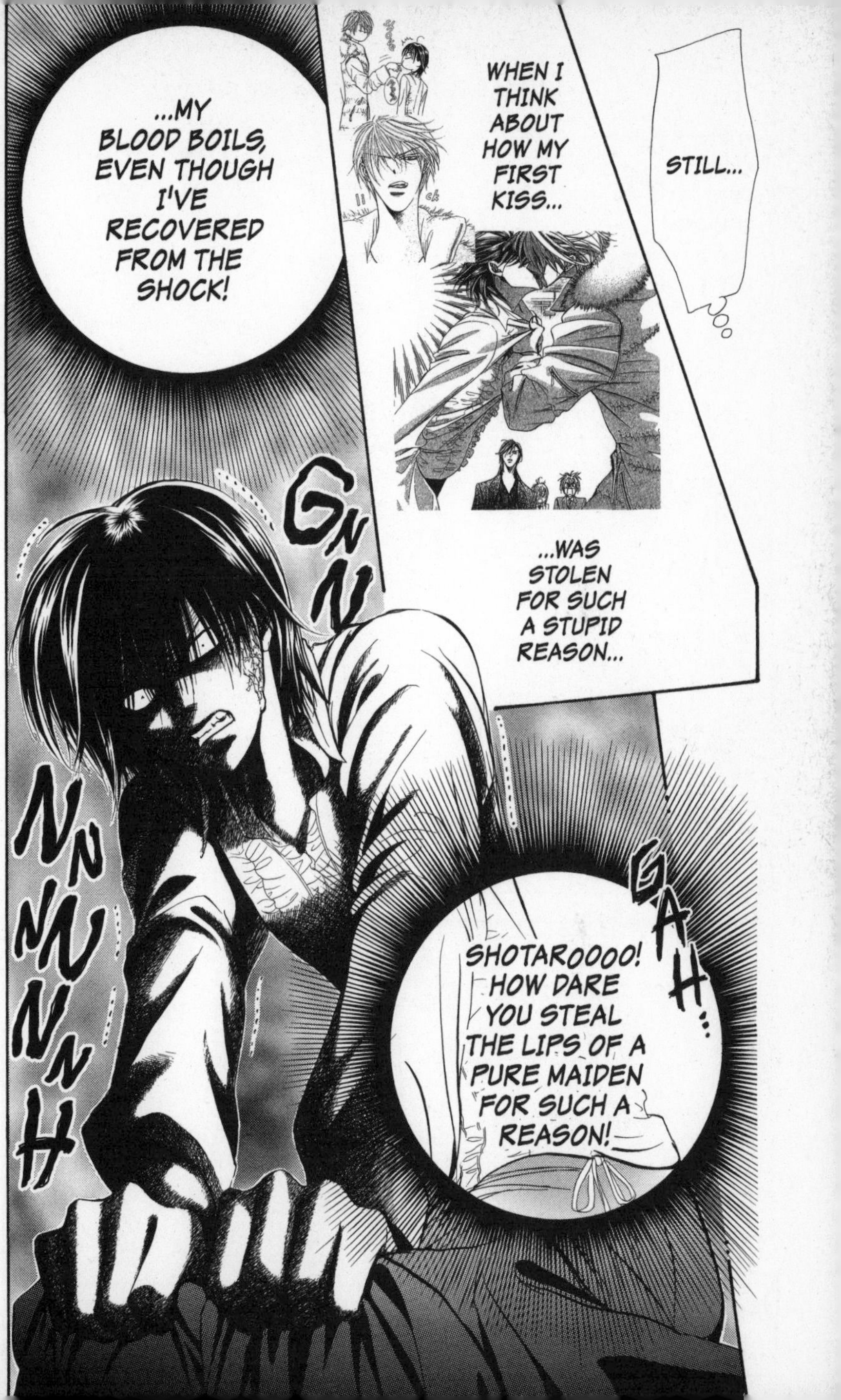
STILL...
WHEN I THINK ABOUT HOW MY FIRST KISS...
...WAS STOLEN FOR SUCH A STUPID REASON...
...MY BLOOD BOILS, EVEN THOUGH I'VE RECOVERED FROM THE SHOCK!
GNN
GAH...
SHOTAROOOO! HOW DARE YOU STEAL THE LIPS OF A PURE MAIDEN FOR SUCH A REASON!
NNNNNNH

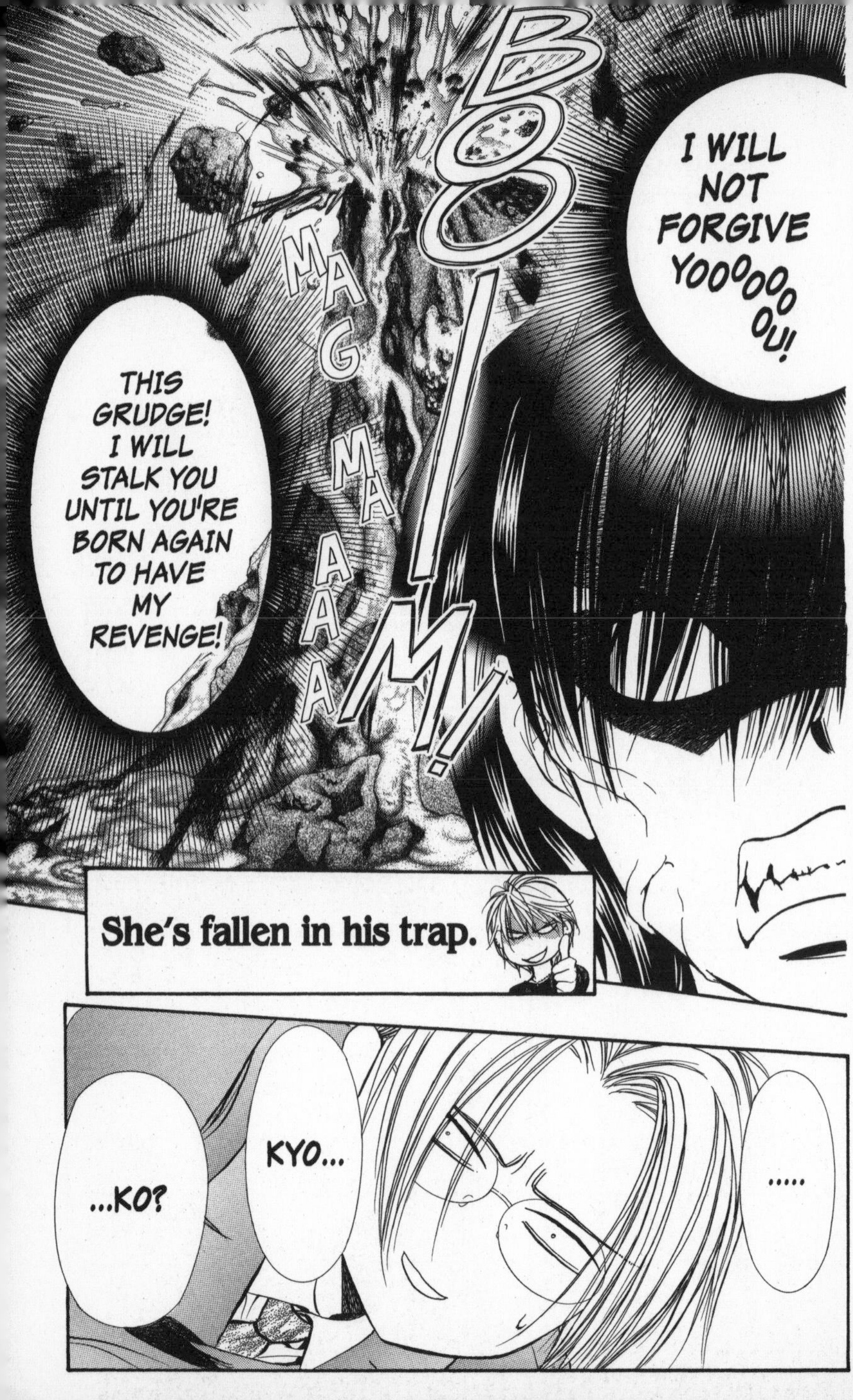
I WILL NOT FORGIVE YOOOOOOOU!
BOOM!
MAGMAAAA
THIS GRUDGE! I WILL STALK YOU UNTIL YOU'RE BORN AGAIN TO HAVE MY REVENGE!
She's fallen in his trap.
.....
KYO...
...KO?

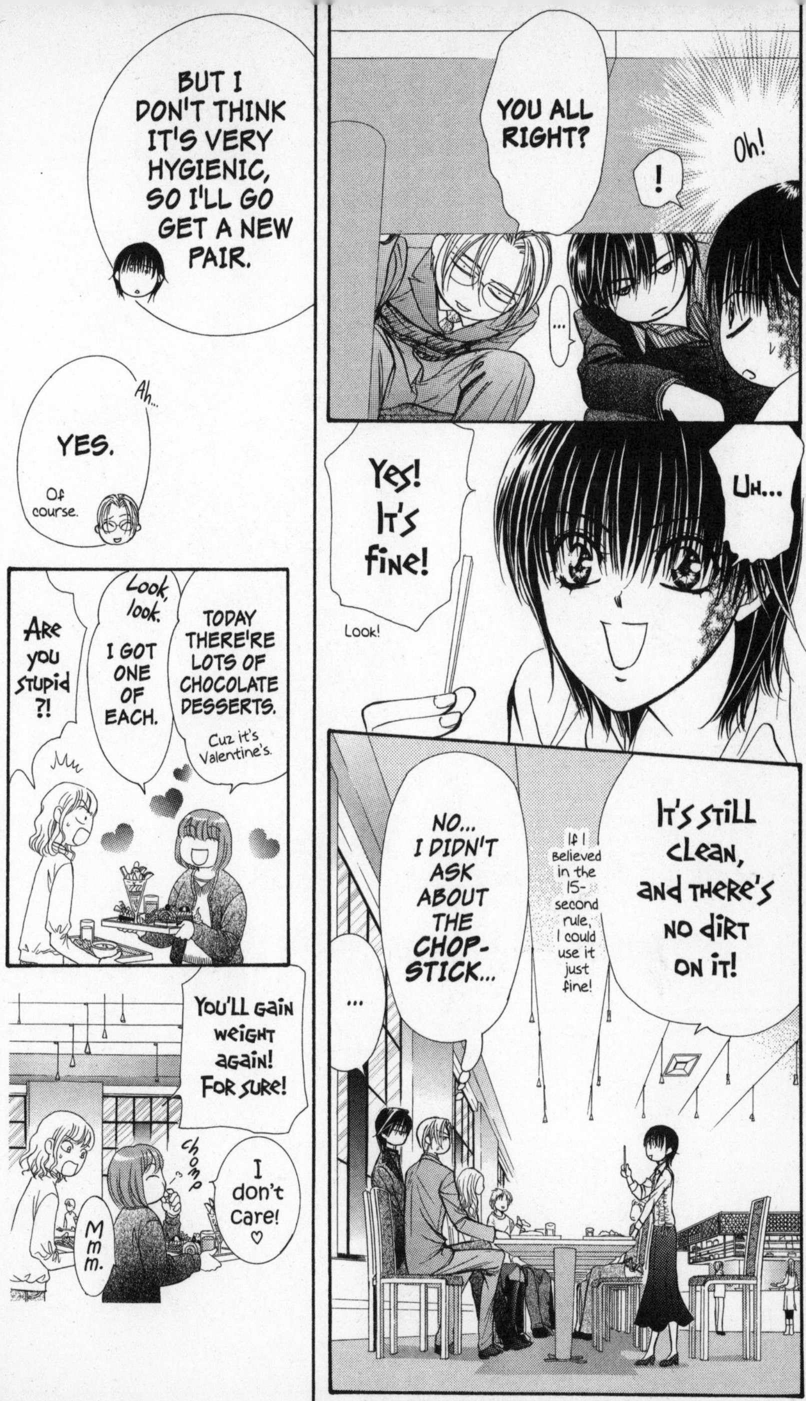

Oh!
!
YOU ALL RIGHT?
...
Uh...
Yes! It's fine!
Look!
It's still clean, and there's no dirt on it!
If I believed in the 15-second rule, I could use it just fine!
NO... I DIDN'T ASK ABOUT THE CHOP-STICK...
...
BUT I DON'T THINK IT'S VERY HYGIENIC, SO I'LL GO GET A NEW PAIR.
Ah... YES.
Of course.
TODAY THERE'RE LOTS OF CHOCOLATE DESSERTS.
Cuz it's Valentine's.
Look, look. I GOT ONE OF EACH.
Are you stupid?!
You'll gain weight again! For sure!
I don't care! ♡
chomp
Mmm.

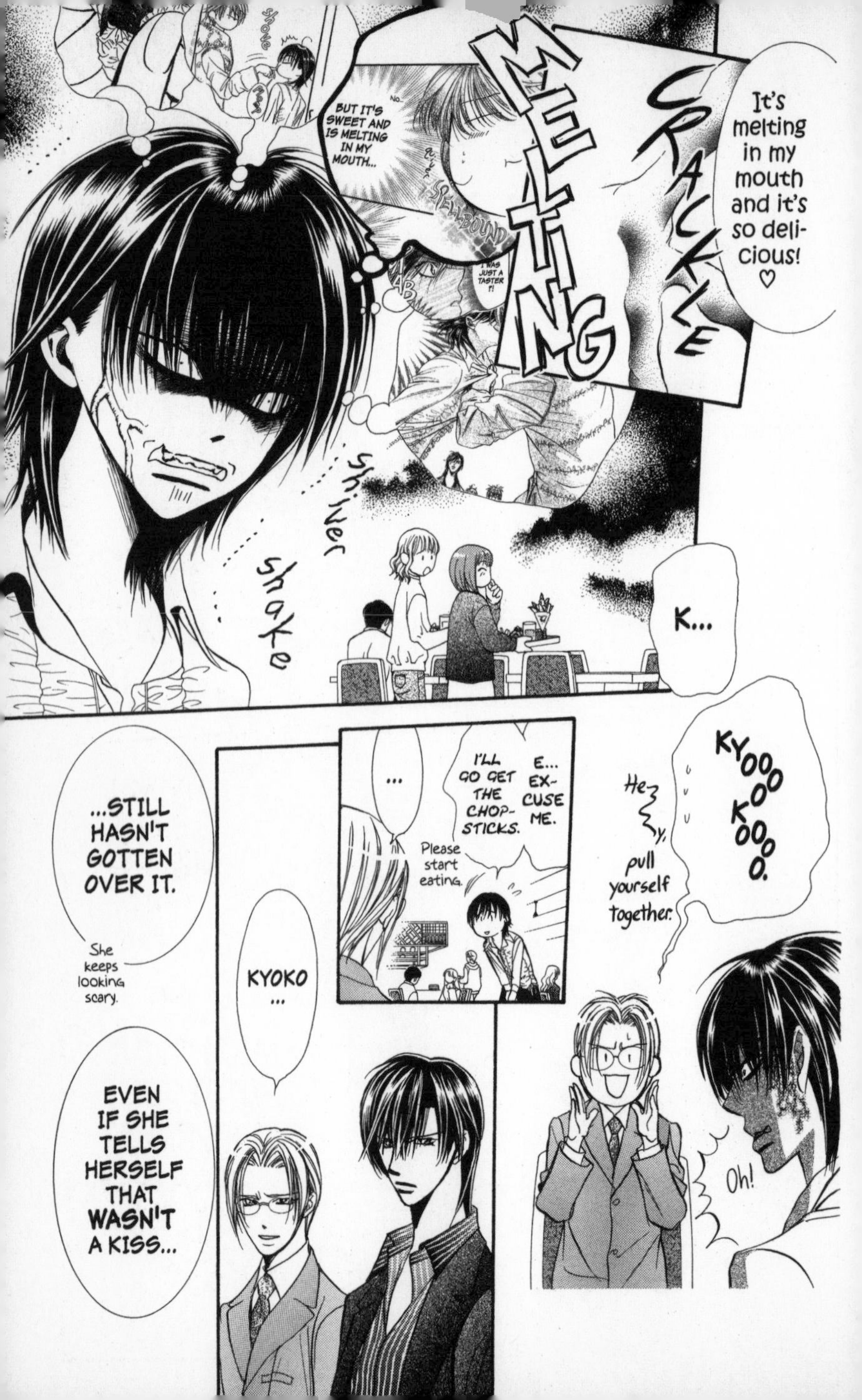

It's melting in my mouth and it's so deli-cious! ♡
CRACKLE
MELTING
BUT IT'S SWEET AND IS MELTING IN MY MOUTH...
No...
quiver
SPELLBOUND
I WAS JUST A TASTER!
shove
shiver
shake
K...
KYOOOOKOOOO.
Hey, pull yourself together.
Oh!
E... EXCUSE ME.
I'LL GO GET THE CHOP-STICKS.
Please start eating.
...
KYOKO...
...STILL HASN'T GOTTEN OVER IT.
She keeps looking scary.
EVEN IF SHE TELLS HERSELF THAT WASN'T A KISS...

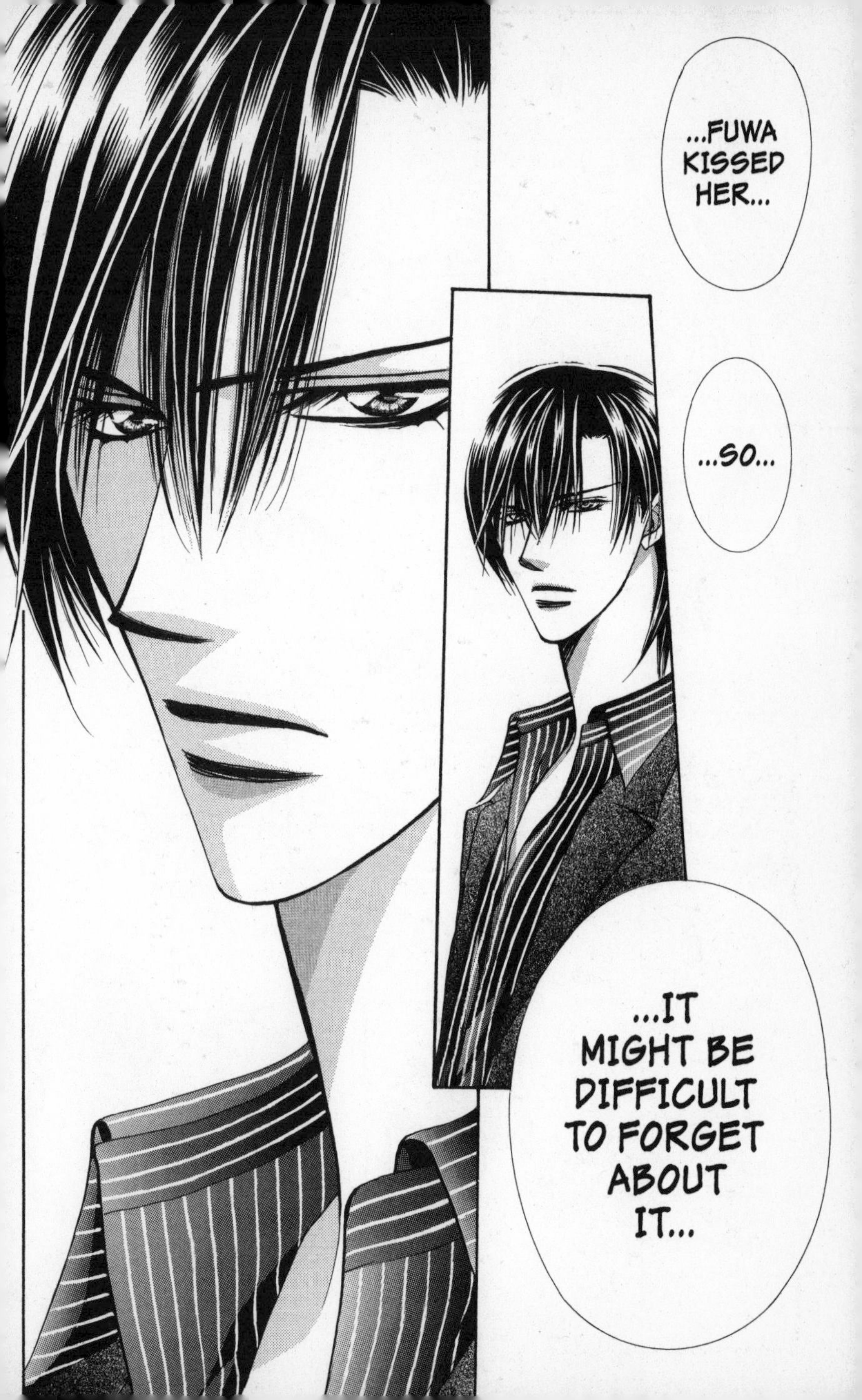
...FUWA KISSED HER...
...SO...
...IT MIGHT BE DIFFICULT TO FORGET ABOUT IT...

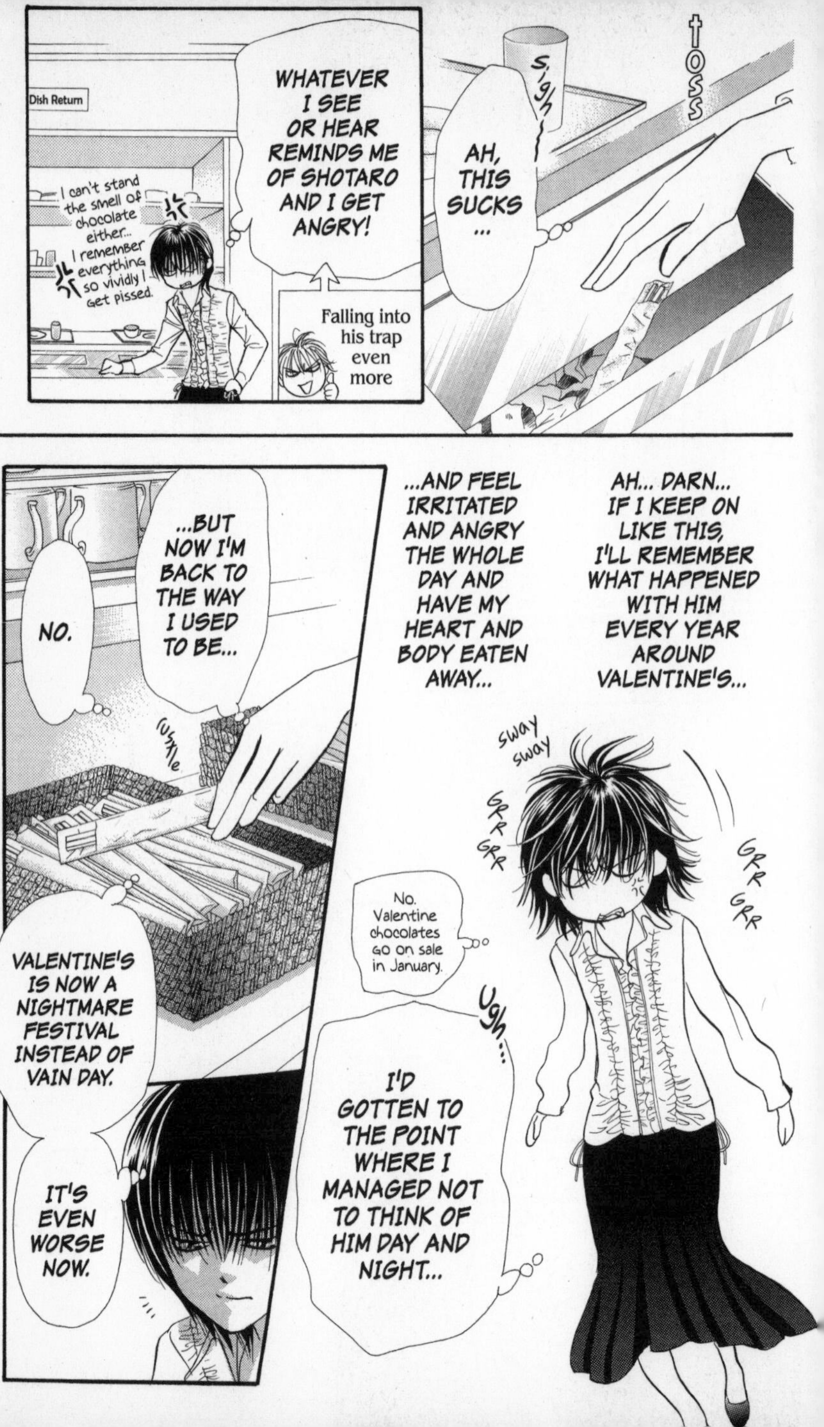
TOSS
Sigh
AH, THIS SUCKS...
WHATEVER I SEE OR HEAR REMINDS ME OF SHOTARO AND I GET ANGRY!
Dish Return
I can't stand the smell of chocolate either... I remember everything so vividly I get pissed.
Falling into his trap even more
AH... DARN... IF I KEEP ON LIKE THIS, I'LL REMEMBER WHAT HAPPENED WITH HIM EVERY YEAR AROUND VALENTINE'S...
...AND FEEL IRRITATED AND ANGRY THE WHOLE DAY AND HAVE MY HEART AND BODY EATEN AWAY...
sway sway
GRR GRR
GRR GRR
No. Valentine chocolates go on sale in January.
Ugh...
I'D GOTTEN TO THE POINT WHERE I MANAGED NOT TO THINK OF HIM DAY AND NIGHT...
...BUT NOW I'M BACK TO THE WAY I USED TO BE...
NO.
rustle
VALENTINE'S IS NOW A NIGHTMARE FESTIVAL INSTEAD OF VAIN DAY.
IT'S EVEN WORSE NOW.

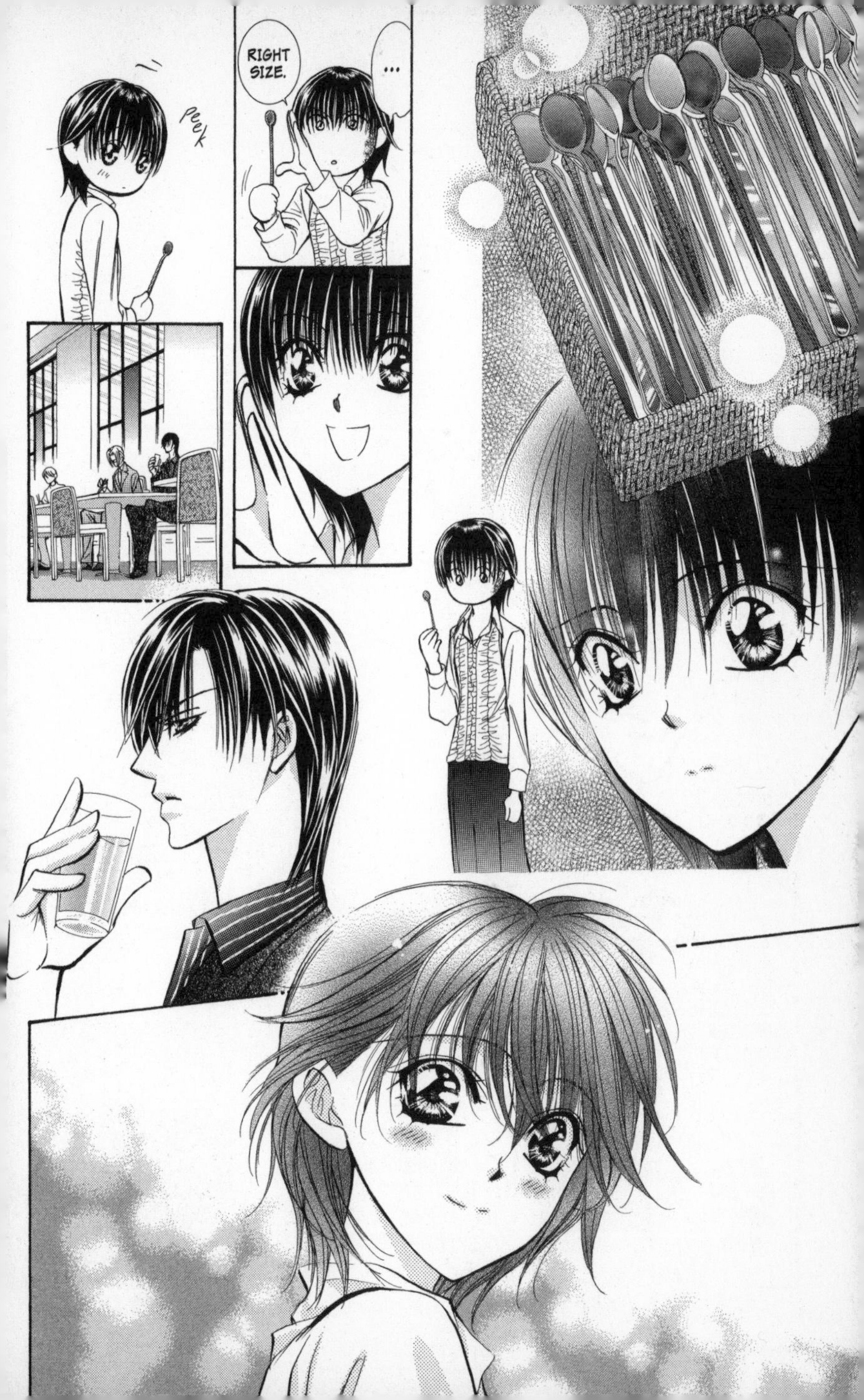
RIGHT SIZE.
...
peek

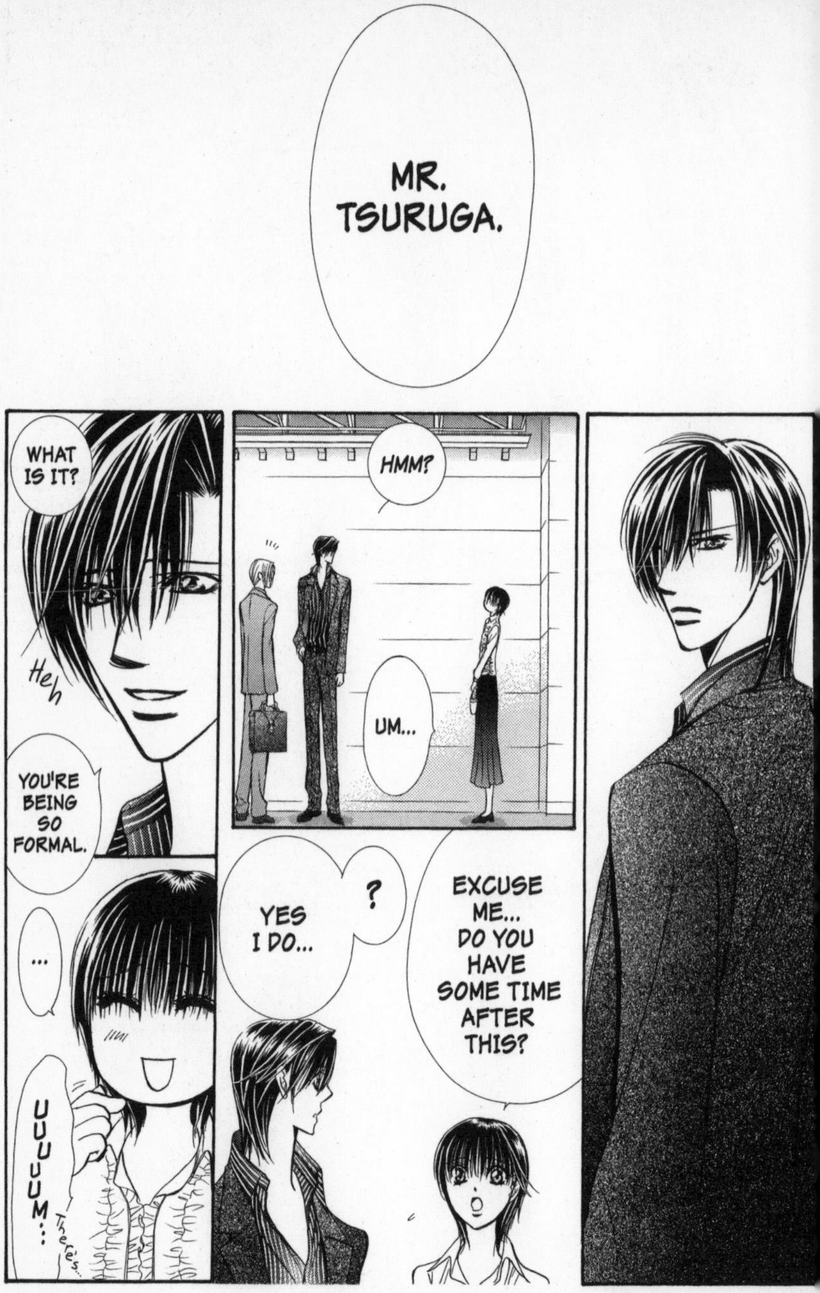
MR. TSURUGA.
HMM?
UM...
WHAT IS IT?
Heh
YOU'RE BEING SO FORMAL.
EXCUSE ME... DO YOU HAVE SOME TIME AFTER THIS?
?
YES I DO...
...
UUUUUM...
There's...

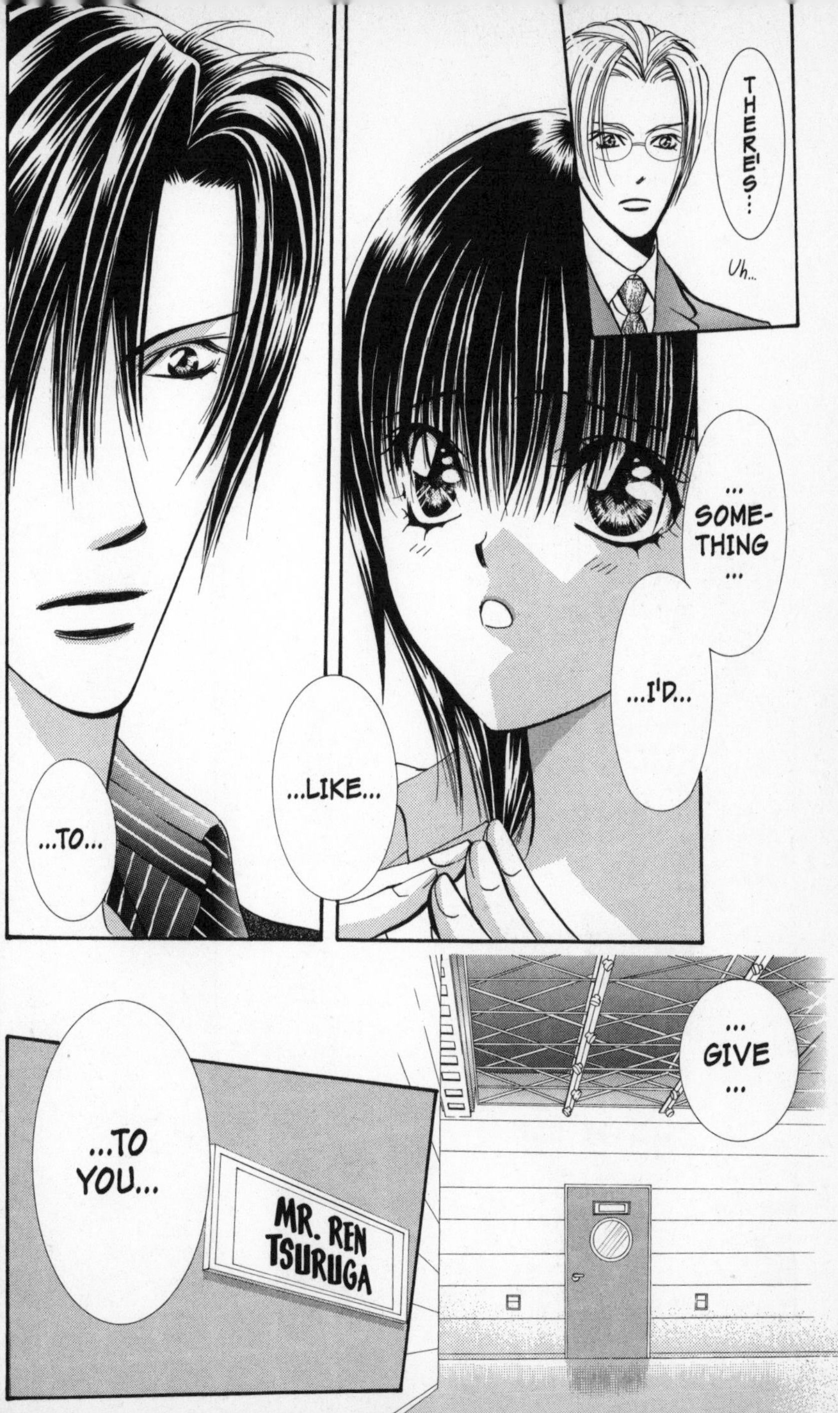
THERE'S...
Uh...
...SOME-THING...
...I'D...
...LIKE...
...TO...
...GIVE...
...TO YOU...
MR. REN TSURUGA

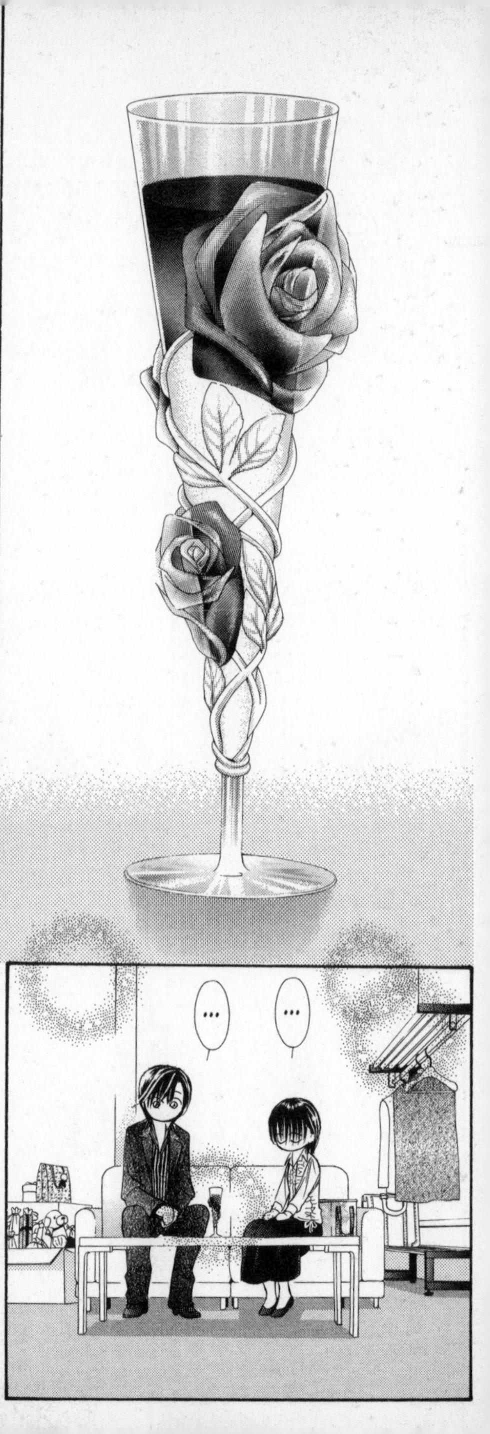
...
...

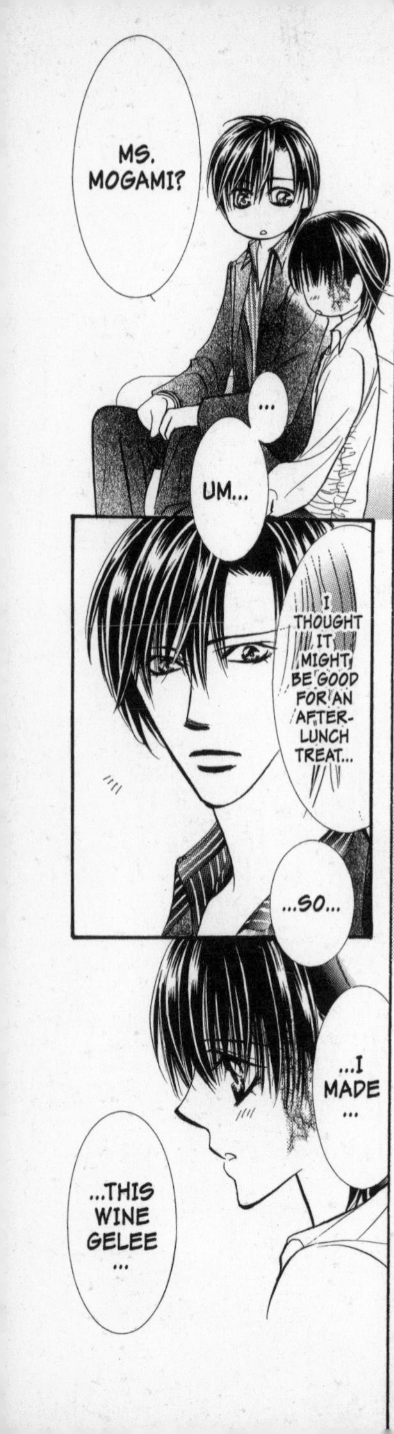
MS. MOGAMI?
...
UM...
I THOUGHT IT MIGHT BE GOOD FOR AN AFTER-LUNCH TREAT...
...SO...
...I MADE ...
...THIS WINE GELEE ...

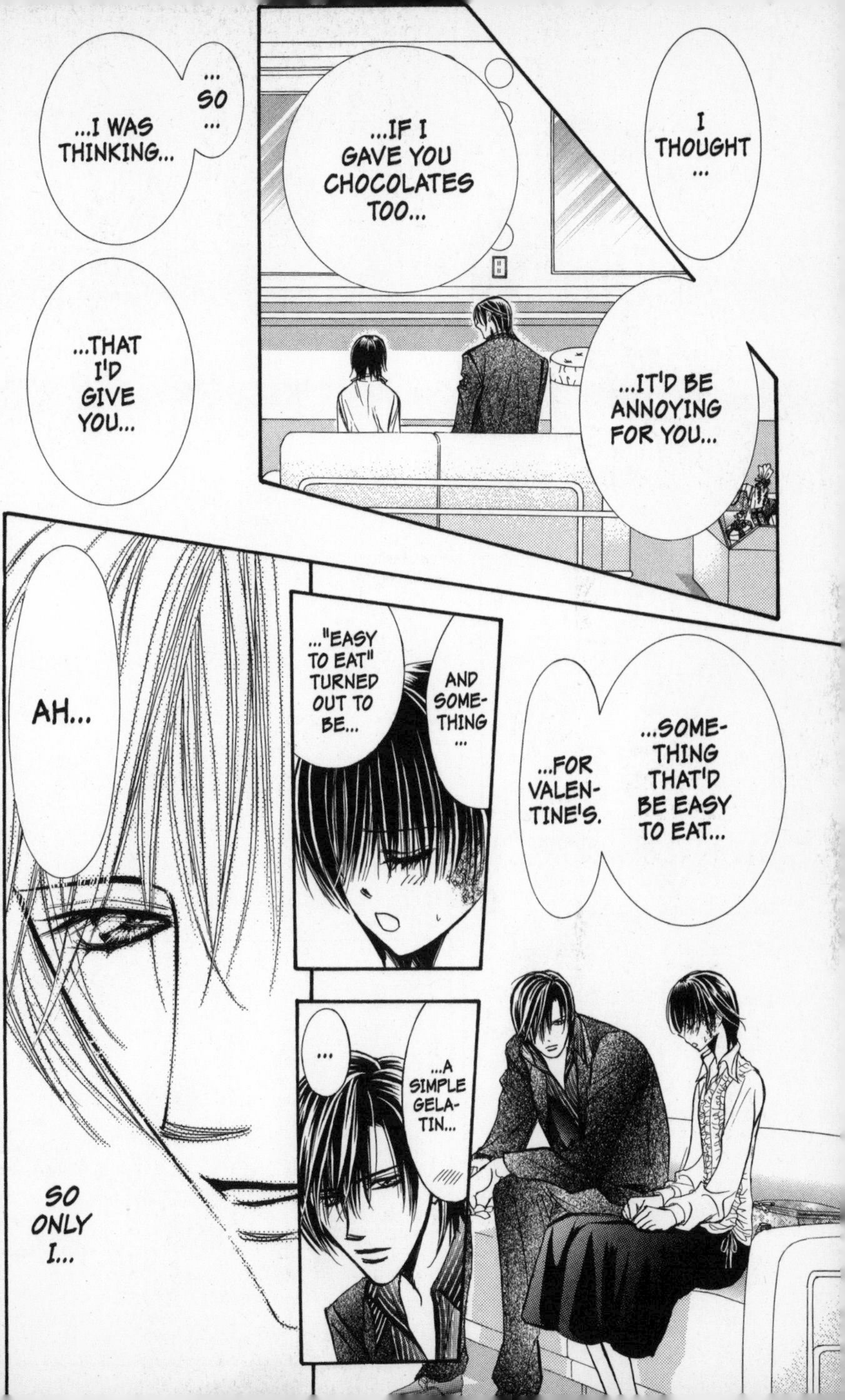
I THOUGHT...
...IF I GAVE YOU CHOCOLATES TOO...
...IT'D BE ANNOYING FOR YOU...
...SO...
...I WAS THINKING...
...THAT I'D GIVE YOU...
...SOMETHING THAT'D BE EASY TO EAT...
...FOR VALENTINE'S.
AND SOMETHING...
..."EASY TO EAT" TURNED OUT TO BE...
...A SIMPLE GELATIN...
...
AH...
SO ONLY I...

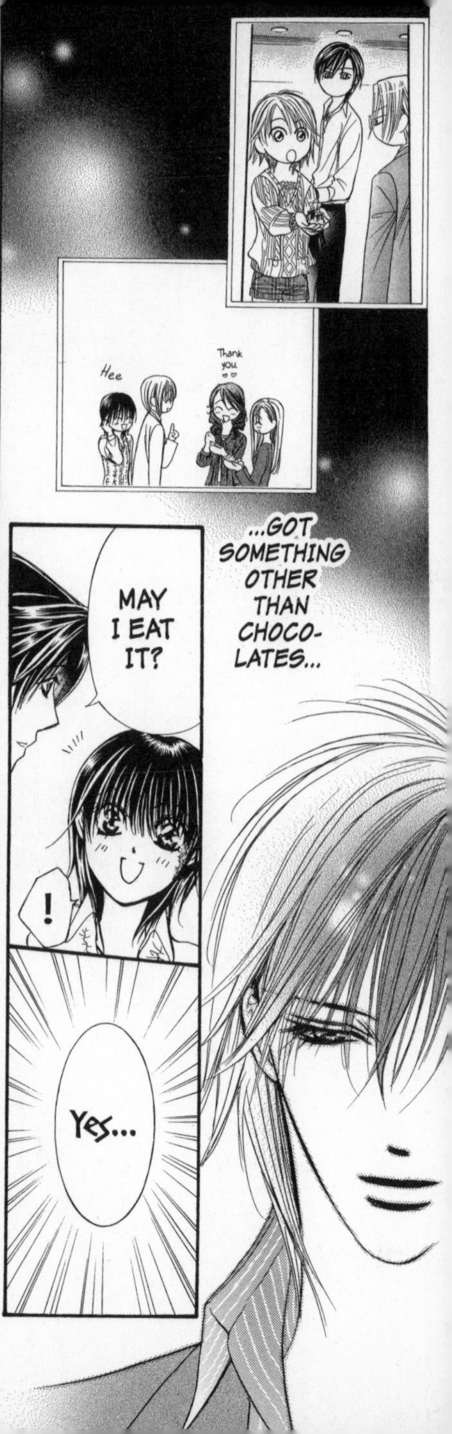
Hee
Thank you
...GOT SOMETHING OTHER THAN CHOCOLATES...
MAY I EAT IT?
!
Yes...
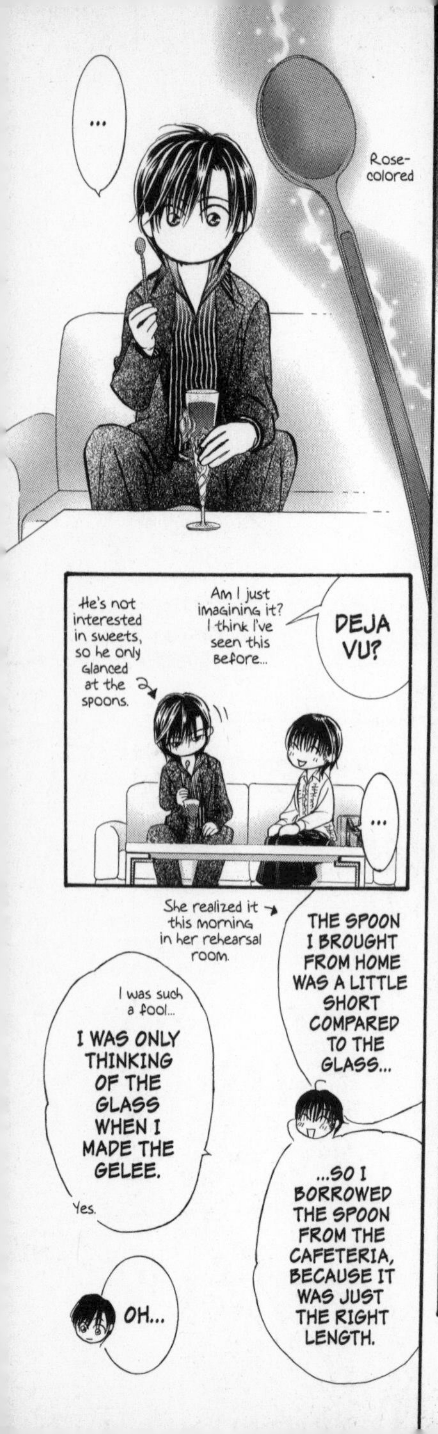
...
Rose-colored
DEJA VU?
Am I just imagining it? I think I've seen this before...
He's not interested in sweets, so he only glanced at the spoons.
...
She realized it this morning in her rehearsal room.
THE SPOON I BROUGHT FROM HOME WAS A LITTLE SHORT COMPARED TO THE GLASS...
I was such a fool...
I WAS ONLY THINKING OF THE GLASS WHEN I MADE THE GELEE.
Yes.
...SO I BORROWED THE SPOON FROM THE CAFETERIA, BECAUSE IT WAS JUST THE RIGHT LENGTH.
OH...

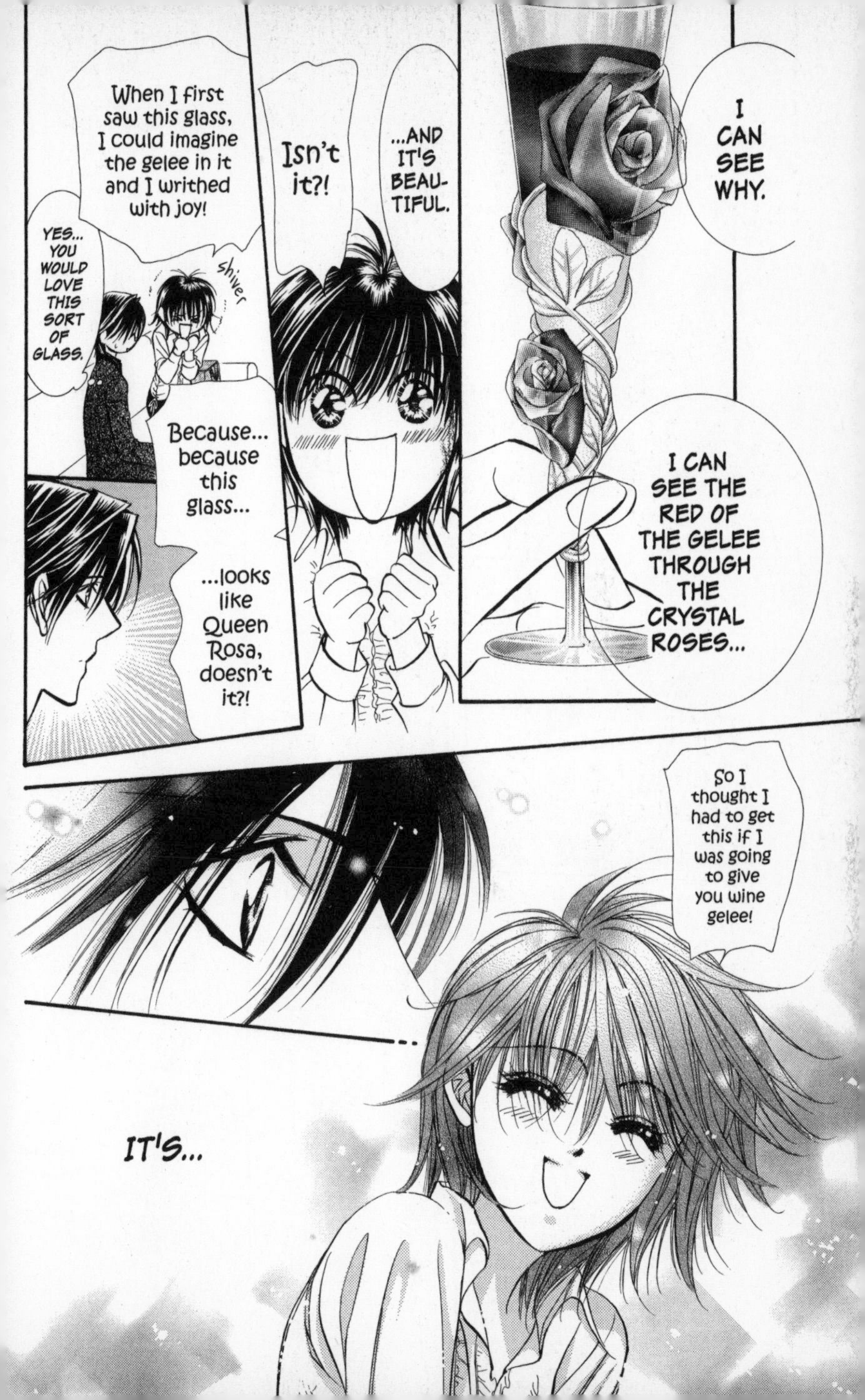
I CAN SEE WHY.
I CAN SEE THE RED OF THE GELEE THROUGH THE CRYSTAL ROSES...
...AND IT'S BEAU-TIFUL.
Isn't it?!
When I first saw this glass, I could imagine the gelee in it and I writhed with joy!
shiver
YES... YOU WOULD LOVE THIS SORT OF GLASS.
Because... because this glass...
...looks like Queen Rosa, doesn't it?!
So I thought I had to get this if I was going to give you wine gelee!
IT'S...

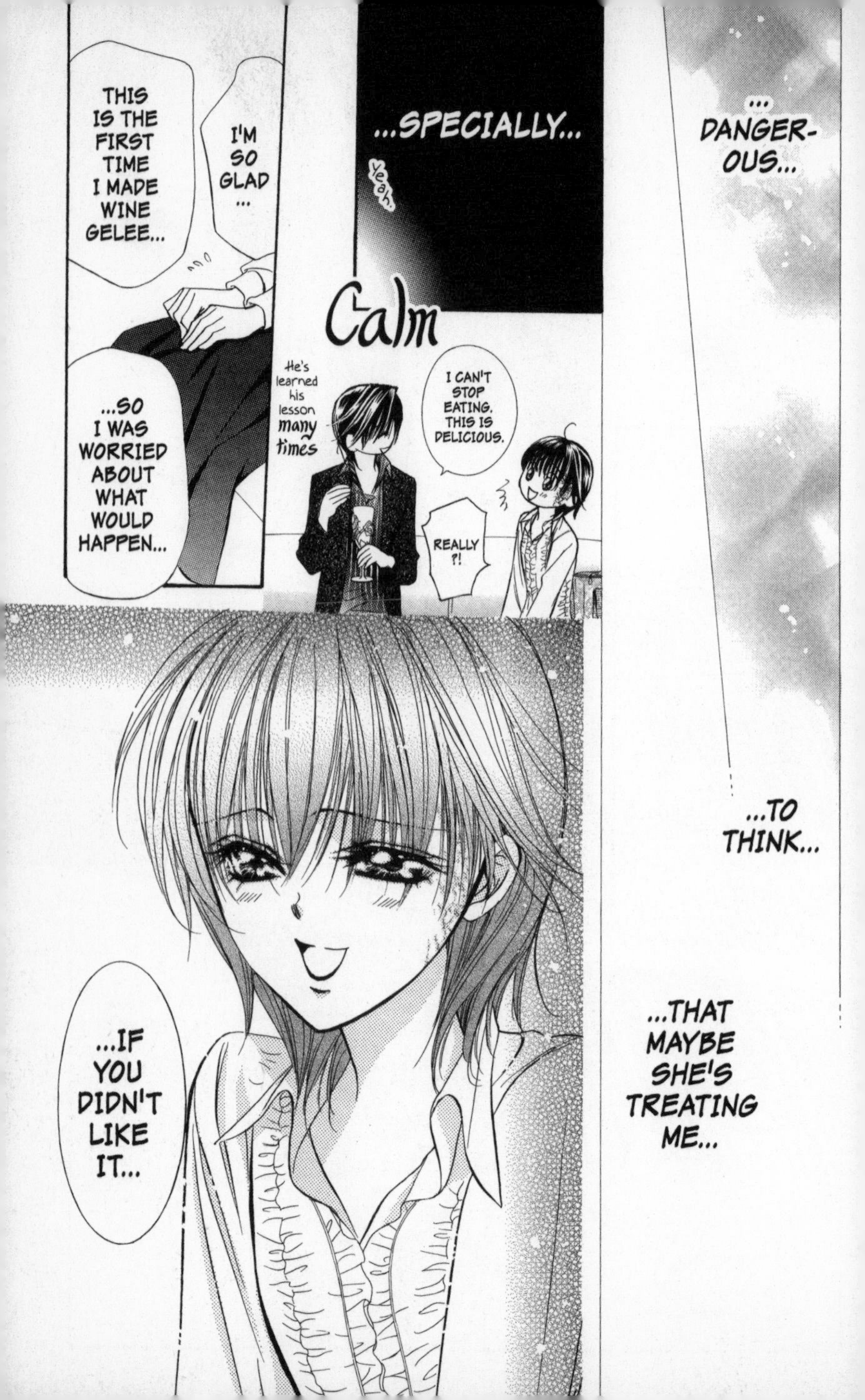
...DANGER-OUS...
...TO THINK...
...THAT MAYBE SHE'S TREATING ME...
...SPECIALLY...
Yeah.
Calm
I CAN'T STOP EATING. THIS IS DELICIOUS.
REALLY?!
He's learned his lesson many times
I'M SO GLAD...
THIS IS THE FIRST TIME I MADE WINE GELEE...
...SO I WAS WORRIED ABOUT WHAT WOULD HAPPEN...
...IF YOU DIDN'T LIKE IT...

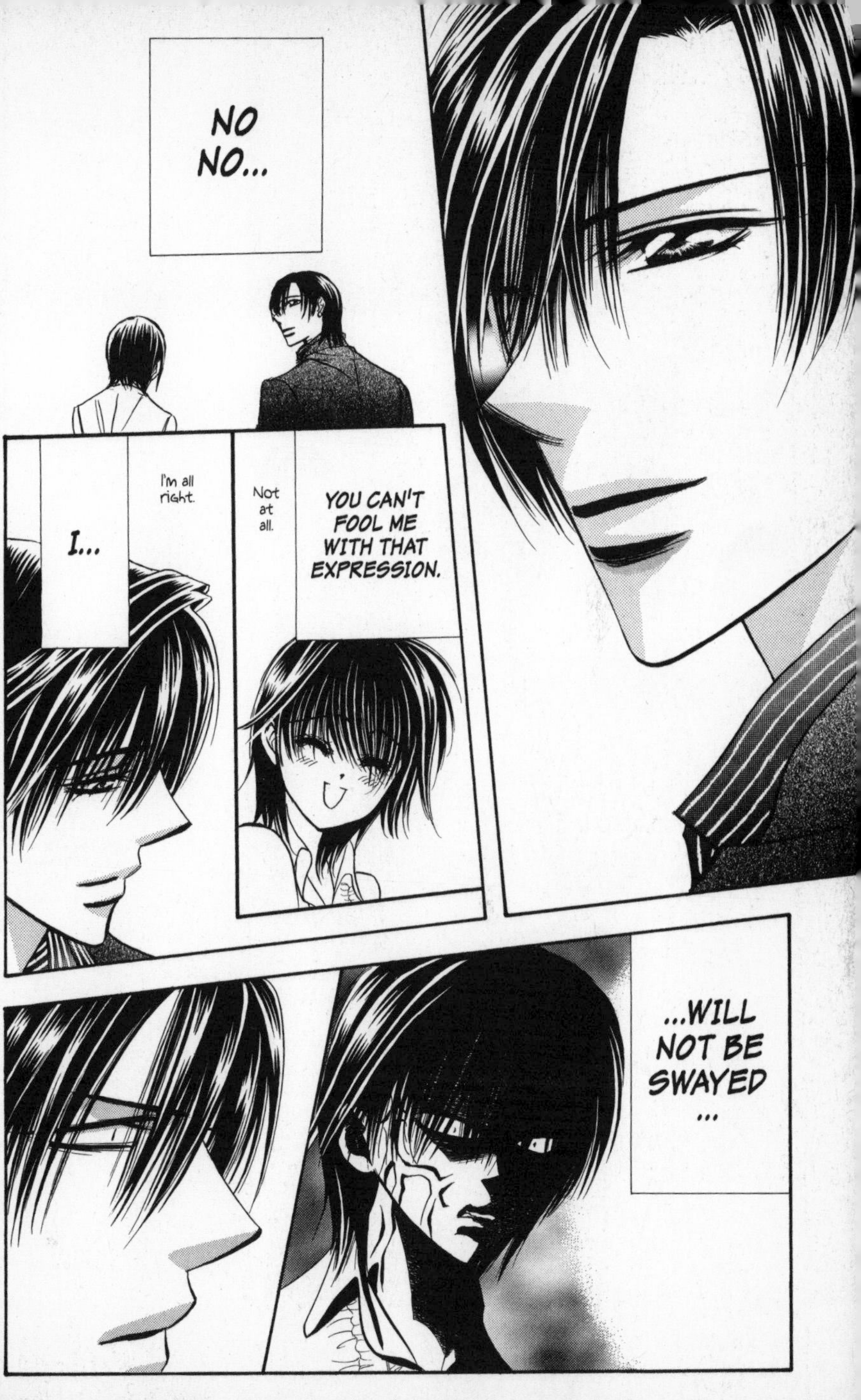
NO NO...
YOU CAN'T FOOL ME WITH THAT EXPRESSION.
Not at all.
I'm all right.
I...
...WILL NOT BE SWAYED ...

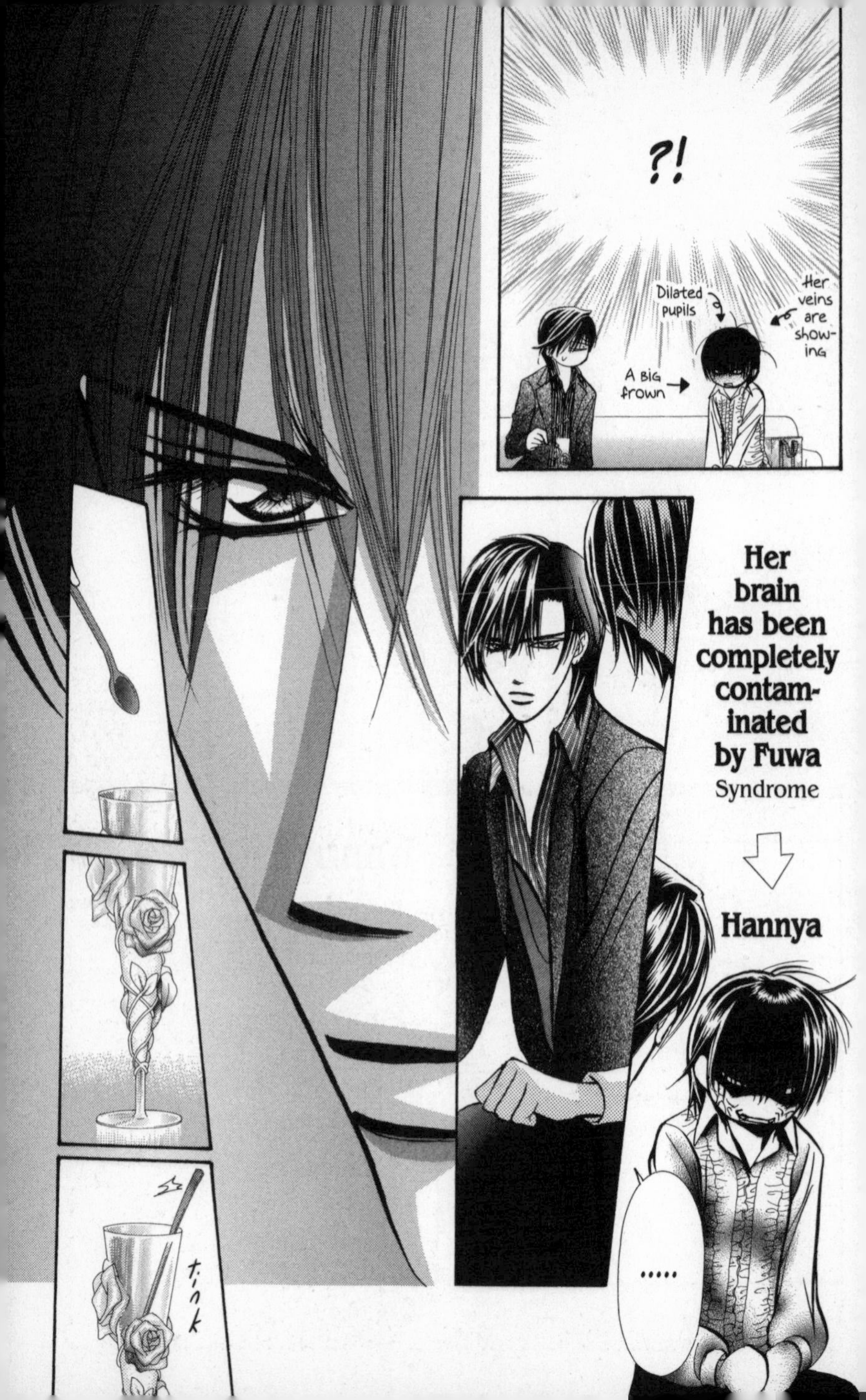
?!
Her veins are showing
Dilated pupils
A BIG frown
Her brain has been completely contaminated by Fuwa Syndrome
Hannya
.....
tink

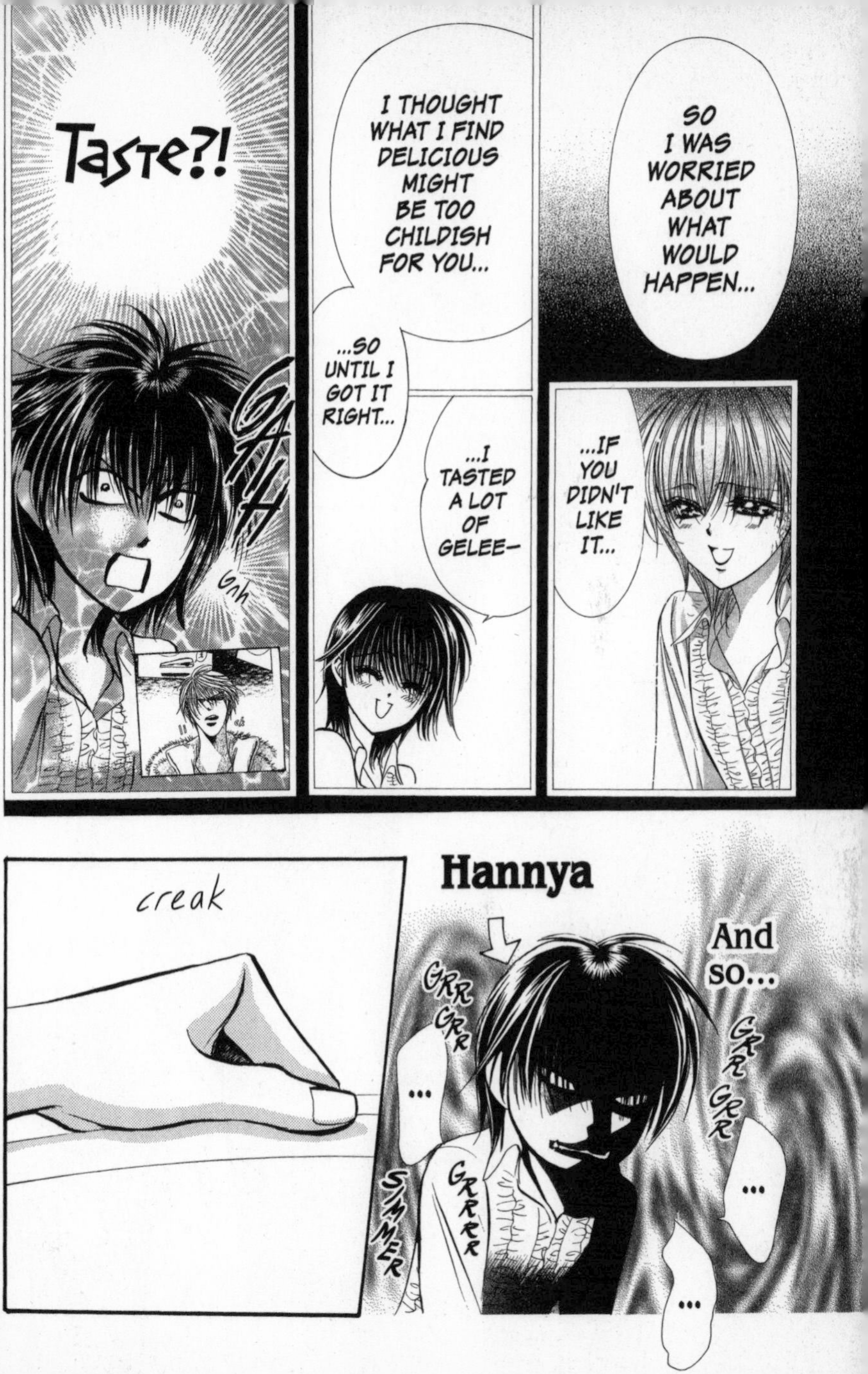
SO I WAS WORRIED ABOUT WHAT WOULD HAPPEN...
...IF YOU DIDN'T LIKE IT...
I THOUGHT WHAT I FIND DELICIOUS MIGHT BE TOO CHILDISH FOR YOU...
...SO UNTIL I GOT IT RIGHT...
...I TASTED A LOT OF GELEE-
Taste?!
Gnh
And so...
Hannya
GRR GRR
GRR GRR
...
GRRRR
SIMMER
...
...
creak

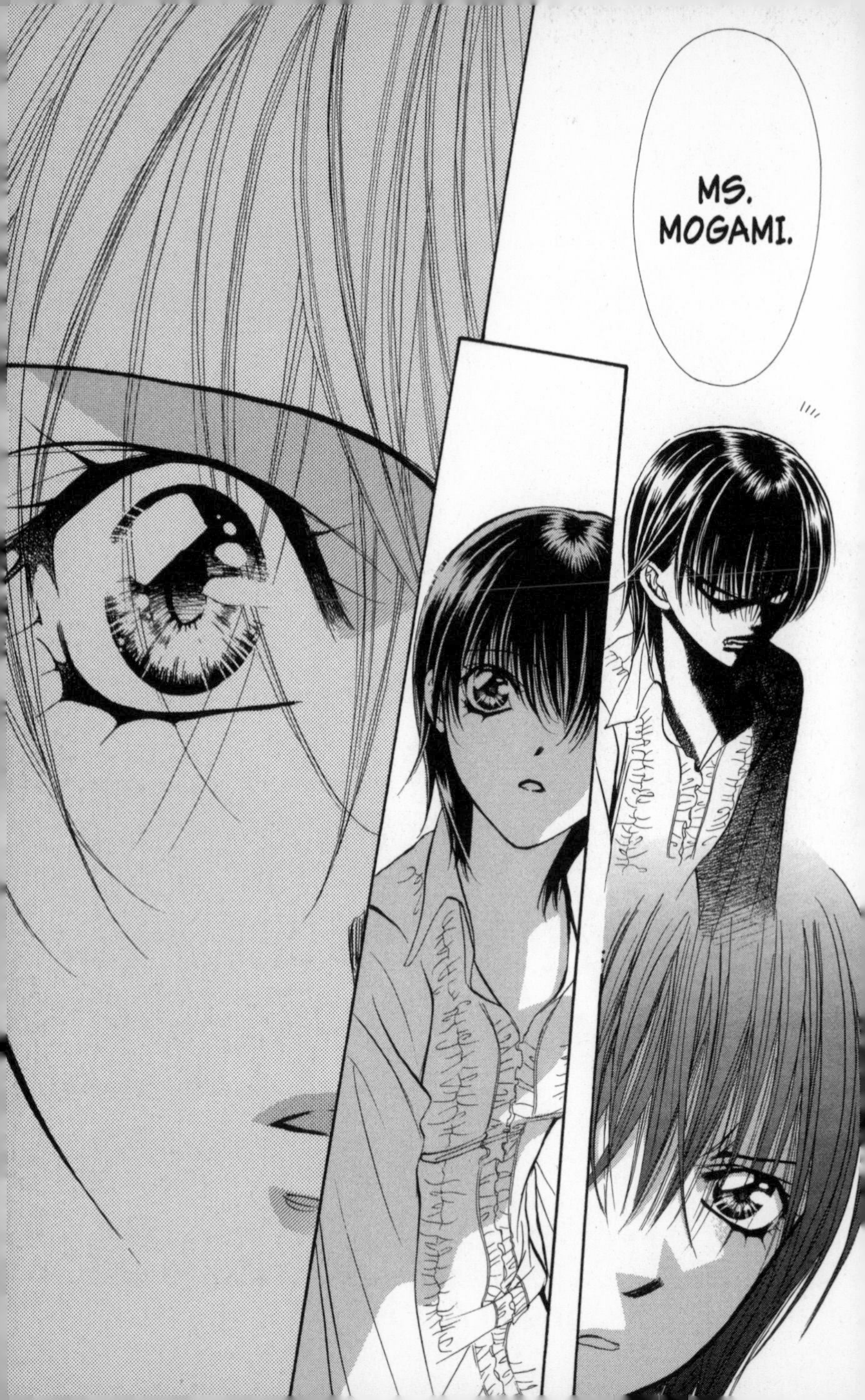
MS. MOGAMI.

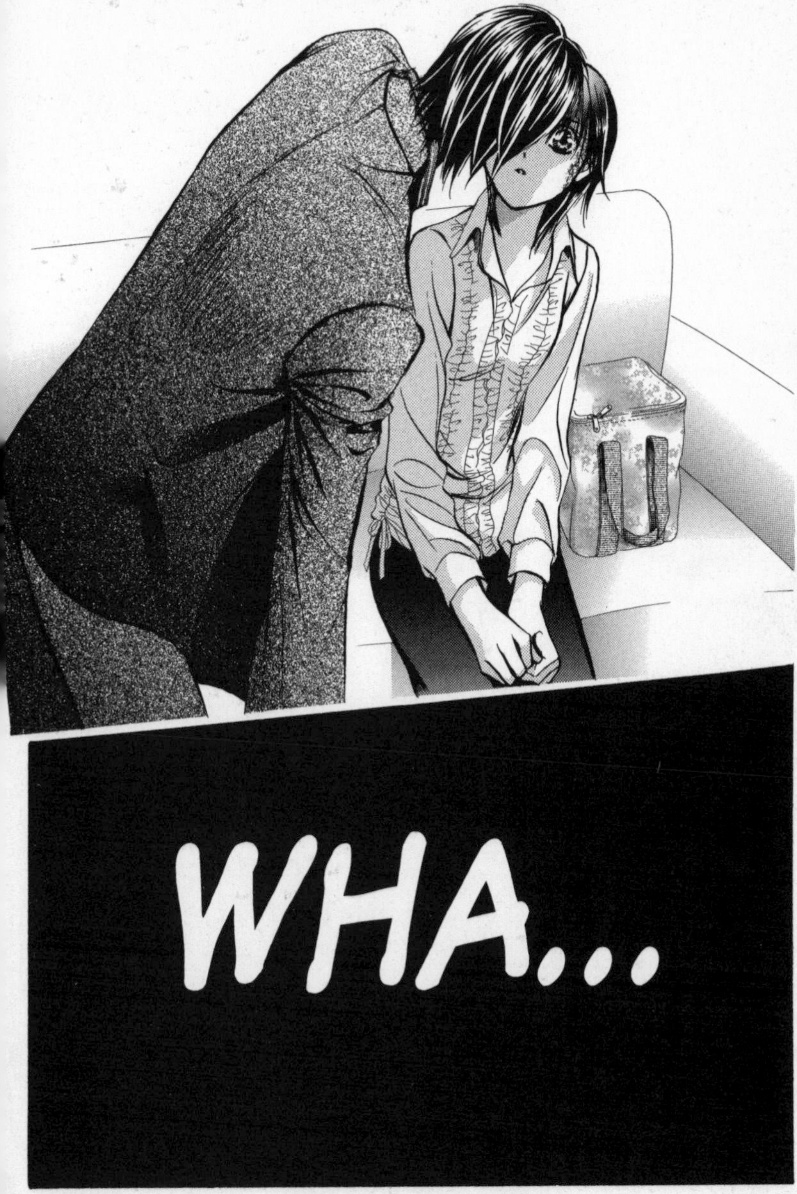
WHA...

End of Act 148

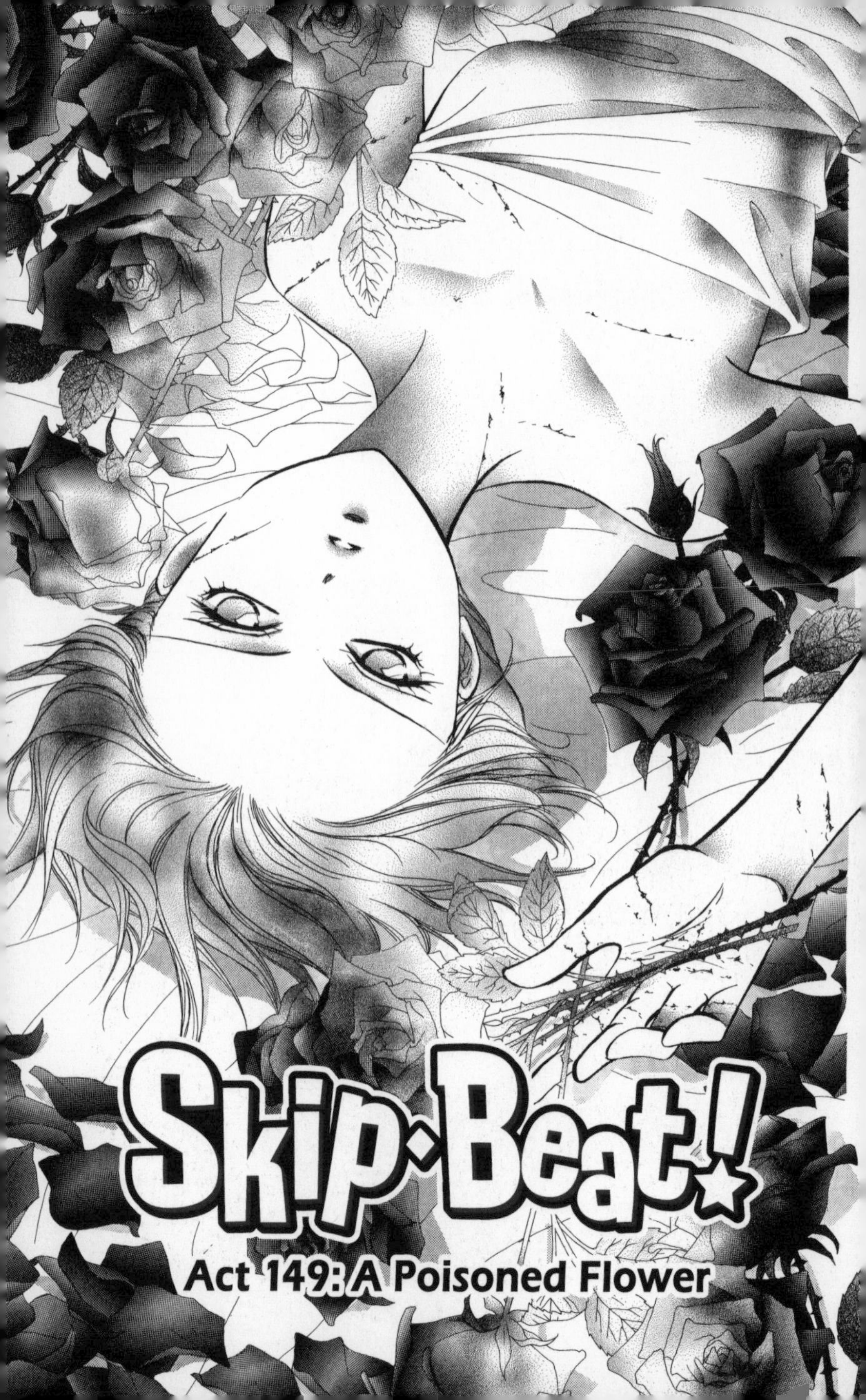
Skip·Beat!
Act 149: A Poisoned Flower

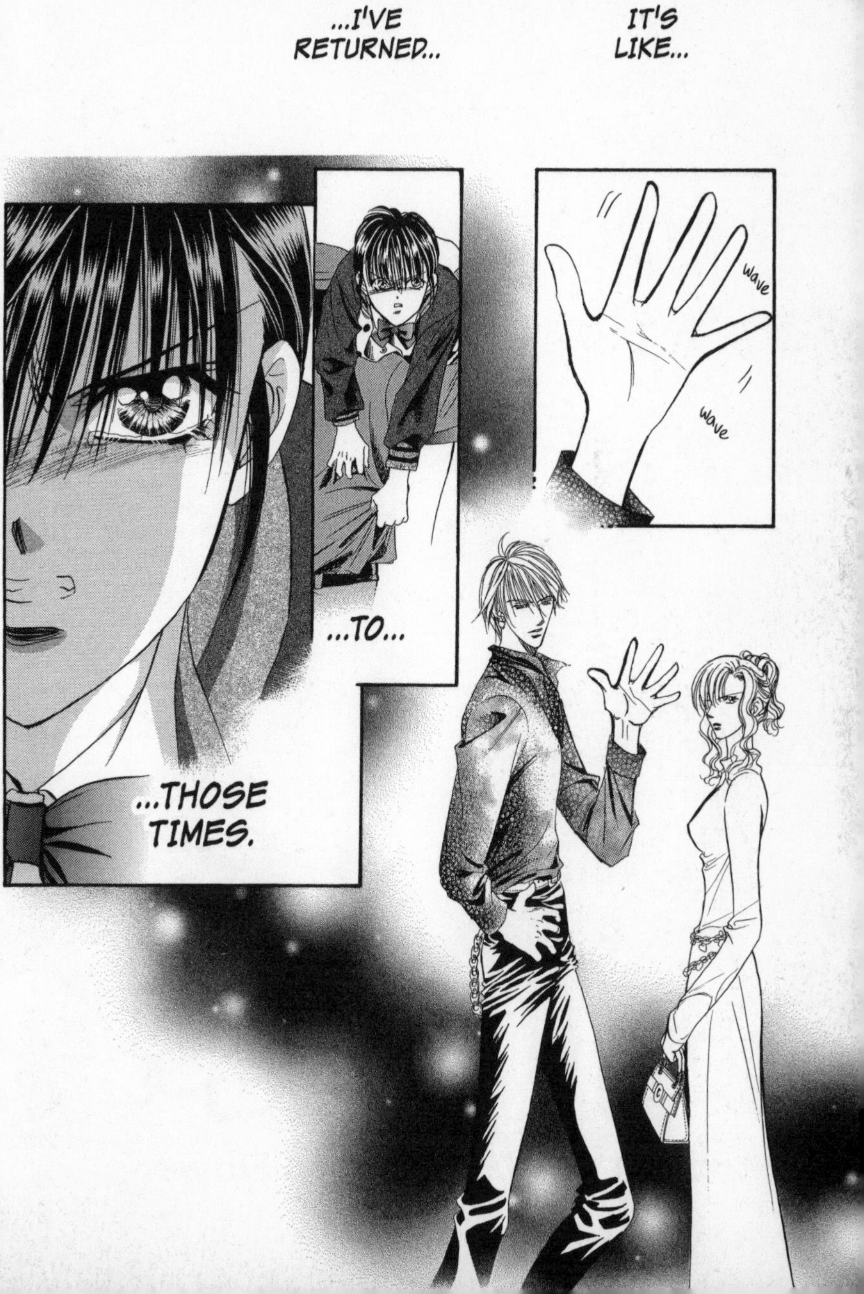
IT'S LIKE...
...I'VE RETURNED...
wave
wave
...TO...
...THOSE TIMES.

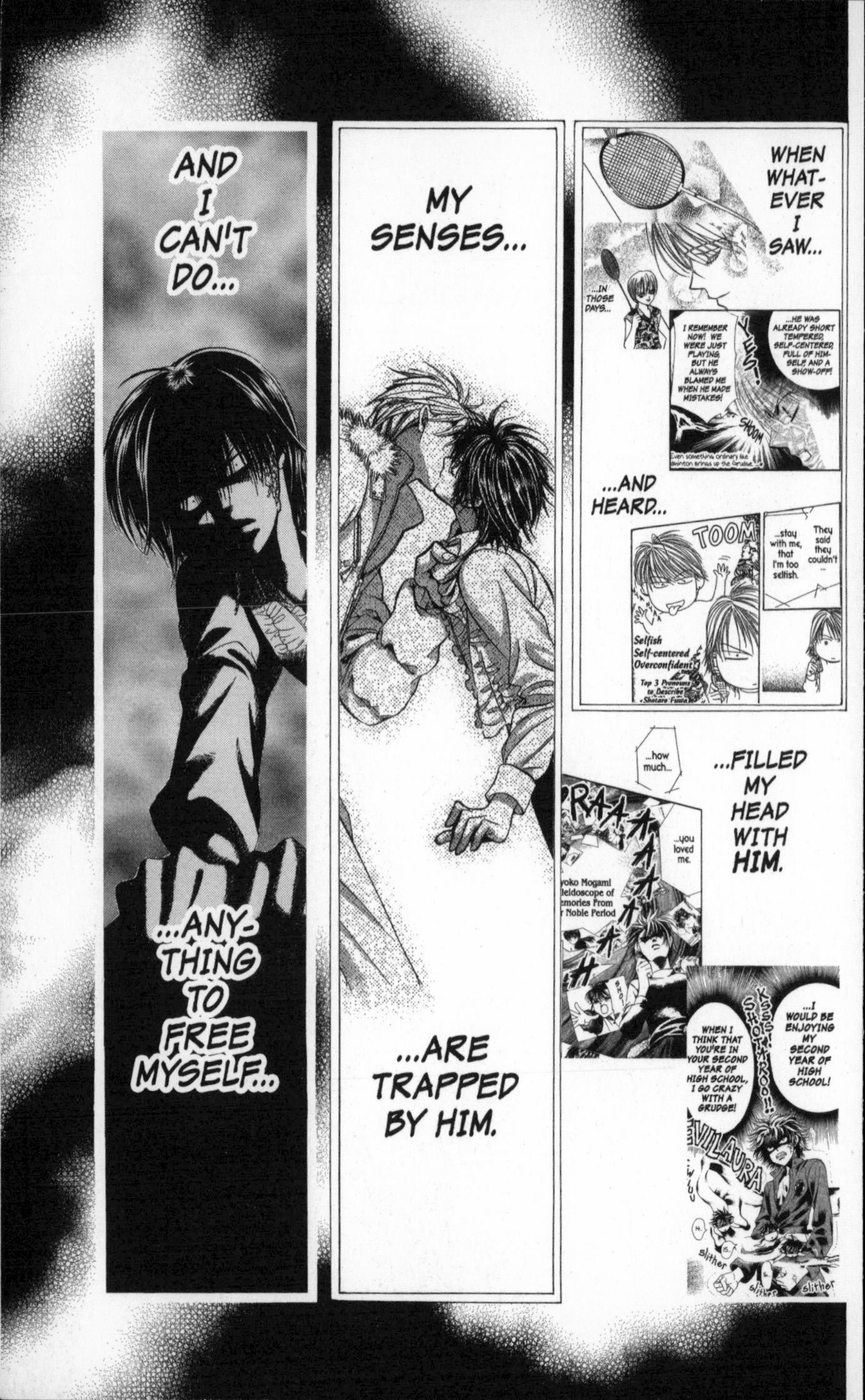
WHEN WHAT-EVER I SAW...
...IN THOSE DAYS...
...HE WAS ALREADY SHORT TEMPERED, SELF-CENTERED, FULL OF HIM-SELF, AND A SHOW-OFF!
YES!
I REMEMBER NOW! WE WERE JUST PLAYING, BUT HE ALWAYS BLAMED ME WHEN HE MADE MISTAKES!
SHOOM
Even something ordinary like dminton brings up the Grudge....
...AND HEARD...
They said they couldn't ...
...stay with me, that I'm too selfish.
TOOM
Selfish
Self-centered
Overconfident
Top 3 Pronouns to Describe Shotaro Fuwa
...FILLED MY HEAD WITH HIM.
...how much...
...you loved me.
RAAAAAAAAH
yoko Mogami
leidoscope of
emories From
r Noble Period
...I WOULD BE ENJOYING MY SECOND YEAR OF HIGH SCHOOL!
SHOTAROO!!
KSSS!
WHEN I THINK THAT YOU'RE IN YOUR SECOND YEAR OF HIGH SCHOOL, I GO CRAZY WITH A GRUDGE!
EVILAURA
slither
slither
slither
MY SENSES...
...ARE TRAPPED BY HIM.
AND I CAN'T DO...
...ANY-THING TO FREE MYSELF...

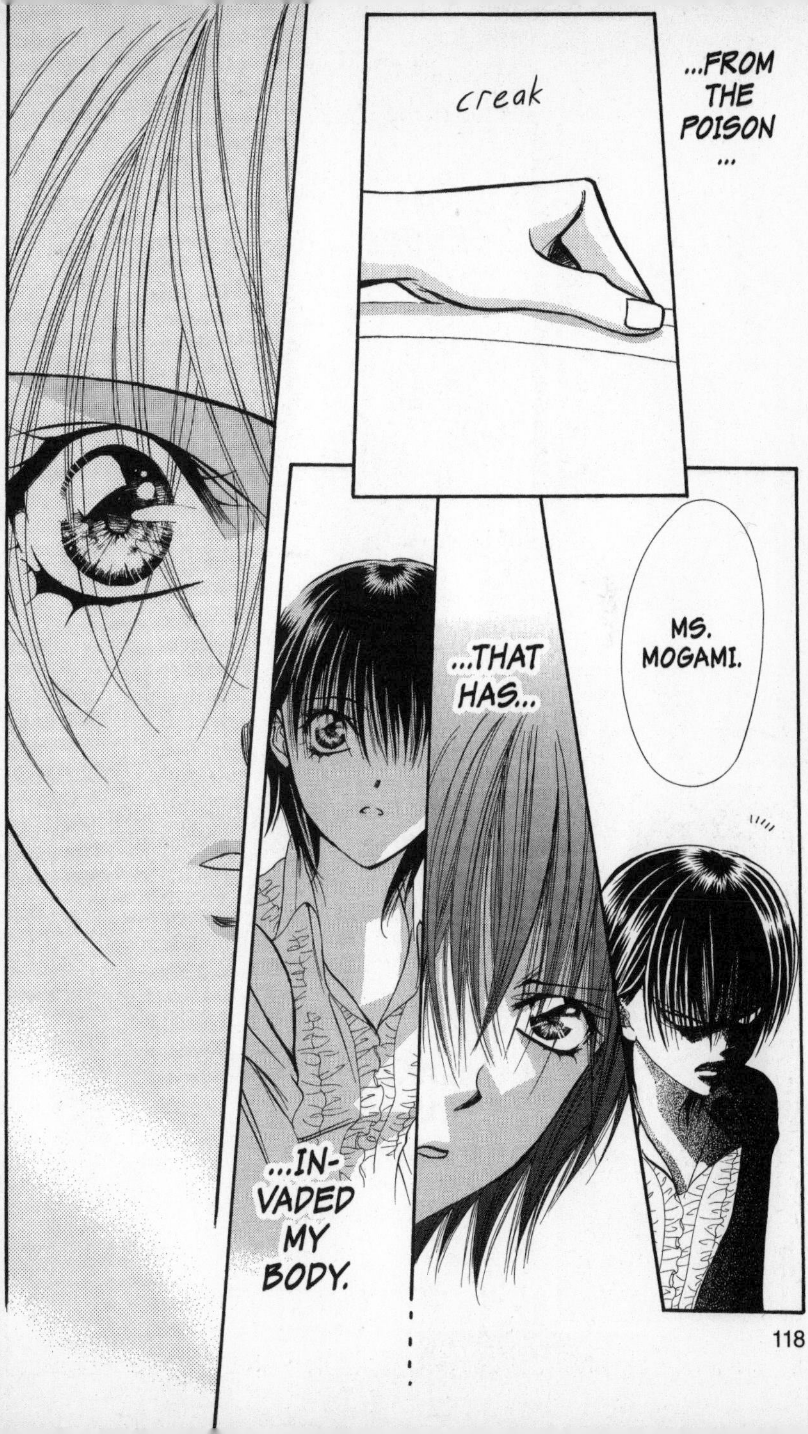
...FROM THE POISON ...
creak
MS. MOGAMI.
...THAT HAS...
...IN-VADED MY BODY.

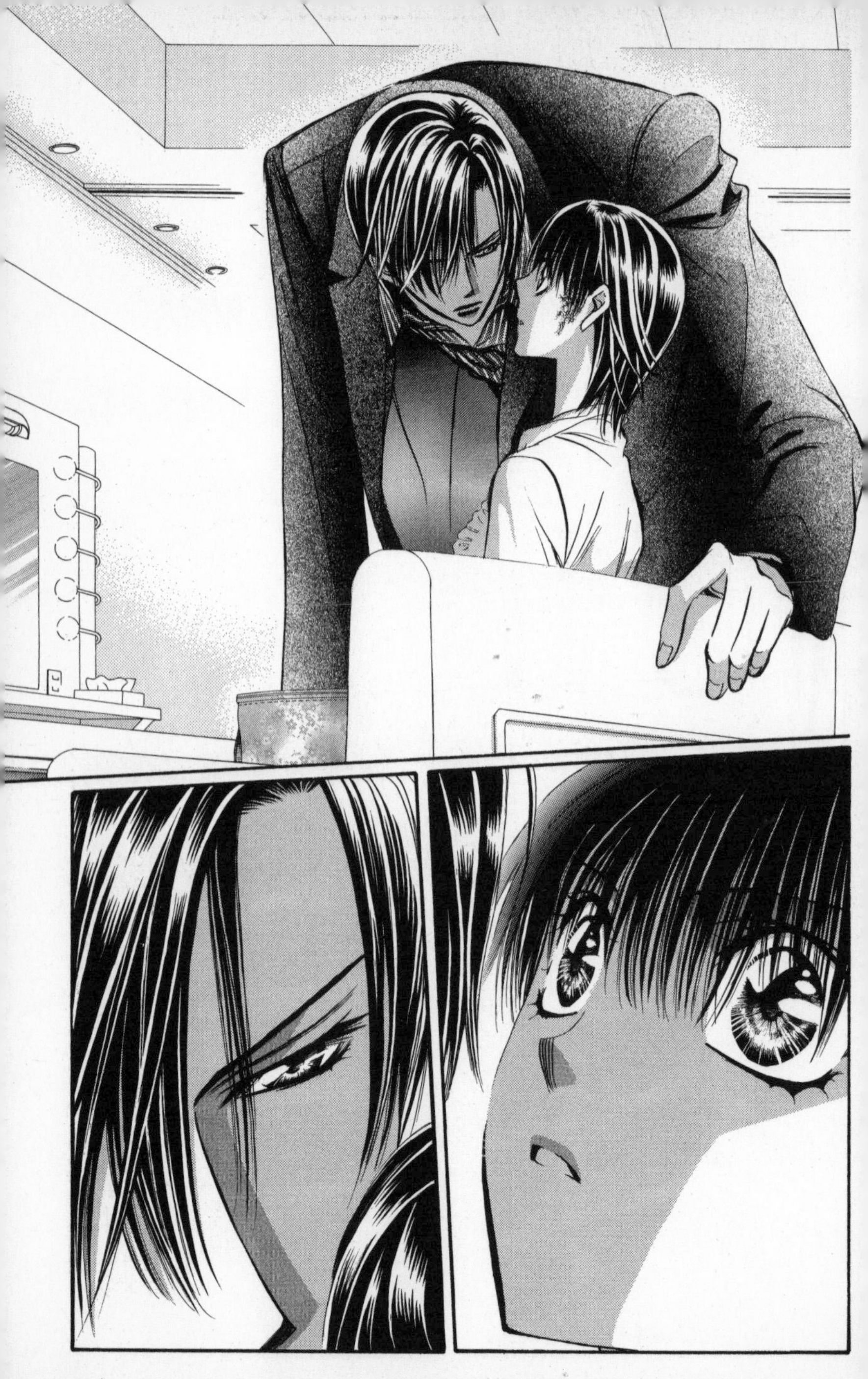

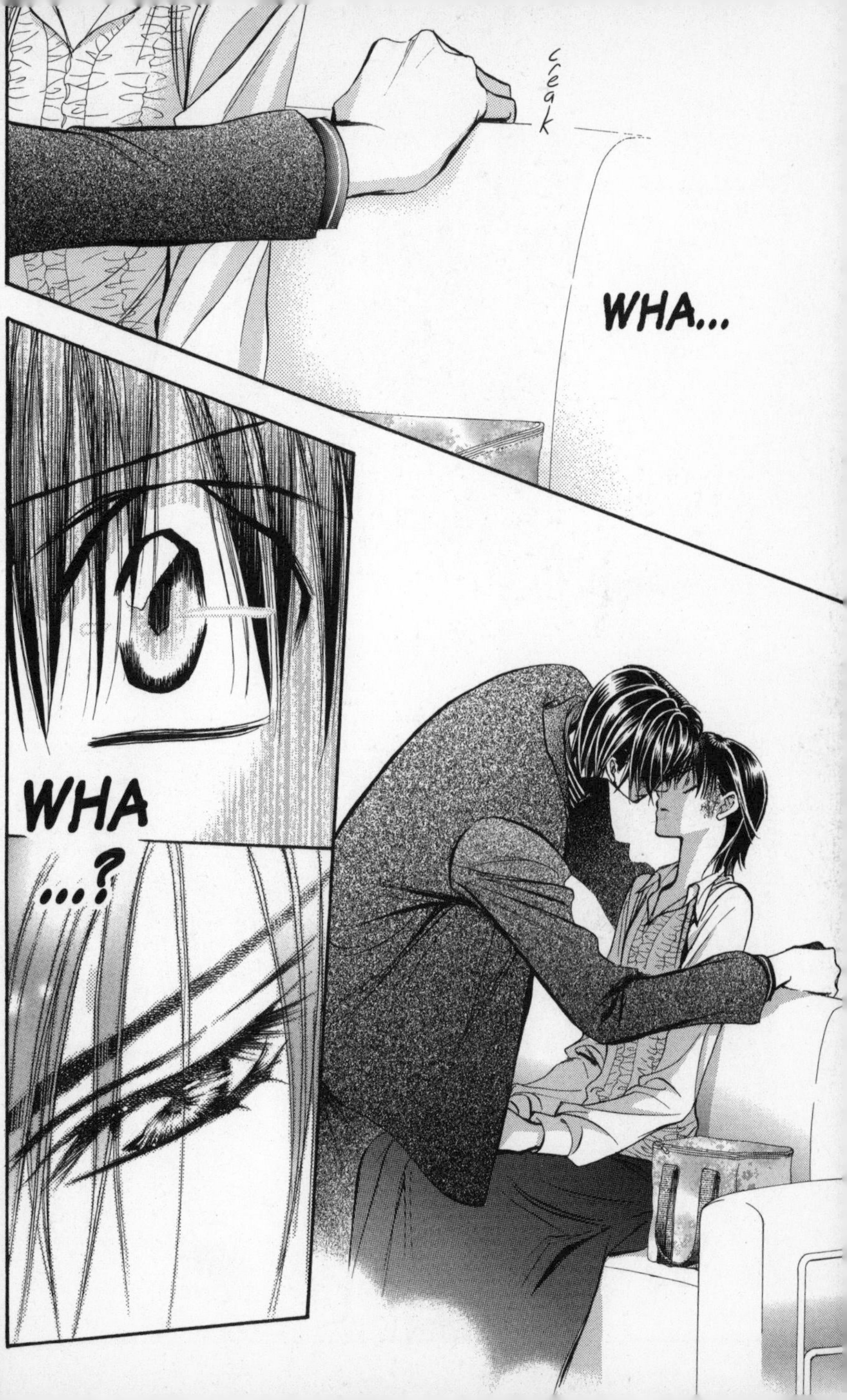
creak
WHA...
WHA
...?

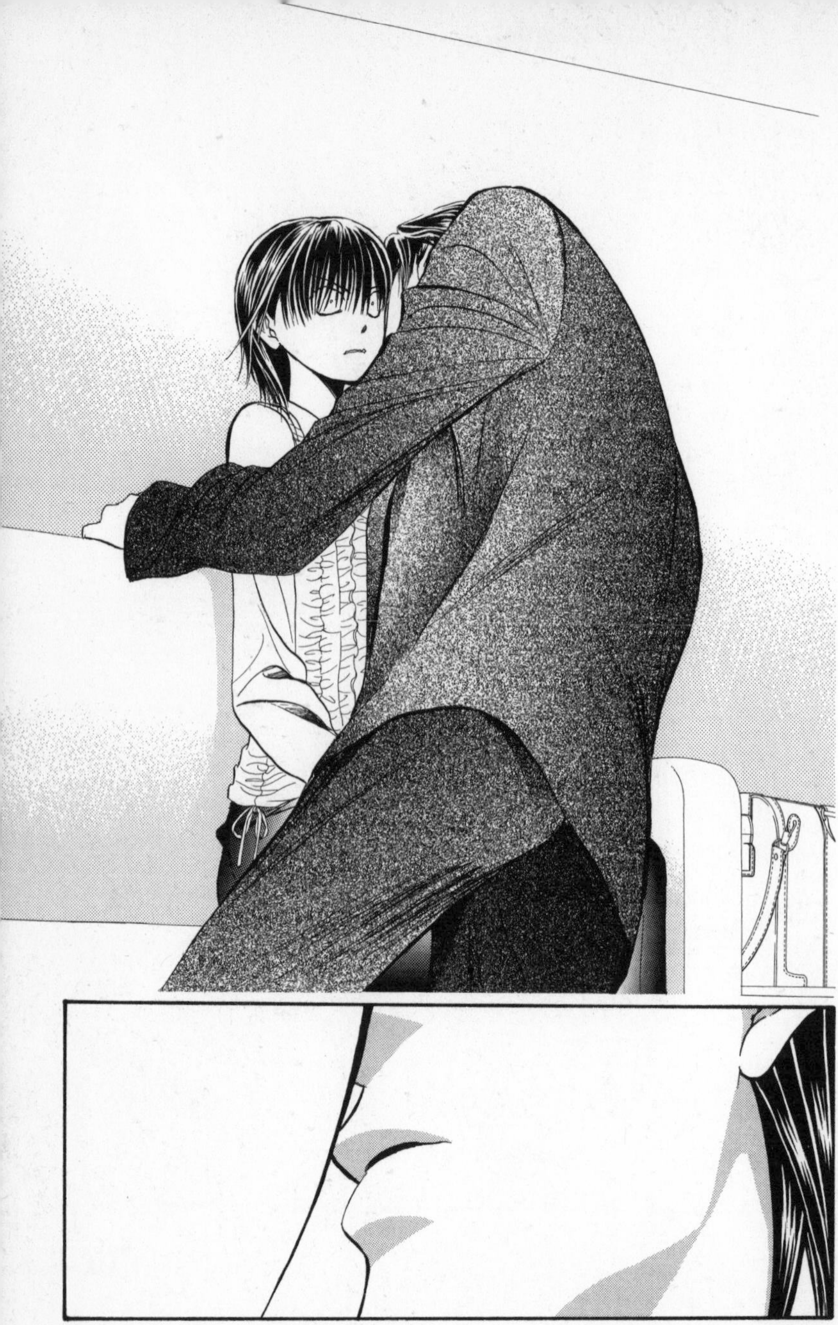

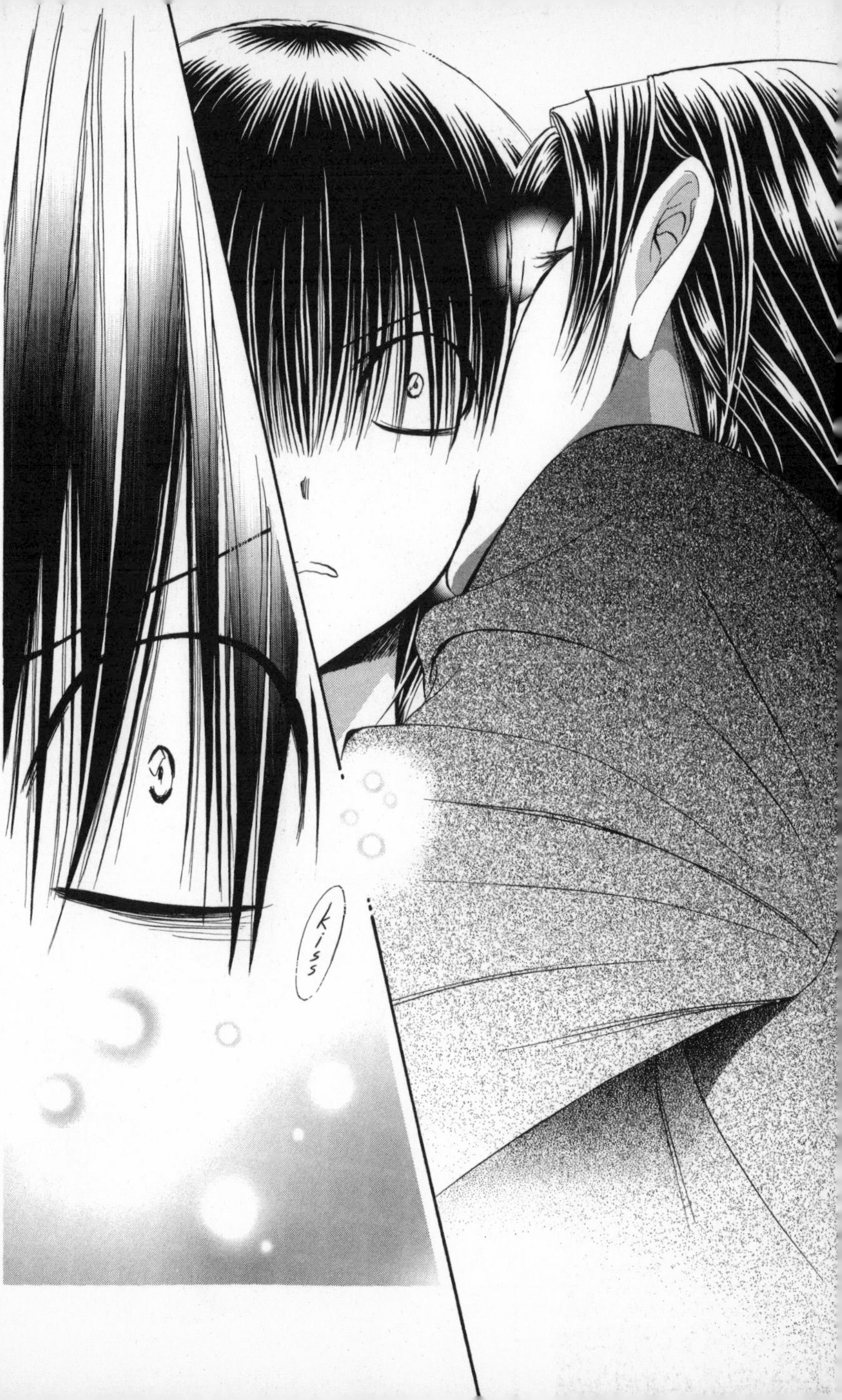
kiss

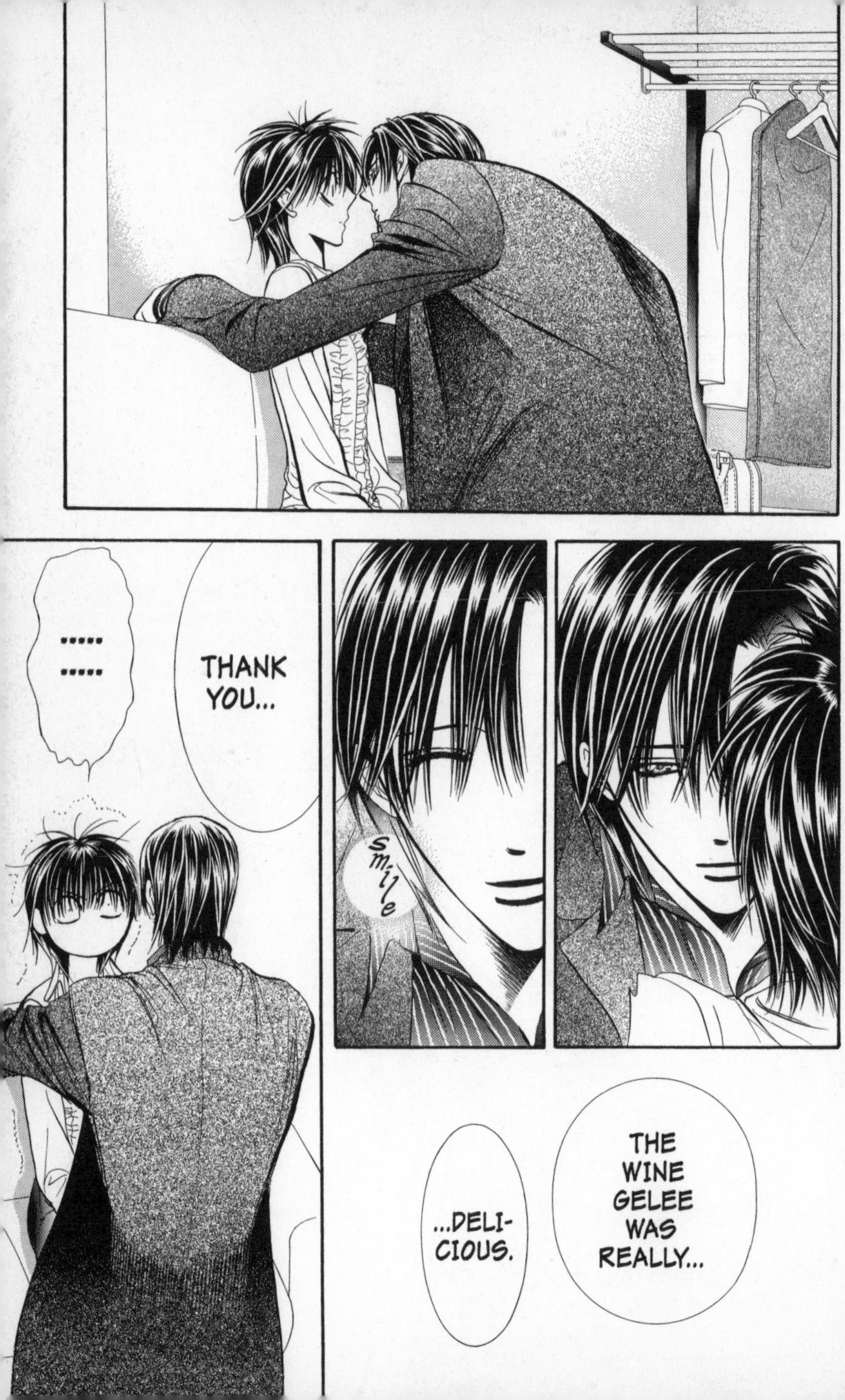
smile
THE WINE GELEE WAS REALLY...
...DELICIOUS.
THANK YOU...
......
......

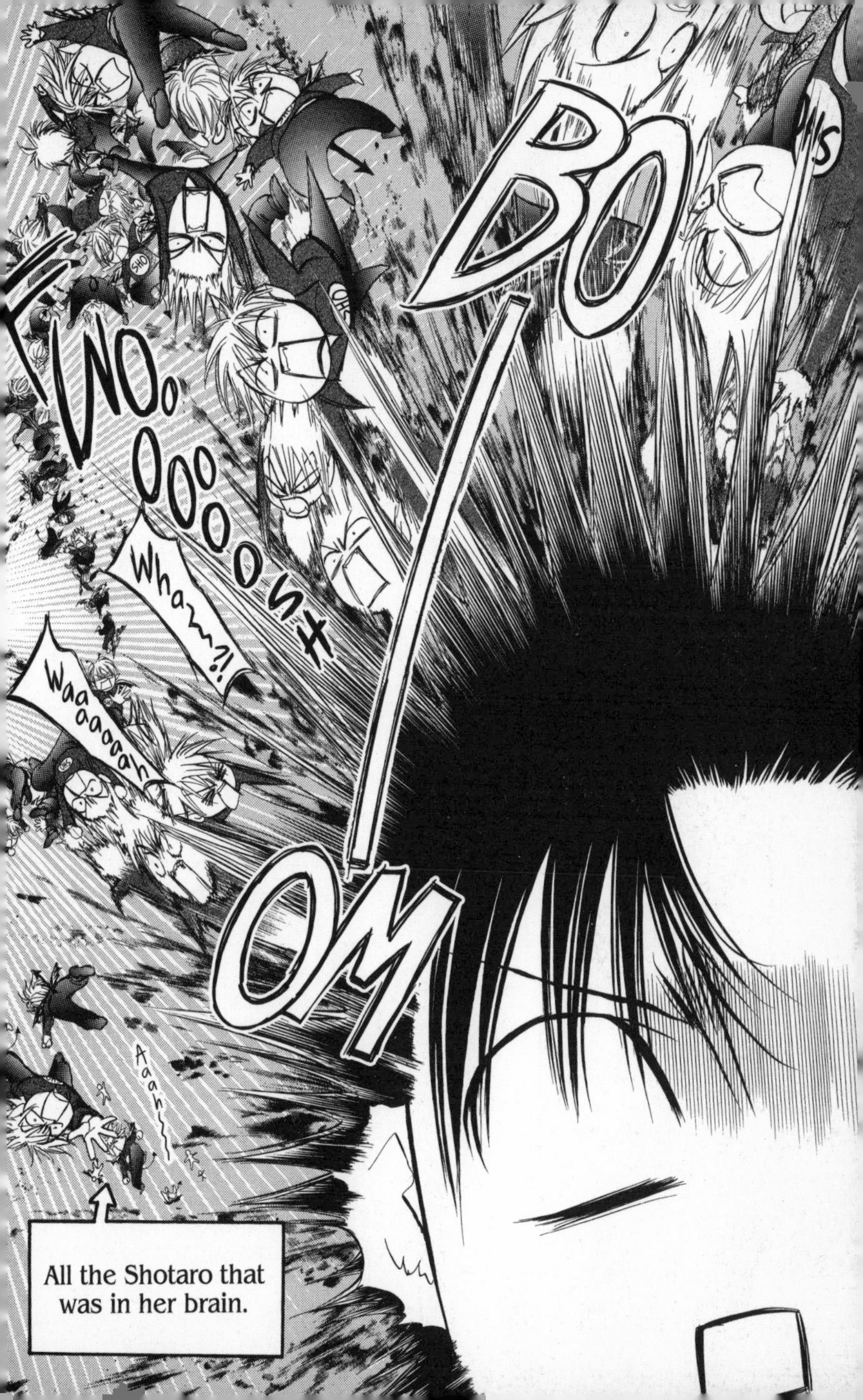
BOOOM
NOOOOOOOOOOOSH
Wham?!
Waaaaaaaah
Aaah~~
All the Shotaro that was in her brain.

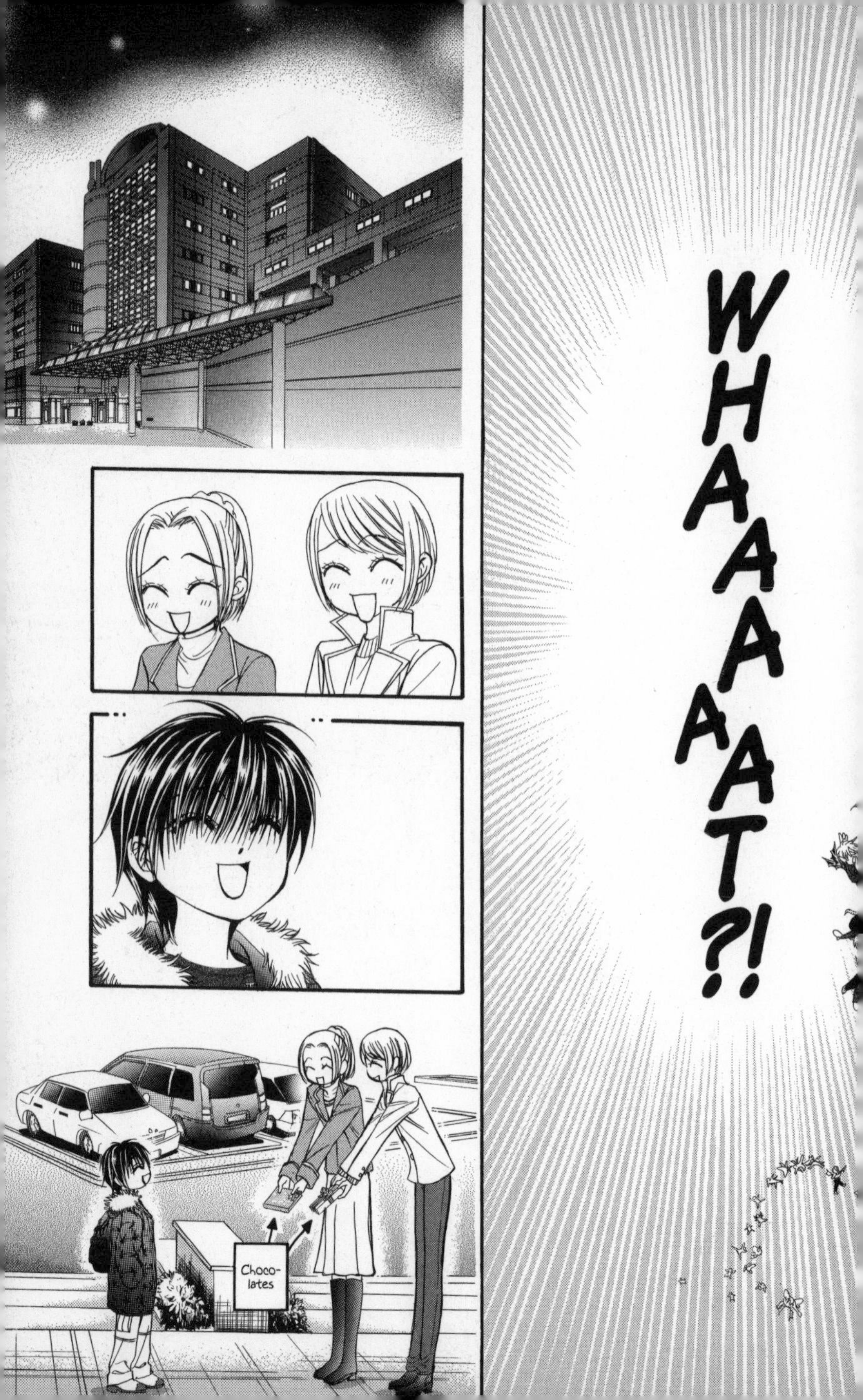
WHAAAAAT?!
Choco-
lates

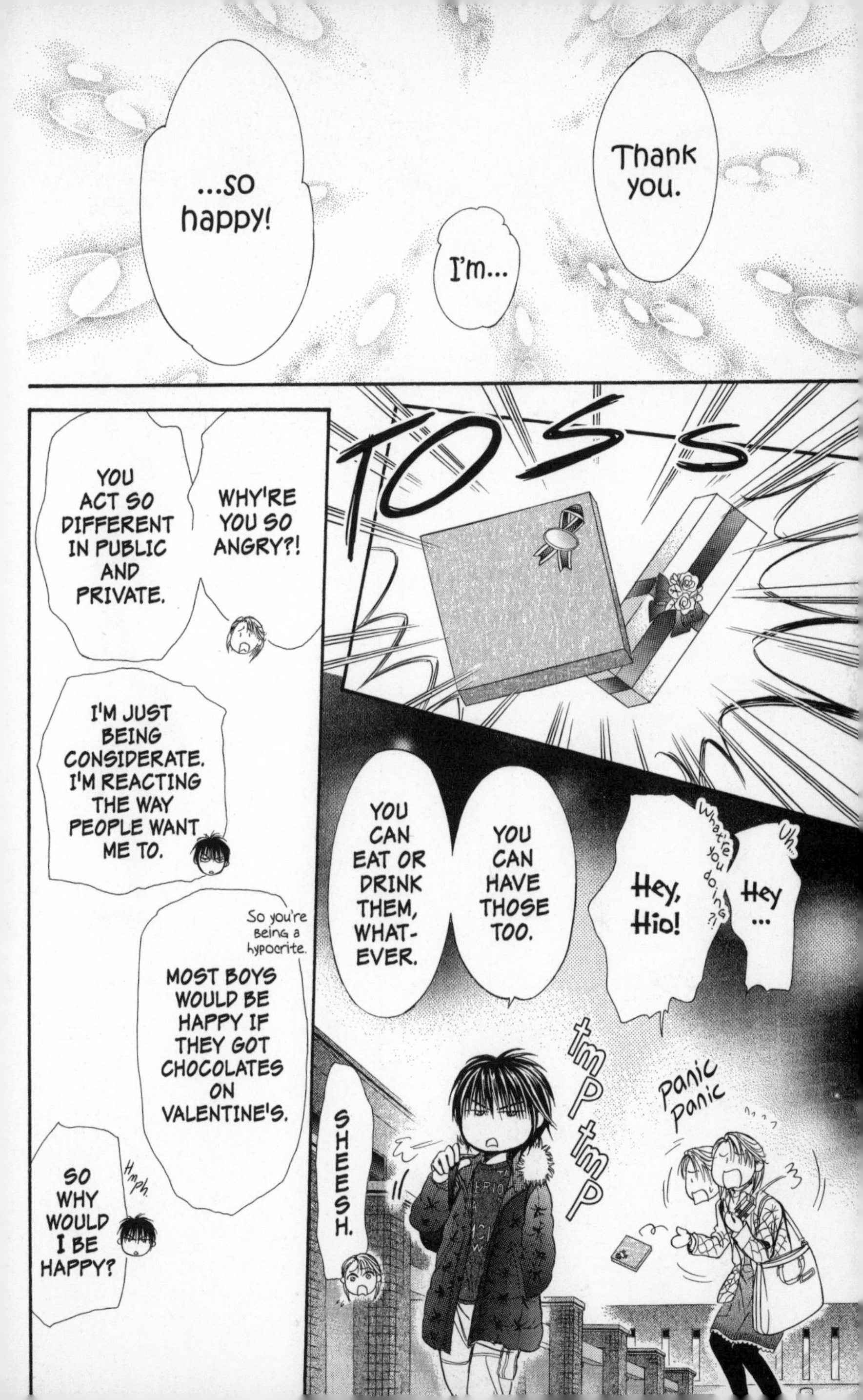
Thank you.
I'm...
...so happy!
TOSS
Uh...
Hey...
What're you doing?!
Hey, Hio!
YOU CAN HAVE THOSE TOO.
YOU CAN EAT OR DRINK THEM, WHATEVER.
tmp tmp
Panic panic
SHEESH.
WHY'RE YOU SO ANGRY?!
YOU ACT SO DIFFERENT IN PUBLIC AND PRIVATE.
I'M JUST BEING CONSIDERATE. I'M REACTING THE WAY PEOPLE WANT ME TO.
So you're being a hypocrite.
MOST BOYS WOULD BE HAPPY IF THEY GOT CHOCOLATES ON VALENTINE'S.
Hmph.
SO WHY WOULD I BE HAPPY?

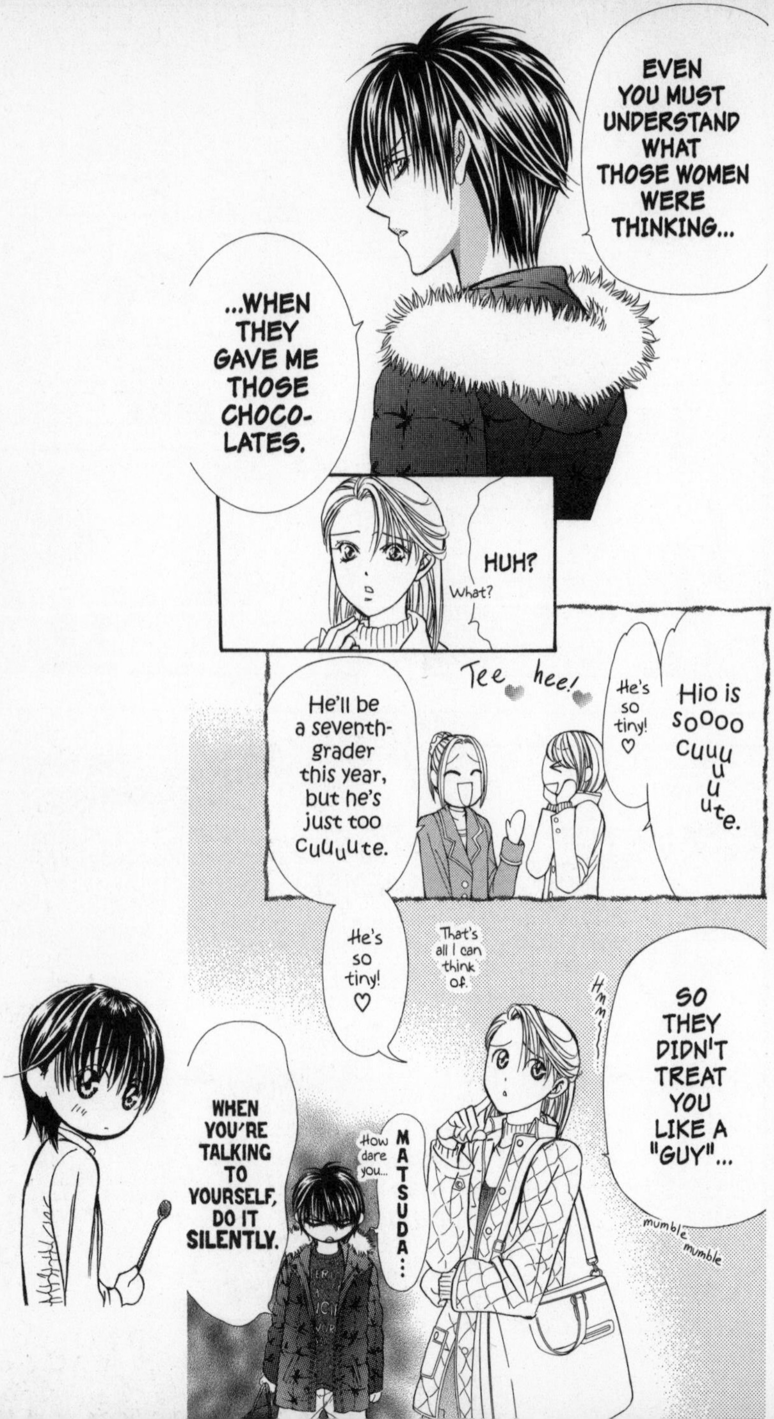
EVEN YOU MUST UNDERSTAND WHAT THOSE WOMEN WERE THINKING...
...WHEN THEY GAVE ME THOSE CHOCOLATES.
HUH?
What?
Hio is sooooo cuuuuuute.
He's so tiny! ♡
Tee hee!
He'll be a seventh-grader this year, but he's just too cuuuute.
He's so tiny! ♡
That's all I can think of.
Hmm~
SO THEY DIDN'T TREAT YOU LIKE A "GUY"...
mumble mumble
MATSUDA...
How dare you...
WHEN YOU'RE TALKING TO YOURSELF, DO IT SILENTLY.

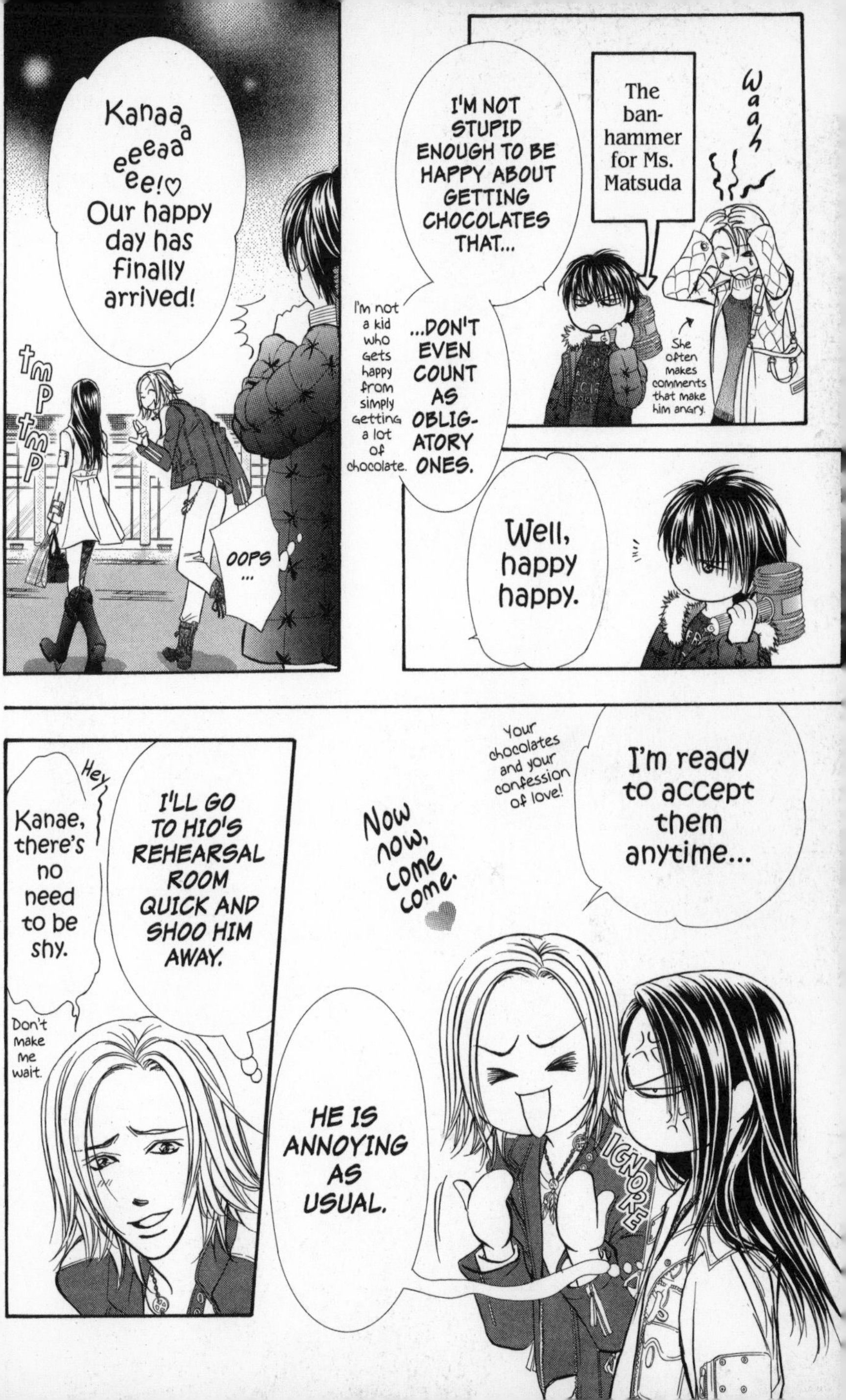
Waah
The ban-hammer for Ms. Matsuda
She often makes comments that make him angry.
I'M NOT STUPID ENOUGH TO BE HAPPY ABOUT GETTING CHOCOLATES THAT...
...DON'T EVEN COUNT AS OBLIGATORY ONES.
I'm not a kid who gets happy from simply getting a lot of chocolate.
Well, happy happy.
Kanaaaeeeaaaee!♡ Our happy day has finally arrived!
tmp tmp
OOPS...
I'm ready to accept them anytime...
Your chocolates and your confession of love!
Now now, come come.
IGNORE
HE IS ANNOYING AS USUAL.
Hey
Kanae, there's no need to be shy.
I'LL GO TO HIO'S REHEARSAL ROOM QUICK AND SHOO HIM AWAY.
Don't make me wait.

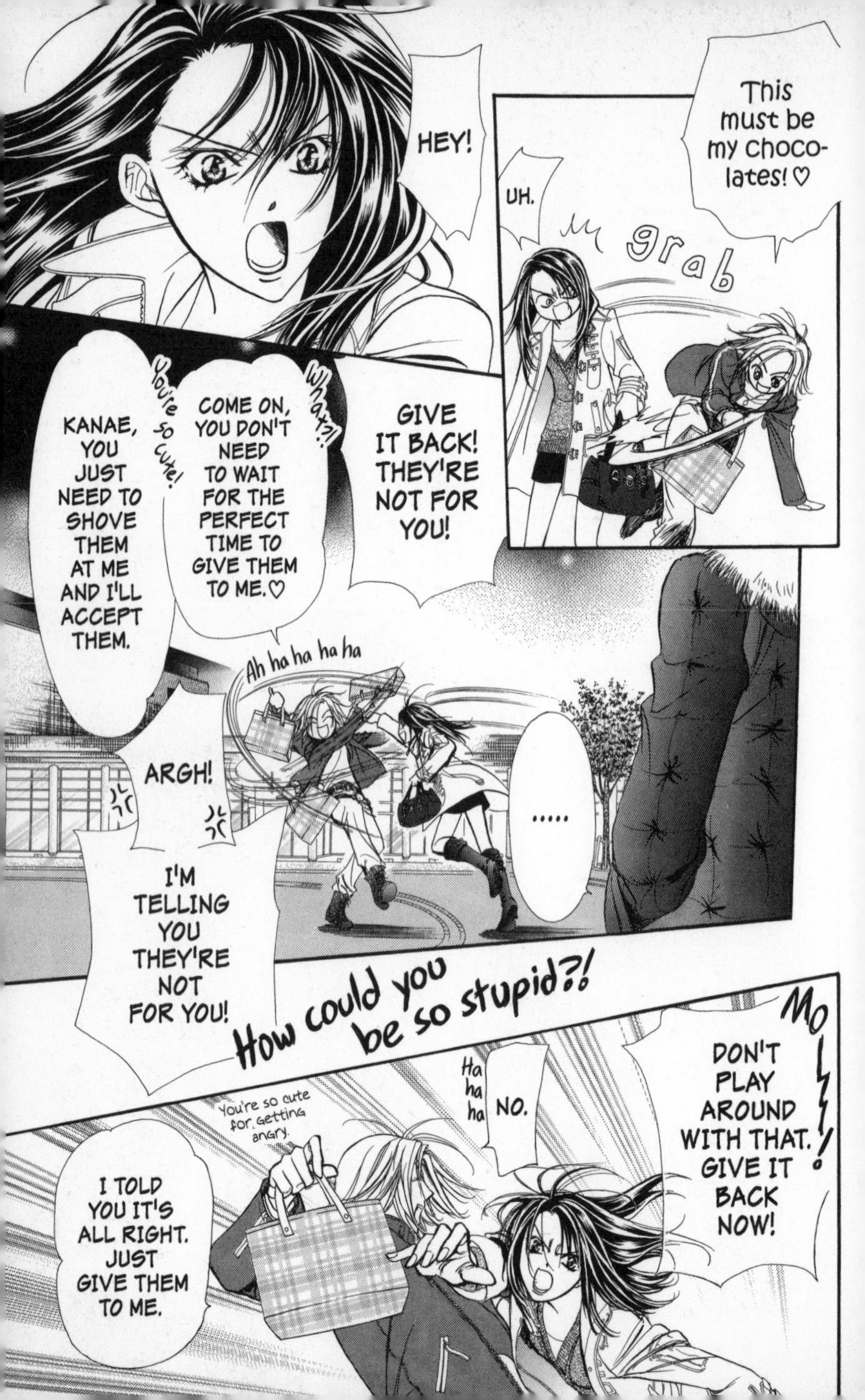
This must be my chocolates! ♡
UH.
grab
HEY!
GIVE IT BACK! THEY'RE NOT FOR YOU!
What?!
COME ON, YOU DON'T NEED TO WAIT FOR THE PERFECT TIME TO GIVE THEM TO ME. ♡
You're so cute!
KANAE, YOU JUST NEED TO SHOVE THEM AT ME AND I'LL ACCEPT THEM.
Ah ha ha ha ha
.....
ARGH!
I'M TELLING YOU THEY'RE NOT FOR YOU!
How could you be so stupid?!
MO!
DON'T PLAY AROUND WITH THAT. GIVE IT BACK NOW!
NO.
Ha ha ha
You're so cute for getting angry.
I TOLD YOU IT'S ALL RIGHT. JUST GIVE THEM TO ME.

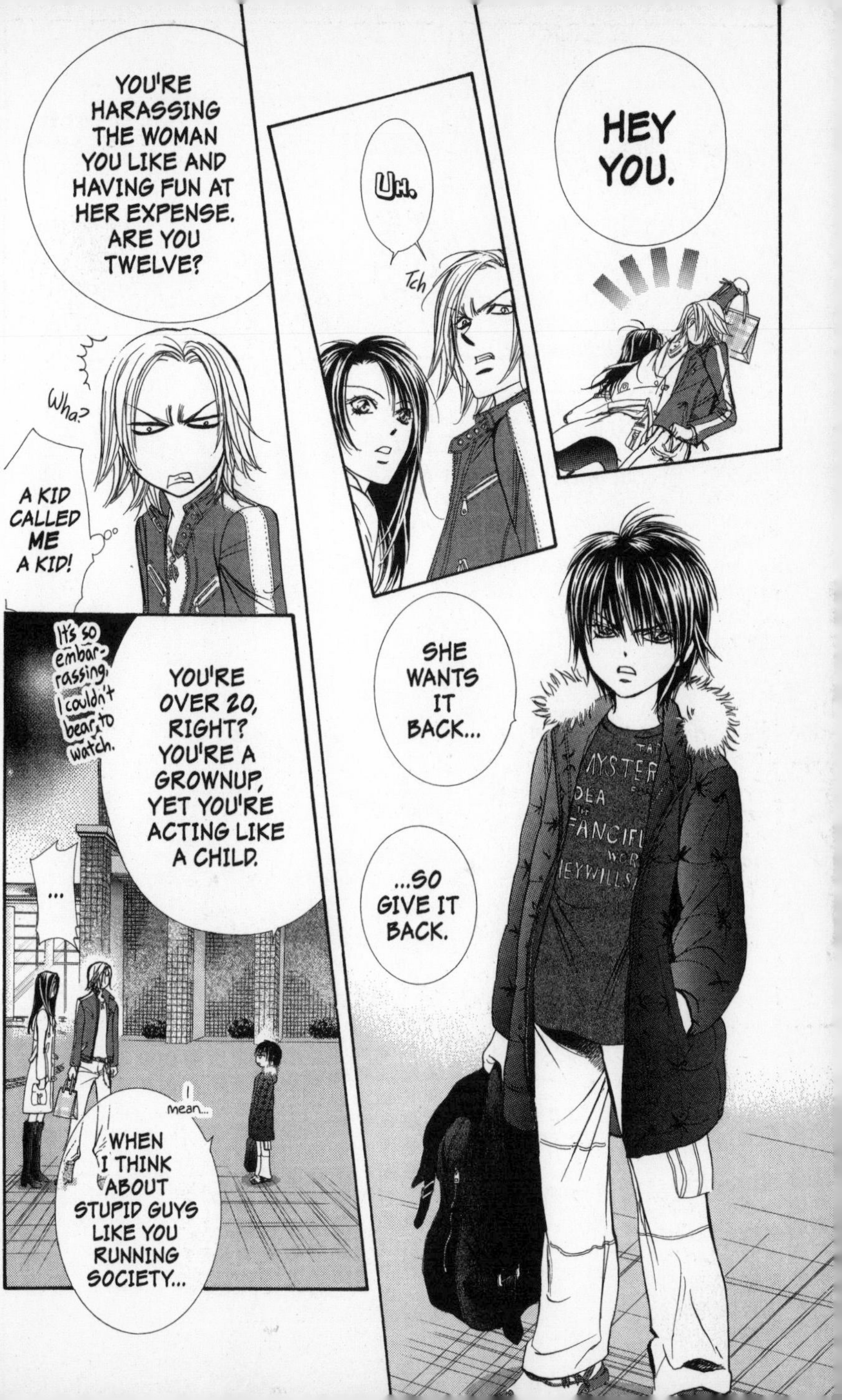
HEY YOU.
UH.
Tch
SHE WANTS IT BACK...
...SO GIVE IT BACK.
YOU'RE HARASSING THE WOMAN YOU LIKE AND HAVING FUN AT HER EXPENSE. ARE YOU TWELVE?
Wha?
A KID CALLED ME A KID!
YOU'RE OVER 20, RIGHT? YOU'RE A GROWNUP, YET YOU'RE ACTING LIKE A CHILD.
It's so embarrassing, I couldn't bear to watch.
...
I mean...
WHEN I THINK ABOUT STUPID GUYS LIKE YOU RUNNING SOCIETY...

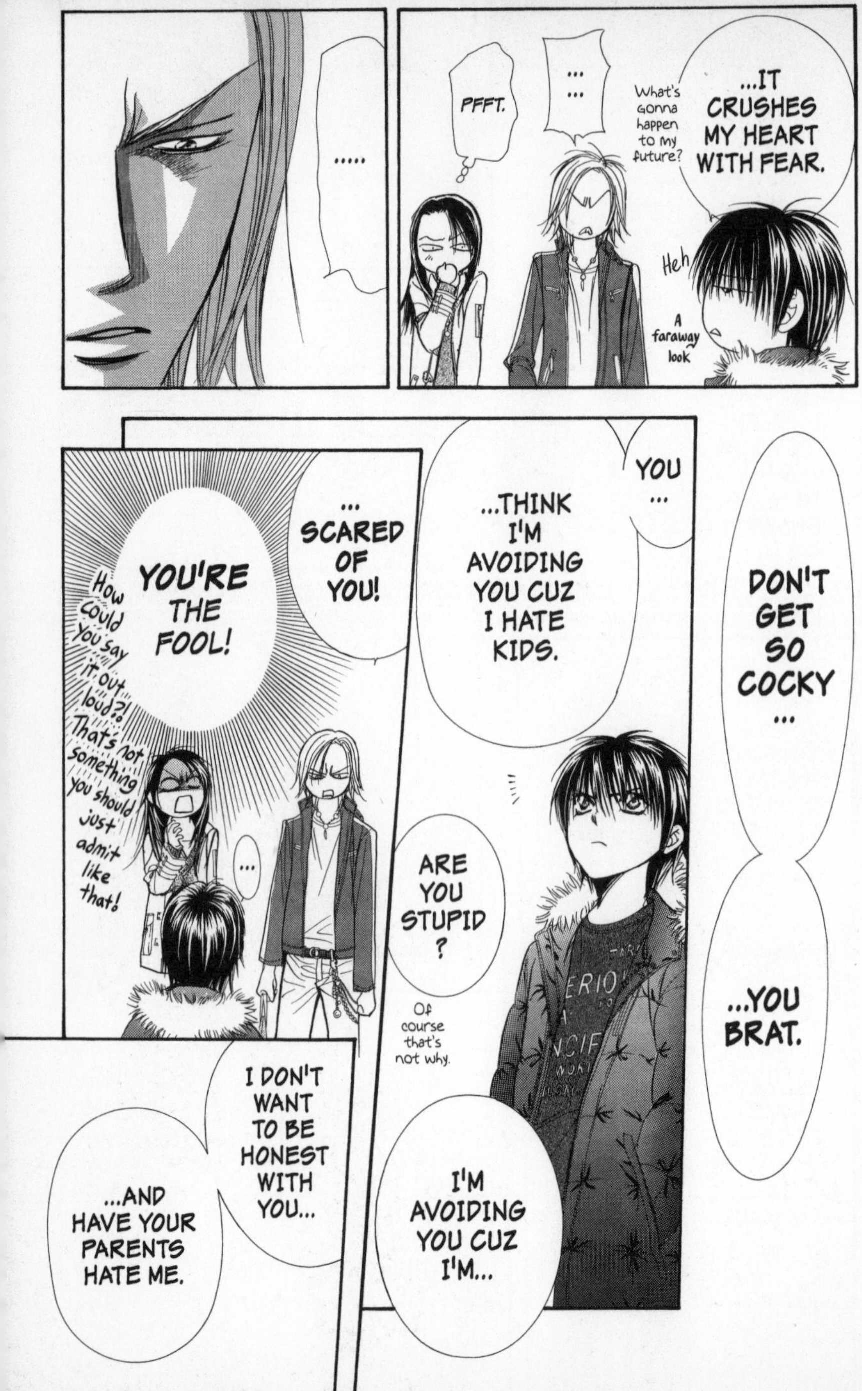
...IT CRUSHES MY HEART WITH FEAR.
What's gonna happen to my future?
Heh
A faraway look
... ...
PFFT.
.....
DON'T GET SO COCKY ...
...YOU BRAT.
YOU ...
...THINK I'M AVOIDING YOU CUZ I HATE KIDS.
ARE YOU STUPID ?
Of course that's not why.
I'M AVOIDING YOU CUZ I'M...
... SCARED OF YOU!
YOU'RE THE FOOL!
How could you say it out loud?! That's not something you should just admit like that!
...
I DON'T WANT TO BE HONEST WITH YOU...
...AND HAVE YOUR PARENTS HATE ME.

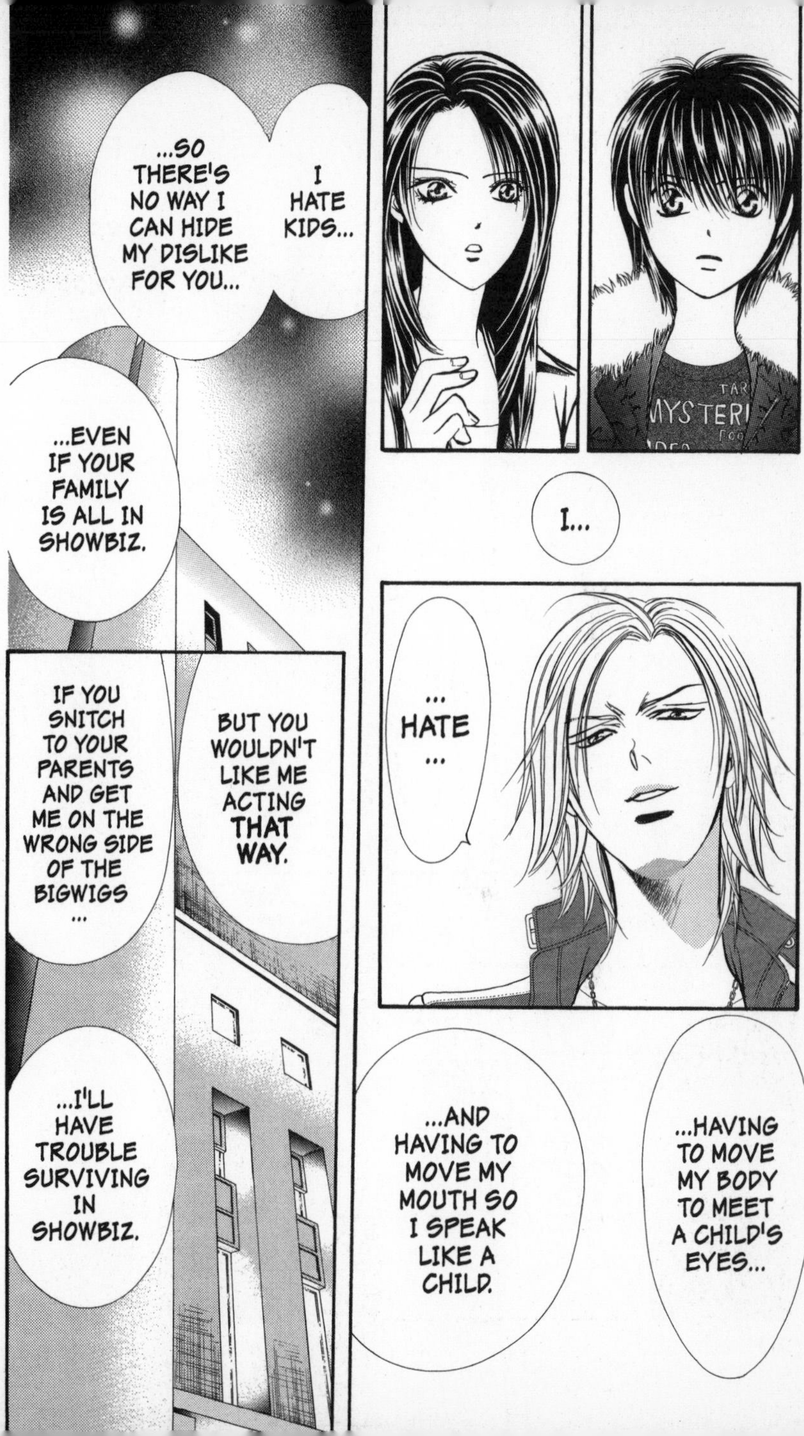
I...
...HATE...
...HAVING TO MOVE MY BODY TO MEET A CHILD'S EYES...
...AND HAVING TO MOVE MY MOUTH SO I SPEAK LIKE A CHILD.
I HATE KIDS...
...SO THERE'S NO WAY I CAN HIDE MY DISLIKE FOR YOU...
...EVEN IF YOUR FAMILY IS ALL IN SHOWBIZ.
BUT YOU WOULDN'T LIKE ME ACTING THAT WAY.
IF YOU SNITCH TO YOUR PARENTS AND GET ME ON THE WRONG SIDE OF THE BIGWIGS...
...I'LL HAVE TROUBLE SURVIVING IN SHOWBIZ.

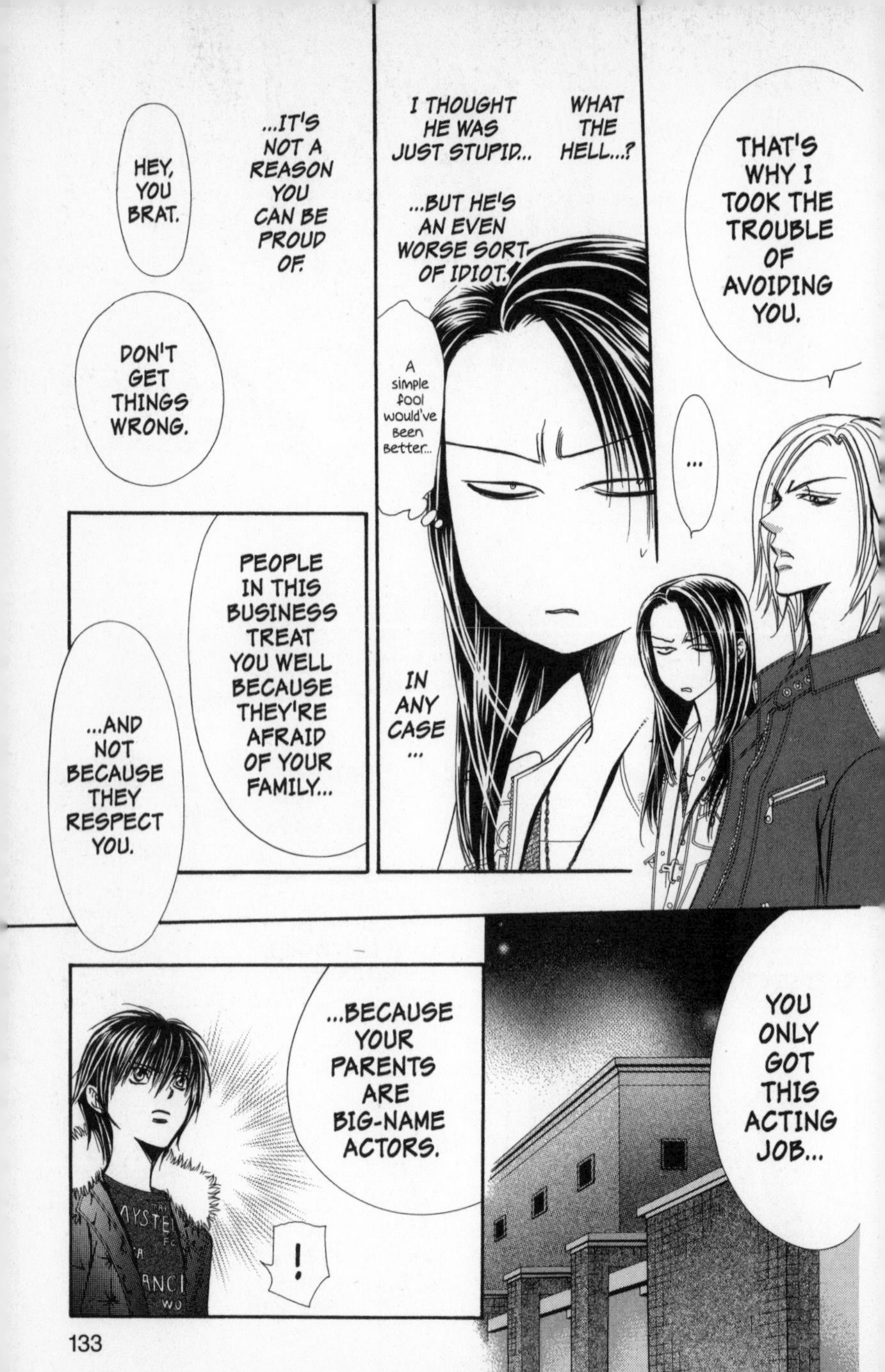
THAT'S WHY I TOOK THE TROUBLE OF AVOIDING YOU.
...
WHAT THE HELL...?
I THOUGHT HE WAS JUST STUPID...
...BUT HE'S AN EVEN WORSE SORT OF IDIOT.
A simple fool would've Been Better...
IN ANY CASE...
...IT'S NOT A REASON YOU CAN BE PROUD OF.
HEY, YOU BRAT.
DON'T GET THINGS WRONG.
PEOPLE IN THIS BUSINESS TREAT YOU WELL BECAUSE THEY'RE AFRAID OF YOUR FAMILY...
...AND NOT BECAUSE THEY RESPECT YOU.
YOU ONLY GOT THIS ACTING JOB...
...BECAUSE YOUR PARENTS ARE BIG-NAME ACTORS.
!

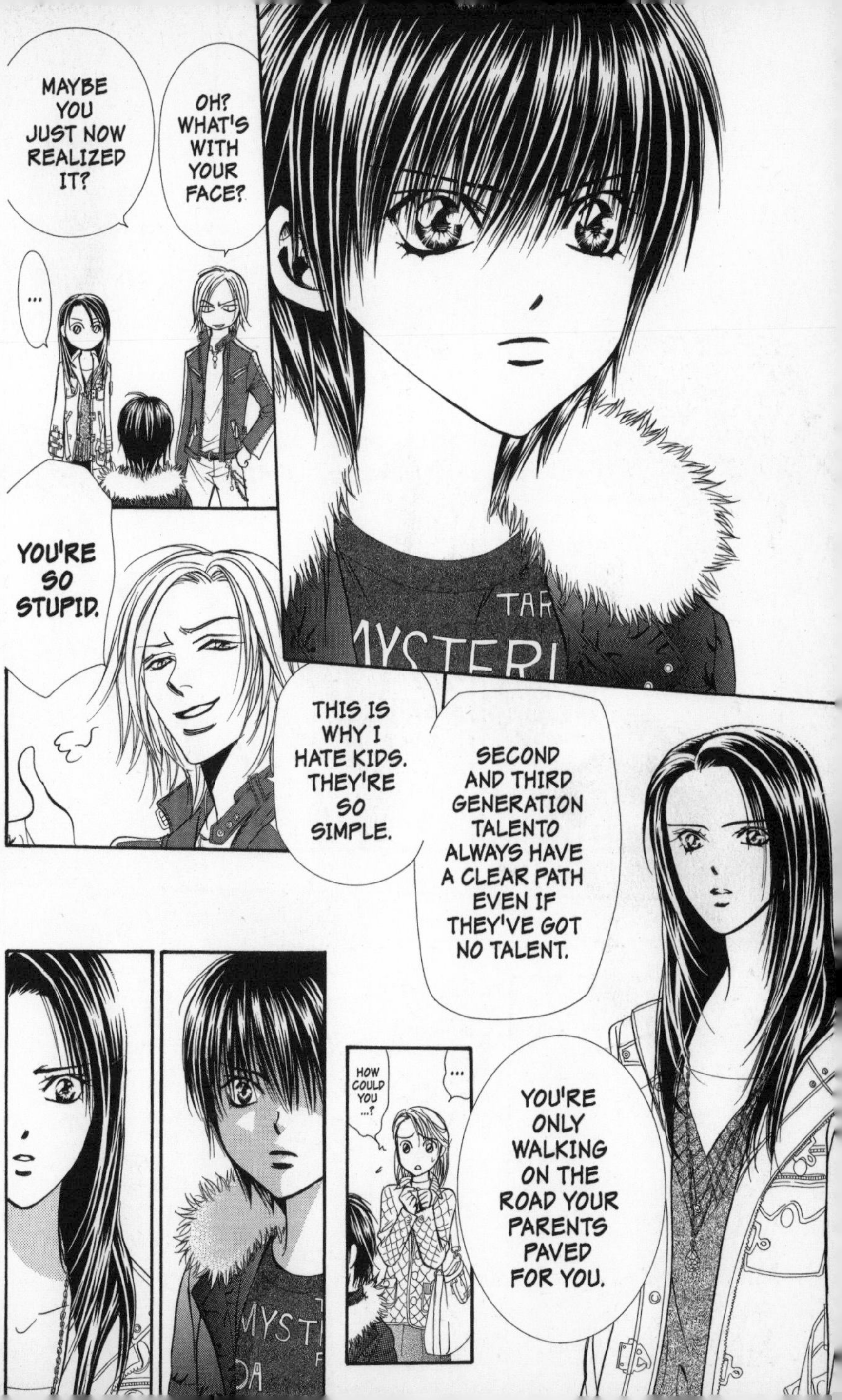
OH? WHAT'S WITH YOUR FACE?
MAYBE YOU JUST NOW REALIZED IT?
...
YOU'RE SO STUPID.
THIS IS WHY I HATE KIDS. THEY'RE SO SIMPLE.
SECOND AND THIRD GENERATION TALENTO ALWAYS HAVE A CLEAR PATH EVEN IF THEY'VE GOT NO TALENT.
YOU'RE ONLY WALKING ON THE ROAD YOUR PARENTS PAVED FOR YOU.
...
HOW COULD YOU ...?

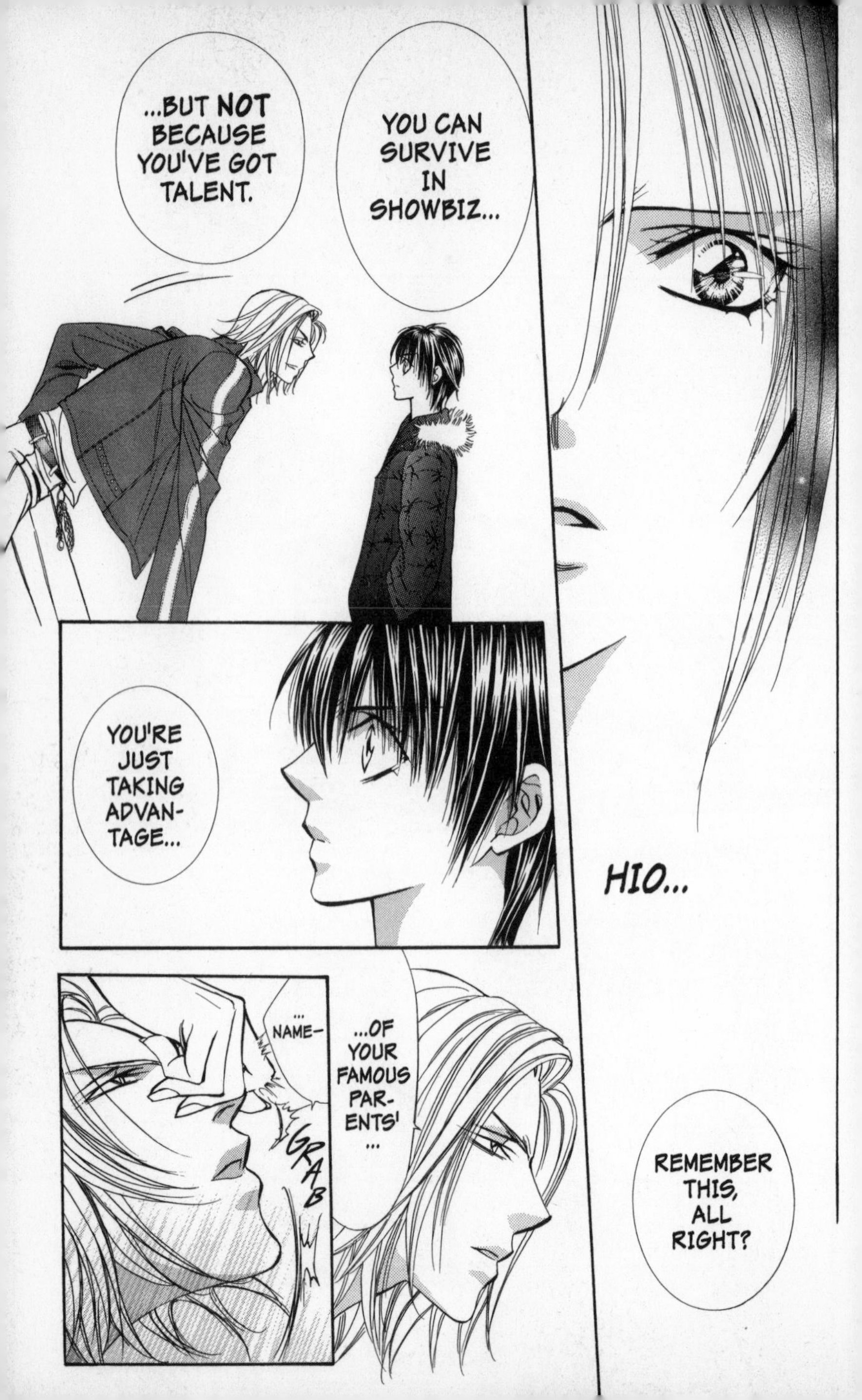
HIO...
REMEMBER THIS, ALL RIGHT?
YOU CAN SURVIVE IN SHOWBIZ...
...BUT NOT BECAUSE YOU'VE GOT TALENT.
YOU'RE JUST TAKING ADVANTAGE...
...OF YOUR FAMOUS PARENTS' ...
... NAME-
GRAB

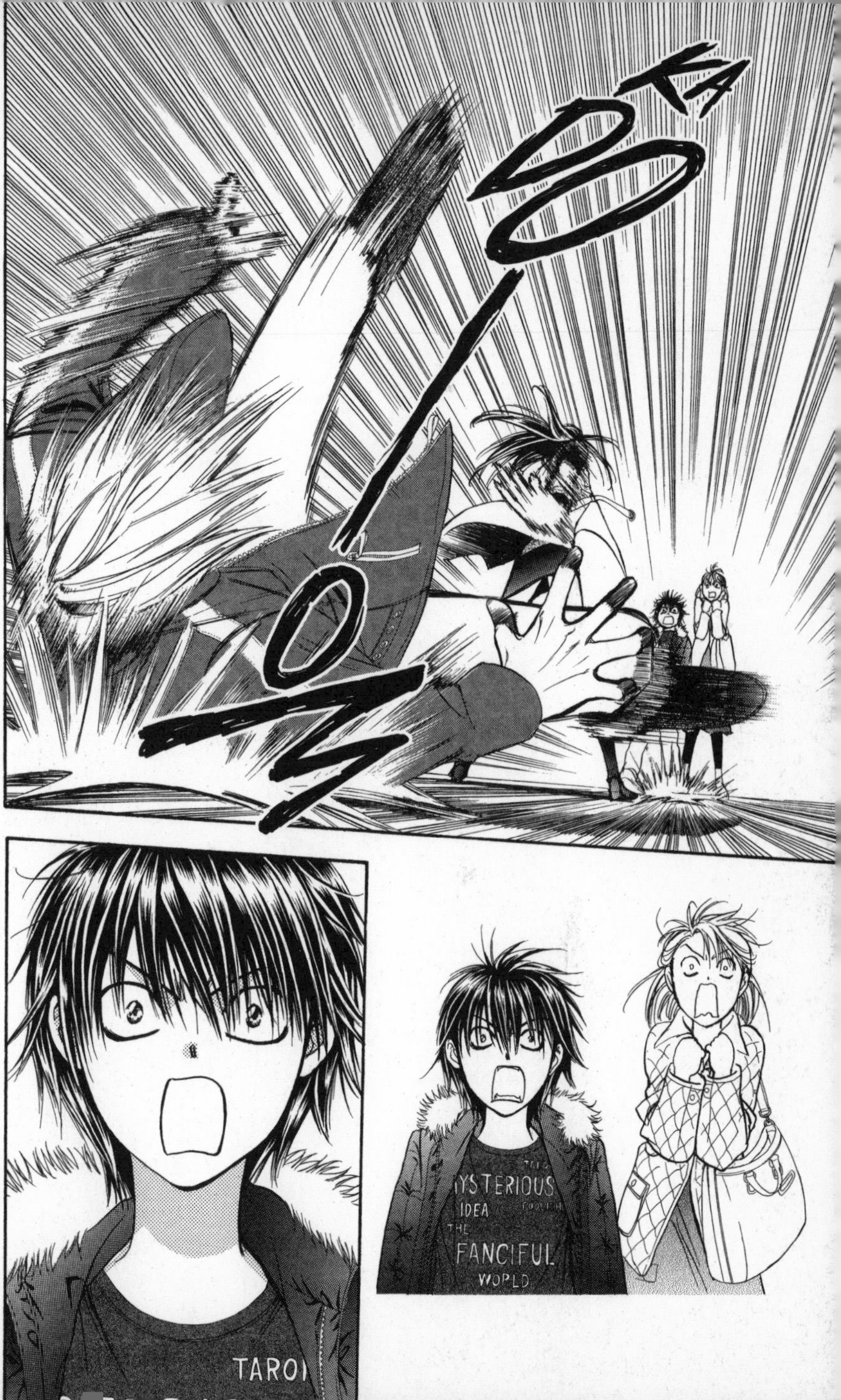
KA
DO-OM
YSTERIOUS
IDEA
THE
FANCIFUL
WORLD
TARO

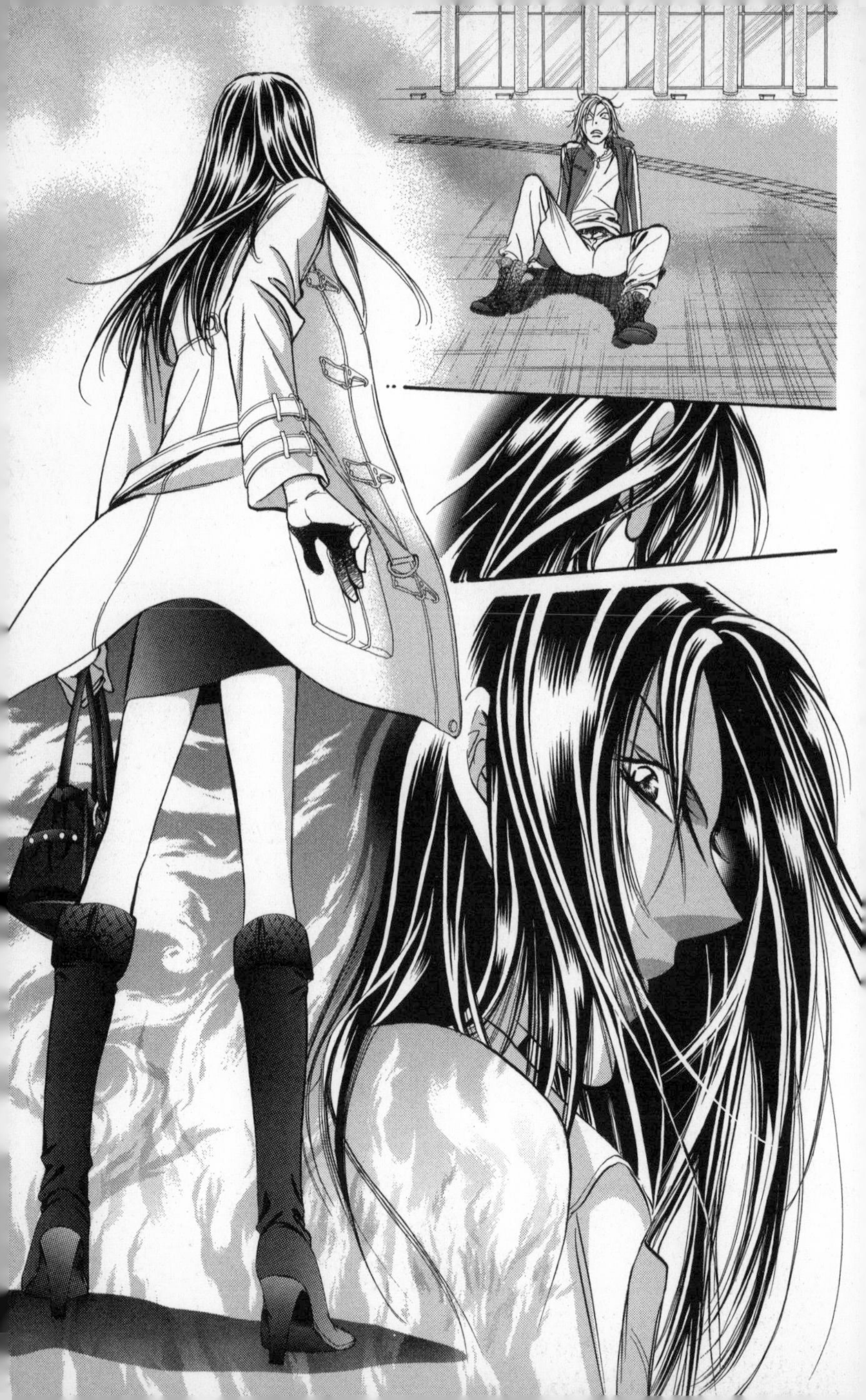

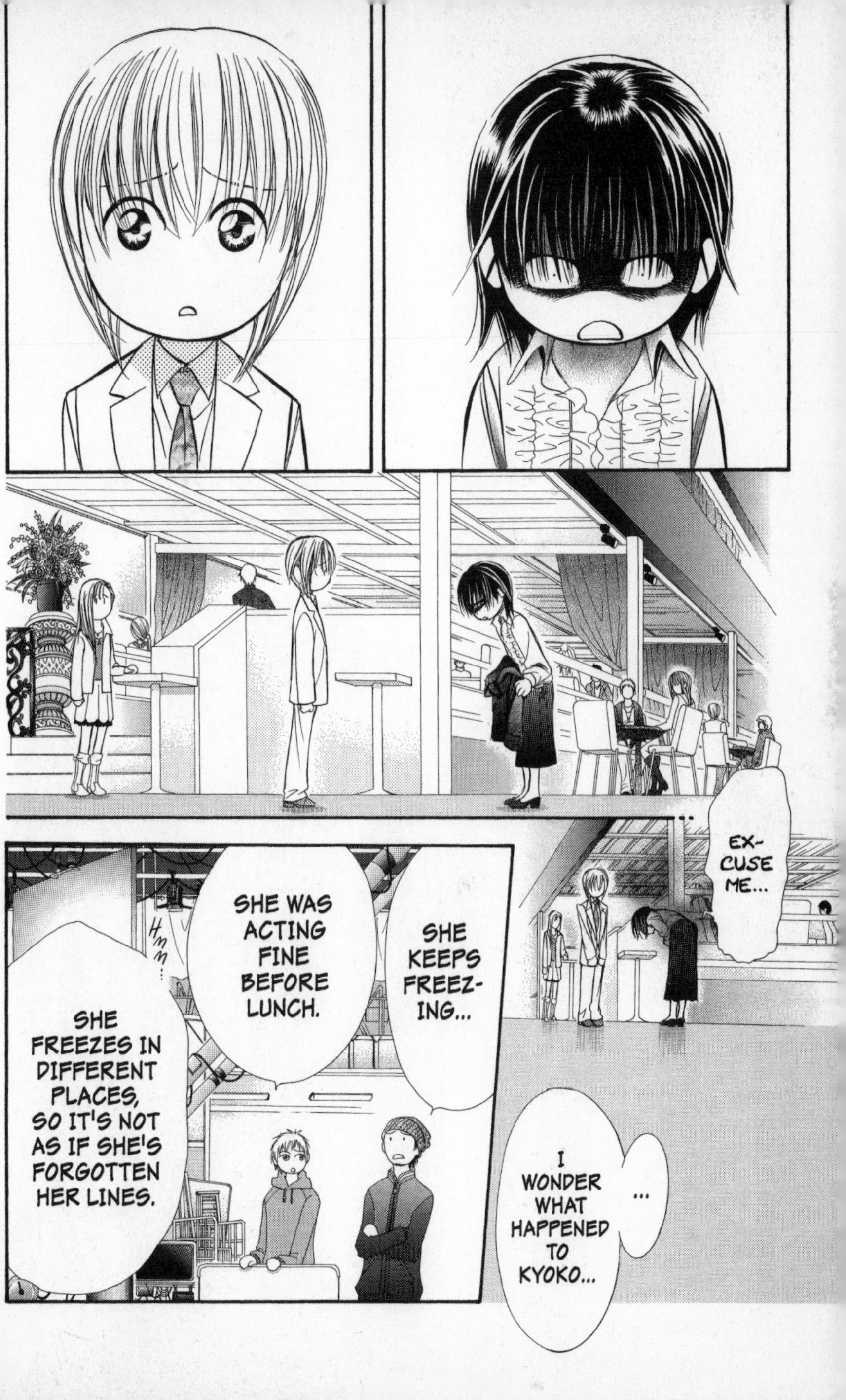
EX-CUSE ME...
SHE KEEPS FREEZ-ING...
SHE WAS ACTING FINE BEFORE LUNCH.
Hmm...
SHE FREEZES IN DIFFERENT PLACES, SO IT'S NOT AS IF SHE'S FORGOTTEN HER LINES.
...
I WONDER WHAT HAPPENED TO KYOKO...

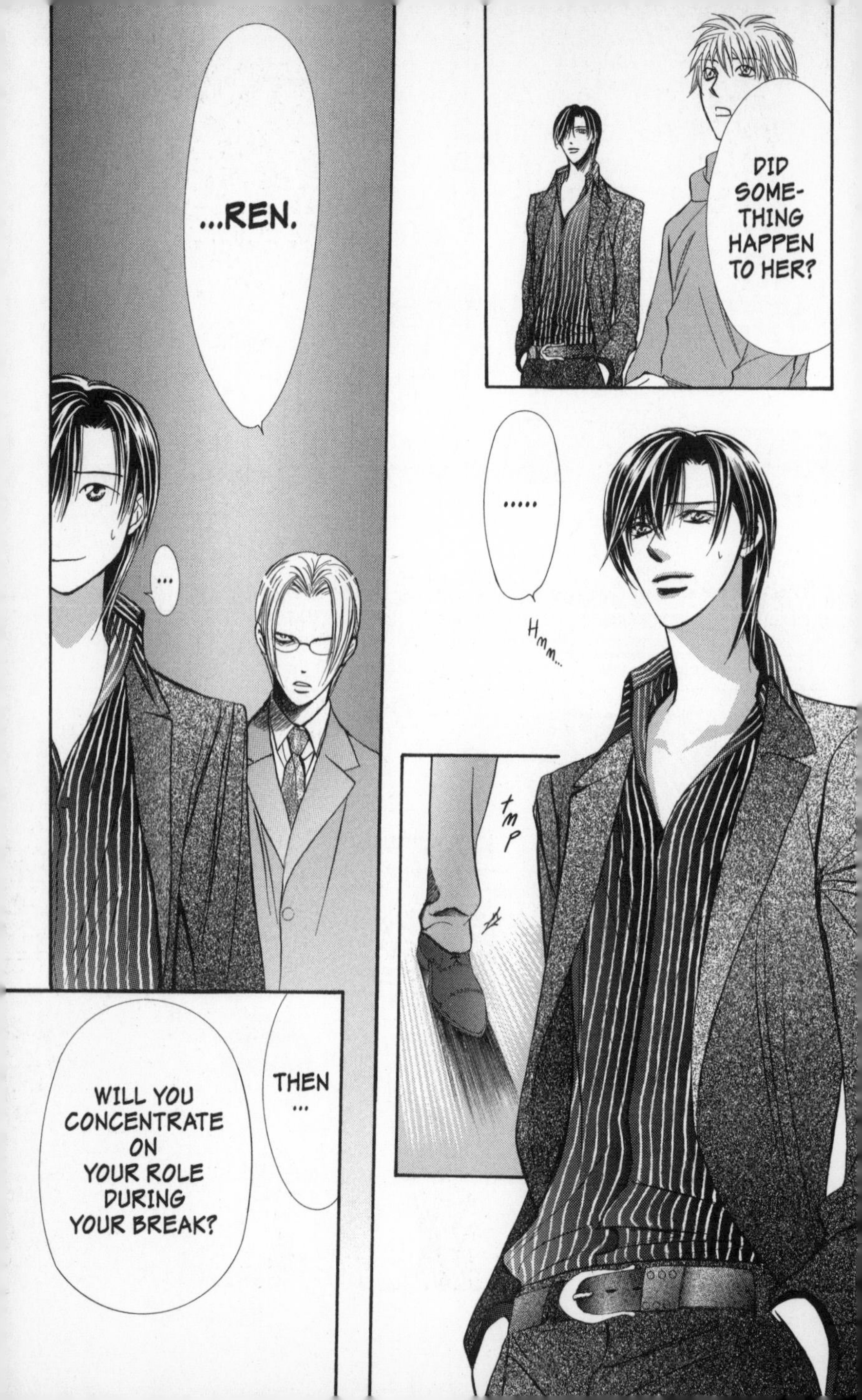
DID SOMETHING HAPPEN TO HER?
.....
Hmm...
tmp
...REN.
...
THEN...
WILL YOU CONCENTRATE ON YOUR ROLE DURING YOUR BREAK?

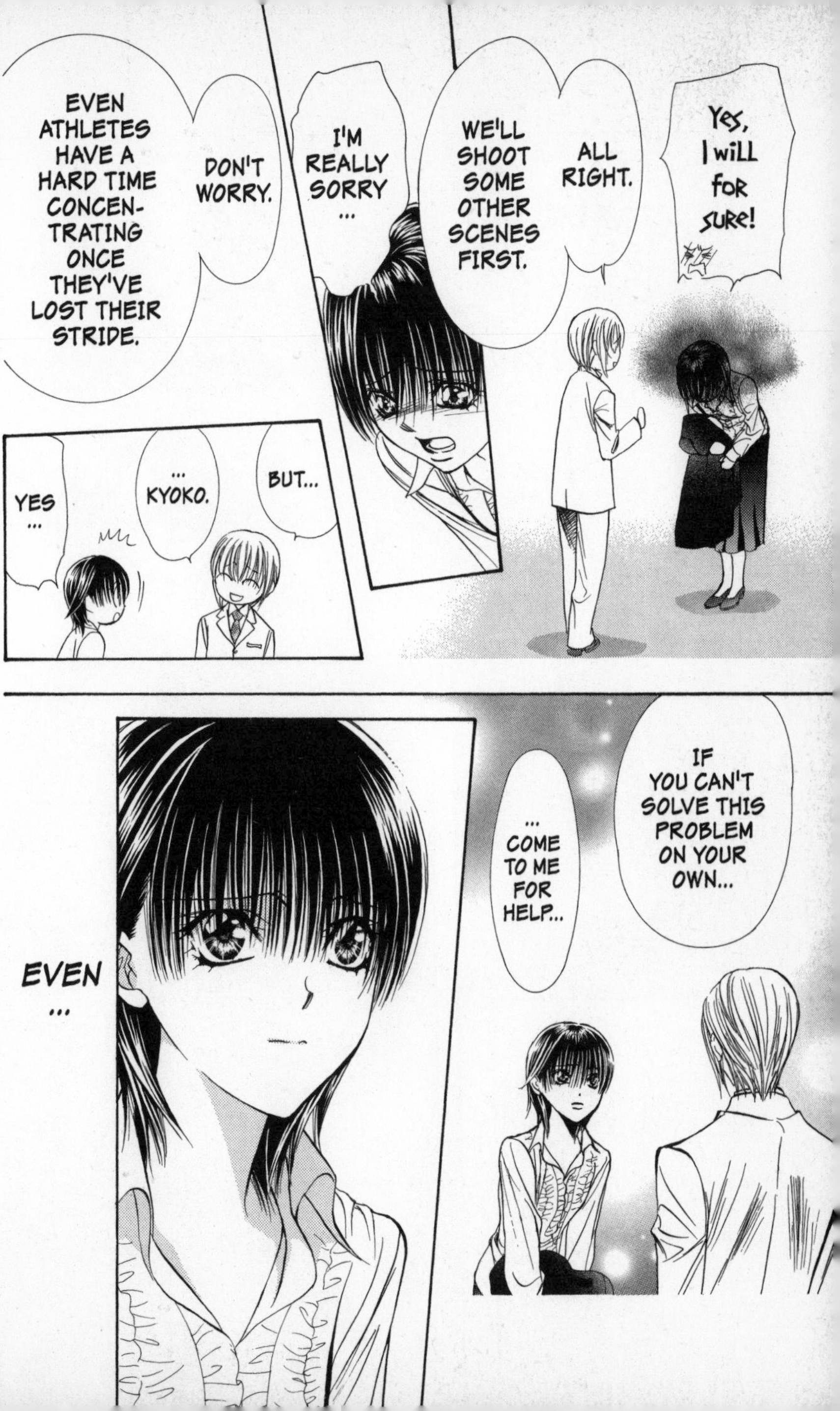
Yes, I will for sure!
ALL RIGHT.
WE'LL SHOOT SOME OTHER SCENES FIRST.
I'M REALLY SORRY ...
DON'T WORRY.
EVEN ATHLETES HAVE A HARD TIME CONCEN-TRATING ONCE THEY'VE LOST THEIR STRIDE.
BUT...
... KYOKO.
YES ...
IF YOU CAN'T SOLVE THIS PROBLEM ON YOUR OWN...
... COME TO ME FOR HELP...
EVEN ...

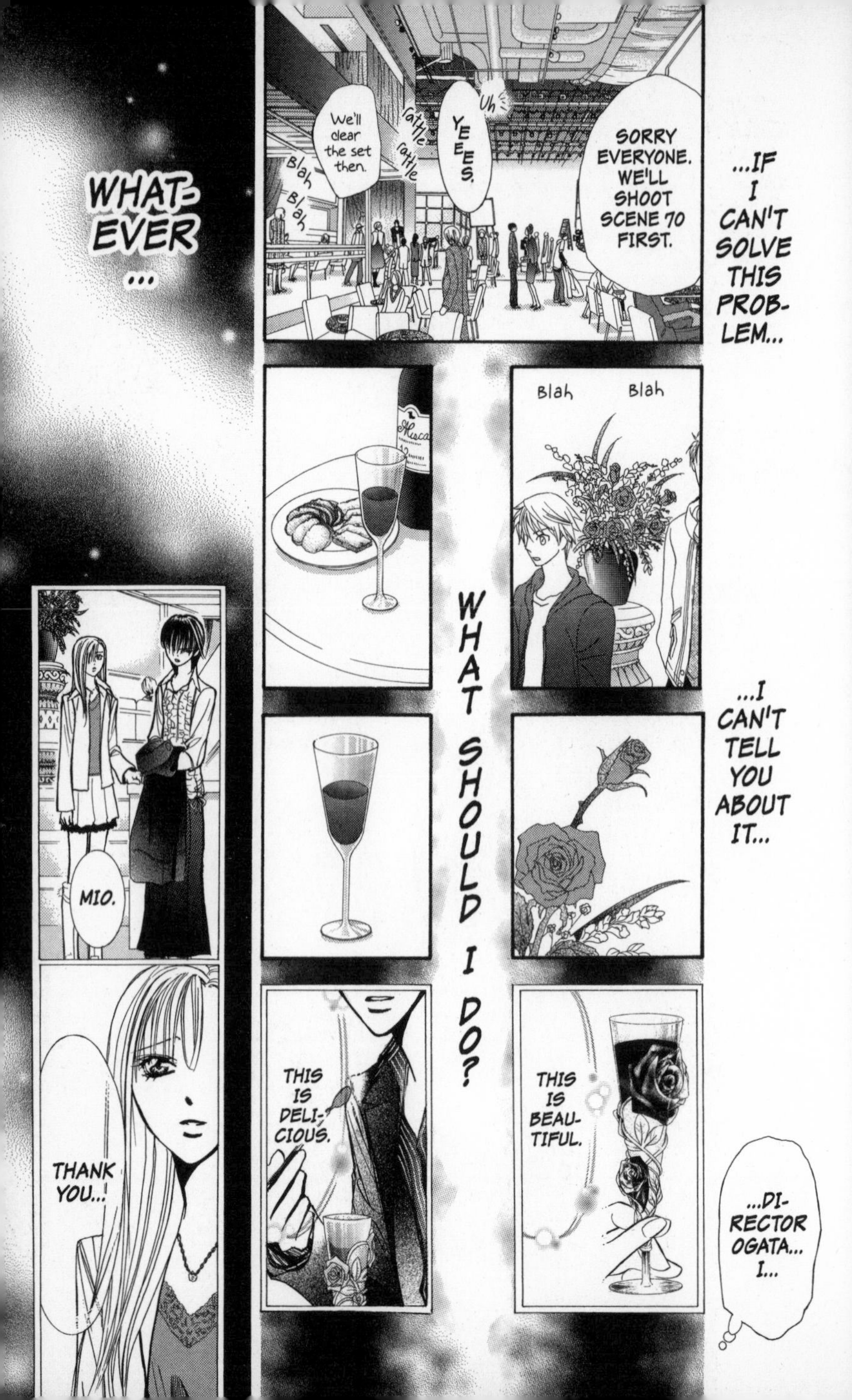
...IF I CAN'T SOLVE THIS PROBLEM...
SORRY EVERYONE. WE'LL SHOOT SCENE 70 FIRST.
Uh
YEEES.
rattle rattle
We'll clear the set then.
Blah Blah
Blah Blah
...I CAN'T TELL YOU ABOUT IT...
WHAT SHOULD I DO?
THIS IS BEAUTIFUL.
THIS IS DELICIOUS.
...DIRECTOR OGATA... I...
WHAT-EVER...
MIO.
THANK YOU...

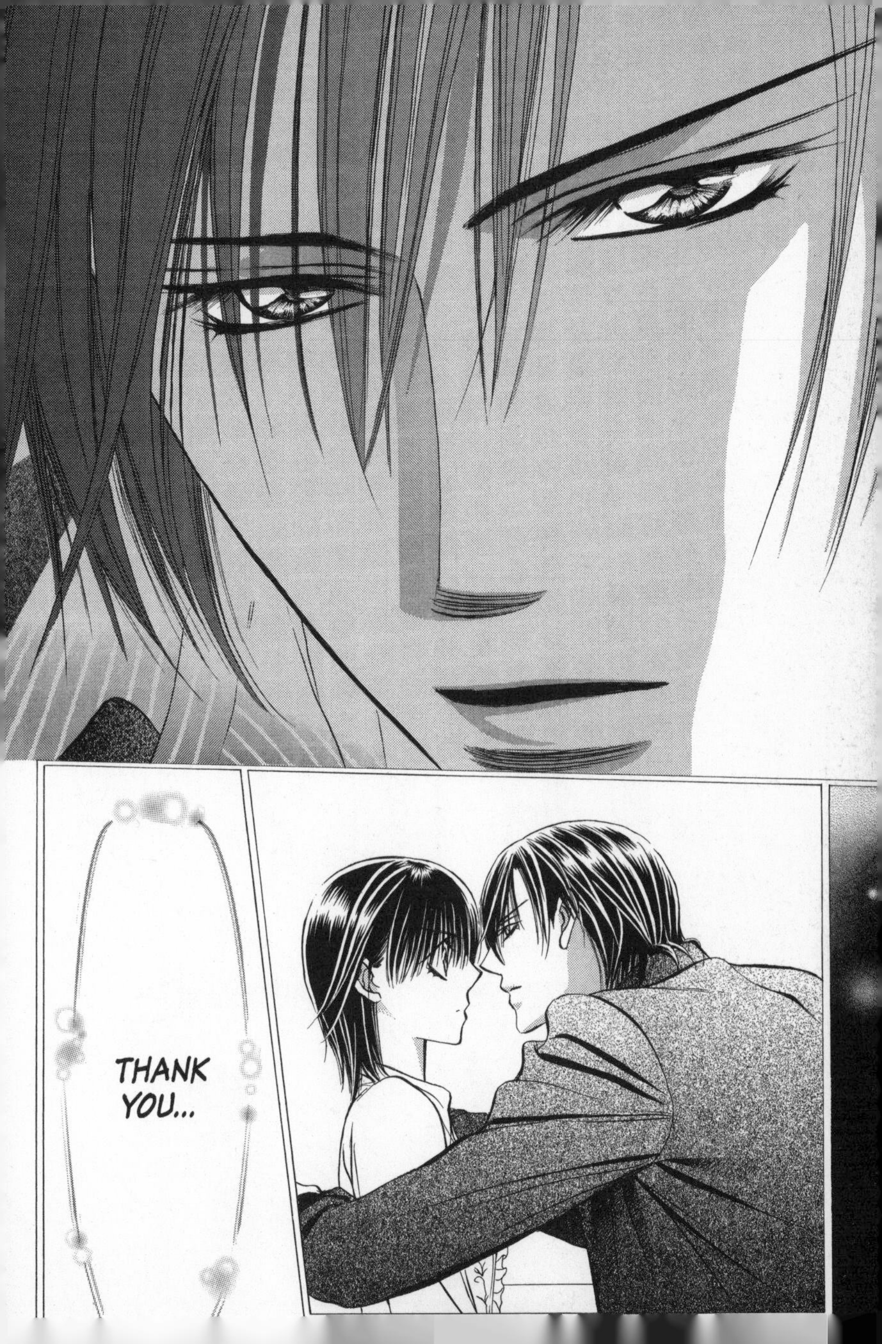
THANK YOU...

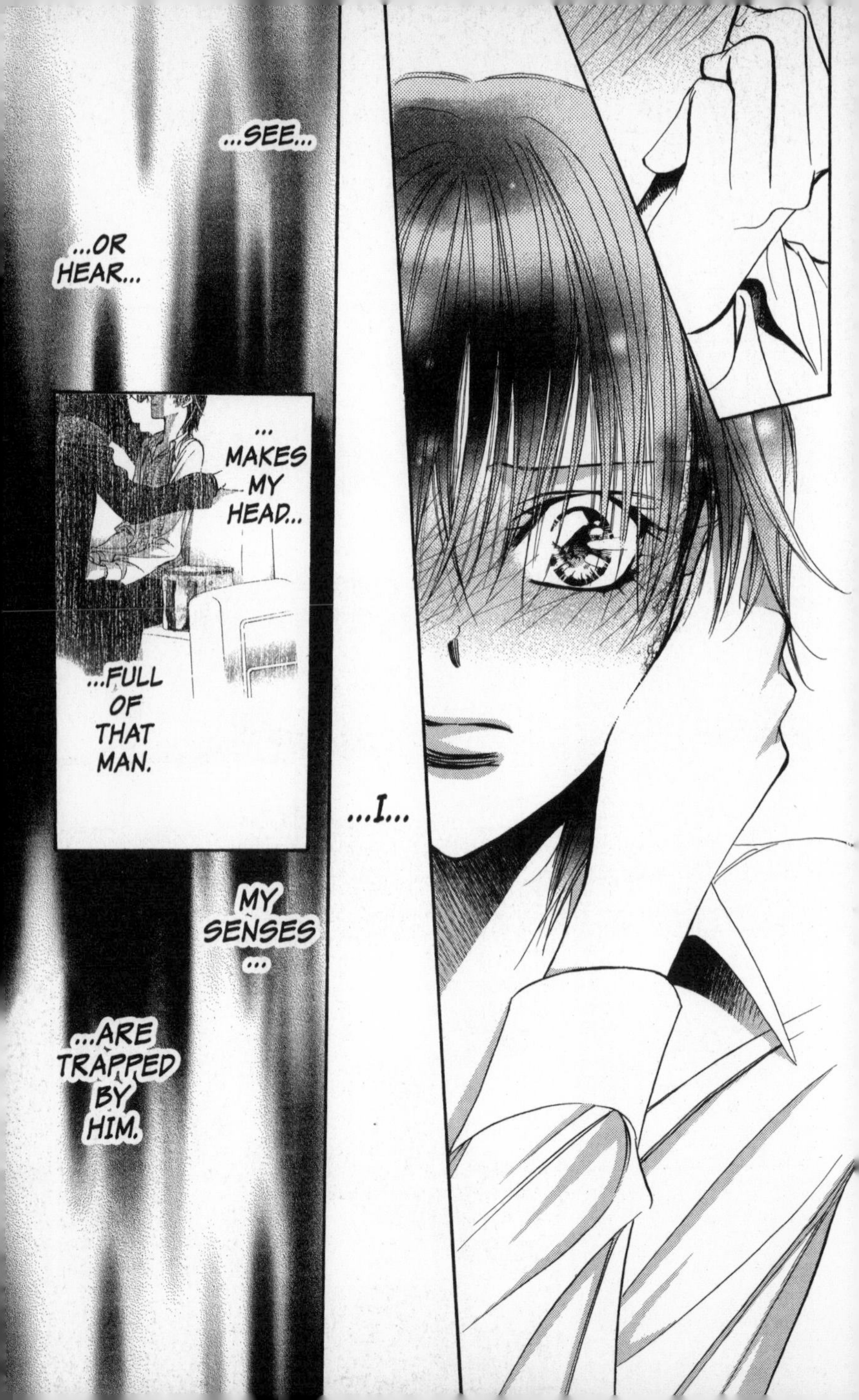
...I...
...SEE...
...OR HEAR...
...MAKES MY HEAD...
...FULL OF THAT MAN.
MY SENSES...
...ARE TRAPPED BY HIM.

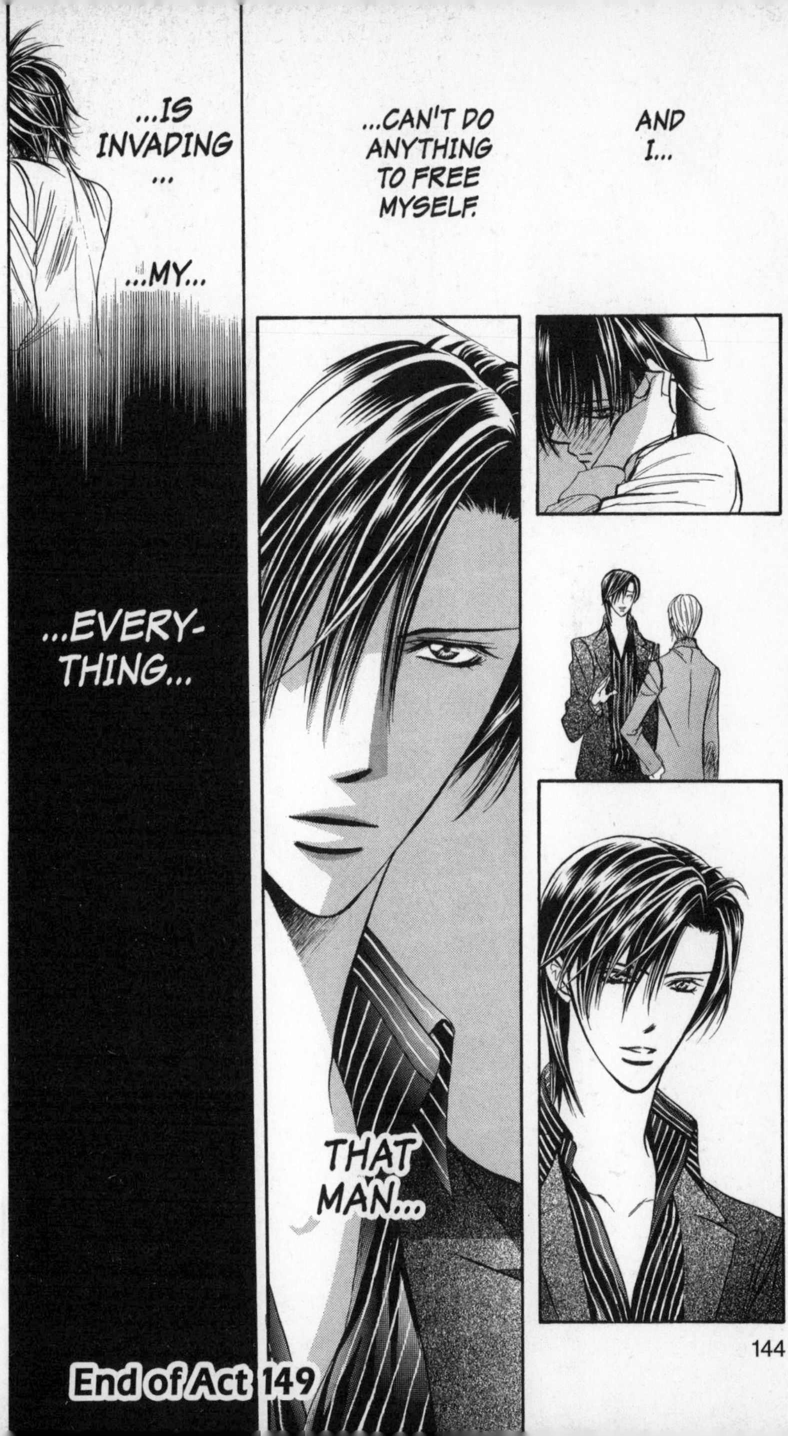
AND I...
...CAN'T DO ANYTHING TO FREE MYSELF.
THAT MAN...
...IS INVADING ...
...MY...
...EVERY-THING...
End of Act 149

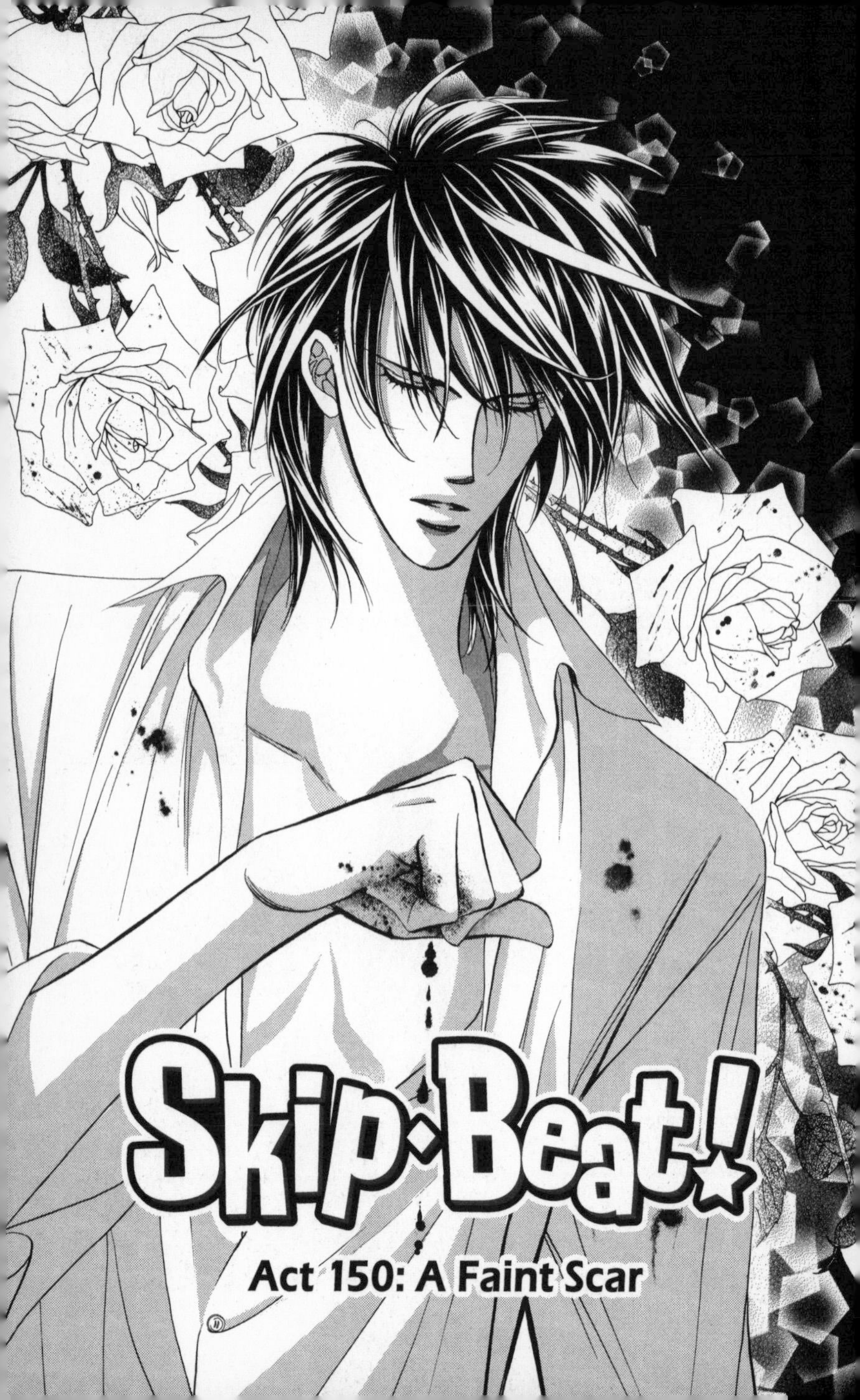
Skip·Beat!
Act 150: A Faint Scar

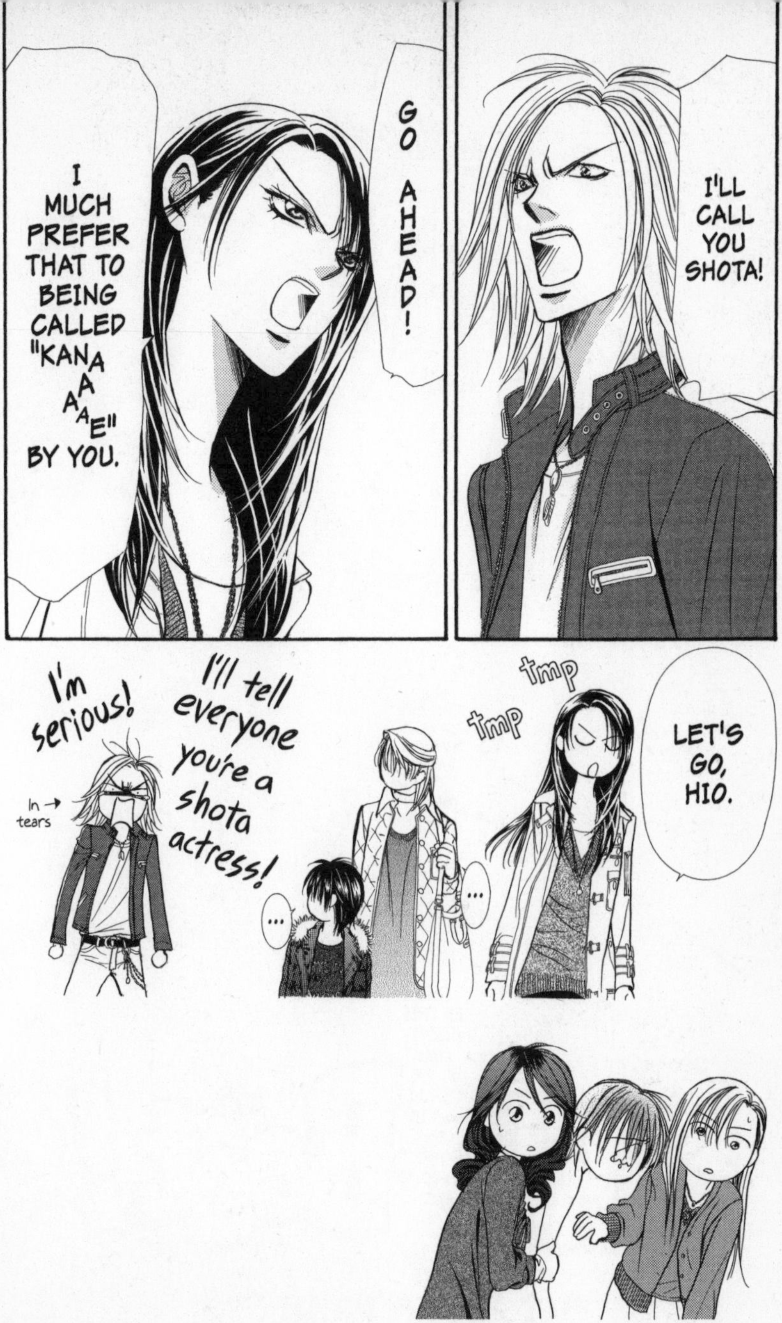
I'LL CALL YOU SHOTA!
GO AHEAD!
I MUCH PREFER THAT TO BEING CALLED "KANAAAAE" BY YOU.
LET'S GO, HIO.
tmp
tmp
...
...
I'll tell everyone you're a shota actress!
I'm serious!
In tears

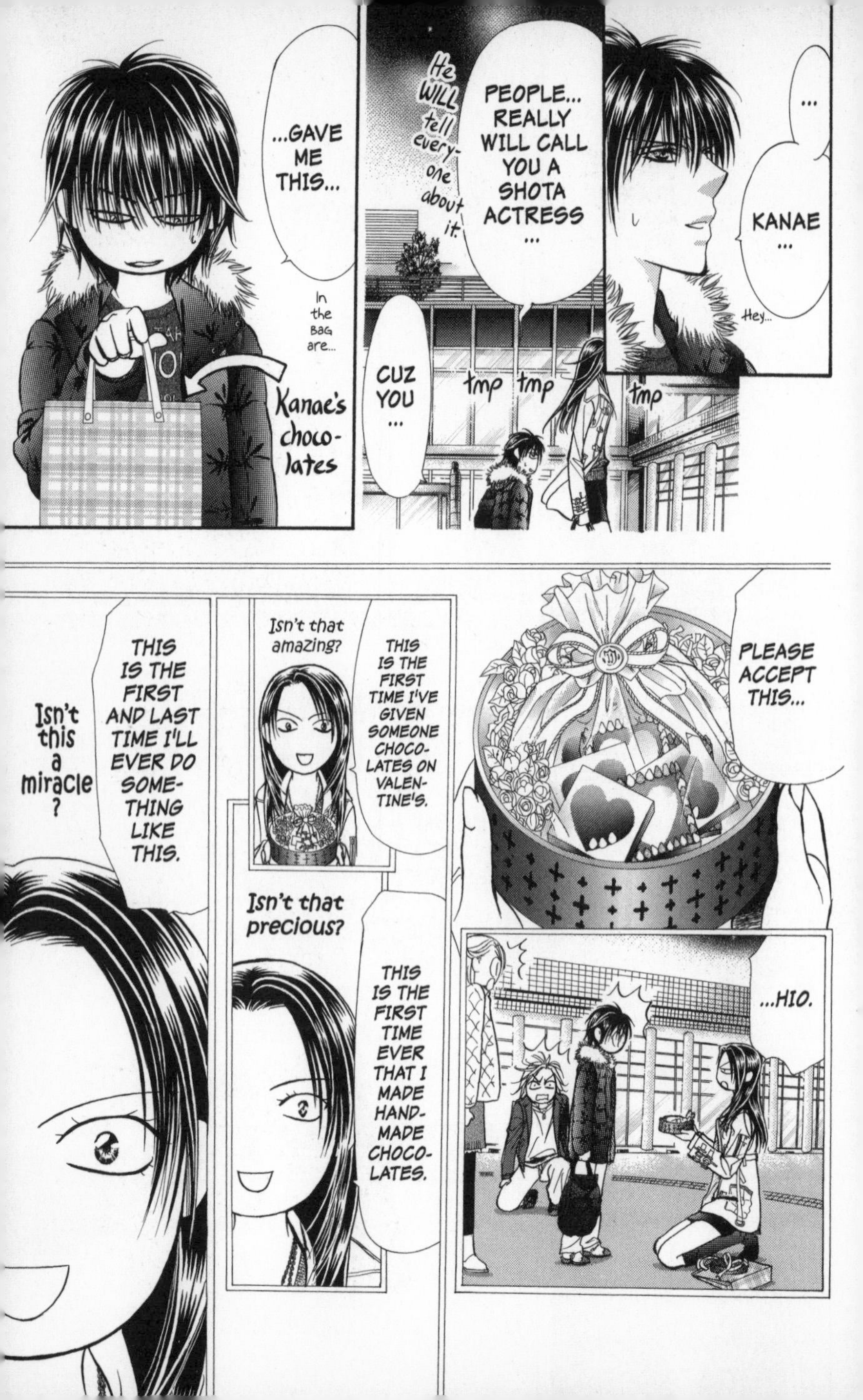
...
KANAE...
Hey...
PEOPLE... REALLY WILL CALL YOU A SHOTA ACTRESS...
He WILL tell every-one about it.
CUZ YOU...
tmp tmp tmp
...GAVE ME THIS...
In the BAG are...
Kanae's choco-lates
PLEASE ACCEPT THIS...
...HIO.
THIS IS THE FIRST TIME I'VE GIVEN SOMEONE CHOCO-LATES ON VALEN-TINE'S.
Isn't that amazing?
THIS IS THE FIRST TIME EVER THAT I MADE HAND-MADE CHOCO-LATES.
Isn't that precious?
THIS IS THE FIRST AND LAST TIME I'LL EVER DO SOME-THING LIKE THIS.
Isn't this a miracle?

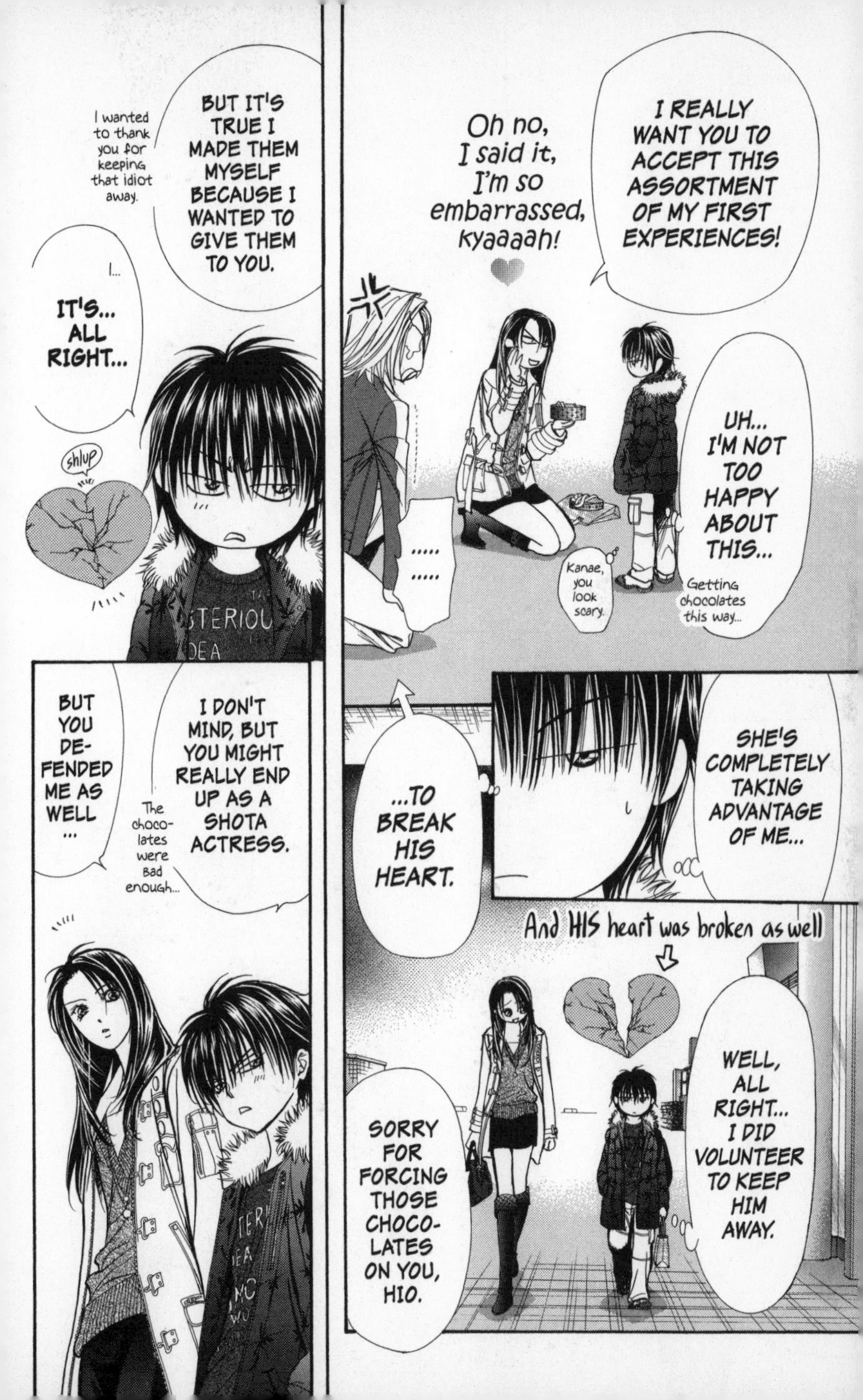
I REALLY WANT YOU TO ACCEPT THIS ASSORTMENT OF MY FIRST EXPERIENCES!
Oh no, I said it, I'm so embarrassed, kyaaaah!
UH... I'M NOT TOO HAPPY ABOUT THIS...
Getting chocolates this way...
Kanae, you look scary.
.....
.....
SHE'S COMPLETELY TAKING ADVANTAGE OF ME...
...TO BREAK HIS HEART.
And HIS heart was broken as well
WELL, ALL RIGHT... I DID VOLUNTEER TO KEEP HIM AWAY.
SORRY FOR FORCING THOSE CHOCO-LATES ON YOU, HIO.
BUT IT'S TRUE I MADE THEM MYSELF BECAUSE I WANTED TO GIVE THEM TO YOU.
I wanted to thank you for keeping that idiot away.
I...
IT'S... ALL RIGHT...
shlup
I DON'T MIND, BUT YOU MIGHT REALLY END UP AS A SHOTA ACTRESS.
The choco-lates were Bad enough...
BUT YOU DE-FENDED ME AS WELL...

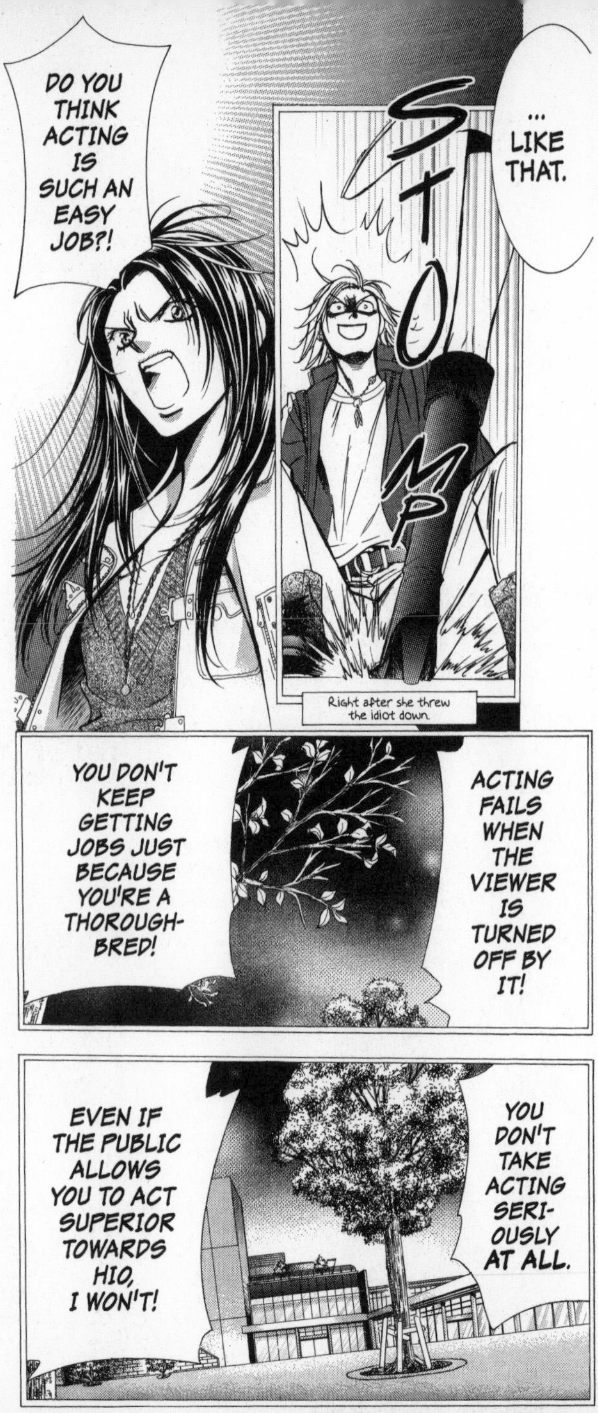

... LIKE THAT.
STOMP
Right after she threw the idiot down.
DO YOU THINK ACTING IS SUCH AN EASY JOB?!
ACTING FAILS WHEN THE VIEWER IS TURNED OFF BY IT!
YOU DON'T KEEP GETTING JOBS JUST BECAUSE YOU'RE A THOROUGH-BRED!
YOU DON'T TAKE ACTING SERI-OUSLY AT ALL.
EVEN IF THE PUBLIC ALLOWS YOU TO ACT SUPERIOR TOWARDS HIO, I WON'T!

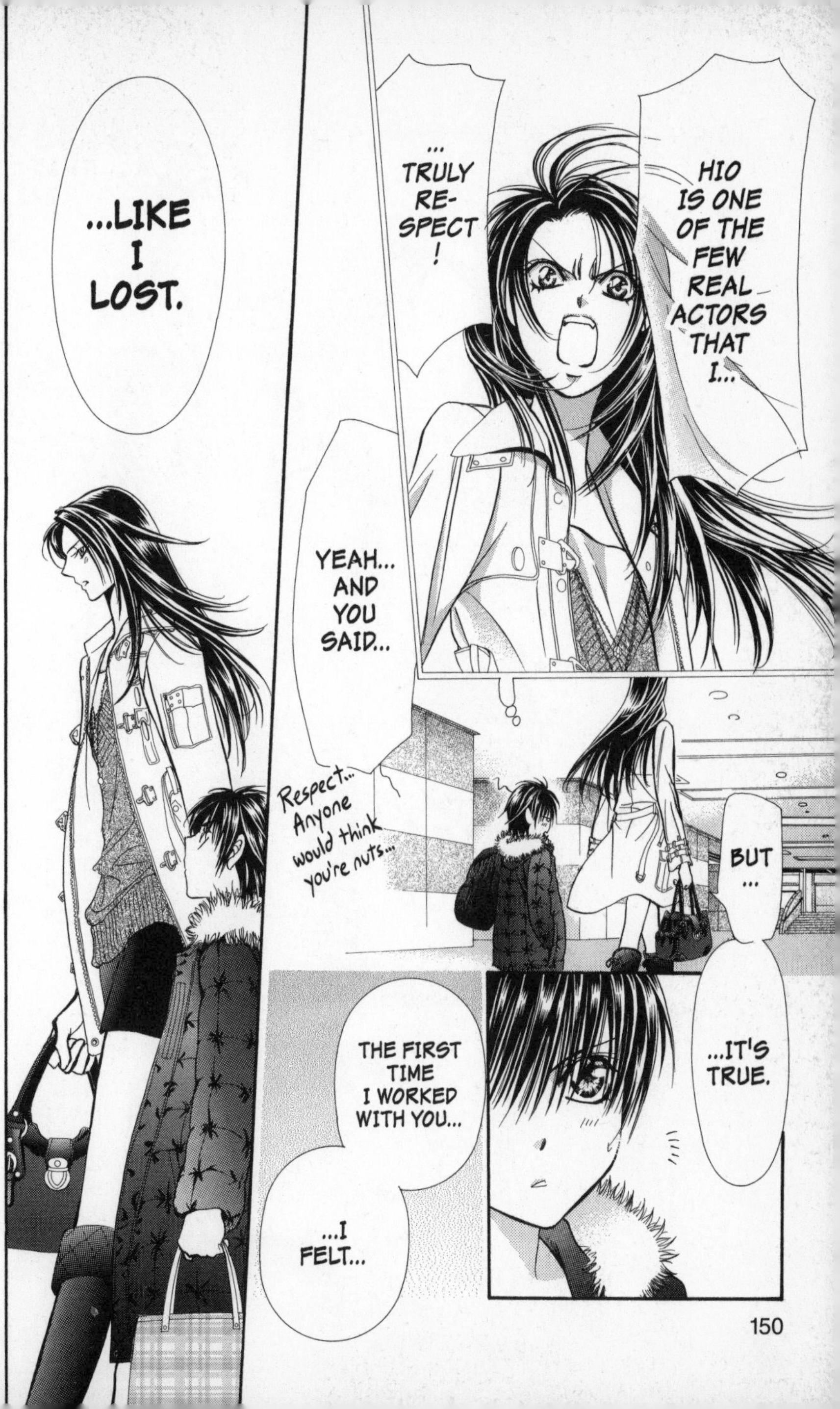
HIO IS ONE OF THE FEW REAL ACTORS THAT I...
...TRULY RE-SPECT!
YEAH... AND YOU SAID...
Respect... Anyone would think you're nuts...
BUT ...
...IT'S TRUE.
THE FIRST TIME I WORKED WITH YOU...
...I FELT...
...LIKE I LOST.

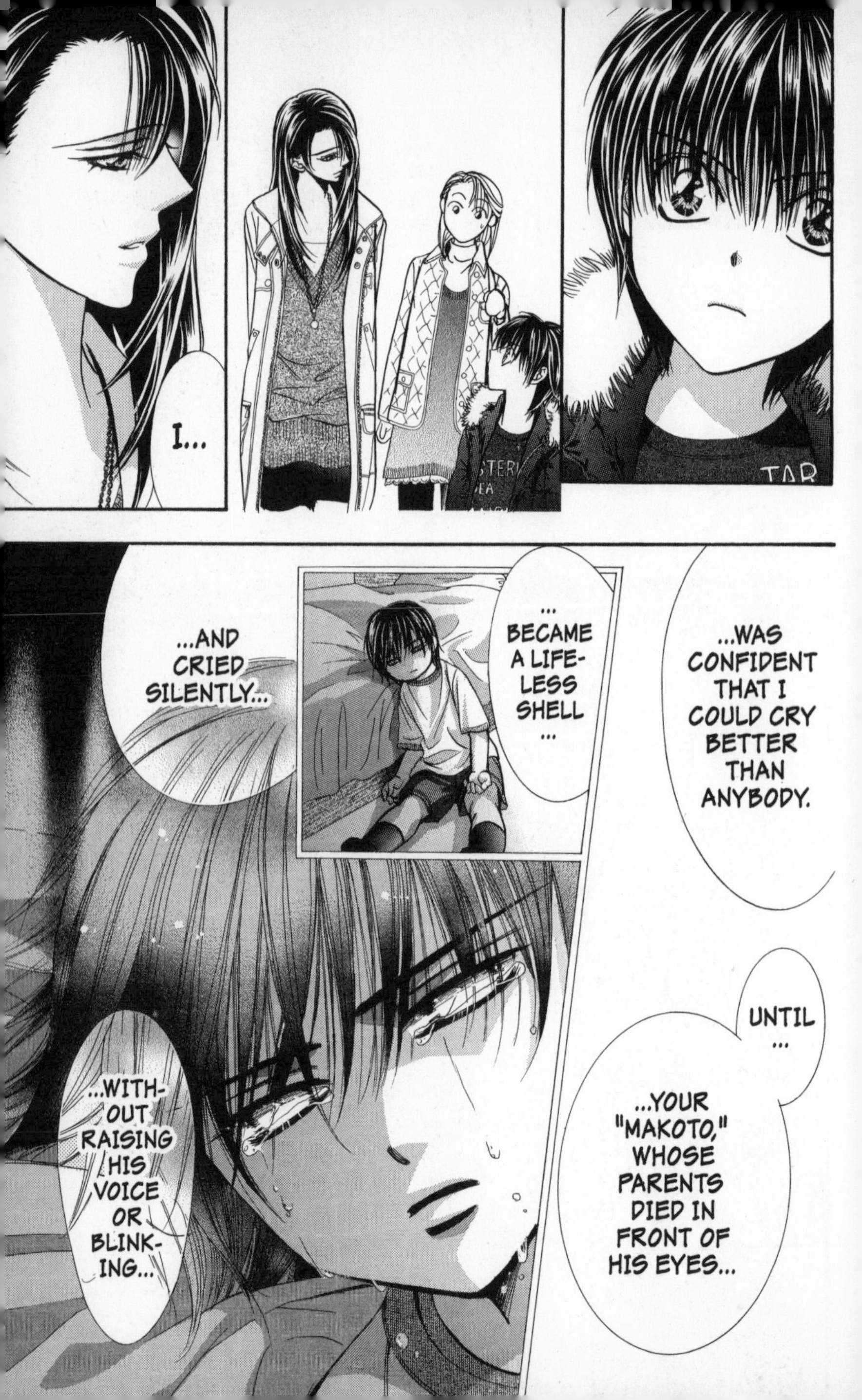
I...
...WAS CONFIDENT THAT I COULD CRY BETTER THAN ANYBODY.
UNTIL...
...YOUR "MAKOTO," WHOSE PARENTS DIED IN FRONT OF HIS EYES...
...BECAME A LIFE-LESS SHELL...
...AND CRIED SILENTLY...
...WITH-OUT RAISING HIS VOICE OR BLINK-ING...

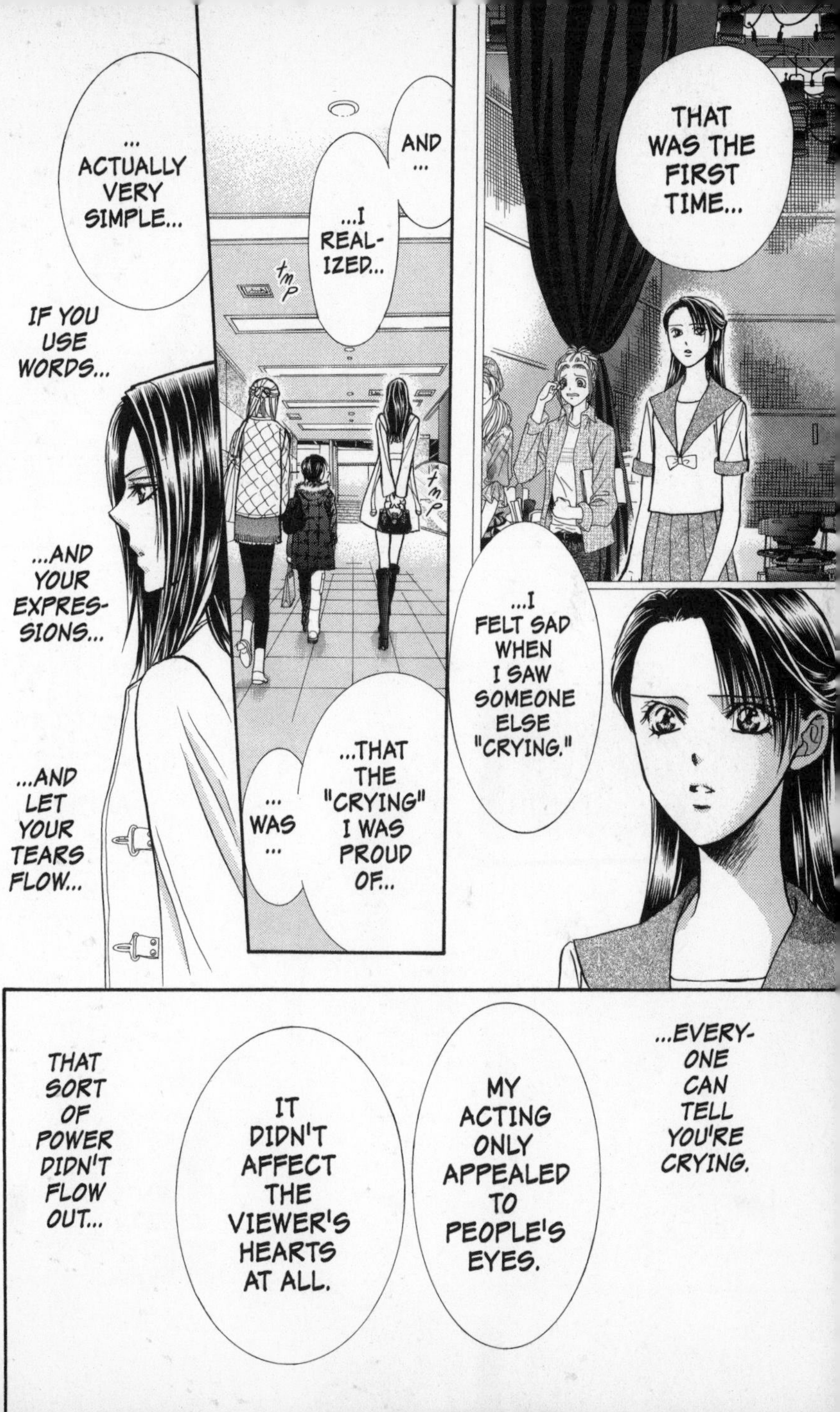
THAT WAS THE FIRST TIME...
...I FELT SAD WHEN I SAW SOMEONE ELSE "CRYING."
AND ...
...I REALIZED...
tmp
tmp
...THAT THE "CRYING" I WAS PROUD OF...
... WAS ...
... ACTUALLY VERY SIMPLE...
IF YOU USE WORDS...
...AND YOUR EXPRESSIONS...
...AND LET YOUR TEARS FLOW...
...EVERYONE CAN TELL YOU'RE CRYING.
MY ACTING ONLY APPEALED TO PEOPLE'S EYES.
IT DIDN'T AFFECT THE VIEWER'S HEARTS AT ALL.
THAT SORT OF POWER DIDN'T FLOW OUT...

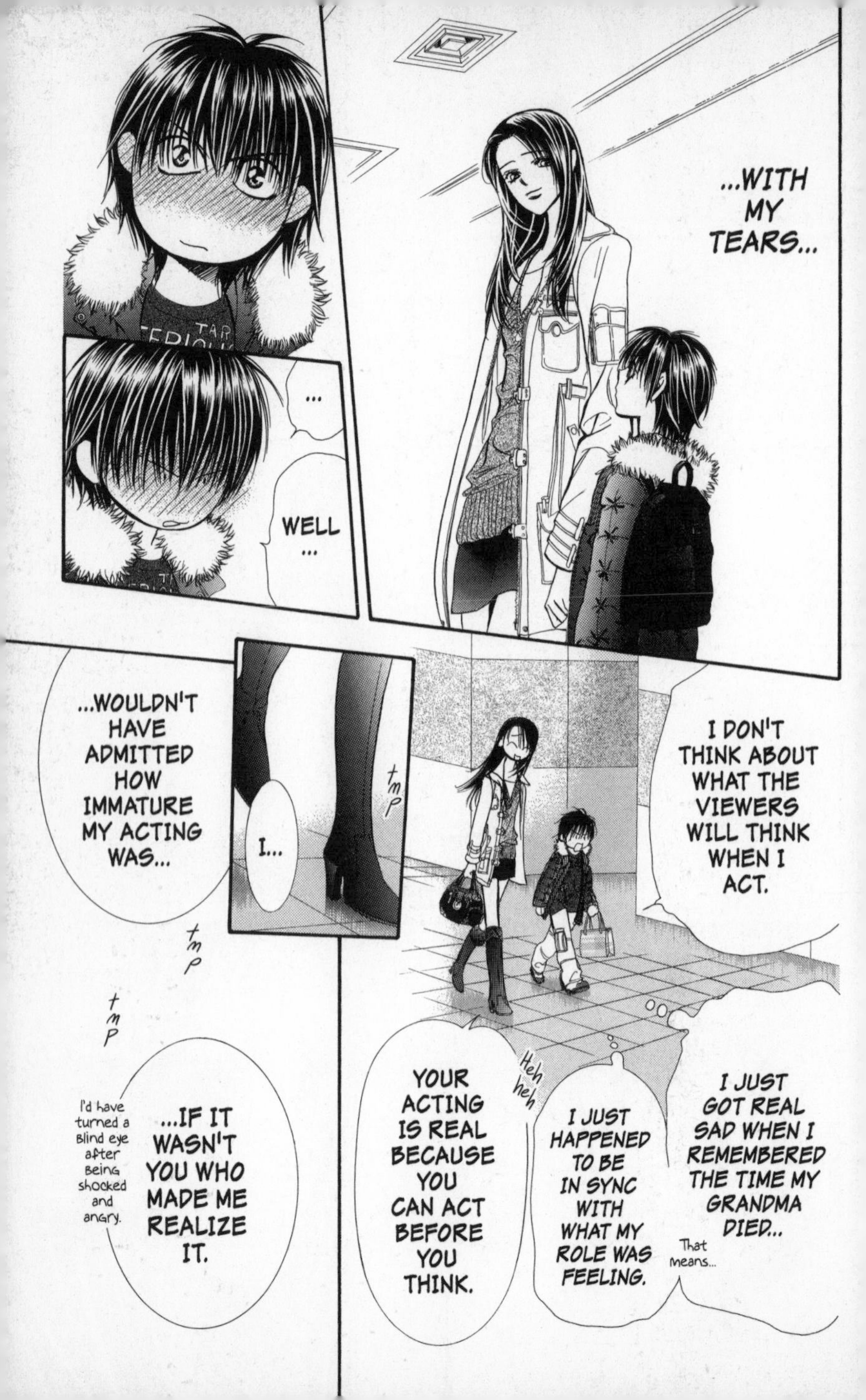
...WITH MY TEARS...
...
WELL ...
I DON'T THINK ABOUT WHAT THE VIEWERS WILL THINK WHEN I ACT.
I JUST GOT REAL SAD WHEN I REMEMBERED THE TIME MY GRANDMA DIED...
That means...
I JUST HAPPENED TO BE IN SYNC WITH WHAT MY ROLE WAS FEELING.
Heh heh
YOUR ACTING IS REAL BECAUSE YOU CAN ACT BEFORE YOU THINK.
tmp
I...
...WOULDN'T HAVE ADMITTED HOW IMMATURE MY ACTING WAS...
tmp
tmp
...IF IT WASN'T YOU WHO MADE ME REALIZE IT.
I'd have turned a blind eye after being shocked and angry.

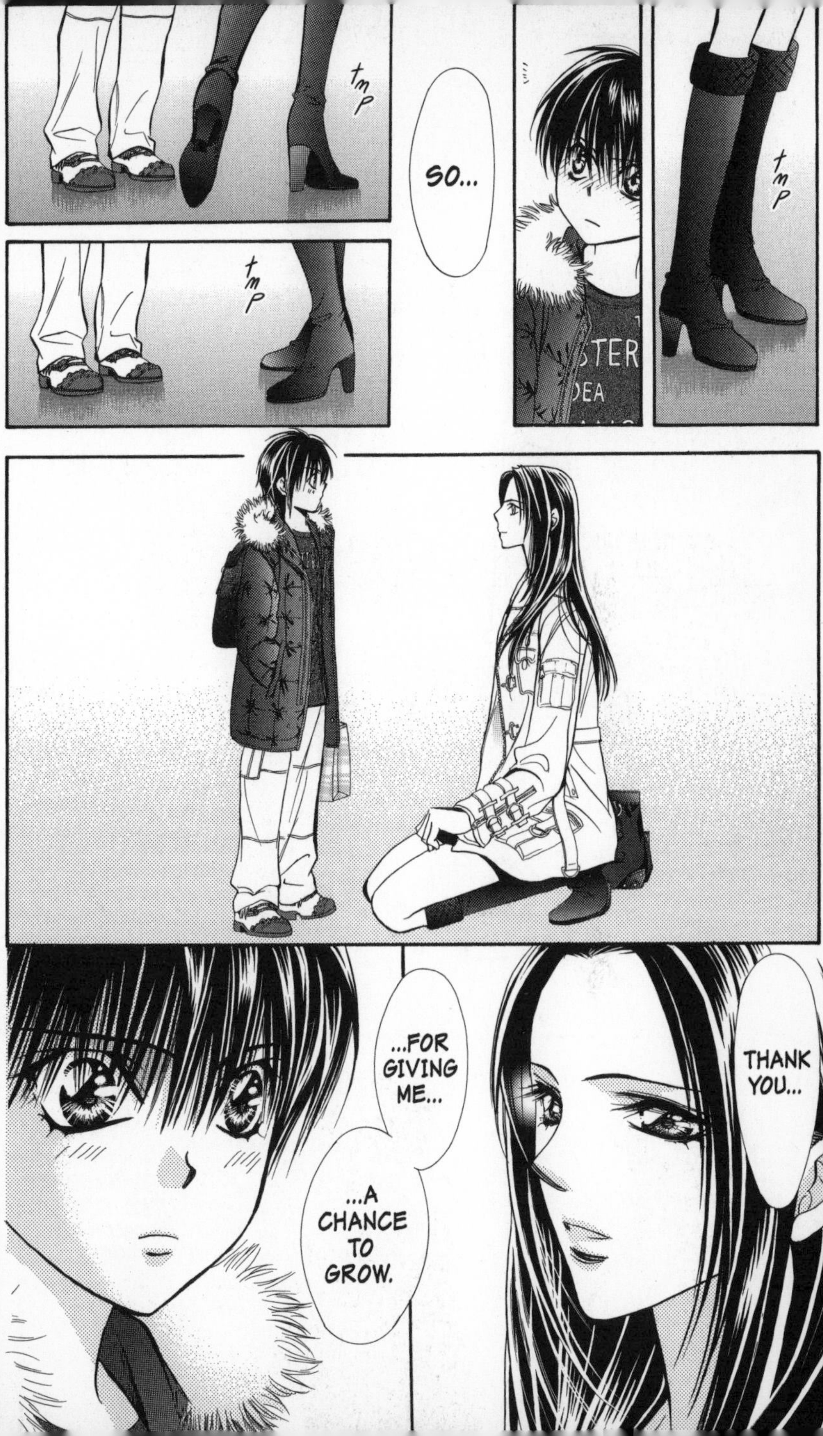
tmp
SO...
tmp
tmp
THANK YOU...
...FOR GIVING ME...
...A CHANCE TO GROW.

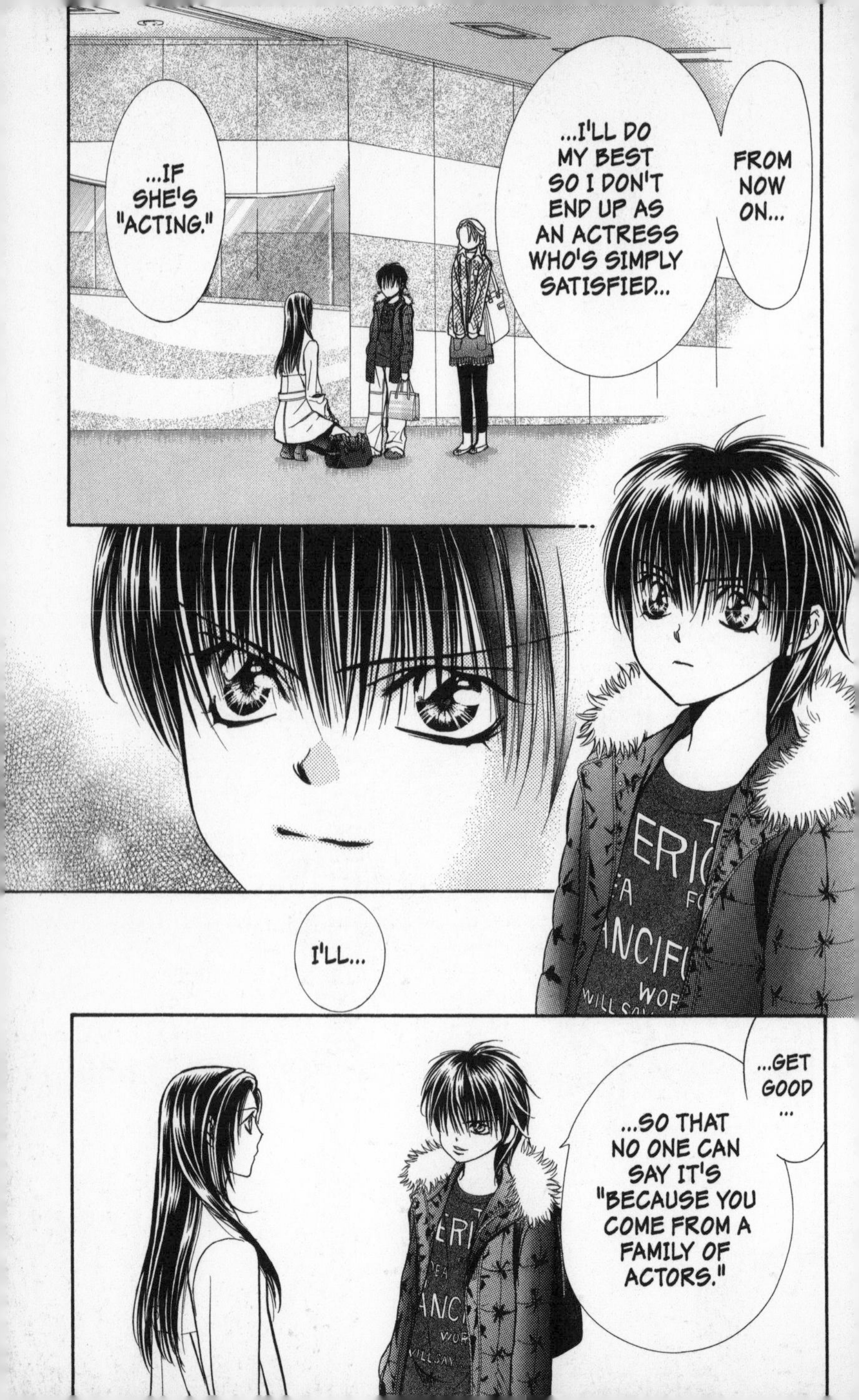
FROM NOW ON...
...I'LL DO MY BEST SO I DON'T END UP AS AN ACTRESS WHO'S SIMPLY SATISFIED...
...IF SHE'S "ACTING."
I'LL...
...GET GOOD ...
...SO THAT NO ONE CAN SAY IT'S "BECAUSE YOU COME FROM A FAMILY OF ACTORS."

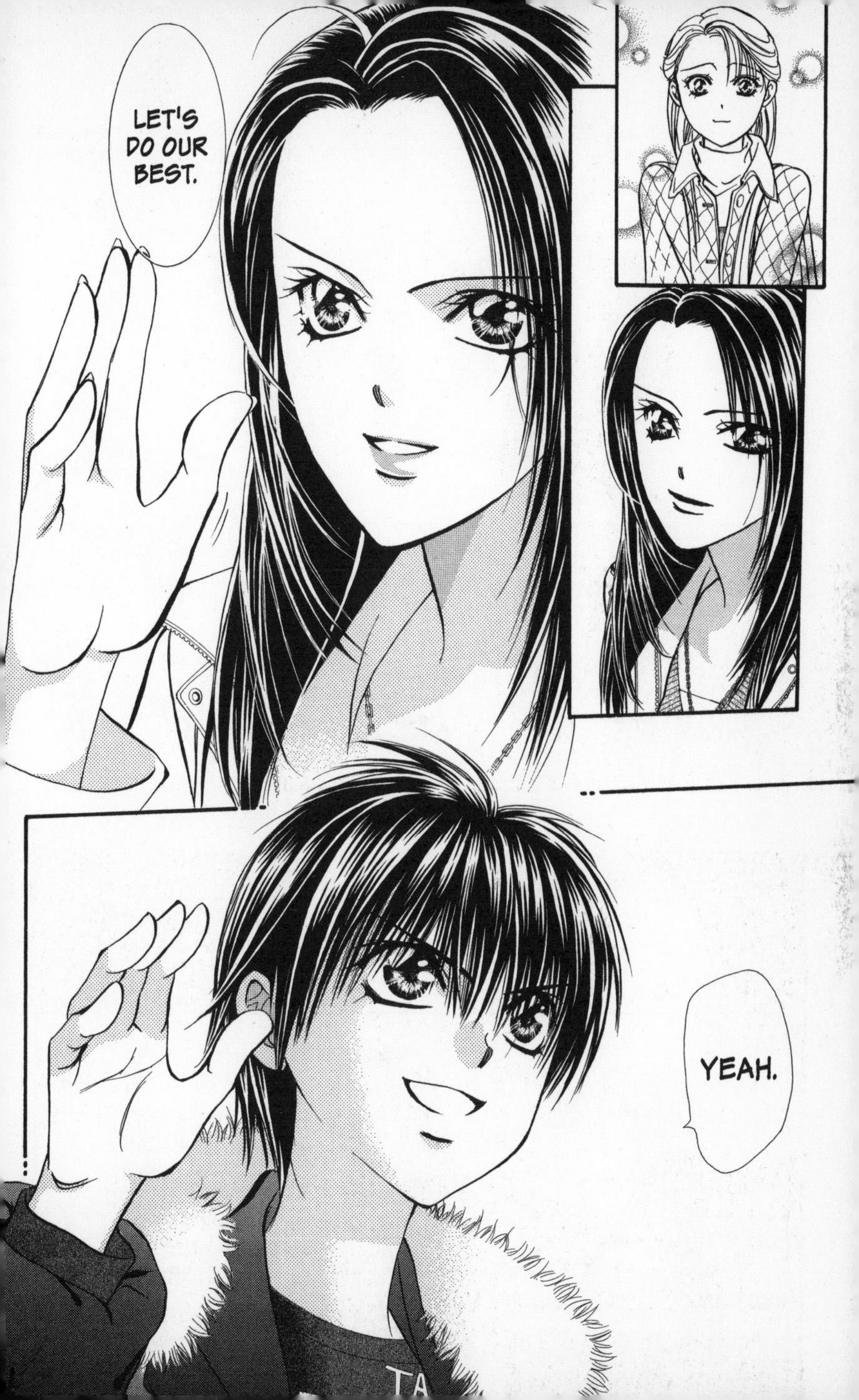
LET'S DO OUR BEST.
YEAH.

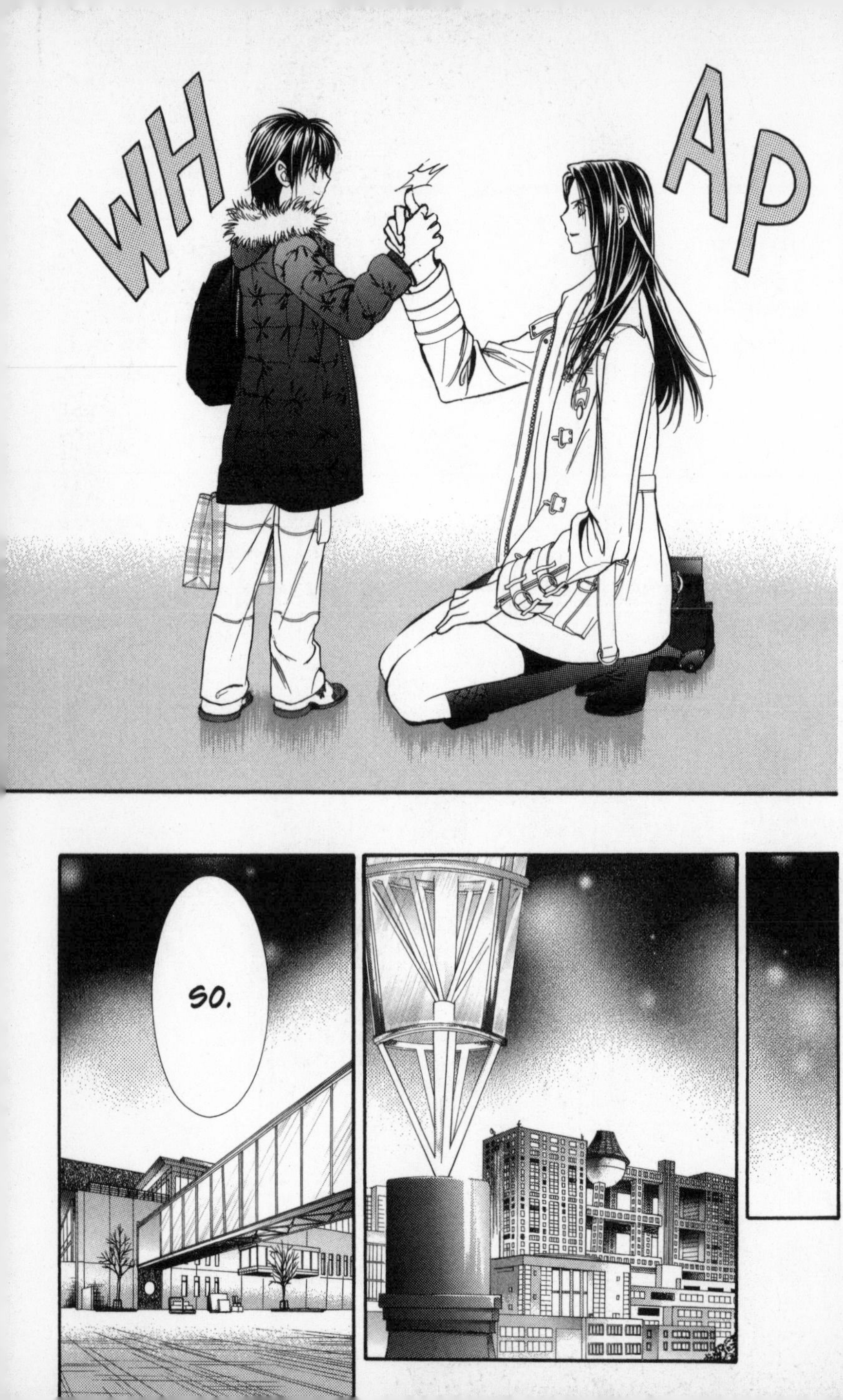
WHAP
SO.

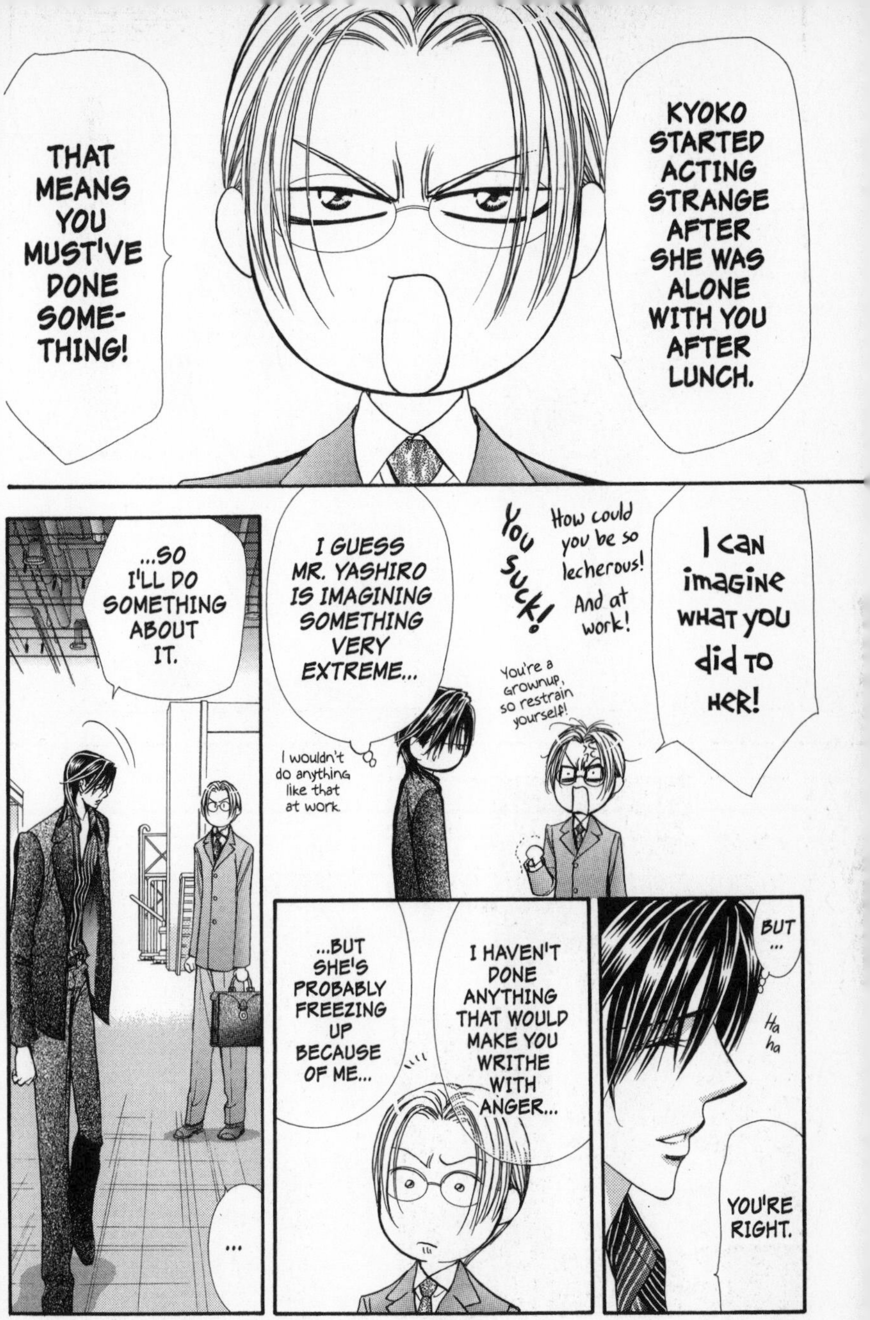
KYOKO STARTED ACTING STRANGE AFTER SHE WAS ALONE WITH YOU AFTER LUNCH.
THAT MEANS YOU MUST'VE DONE SOME-THING!
I can imagine what you did to her!
How could you be so lecherous! And at work!
You suck!
You're a grownup, so restrain yourself!
I GUESS MR. YASHIRO IS IMAGINING SOMETHING VERY EXTREME...
I wouldn't do anything like that at work.
BUT ...
Ha ha
YOU'RE RIGHT.
I HAVEN'T DONE ANYTHING THAT WOULD MAKE YOU WRITHE WITH ANGER...
...BUT SHE'S PROBABLY FREEZING UP BECAUSE OF ME...
...SO I'LL DO SOMETHING ABOUT IT.
...

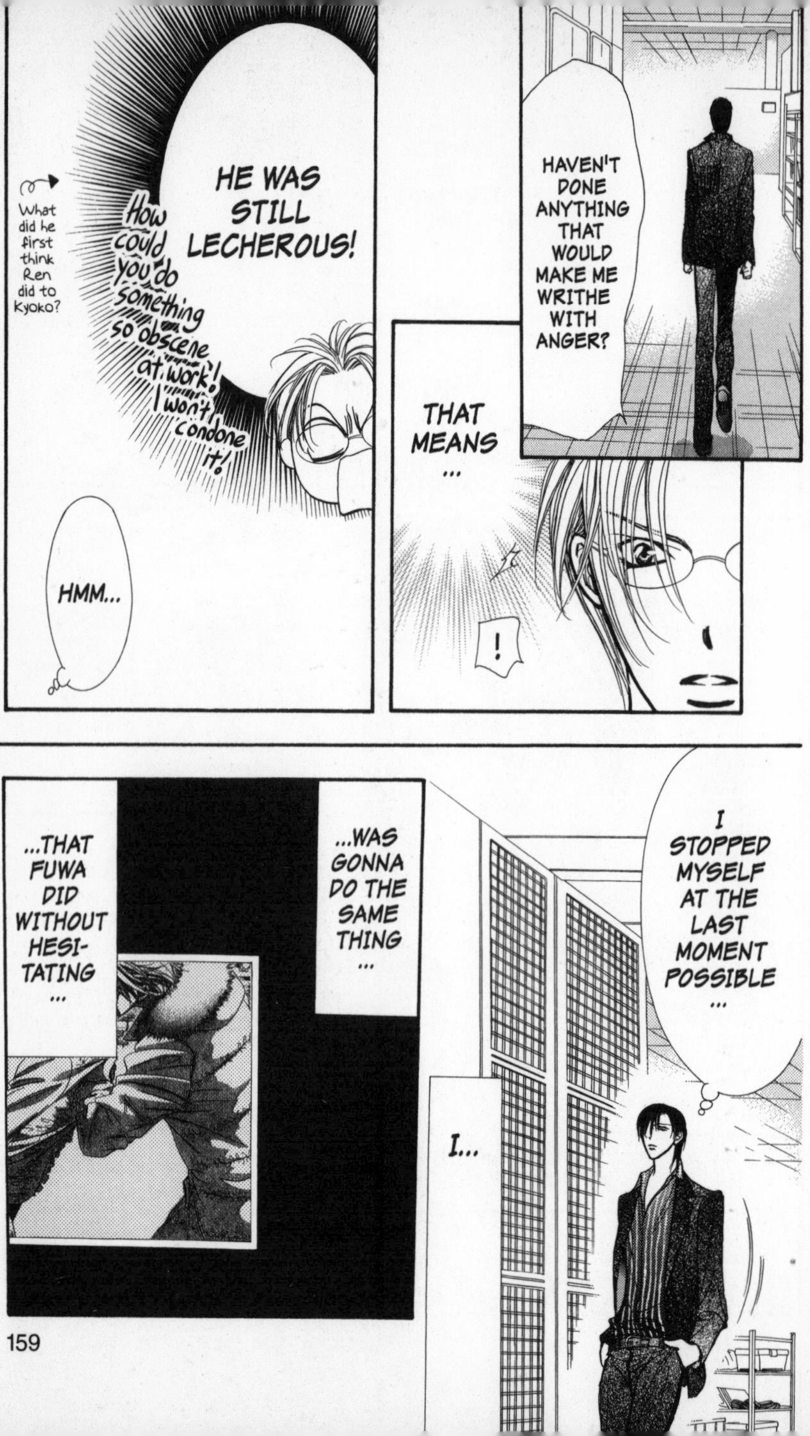
HAVEN'T DONE ANYTHING THAT WOULD MAKE ME WRITHE WITH ANGER?
THAT MEANS ...
!
HE WAS STILL LECHEROUS!
How could you do something so obscene at work! I won't condone it!
What did he first think Ren did to Kyoko?
HMM...
I STOPPED MYSELF AT THE LAST MOMENT POSSIBLE ...
I...
...WAS GONNA DO THE SAME THING ...
...THAT FUWA DID WITHOUT HESI-TATING ...

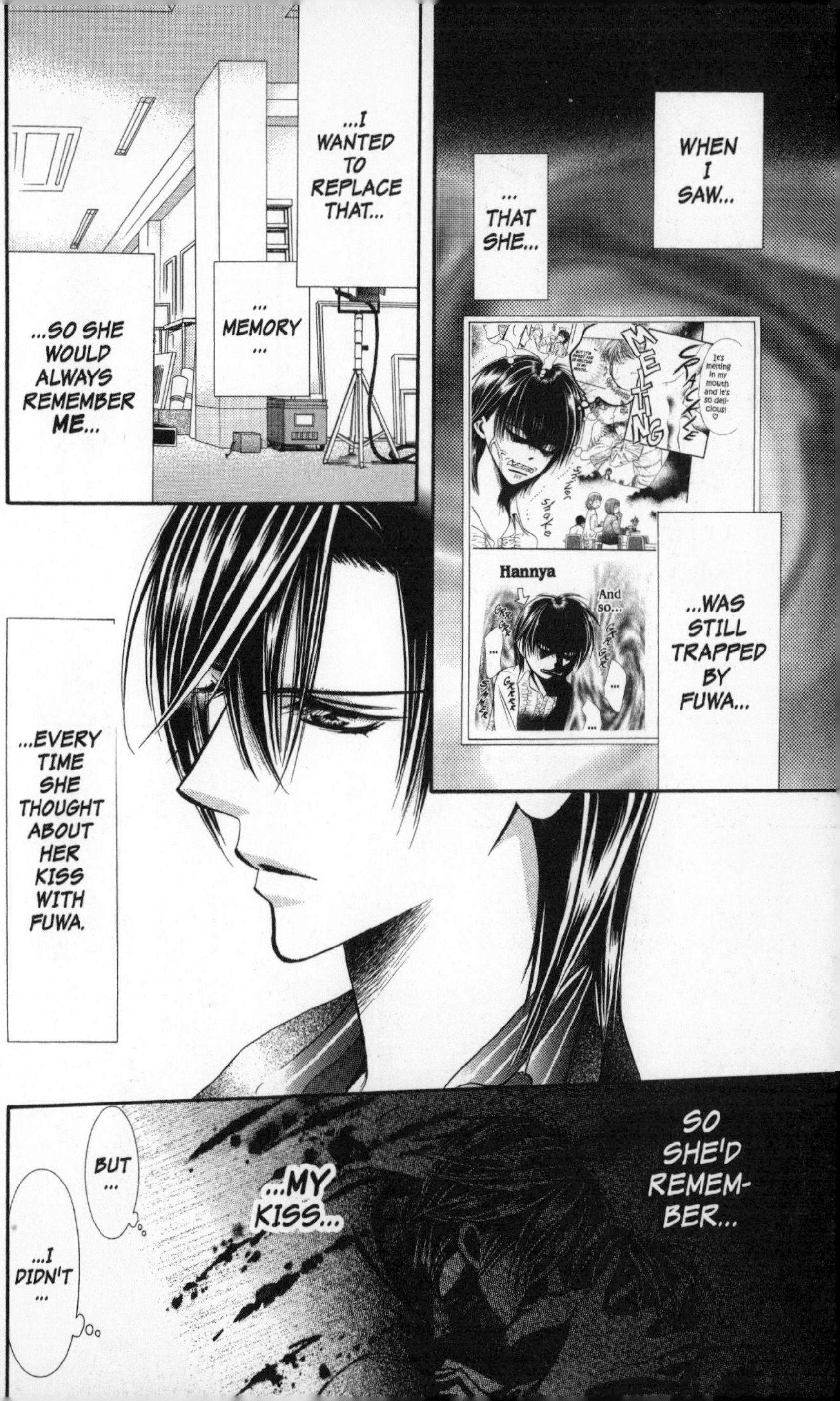
WHEN I SAW...
... THAT SHE...
MELTING
CRACKLE
It's melting in my mouth and it's so delicious! ♡
Shiver
Shake
Hannya
And so...
...WAS STILL TRAPPED BY FUWA...
...I WANTED TO REPLACE THAT...
... MEMORY ...
...SO SHE WOULD ALWAYS REMEMBER ME...
...EVERY TIME SHE THOUGHT ABOUT HER KISS WITH FUWA.
SO SHE'D REMEMBER...
...MY KISS...
BUT ...
...I DIDN'T ...

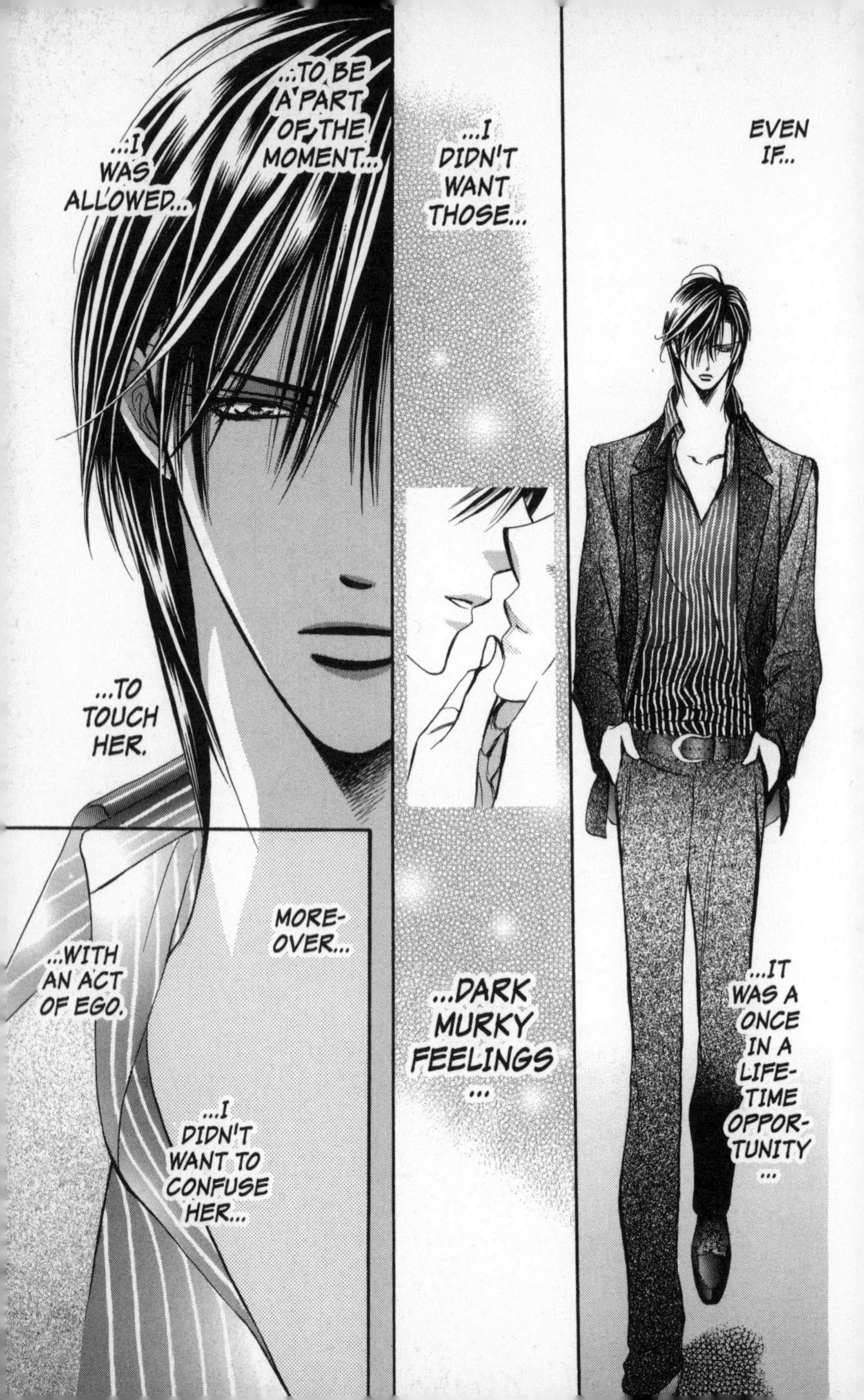
EVEN IF...
...IT WAS A ONCE IN A LIFE-TIME OPPOR-TUNITY...
...I DIDN'T WANT THOSE...
...DARK MURKY FEELINGS...
...TO BE A PART OF THE MOMENT...
...I WAS ALLOWED...
...TO TOUCH HER.
MORE-OVER...
...WITH AN ACT OF EGO.
...I DIDN'T WANT TO CONFUSE HER...

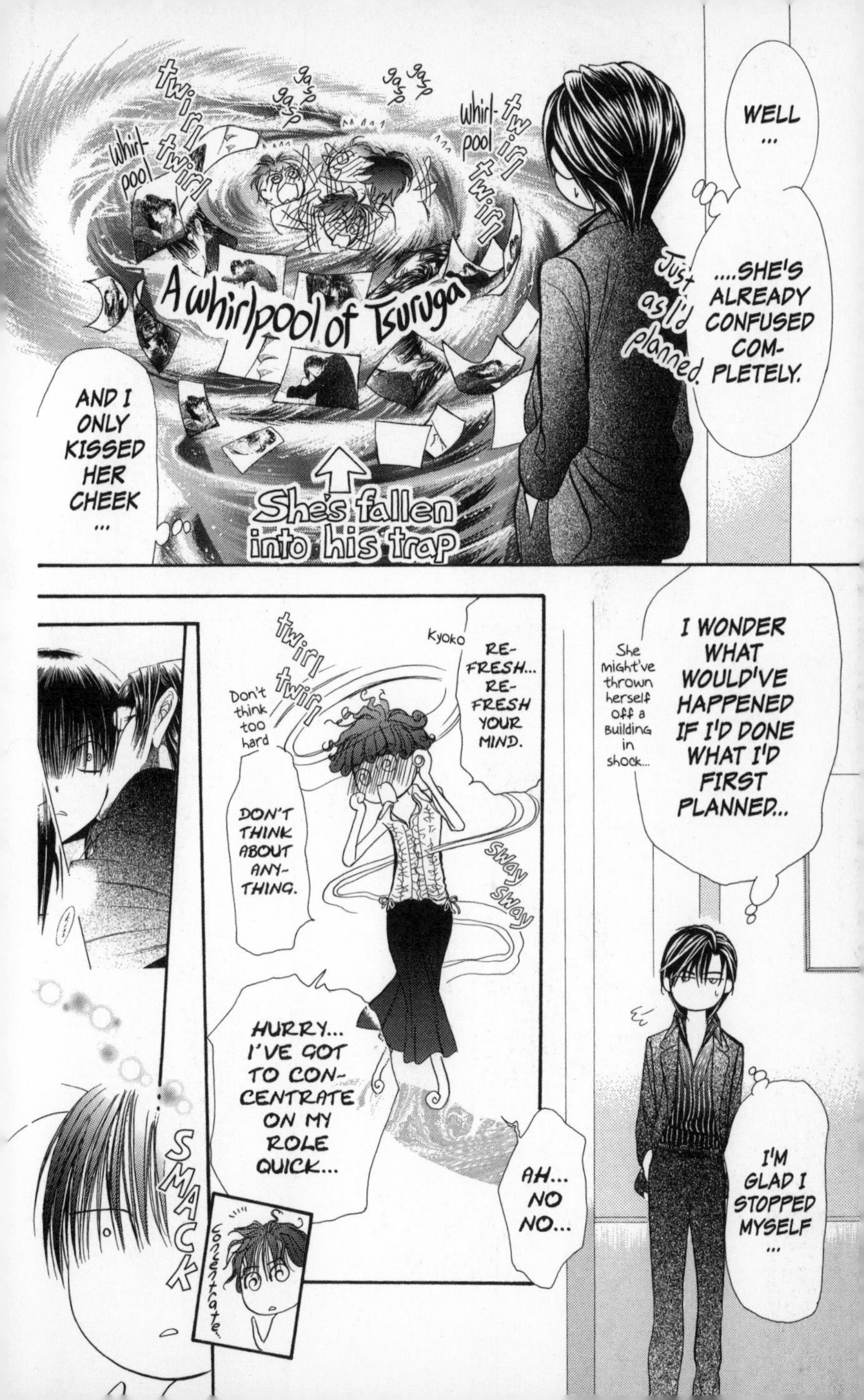
WELL ...
....SHE'S ALREADY CONFUSED COMPLETELY.
Just as I'd planned.
whirlpool
twirl twirl
gasp gasp
gasp
whirlpool
twirl twirl
A whirlpool of Tsuruga
She's fallen into his trap
AND I ONLY KISSED HER CHEEK ...
I WONDER WHAT WOULD'VE HAPPENED IF I'D DONE WHAT I'D FIRST PLANNED..
She might've thrown herself off a building in shock...
I'M GLAD I STOPPED MYSELF ...
Kyoko
REFRESH... REFRESH YOUR MIND.
twirl twirl
Don't think too hard
DON'T THINK ABOUT ANYTHING.
sway sway
HURRY... I'VE GOT TO CONCENTRATE ON MY ROLE QUICK...
AH... NO NO...
SMACK
Concentrate...

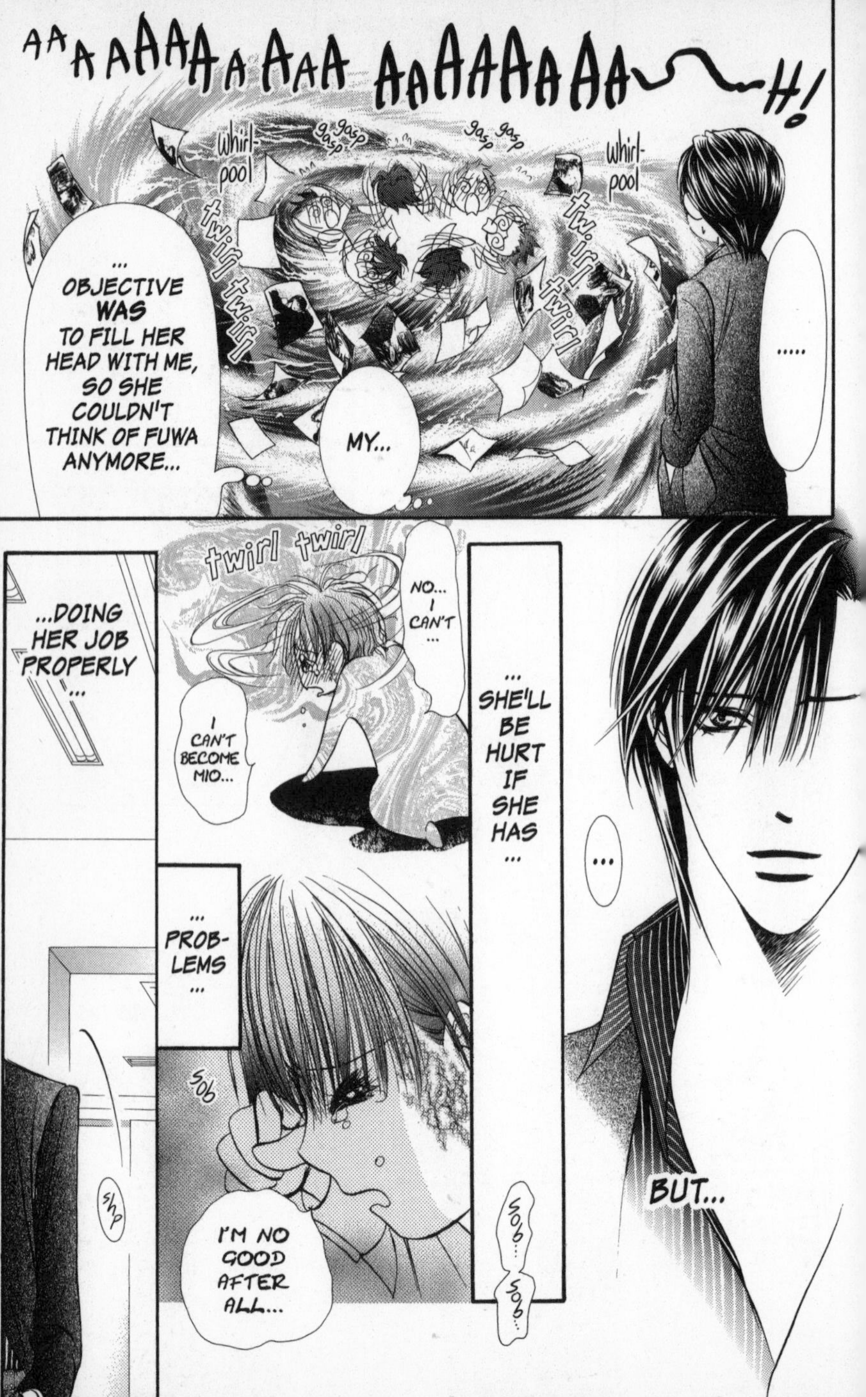
AAAAAAAAAAAAAAAAAAAAA~~H!
.....
whirl-pool
gasp gasp
gasp gasp
twirl twirl
twirl twirl
whirl-pool
MY...
... OBJECTIVE WAS TO FILL HER HEAD WITH ME, SO SHE COULDN'T THINK OF FUWA ANYMORE...
...
BUT...
... SHE'LL BE HURT IF SHE HAS ...
twirl twirl
NO... I CAN'T ...
I CAN'T BECOME MIO...
... PROB-LEMS ...
sob
I'M NO GOOD AFTER ALL...
sob... sob...
...DOING HER JOB PROPERLY ...
shp

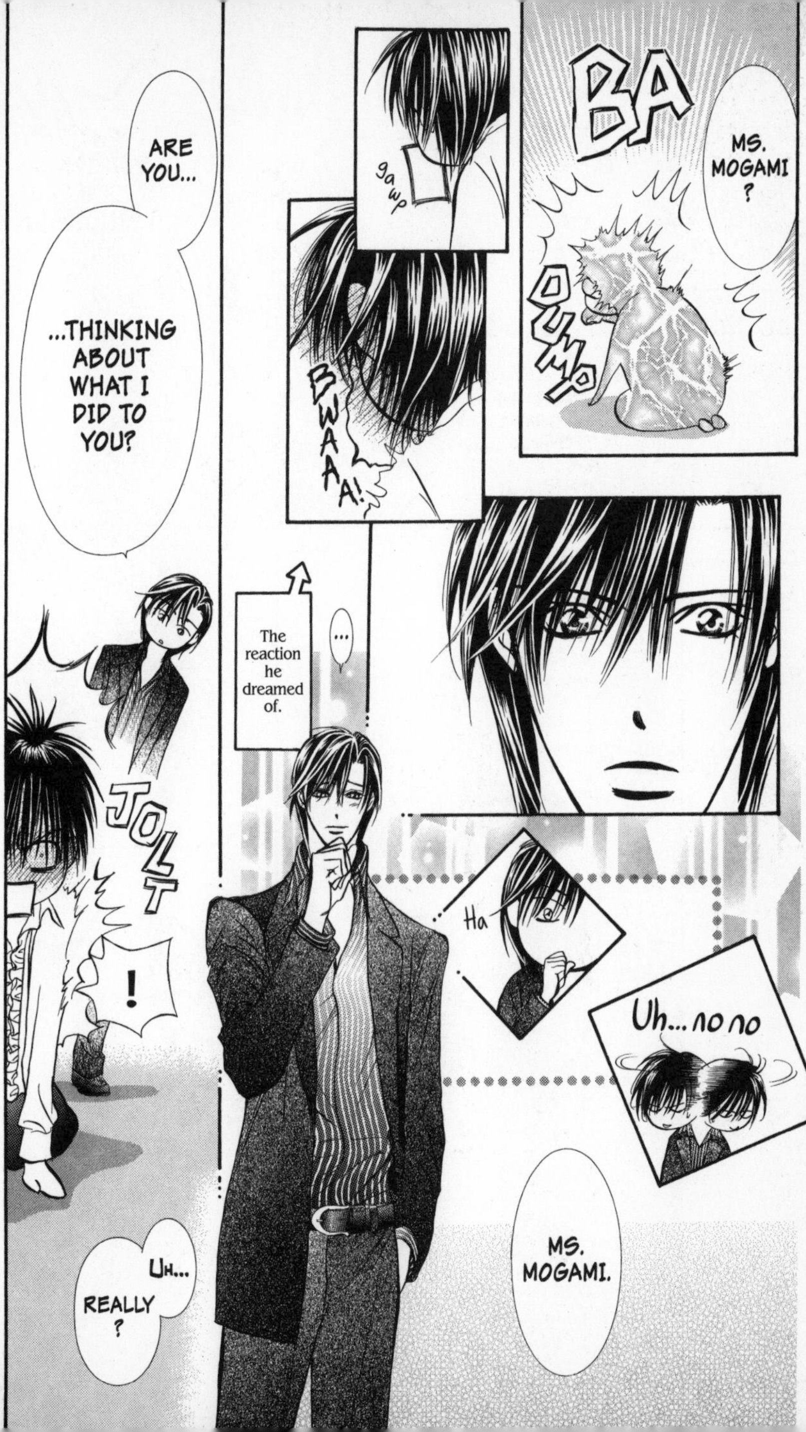
MS. MOGAMI?
BA
DUMP
gawp
BWAAAA!
...
The reaction he dreamed of.
Ha
Uh... no no
MS. MOGAMI.
ARE YOU...
...THINKING ABOUT WHAT I DID TO YOU?
JOLT
!
UH... REALLY?

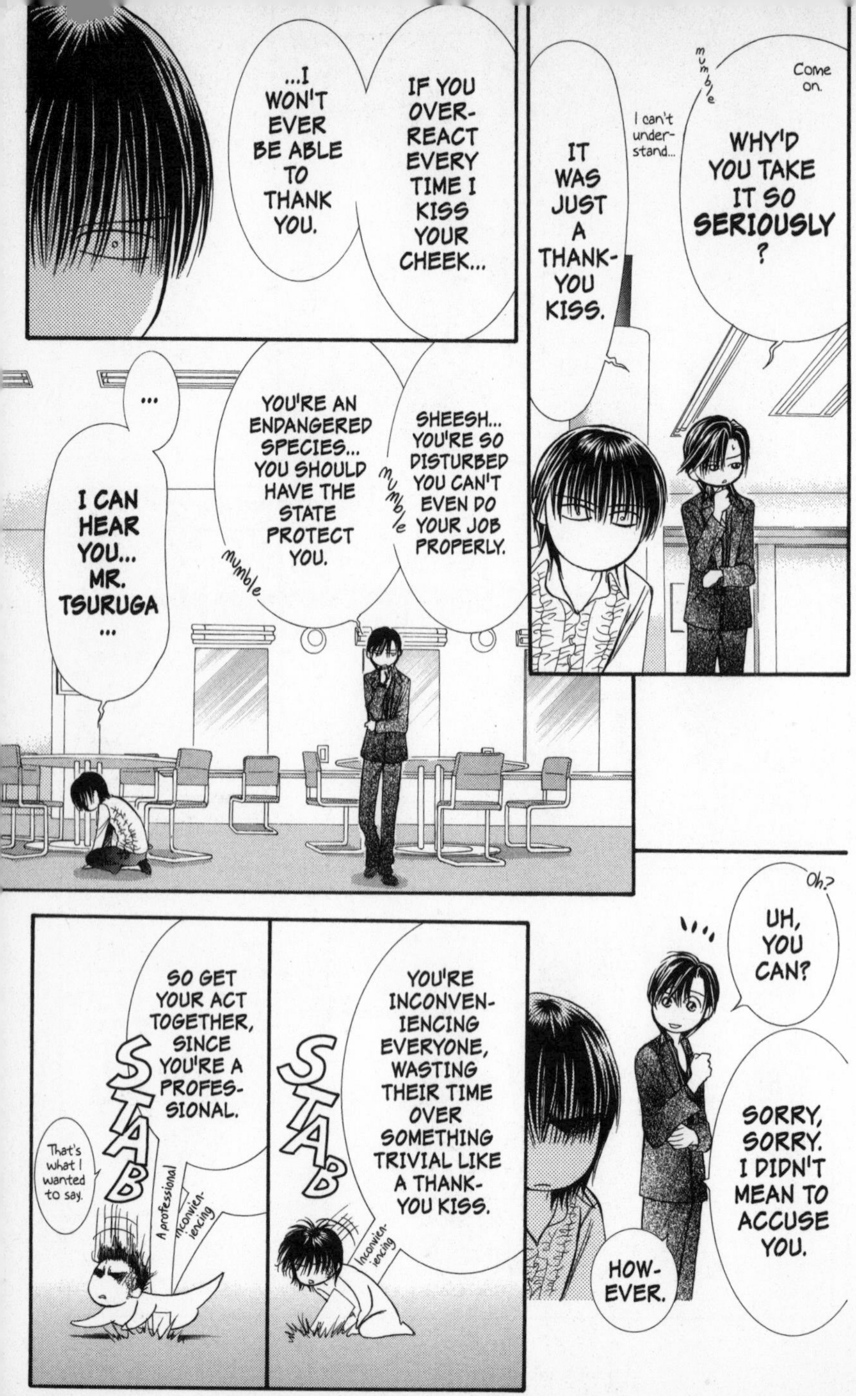
Come on.
mumble
WHY'D YOU TAKE IT SO SERIOUSLY?
I can't understand...
IT WAS JUST A THANK-YOU KISS.
IF YOU OVERREACT EVERY TIME I KISS YOUR CHEEK...
...I WON'T EVER BE ABLE TO THANK YOU.
SHEESH... YOU'RE SO DISTURBED YOU CAN'T EVEN DO YOUR JOB PROPERLY.
mumble
YOU'RE AN ENDANGERED SPECIES... YOU SHOULD HAVE THE STATE PROTECT YOU.
mumble
...
I CAN HEAR YOU... MR. TSURUGA...
Oh?
UH, YOU CAN?
SORRY, SORRY. I DIDN'T MEAN TO ACCUSE YOU.
HOW-EVER.
YOU'RE INCONVENIENCING EVERYONE, WASTING THEIR TIME OVER SOMETHING TRIVIAL LIKE A THANK-YOU KISS.
STAB
Inconvien-iencing
SO GET YOUR ACT TOGETHER, SINCE YOU'RE A PROFESSIONAL.
STAB
A professional
Inconvien-iencing
That's what I wanted to say.

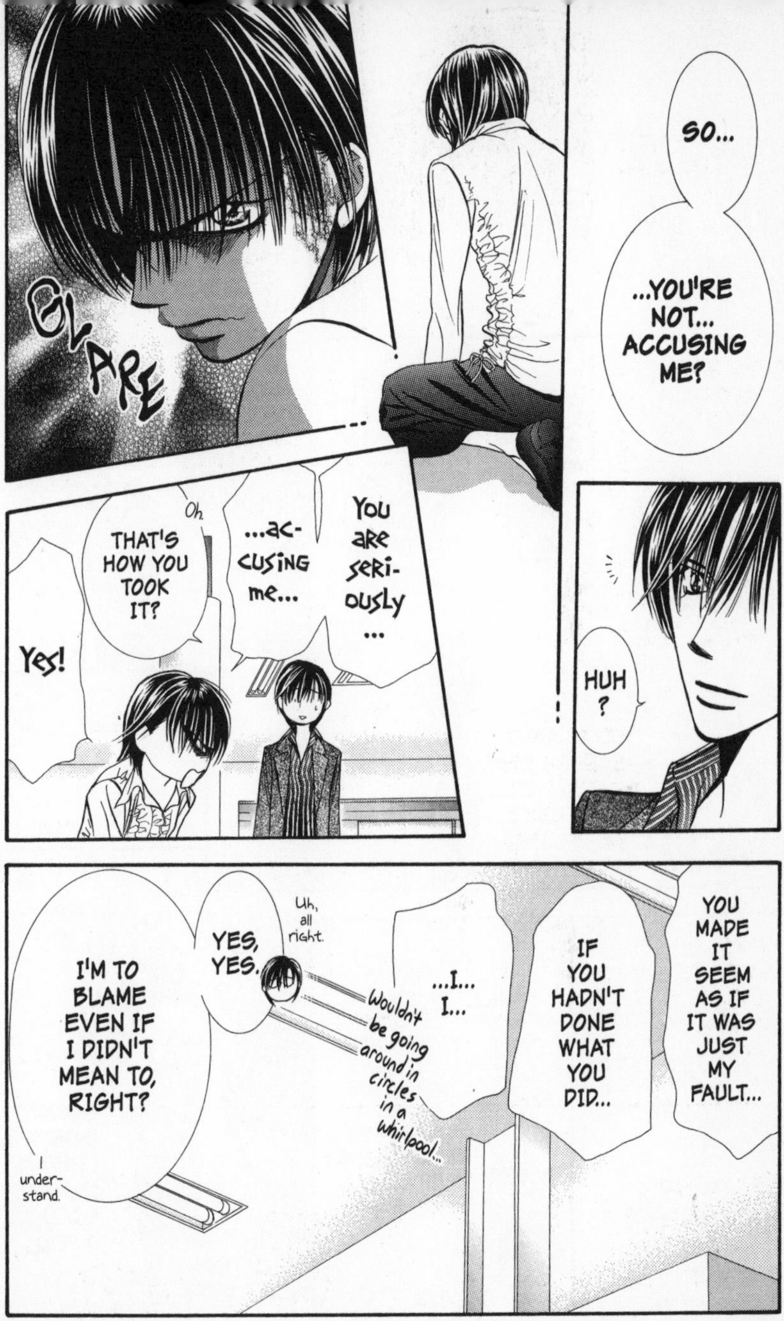
SO...
...YOU'RE NOT... ACCUSING ME?
GLARE
HUH?
You are seriously...
...accusing me...
Oh.
THAT'S HOW YOU TOOK IT?
Yes!
YOU MADE IT SEEM AS IF IT WAS JUST MY FAULT...
IF YOU HADN'T DONE WHAT YOU DID...
...I... I...
Wouldn't be going around in circles in a whirlpool...
Uh, all right.
YES, YES.
I'M TO BLAME EVEN IF I DIDN'T MEAN TO, RIGHT?
I understand.

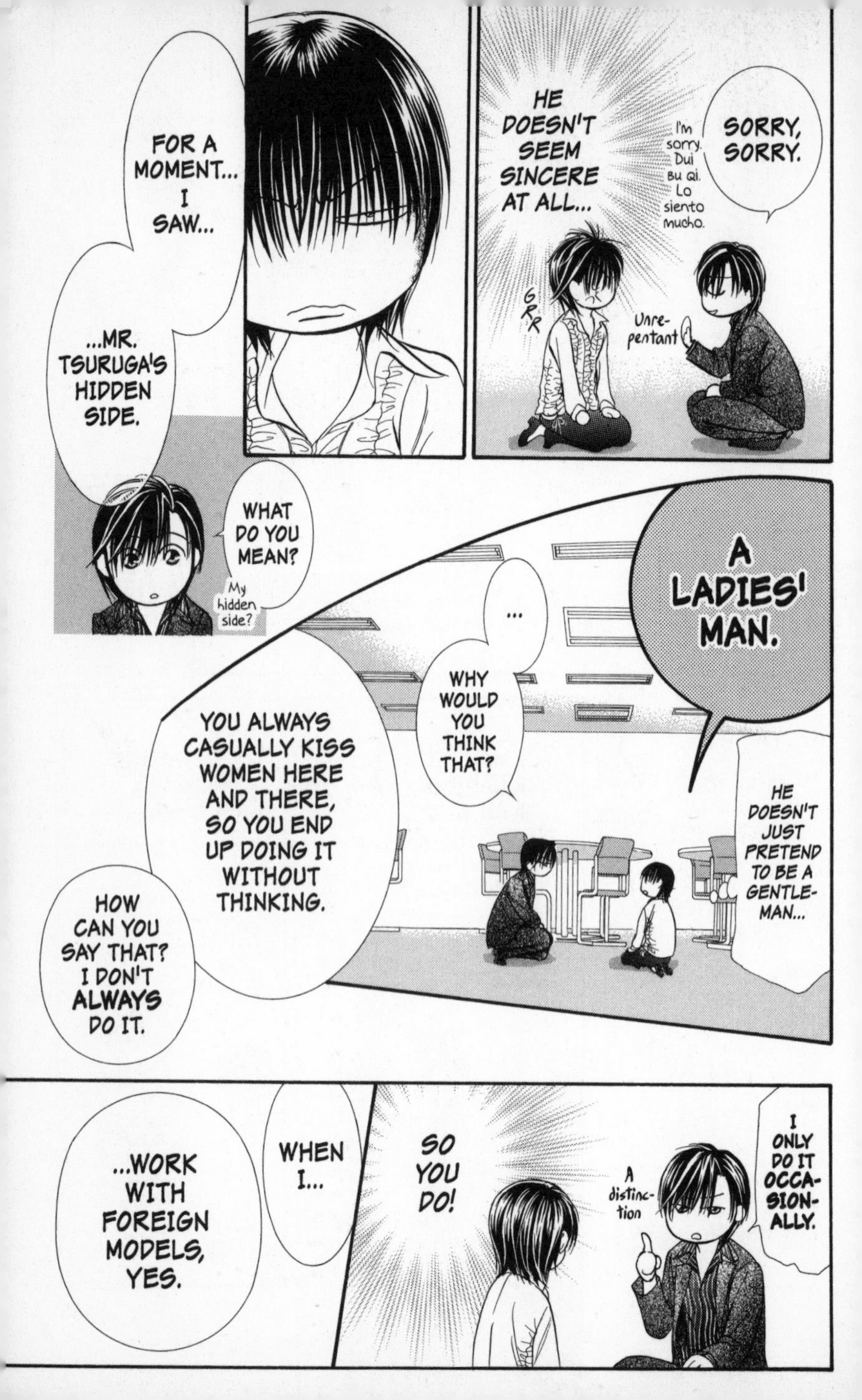
SORRY, SORRY.
I'm sorry. Dui Bu Qi. Lo siento mucho.
HE DOESN'T SEEM SINCERE AT ALL...
GRR
Unre-pentant
FOR A MOMENT... I SAW...
...MR. TSURUGA'S HIDDEN SIDE.
WHAT DO YOU MEAN?
My hidden side?
A LADIES' MAN.
HE DOESN'T JUST PRETEND TO BE A GENTLE-MAN...
...
WHY WOULD YOU THINK THAT?
YOU ALWAYS CASUALLY KISS WOMEN HERE AND THERE, SO YOU END UP DOING IT WITHOUT THINKING.
HOW CAN YOU SAY THAT? I DON'T ALWAYS DO IT.
I ONLY DO IT OCCA-SION-ALLY.
A distinc-tion
SO YOU DO!
WHEN I...
...WORK WITH FOREIGN MODELS, YES.

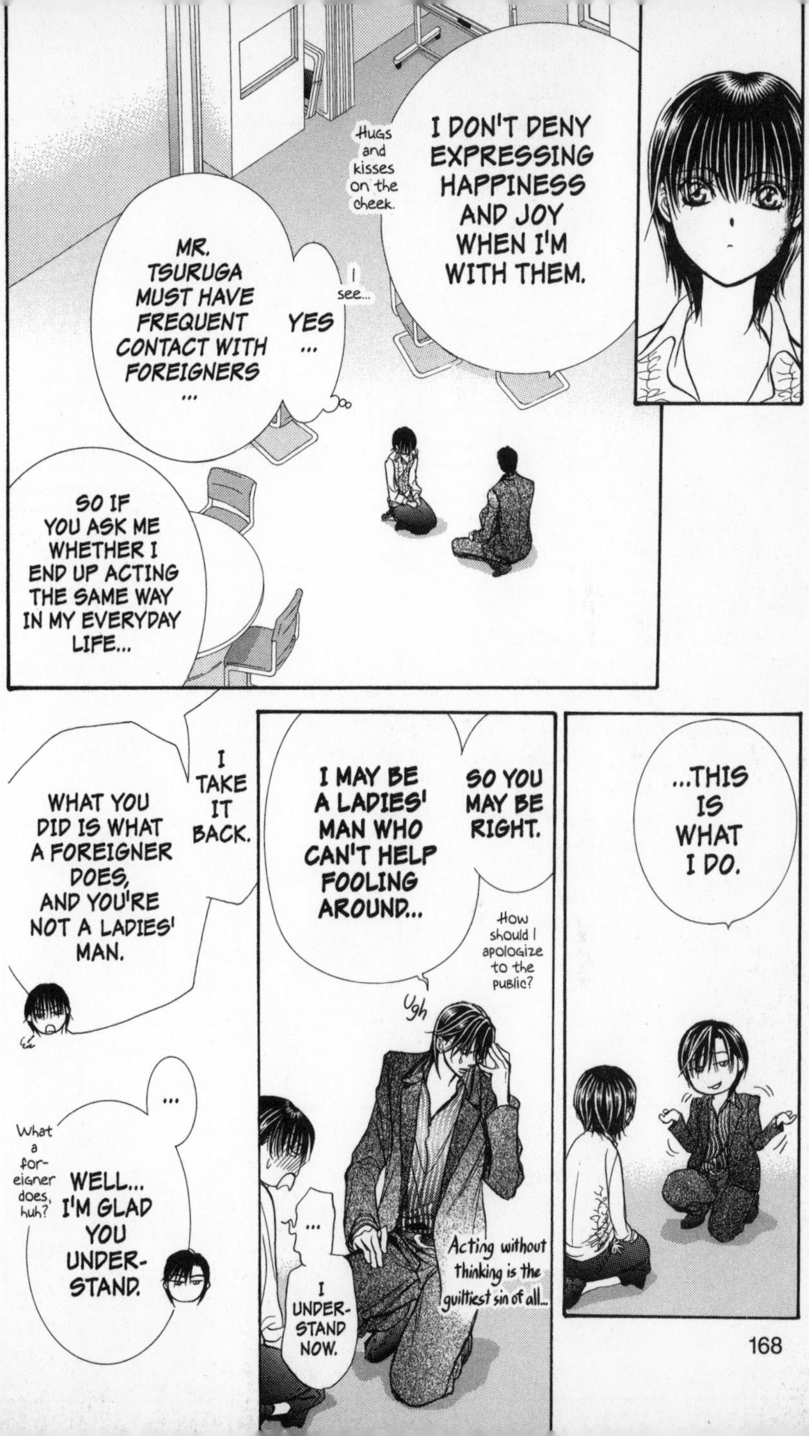

I DON'T DENY EXPRESSING HAPPINESS AND JOY WHEN I'M WITH THEM.
Hugs and kisses on the cheek.
I see...
YES ...
MR. TSURUGA MUST HAVE FREQUENT CONTACT WITH FOREIGNERS ...
SO IF YOU ASK ME WHETHER I END UP ACTING THE SAME WAY IN MY EVERYDAY LIFE...
...THIS IS WHAT I DO.
SO YOU MAY BE RIGHT.
I MAY BE A LADIES' MAN WHO CAN'T HELP FOOLING AROUND...
How should I apologize to the public?
Ugh
Acting without thinking is the guiltiest sin of all...
...
I UNDERSTAND NOW.
I TAKE IT BACK.
WHAT YOU DID IS WHAT A FOREIGNER DOES, AND YOU'RE NOT A LADIES' MAN.
...
What a foreigner does, huh?
WELL... I'M GLAD YOU UNDERSTAND.

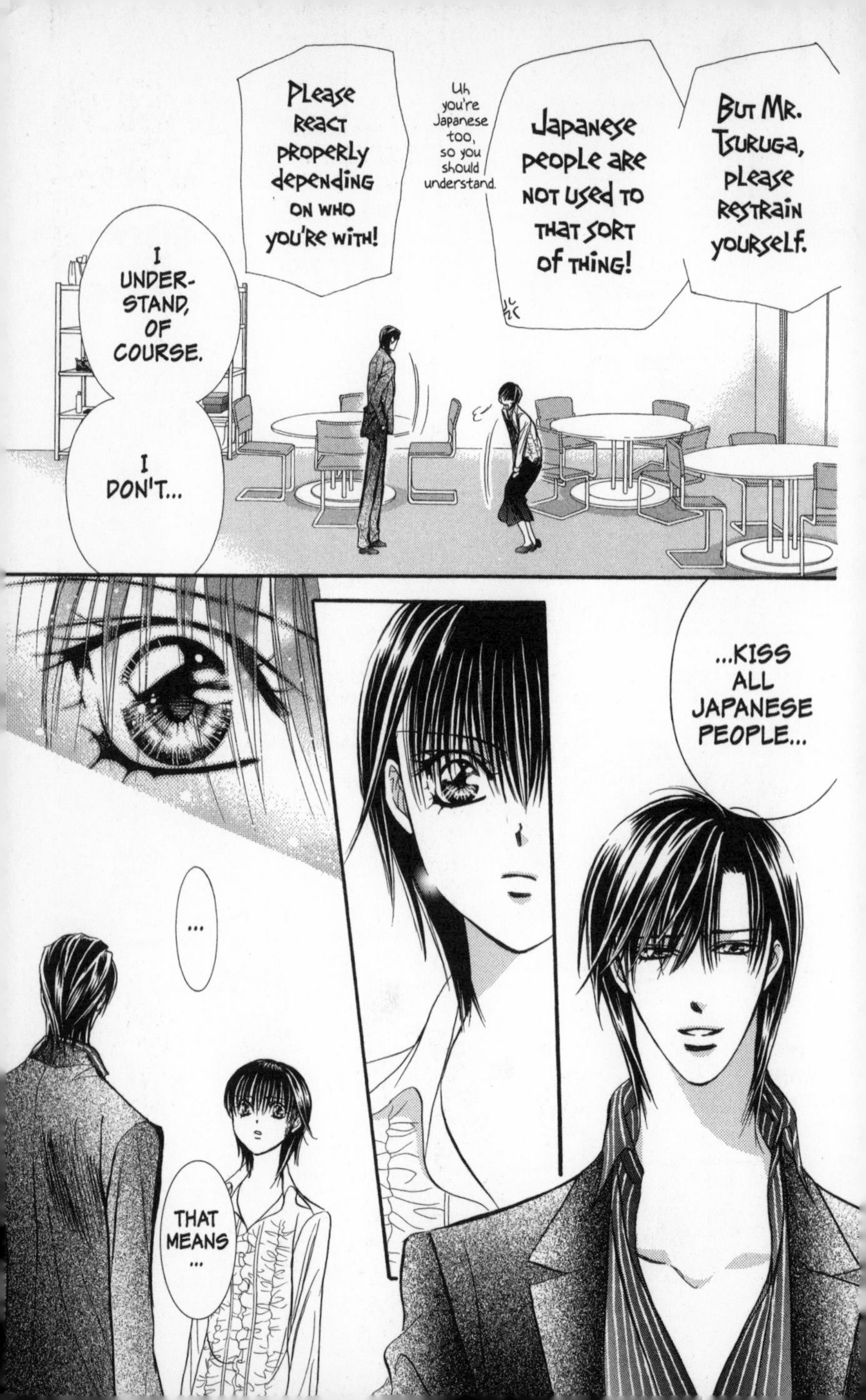
But Mr. Tsuruga, please restrain yourself.
Japanese people are not used to that sort of thing!
Uh you're Japanese too, so you should understand.
Please react properly depending on who you're with!
I understand, of course.
I don't...
...Kiss all Japanese people...
...
That means ...

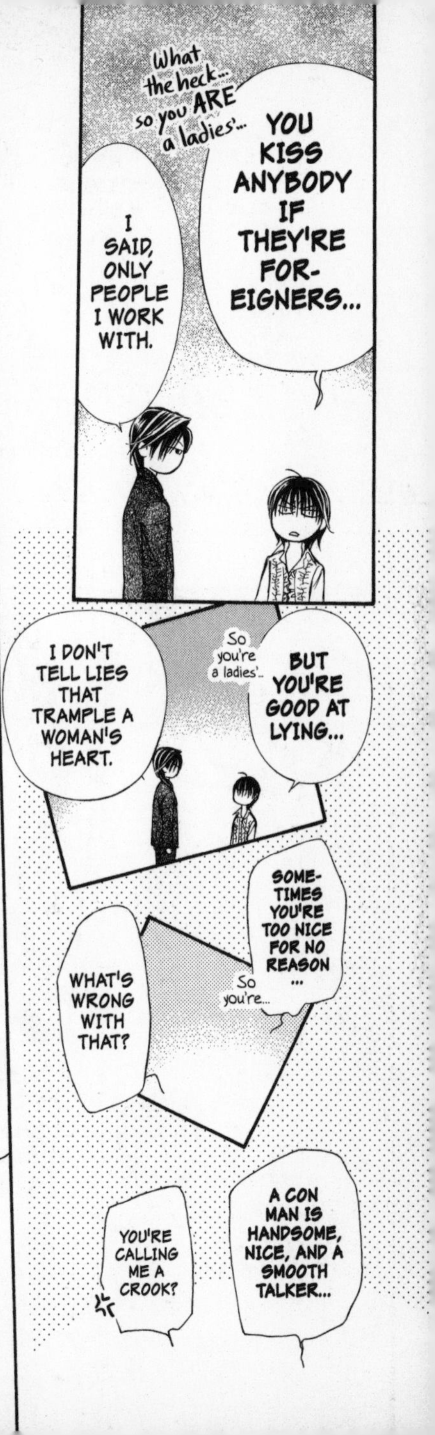
YOU KISS ANYBODY IF THEY'RE FOR-EIGNERS...
What the heck... so you ARE a ladies'...
I SAID, ONLY PEOPLE I WORK WITH.
BUT YOU'RE GOOD AT LYING...
So you're a ladies'...
I DON'T TELL LIES THAT TRAMPLE A WOMAN'S HEART.
SOME-TIMES YOU'RE TOO NICE FOR NO REASON...
So you're...
WHAT'S WRONG WITH THAT?
A CON MAN IS HANDSOME, NICE, AND A SMOOTH TALKER...
YOU'RE CALLING ME A CROOK?
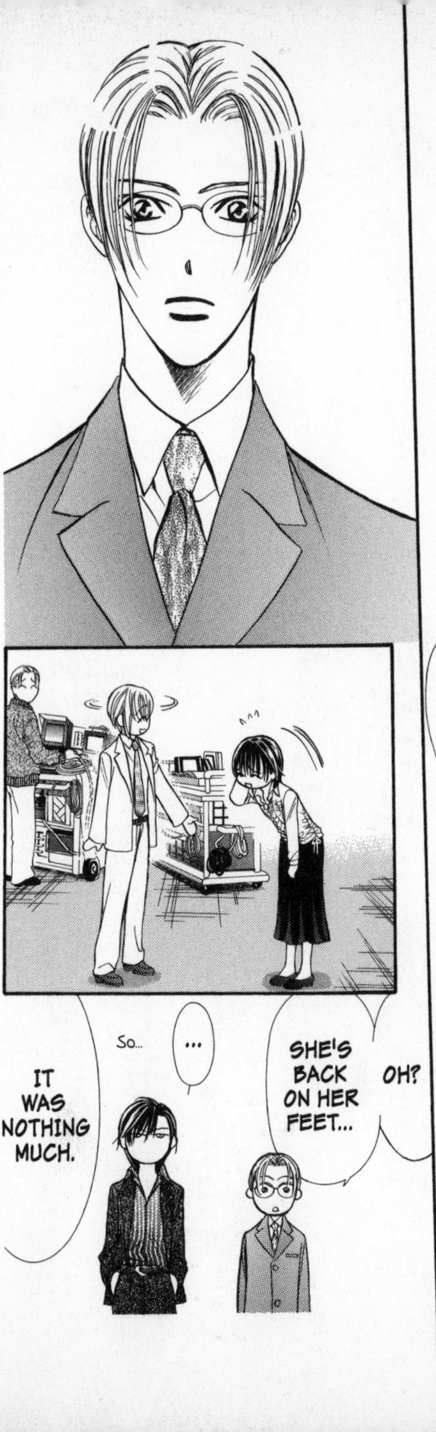
OH?
SHE'S BACK ON HER FEET...
...
So...
IT WAS NOTHING MUCH.

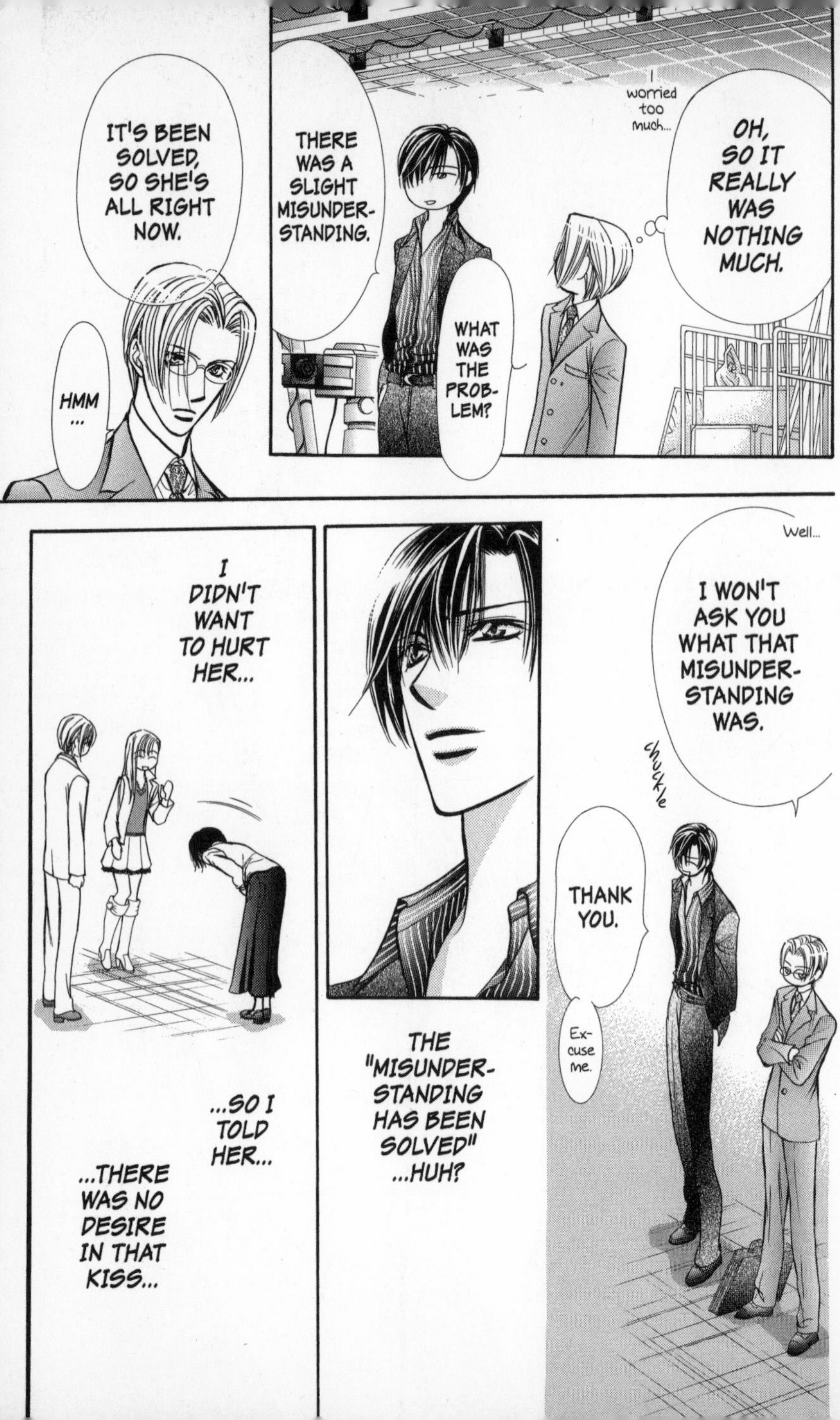
OH, SO IT REALLY WAS NOTHING MUCH.
I worried too much...
THERE WAS A SLIGHT MISUNDERSTANDING.
WHAT WAS THE PROBLEM?
IT'S BEEN SOLVED, SO SHE'S ALL RIGHT NOW.
HMM...
Well...
I WON'T ASK YOU WHAT THAT MISUNDERSTANDING WAS.
chuckle
THANK YOU.
Ex-cuse me.
THE "MISUNDERSTANDING HAS BEEN SOLVED" ...HUH?
I DIDN'T WANT TO HURT HER...
...SO I TOLD HER...
...THERE WAS NO DESIRE IN THAT KISS...

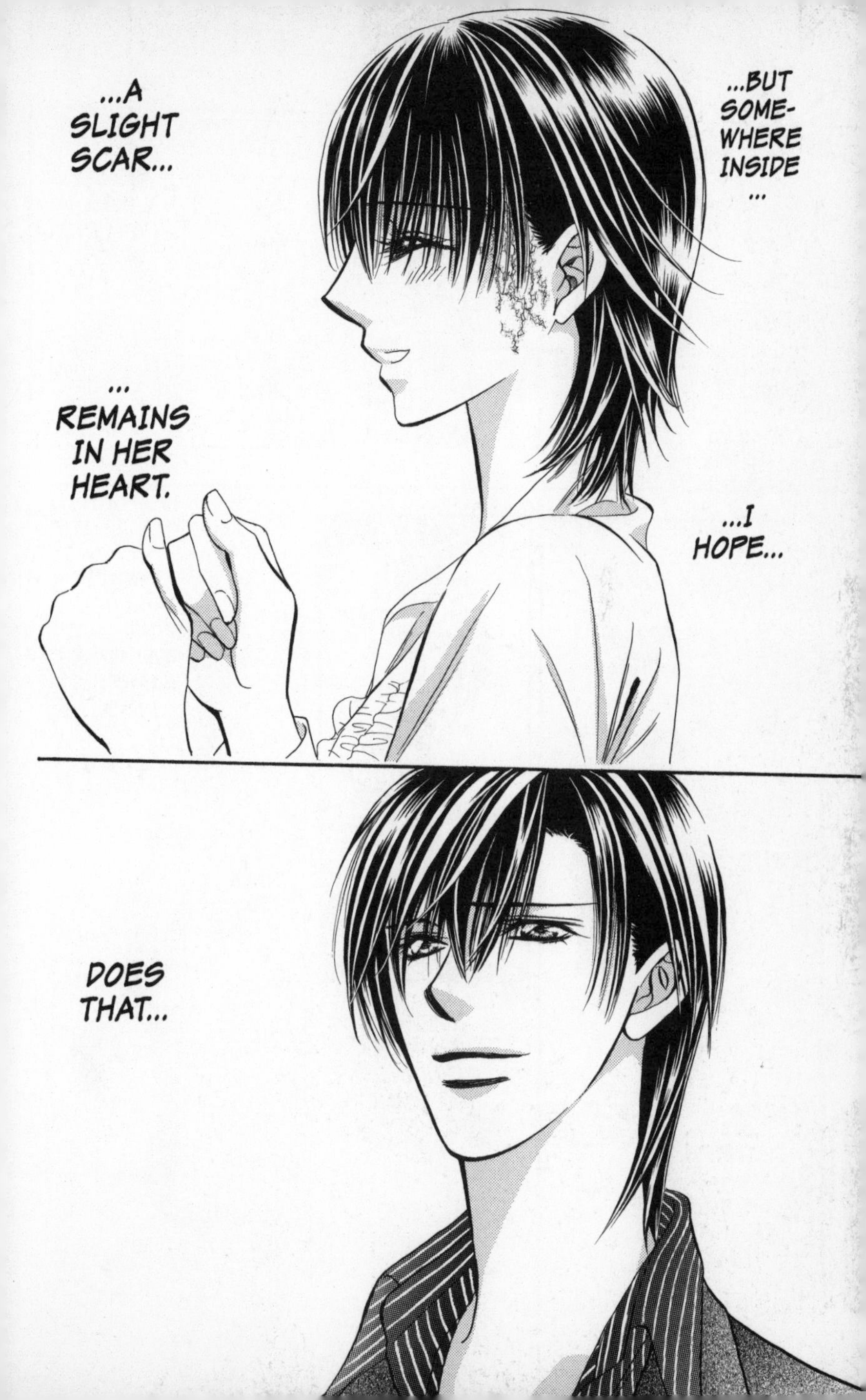
...BUT SOMEWHERE INSIDE ...
...A SLIGHT SCAR...
... REMAINS IN HER HEART.
...I HOPE...
DOES THAT...

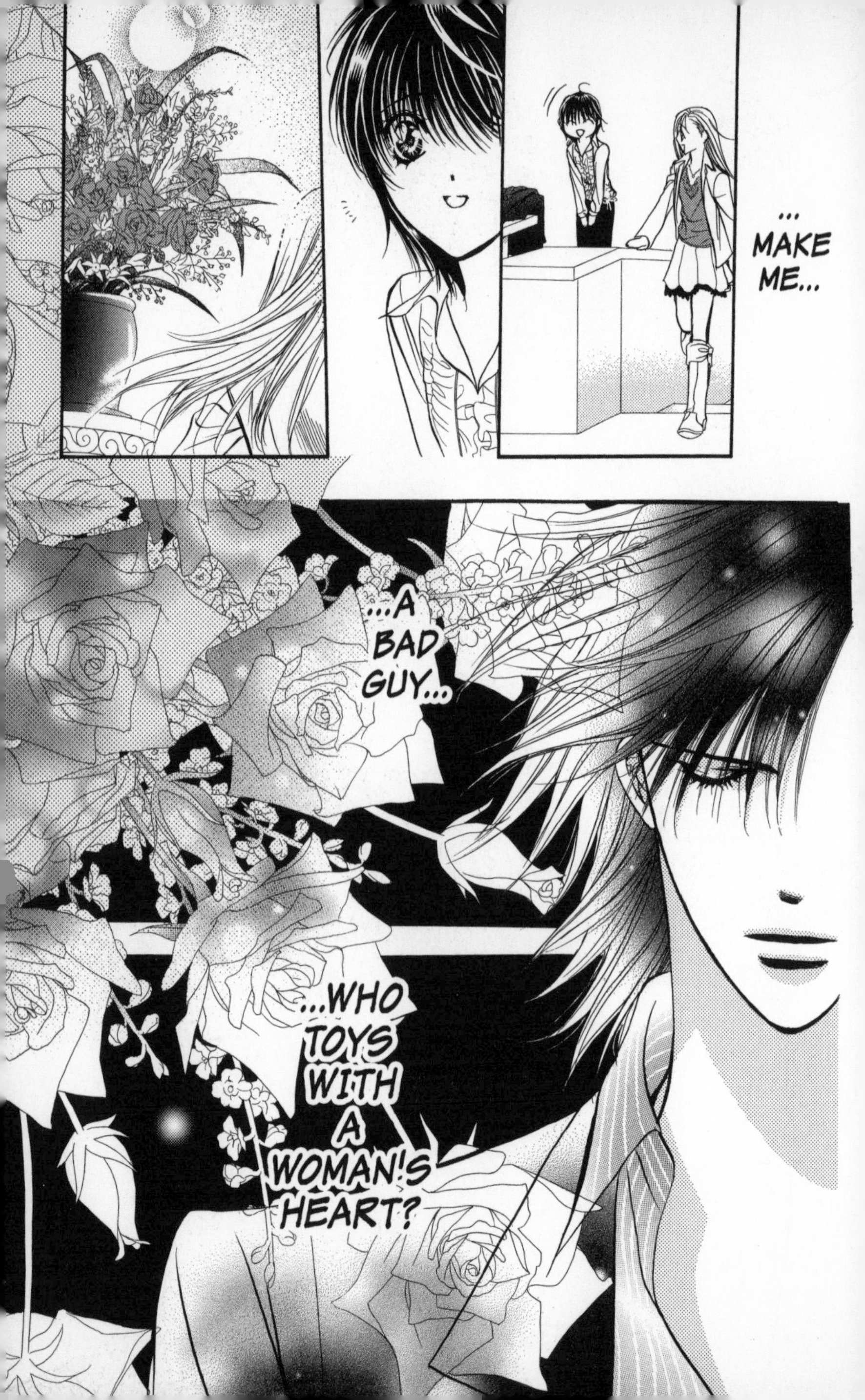
... MAKE ME...
...A BAD GUY...
...WHO TOYS WITH A WOMAN'S HEART?

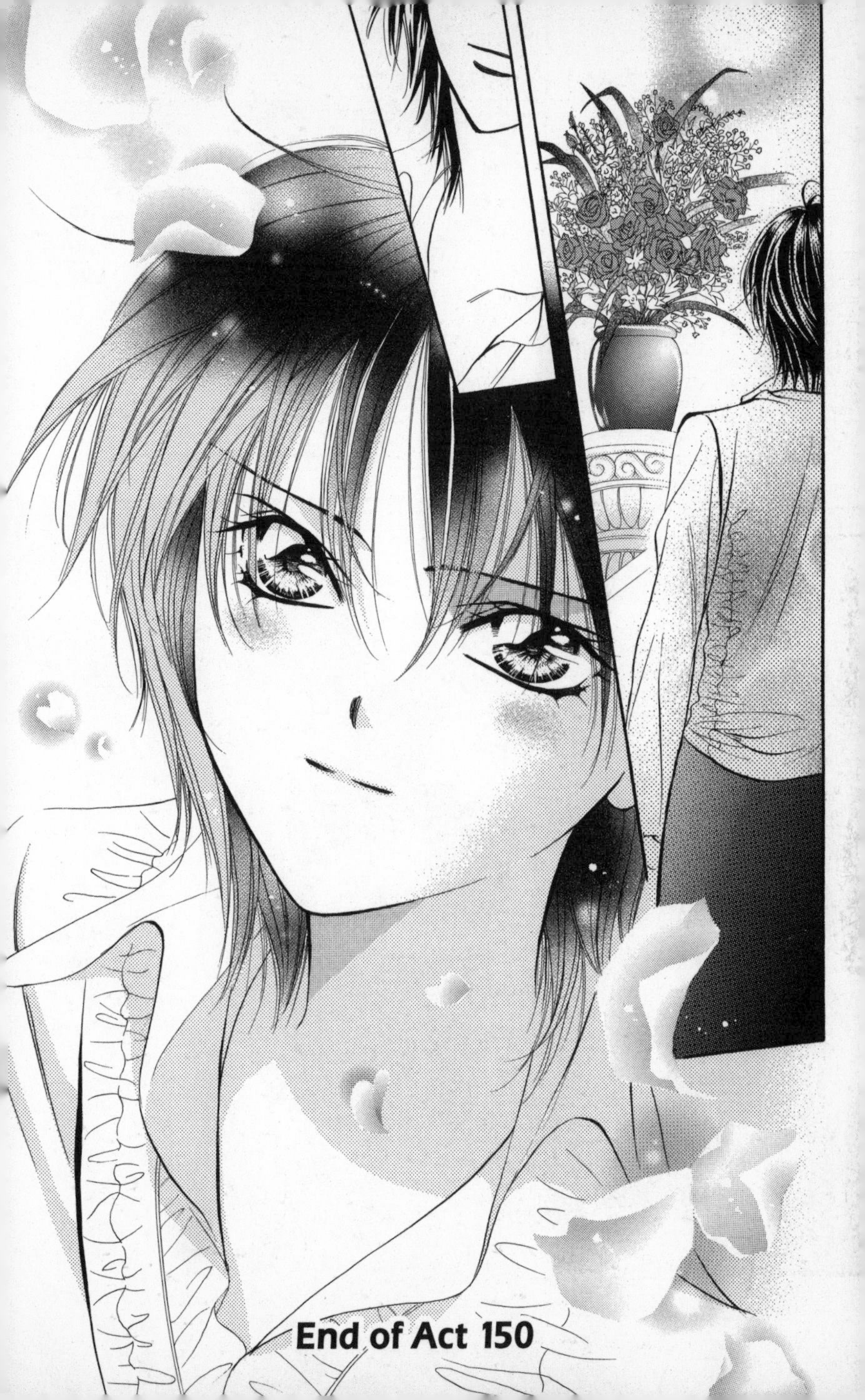
End of Act 150

A Mysterious Valentine's Incident vs Reino

This happened the day before Valentine's Day

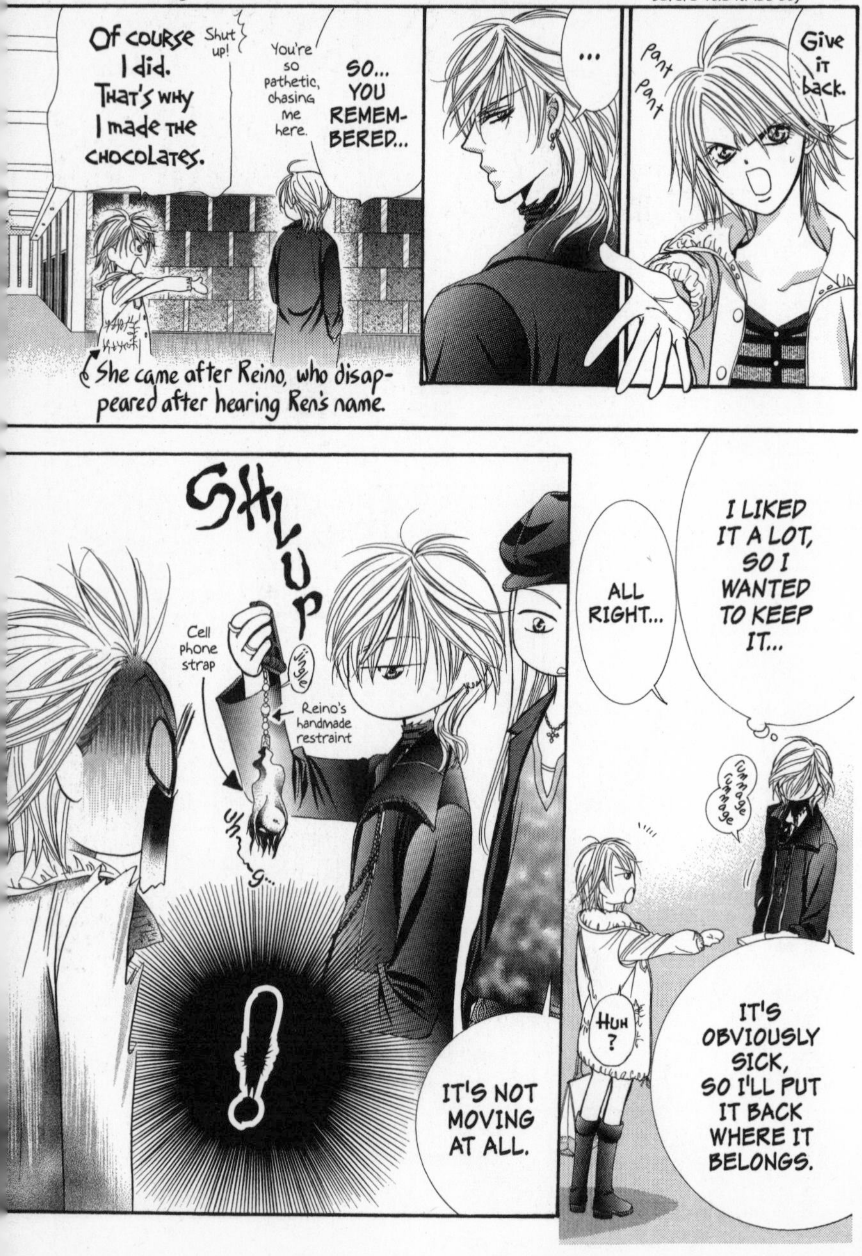
Give it back.
Pant pant
...
SO... YOU REMEMBERED...
You're so pathetic, chasing me here.
Shut up!
Of course I did. That's why I made the chocolates.
She came after Reino, who disappeared after hearing Ren's name.
I LIKED IT A LOT, SO I WANTED TO KEEP IT...
ALL RIGHT...
rummage rummage
Huh?
IT'S OBVIOUSLY SICK, SO I'LL PUT IT BACK WHERE IT BELONGS.
SHLUP
jingle
Cell phone strap
Reino's handmade restraint
IT'S NOT MOVING AT ALL.

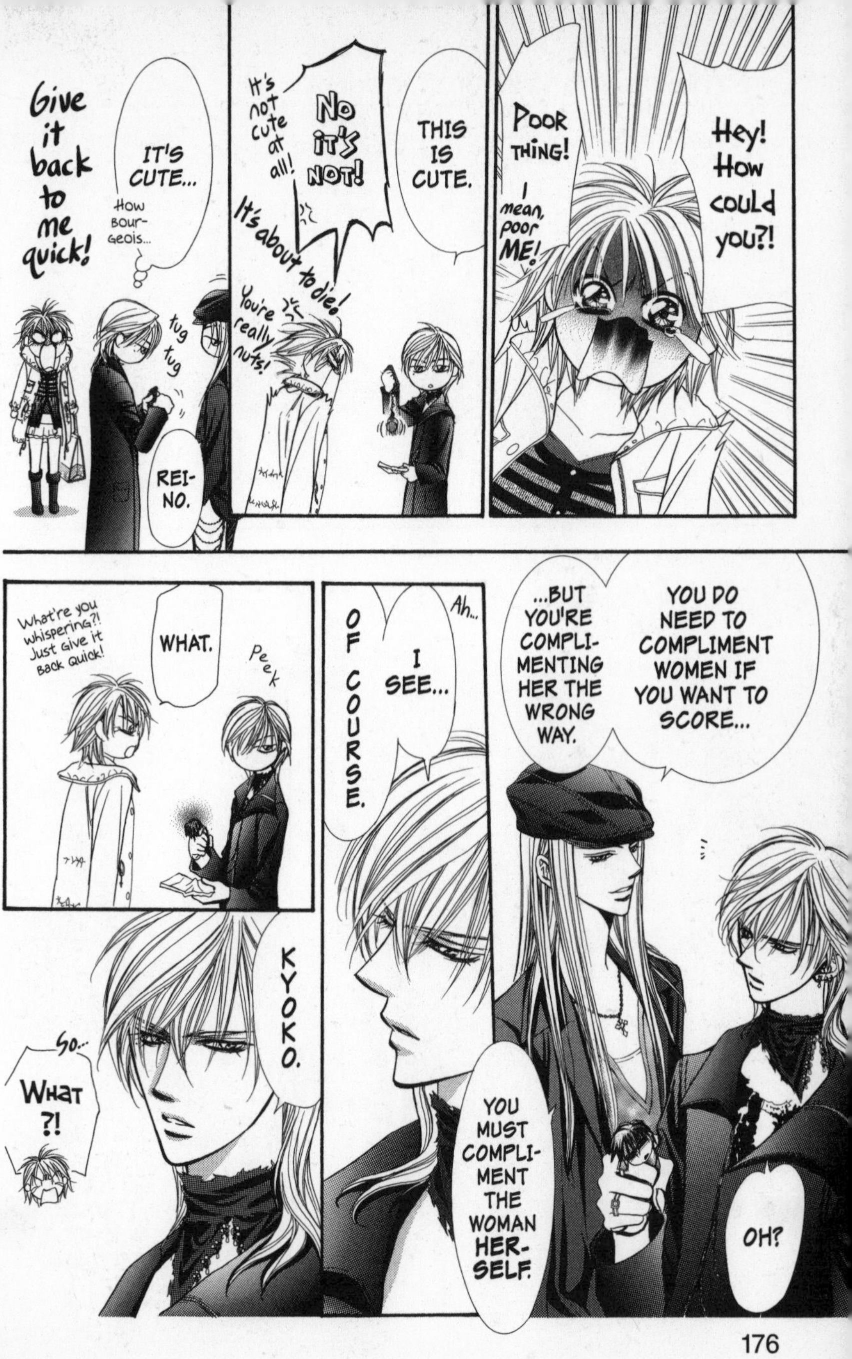

Hey! How could you?!
POOR THING!
I mean, poor ME!
THIS IS CUTE.
NO IT'S NOT!
It's not cute at all!
It's about to die!
You're really nuts!
IT'S CUTE...
How bour-geois...
Give it back to me quick!
tug tug
REI-NO.
YOU DO NEED TO COMPLIMENT WOMEN IF YOU WANT TO SCORE...
...BUT YOU'RE COMPLI-MENTING HER THE WRONG WAY.
Ah...
I SEE...
OF COURSE.
YOU MUST COMPLI-MENT THE WOMAN HER-SELF.
OH?
WHAT.
Peek
What're you whispering?! Just give it back quick!
KYOKO.
So...
WHAT ?!

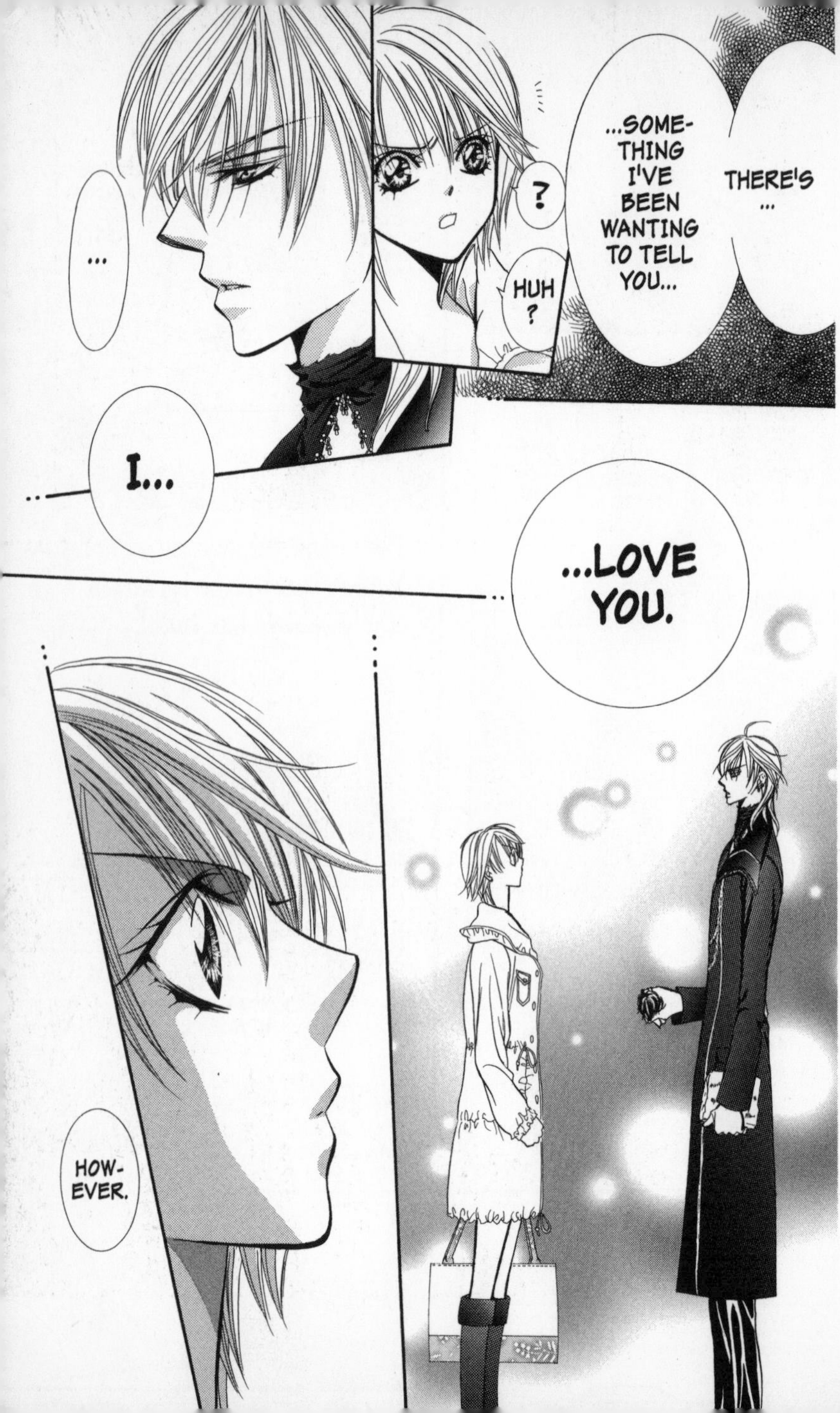
THERE'S ...
...SOME-THING I'VE BEEN WANTING TO TELL YOU...
?
HUH?
...
I...
...LOVE YOU.
HOW-EVER.

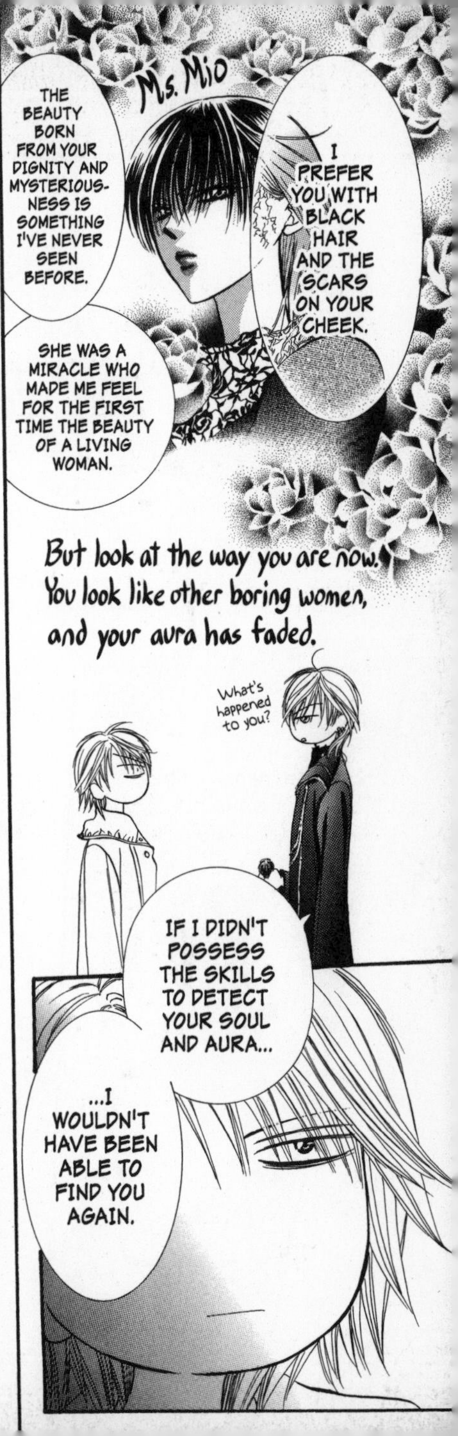
I PREFER YOU WITH BLACK HAIR AND THE SCARS ON YOUR CHEEK.
Ms. Mio
THE BEAUTY BORN FROM YOUR DIGNITY AND MYSTERIOUS-NESS IS SOMETHING I'VE NEVER SEEN BEFORE.
SHE WAS A MIRACLE WHO MADE ME FEEL FOR THE FIRST TIME THE BEAUTY OF A LIVING WOMAN.
But look at the way you are now. You look like other boring women, and your aura has faded.
What's happened to you?
IF I DIDN'T POSSESS THE SKILLS TO DETECT YOUR SOUL AND AURA...
...I WOULDN'T HAVE BEEN ABLE TO FIND YOU AGAIN.

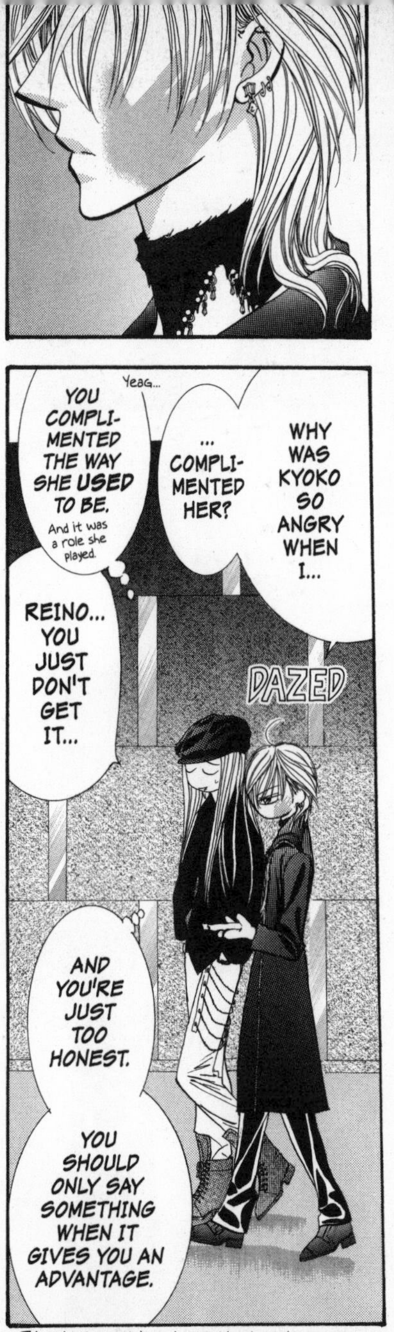
WHY WAS KYOKO SO ANGRY WHEN I...
...COMPLI-MENTED HER?
Yeag...
YOU COMPLI-MENTED THE WAY SHE **USED** TO BE.
And it was a role she played.
REINO... YOU JUST DON'T GET IT...
DAZED
AND YOU'RE JUST TOO HONEST.
YOU SHOULD ONLY SAY SOMETHING WHEN IT GIVES YOU AN ADVANTAGE.

This episode couldn't be included in the main story. Reino rubbed Kyoko the wrong way with the Grudge Kyoko cell phone strap and his confession of love.

Skip-Beat! End Notes
Everyone knows how to be a fan, but sometimes cool things from other cultures need a little help crossing the language barrier.

Page 59, panel 1: 5,000 yen
About $61 U.S.

Page 86, panel 3: Nio statue
Statues of guardian gods that are placed at temple gates. One is the Agyo (with its mouth open), and the other is the Ungyo (with its mouth closed).

Page 111, panel 2: Hannya
One of the masks used in Noh theater. It represents a female demon or ogre.

Page 146, panel 1: Shota
Short for Shotacon, or Shotaro Complex. An interest in young boys. The opposite is Lolicon, or Lolita Complex.

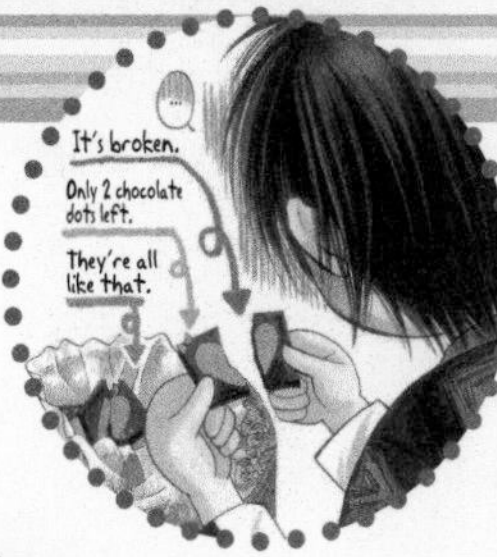
It's broken.
Only 2 chocolate dots left.
They're all like that.

Yoshiki Nakamura is originally from Tokushima Prefecture. She started drawing manga in elementary school, which eventually led to her 1993 debut of *Yume de Au yori Suteki* (Better than Seeing in a Dream) in *Hana to Yume* magazine. Her other works include the basketball series *Saint Love, MVP wa Yuzurenai* (Can't Give Up MVP), *Blue Wars* and *Tokyo Crazy Paradise*, a series about a female bodyguard in 2020 Tokyo.

Shojo Beat

SKIP·BEAT!

Vol. 25

Shojo Beat Edition

STORY AND ART BY YOSHIKI NAKAMURA

English Translation & Adaptation/Tomo Kimura
Touch-up Art & Lettering/Sabrina Heep
Design/Ronnie Casson
Editor/Pancha Diaz

Printed in the U.S.A.

Published by VIZ Media, LLC
P.O. Box 77010
San Francisco, CA 94107

10 9 8 7 6 5 4 3 2 1
First printing, October 2011

www.viz.com

www.shojobeat.com

RATED T FOR TEEN

PARENTAL ADVISORY
SKIP·BEAT! is rated T for Teen and is recommended for ages 13 and up. This volume contains a grudge.

ratings.viz.com

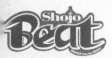

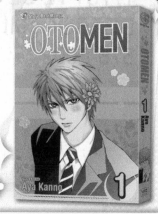
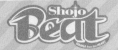

library wars
Love & War

STORY & ART BY Kiiro Yumi ORIGINAL CONCEPT BY Hiro Arikawa

Winning the war on information, one book at a time

When the federal government tries to rid society of "unsuitable" books, an underground group of librarians and bibliophiles vows to fight back.

They are the Library Forces. And this is their story.

library wars
Love & War
1

$9.99 USA / $12.99 CAN *
ISBN: 978-1-4215-3

Toshokan Sensou LOVE&WAR

* Prices subject to change

RATED T+ FOR OLDER TEEN ratings.viz.com

VIZ media www.viz.com